WHAT PROFESSIONALS HAVE SAID ABOUT
THE FIRST EDITION OF THIS BOOK ...

"Dr. Dayhoff has done a remarkable job researching the current literature on social anxiety and its disorder. The text is well written and comprehensive. I enjoyed the use of humor"

> Stefan G. Hofmann, Ph.D., Director, Social Phobia Program, Boston University

"Dr. Dayhoff has done an excellent job covering ... social anxiety, and [her] book will be valuable to both therapists and self-help readers. I definitely recommend it."

> Albert Ellis, Ph.D., Albert Ellis Institute for Rational Emotive Behavioral Therapy

"Signe Dayhoff combines the best of both worlds – the knowledge and expertise of the professional and the insight and understanding of the consumer – and communicates these strengths to her reader. This is a winning recipe."

> Ronald M. Rapee, Ph.D., Psychology Professor, Macquarie University, Australia, author of *Overcoming Shyness and Social Phobia: A Step by Step Guide*

"Finally here's a book that deals with SA/SP from the ... insider's perspective on this long-neglected anxiety problem. Because Dr. Dayhoff has lived through social anxiety herself, she is able to comprehensively cover both the personal concerns of sufferers and current research and treatment options. I recommend it."

> Thomas A. Richards, Director, The Social Anxiety Institute Phoenix, Arizona

"This is a highly readable book and gives good concrete examples and exercises. I particularly like the part about how to find a suitable therapist or treatment setting. That can be a real challenge for shy people. I am happy to endorse it."

> Lynn Henderson, Ph.D., Director, The Shyness Clinic Menlo Park, California

ii

SECOND EDITION

DIAGONALLY-PARKED IN A PARALLEL UNIVERSE:

WORKING THROUGH SOCIAL ANXIETY

SIGNE A. DAYHOFF, PH.D.

Effectiveness-Plus Publications LLC
Placitas, New Mexico
www.effectiveness-plus.com

Diagonally-Parked in a Parallel Universe:
Working Through Social Anxiety (2ND Edition)
By Signe A. Dayhoff, Ph.D.

Copyright © 2010 by Signe A. Dayhoff, Ph.D.

Published by Effectiveness-Plus Publications LLC
P.O. Box 340
Placitas, New Mexico 87043

Cover design and illustrations by Signe A. Dayhoff

Printed in the United States of America

**Publisher's Cataloging-in-Publication
(Provided by Quality Books, Inc.)**

Dayhoff, Signe A.
    Diagonally parked in a parallel universe:
    working through social anxiety / Signe A. Dayhoff.
  -- 2nd ed.
    p. cm.
    Includes index.
    LCCN: 2009934961
    ISBN: 978-0-9671265-1-7

    Social phobia. 2. Anxiety. 3. Bashfulness.

    I. Title

RC552.S62D39 2010   616.85'225
                              QBI99-1021

    Printing number
    10 9 8 7 6 5 4 3 2

TABLE OF CONTENTS

APPROACHING RECOVERY 105

TARGETING AROUSAL 141

MODIFYING THOUGHTS AND BEHAVIORS 165

ABOUT THE AUTHOR

Signe A. Dayhoff, Ph.D., M.A., M.Ed., is a Social Psychologist with post-graduate training in counseling. She received her doctorate from Boston University where she studied ways to increase personal and professional presentation and self-promotion effectiveness. For the last 25+ years she has taught individuals how to transform presentation anxiety and marketing reluctance into confident social effectiveness and dignified, profitable marketing.

Currently she is president of Effectiveness-Plus LLC, which provides educational products and services. A Certified Graduate of Authentic Happiness Coaching, she coaches internationally and is a member of International Coach Federation and International Association of Coaches.

Prior to this, she was president of The Mentoring Network, which provided mentoring and training in interpersonal skills for career development. She also has taught psychology at Boston University, University of Massachusetts, and Framingham State College

Author of four other books: *How to Win in a Tough Job Market: Successful Strategies for Getting the Job You Want; Create Your Own Career Opportunities; Get the Job You Want: Successful Strategies For Selling Yourself in the Job Market;* and *Decision Making For Managers,* she also contributed to David Riklan's *101 Great Ways to Improve Your Life (Vol. 2)* and Steven J. Bennett's *Executive Chess: Creative Problem Solving By 45 of America's Top Business Leaders and Thinkers.*

With over 150 published newspaper and magazine articles, she has been quoted e.g. in *Time Out New York, Boston Business Journal, Mass High Tech, Shape, Industry Week, Wall Street Journal, Success,* and *Cosmopolitan.*

For over four years she hosted and produced Continental Cablevision's career education program, *The Inside Track,* for which she received a Conti Award nomination. She has appeared on radio, television, teleseminars, and presented for many diverse organizations.

ACKNOWLEDGMENTS

Many individuals generously contributed their time and effort to the making of this book. First, I'd like to thank all those SA/SP sufferers who have shared their experiences, issues, and concerns with me over the years.

Second, I want to thank those experts who reviewed early drafts of the first edition for accuracy and completeness and offered invaluable comments and suggestions:

Albert Ellis, Ph.D., Founder of Albert Ellis Institute and Rational-Emotive-Behavioral Therapy

Richard G. Heimberg, Ph.D., Adult Anxiety Clinic, Social Phobia Program, Department of Psychology, Temple University

Stefan G. Hofmann, Ph.D., Center for Anxiety and Related Disorders, Boston University

Mark R. Leary, Ph.D., Department of Psychology, Wake-Forest University

Neil F. Neimark, M.D., Department of Family Practice, University of California, Irvine, and The Mind/Body Connection

Daniel Perlman, Ph.D., Family Studies and Nutrition Science, University of British Columbia

Thomas A. Richards, Ph.D., The Social Anxiety Institute

Suzanne M. Sutherland, M.D., Department of Psychiatry and Behavioral Sciences, Duke University

Timo Telaranta, M.D., Privatix Clinic.

Third, I want to thank those who answered questions and provided information: Kathryn L. Blackmon. Ph.D., Christer Drott, M.D., James S. Garza, M.D., Amy S. Kloeblen, M.P.H., R.D., Robert C. Meyer, M.D., and Clifford B. Saper, M.D., Ph.D.

INTRODUCTION

Dear Social Anxiety Sufferers (Your Friends and Family),

Everyone has experienced fleeting moments of anxiety in social situations. But sometimes this social anxiety happens more frequently. Sometimes it's severe and debilitating because it insinuates itself into one or more important aspects of your life.

You may suffer from the agonizing pangs of self-consciousness about being on public view or the center of attention ... making a mistake, leaving you humiliated. You may dread meeting people, making small talk, giving a speech, using a public restroom, or eating in public. You may quake when talking to your boss or when your social skills and/or work are being observed ... or your competence assessed. You may feel threatened in a new social situation where you don't know the "rules."

In general, when you have social anxiety, you avoid such situations altogether or just want to escape. However you experience this anxiety, you need to know *you are* **not** *alone*. While each sufferer experiences social anxiety a little differently, you're all riding the same fearful, skittish horse.

When your social fears are intense and persistent, you have what's called *Social Anxiety Disorder/Social Phobia* (SA/SP—"sasp" for short). This means every day you're forced to confront the pain of being in the spotlight, being evaluated, and being embarrassed by the very social situations you long to embrace.

Socially you find yourself on the periphery of life's dance, trying to follow the choreographed patterns and rhythm. But, usually you seem to be one beat out of synch, zigging when you should zag. Often you feel like the butt of a cosmic joke. You see yourself as the ball in a pinball machine, bouncing from bumper to bumper, missing targets, and always on the verge of "tilt." This is the essence of being *diagonally-parked in a parallel universe.*

Clinically too, having SA/SP puts you in another dimension. SA/SP is the most common anxiety disorder and the third most common psychiatric disorder after depression and alcoholism. Yet, until the late 1990s, it was the least-diagnosed, least-widely understood, and most under-treated disorder. Still, few mental health professionals are fully appreciative of the broad range of the condition or are fully experienced in the different approaches to its treatment … even as the number of sufferers continues to increase.

Making your situation worse, many of you with SA/SP don't know you have a *treatable* disorder. But even when you understand this, you're often reluctant to seek professional help.

You're ashamed of the fear and worried that your complaints won't be taken seriously. And, when you finally do muster the courage to seek help, you're often hobbled by the very anxiety for which you seek help: Your fear of talking with and being evaluated by others. Together, these factors help keep this major health problem less visible… but no less painful.

This book was written to comprehensively show you how you can

- Significantly and effectively alleviate your SA/SP pain;
- Significantly improve your daily functioning; and
- Effectively work toward your social effectiveness and other potential.

You benefit from the uniqueness of my perspective. I'm a clinically-trained social psychologist working in the areas of social confidence, competence, and effectiveness. I am someone who struggled for 22 years to successfully overcome SA/SP.

I used to worry endlessly about what others might think about me and whether I was meeting their expectations. As a result, I understand how it feels to be living- and working through this often-incapacitating disorder. I also know where you need to specifically concentrate your efforts to improve your life *multi-dimensionally*.

You benefit from my knowledge of SA/SPers' concerns, issues, and desires that results from nearly 10 years of coaching SA/SPers, as well as talking with and listening to them online and offline.

You benefit from my research, teaching, consulting, training, and coaching experience, as well as my association with professionals in the SA/SP therapy and clinical research trenches.

To make your SA/SP more understandable and amenable to change, this book provides you with *everything* you need: theories and salient research on its origin and development, its anxiety triggers and anxiety maintaining mechanisms, and a broad range of standard and alternative clinical approaches (including medications and therapies), life strategies, interpersonal, communication, motivational exercises, and empathy.

To help you empower yourself and succeed, this book takes you back to square one. It gives you the psychological preparation you need to jump-start, enable, and maintain your recovery process.

Because SA/SPers tend to have difficulties with clinicians, this book takes the mystery and risk out of locating and talking to them. Moreover, it guides you through the process. It shows you how to initiate your search and survive your first appointment. It tells you what to expect and how to prepare for it.

Because SA/SPers struggle with presenting themselves socially (communicating, socializing, or dating), this book addresses each significant life activity. It breaks each of them into digestible, sequential chunks so you can absorb, assimilate, and achieve each chunk (and the whole) more easily.

And, because the Internet has great importance and value for SA/SPers as one of the few means of establishing relationships and comfortable communication you have, the book pinpoints services and resources available for those with SA/SP.

How you think, believe, feel, and behave determines how you interact with your environment (and how your environments perceive and respond to you). Consequently, this book focuses on your perceptions, emotions, attitudes, beliefs, and self-presentation.

Using real-life stories, typical problems, and their solutions, its user-friendly format takes you logically, incrementally, step-by-baby-step through your recovery process. It takes you from foundation-building basics to advanced applications.

Through concise explanations, thought questions, self-quizzes, and exercises, you systematically develop and apply your cognitive and behavioral strategies to achieve your recovery goals.

In this process you'll assess your social anxiety, determine where you're headed, how to get there, and how you'll know when you've arrived. You'll act as a scientist doing experiments. You'll learn by trial and error what works best for you as a unique individual.

You'll discover, learn, practice, and apply new skills. You'll constructively change the way you think about and cope with your SA/SP and the world outside yourself. You'll monitor your progress as you make positive changes and reward yourself for them.

However, it's important to note, just *reading* this book isn't likely to ameliorate your SA/SP. Not any more than just watching others exercise will cause you to lose weight and tone your body

The book's recovery program is *action-oriented*. It requires your active, committed, persistent participation. This is necessary if you are to alter all those factors that contribute to your SA/SP. These factors include your automatic fear arousal, negative thoughts, mistaken beliefs and assumptions, unrealistic expectations, and counter-productive behaviors.

Note: As much as you may wish it, there is no finger-snapping, lamp-rubbing, "Shazaam!" magical solution to SA/SP. It took many factors interacting over many years to bring you to your present state. So recovery will not be instantaneous. But if you take the time to make the necessary structured effort toward recovery, you will quickly begin to experience small but significant changes in your thoughts, feelings, and behavior. You'll glimpse what it'll be like "without SA/SP." You'll feel the freedom to be the *real* you!

Essential to your SA/SP recovery will be empathy, patience, and your acceptance of yourself as you are. You must feel and believe that you're worthy of becoming better. You must believe that you're not to blame for this problem ... but that you are responsible for its solution.

The goal of this book is not to make you wildly extroverted or a party animal. Unless you're an extrovert lurking under the heavy cloak of SA/SP, that's not likely to happen. What is likely is when that leaden SA/SP mantle is slipped from your shoulders, your submerged personality, whatever that may be, will be liberated to fly and soar.

The goal of this book is not to make you a "success" at everything you try. It's not to get you everything you want. It's not to make your life totally perfect and totally satisfying. That's unrealistic.

The goal is to substitute functional habits for dysfunctional habits. It's to give you the knowledge, skills, insights, and tools you need to succeed interpersonally and socially.

The goal is to help you significantly and effectively alleviate your SA/SP pain, significantly improve your daily functioning, and effectively and successfully work toward meeting your potential. It will help effect your *recovery*.

Your purposeful actions toward recovery will give you the necessary success experience, confidence, and solution-finding strategies you'll need for your new life. They'll give you coping and social effectiveness skills. They will give you a new perspective on yourself, others, and social interaction.

Important: The first four chapters of this book are educational, providing you with a comprehensive, in-depth understanding of the many aspects of SA/SP: its origins, triggers, maintainers, and its clinical and social manifestations. Chapter 5 then takes you through, and prepares you for, the process of recovery. The treatment section begins with Chapter 6.

Because you are understandably eager to start working directly on your SA/SP, you might possibly consider skipping the first five chapters. I strongly urge you **not** to do so. The more informed you are about the making of SA/SP and how it affects people generally and you particularly, the better able you'll be to determine your unique SA/SP goals, make your plan to achieve them, and then do whatever is necessary to accomplish it.

Whether you use this book as a guide to work on your SA/SP on your own or as an adjunct to therapy, the thirteen chapters will provide you with everything you need to spark your action and relieve your anxiety.

I want you to always remember: Your social anxiety is merely a dysfunctional over-expression of your highly-tuned sensitivity, empathy, and imagination. These are *special gifts*. They are to be valued, cultivated, and nurtured. Yes, you CAN discover how to delight in these gifts … and share them with others.

I invite you to join me and enjoy finally being *parallel-parked in a parallel universe*.

Yours in social confidence, competence, and effectiveness,

Signe A. Dayhoff, Ph.D. ("Dr. Signe")

Placitas, New Mexico

1

"LIONS AND TIGERS AND BEARS, OH MY!"

"He flung himself from the room, flung himself upon his horse, and rode off in all directions."
(Stephen Leacock, *Nonsense Novels*, 1911)

JOANNA'S TALE

Joanna's heart galloped, the surging blood thundering in her ears, painting her face and neck crimson. The butterflies in her knotted stomach were flapping their wings with greater force as the time drew near. Sweat trickled down her. She was sure everyone could see her soggy, wrinkled blouse, even with her jacket on.

Perched on the edge of her chair in her college English class, 35-year-old Joanna had started the countdown for the instructor's call for the students' five-minute presentations to begin. It was always the same. Whenever she had to speak before a group, her mouth instantaneously became parched. Her tongue stuck to her hard palate. Words caught in her throat. And those incomprehensible phrases that managed to escape flooded the audience in a tidal wave of croaked stutters and stammers. All the while she gasped for breath, quaking. You're a mess, girl, she chided herself.

Joanna knew she couldn't present for even five minutes without looking like a laughingstock. Her mindless sense of dread was one reason she was still in the process of trying to get through school. Fear of public speaking seemed to malevolently greet her in every subject, rendering her unable to stick with one major and finish her college degree.

Just standing before the group of confident 19-year-olds reduced her to quivering jelly. Having to speak on top of that totally liquefied her resolve. She already knew how the audience would respond: They'd either look disgusted at this pathetic old person or smirk and snicker at the absurdity of her trying to pull it off.

Once again she'd be embarrassed, ... no, humiliated. Every last one of them, including the instructor, would write her off as being a loser. Once again, she sighed with a grimace, I'm a failure.

Like a coyote-cornered rabbit she felt on the verge of panic ... again. Something primitive, ancestrally wired in her brain, made her want to run and escape. But, no, she couldn't do that. Crazy behavior like that would only draw attention to her. Joanna mulled it over. A room this packed is a minefield. It was not something to try to navigate in a hurry.

She chewed her lip and sighed. Maybe I can find another excuse to get me out of the rest of this class period and the presentation. But as she sat jiggling her crossed leg, her mind was blank.

Compounding her immediate distress was the knowledge that she needed to do this presentation for her grade. She'd already skipped the others, one way or another. This would leave her teacher, who'd tried to talk with her about it, with no other conclusion than Joanna just didn't care.

And her grade-point average, which she'd struggled to keep high despite these self-presentation obstacles, depended on her doing well in this class. What was she to do? To Joanna it was a rattlesnake roundup from the perspective of the snake: a lose-lose situation. At this point she couldn't tell which failure was worse.

As she bounced her leg under her desk, her foot brushed her backpack, which fell open, revealing the fifth of Jack Daniels she'd stashed there for emergencies. A fleeting flash of relief played across her face. Her eyes drinking in the label gave her courage. Emergency. She grabbed the bag and its precious cargo and took a deep breath. With her head bowed, she cautiously and slowly threaded her way to the door, avoiding curious eyes. Once outside the classroom, she bolted for the restroom.

After a couple of healthy swigs, Joanna felt a warming calm wash over her. Ah, yes, that's better. She was alone, away from scrutiny. Her hyperventilation was fading in the glow. This can't continue. I've got to find some way to make it work out, she sighed dispiritedly. Her heart palpitations were leveling off too. Sinking to a sitting position on the gray tiled floor, Joanna leaned against the wall and took another drink.

BARRY'S TALE

With knuckles showing white, Barry finally dragged himself to the Lucky U singles' bar on Saturday night. It had taken him months of pep talks and false starts to steel himself to do it. At twenty-eight, slim with Clint Eastwood intensity, he still had never really dated.

Searching his memory, he chuckled and shook his head. After all, you can't count the time my mother arranged for me to take Judy Jones, a 9th-grade classmate and next-door neighbor, Christmas caroling with our church group. And, he had to confess, that much to his humiliation, he was still a virgin.

He didn't date because approaching women was like circumnavigating the globe in a kayak and concrete booties. It was not something a sane person would contemplate. He didn't know the "rules of the game." Since he hadn't read the latest prescription, he was sure that the women at the Lucky U would catch the scent of his inadequacy the moment he crossed the threshold and be lying in wait for their prey.

In the movie he played and replayed in his mind he saw them in groups, carefully appraising each male who walked by, sizing him up. They would tick off his pluses and minuses and put him in the "discard" pile. And when he didn't stack up to their high standards, he was certain they'd make sure he knew it. Barry was convinced they'd take one look at him, and, without so much as a word, label him a jerk: an object of derision and laughter.

As he stood at the bar in his freshly pressed chinos, oxford cloth shirt, with a Michelob in hand, he fantasized about having a magic lamp. One rub and ... poof! ... he would mentally download the "The Successful Stud's Dating Manual." Another rub and he'd be so cool he was hot.

He began to survey the crowd. All I really want, he thought, is to meet someone nice. You know, someone who would appreciate me for my thoughtfulness and sensitivity. Hey, he wanted to shout, I don't see women as notches in my belt or slabs of beef in a meat locker. But every time he spotted someone who might fill the bill, his indecisiveness punched him in the gut. His thoughts of failure overwhelmed him, cementing him to the ground.

I can't talk to her, he'd respond plaintively to himself. What would I say? I always sound so dull and stupid when I try. Before I could get out what I wanted to say, she'd get bored and leave. Nobody really wants to listen to me ... and I can't blame them.

Even when a woman returned his gaze and his infrequent, tentative smile, like the vivacious assistant in marketing at his company, he found himself unable to follow through. It was always the same. His face flushed magenta and then he began to stammer. And when he wasn't blushing, he was agonizing over its prospect and the bad first-impression he was sure he had already made on her. It had him coming and going.

When he spied her, even though she was forty-five feet away at the end of the hall, he averted his eyes to avoid meeting her gaze. But with or without eye contact, his face continued to glow in her presence. He was at its mercy. Soon he became so obsessed with the possibility of their meeting that he was ever on the lookout for her. Armed with evasive strategies, he waited around corners for her to pass. He took the stairs when she took the elevator. He did whatever he could to try to preempt accidental contact.

Suddenly Barry was shaken from his reverie by the three-piece band starting its set. As he turned his attention toward the music, his eyes swept a young woman with long, dark hair, some twenty feet away from him. She was standing and chatting with two other women, but looking directly at him. She was smiling sweetly.

His face became a warning beacon as his heart began to throb. What should I do? He asked himself. Smile back? Go over? And what about the other two women? He began to breathe more rapidly and shallowly. Should I talk to them? Ignore them? What if the one with the sweet smile is trying to play a joke on me? I'd be humiliated in front of everyone. With a laundry list of negative what-ifs spinning in his head, Barry felt immobilized, glued to the spot at the bar where he stood.

JOE'S TALE

Eighteen-year-old Joe sat rigidly behind the wheel of his pre-owned Camry, concentrating on staring straight ahead as the bumper-to-bumper commuter traffic jockeyed around him for position. As much as he loved the independence of driving, he hated being in this automotive fishbowl with no place to hide and no way to escape.

When he was caught in traffic, he was on display. He was like a street mime, just hanging out there where all could observe him and judge his performance.

Under his Grand Ole Opry T-shirt, his muscular shoulders and neck ached with tension as he calculated his options. If I casually look around and catch the eye of other drivers, they'll start to watch me. They'll think what's that dumb kid think he's doing. While that was bad enough, what chilled Joe's bones even more was glancing over and discovering that people in the other cars were already scrutinizing and judging him.

At critical moments like this Joe always launched into a dialogue with himself. What if that happened? He asked and replied, I'd look stupid. No matter what he did, he felt his reaction would be awkward at best. And then, what if that happened? Well, I'd do what I usually do and embarrass and humiliate myself. And they'd think I was a real loser.

Whenever other vehicles were moving slowly or running along side the Camry, Joe adopted a look of deep contemplation as he began to fiddle with the radio. He'd pretend to be looking for a specific station or tuning it in. His look of rapt attention was intended to convey that he had serious matters on his mind and certainly didn't have the time to rubberneck to see what others were doing.

At traffic lights, Joe would try to stop a half-length behind the car beside him, thereby making observation less likely. But when there were cars covering both his flanks, he resorted to his radio station button-punching ploy. If he had been listening prior to stopping, he immediately turned the sound down so no one could hear and evaluate his music choice.

Driving wasn't the freewheeling expression of teenage freedom he had expected. Instead, it was just an exhausting activity. When he wasn't thinking about driving defensively and maintaining the speed limit so the police wouldn't pull him over, he was focusing all his energies on managing the impression he was making on other drivers.

But Joe's fear wasn't confined to his driving. He couldn't bring himself to stand in any line, like a line at the bank or the grocery store, sit in the doctor's office, or ride the bus without feeling cold and clammy. Dozens of pairs of eyes were "boring" into him. He knew it made no sense, but that's how he felt.

Rather than use a public restroom where someone could see or hear him, he tried never to be too far from home so he could hurry back when urgency called. Being on a plane for more than two hours left in him in leg-crossing agony. Because he couldn't use a restroom urinal he would use a stall instead. However, if someone entered the restroom before he started to urinate, his anxiety went into overdrive and totally blocked his bladder, leaving him dancing in pain.

Once he tried using a Walkman so he couldn't hear himself or others in the bathroom. But, unfortunately, he turned the volume up so high that he inadvertently attracted the attention of all the other patrons as they entered the bathroom. Thus, as he emerged from the stall, assuming his usual blasé pose, he found pairs of eyes turned in his direction. They were taking in his 250-pound, six-foot weightlifter's body with his ginger hair poking out around the tiny blasting Sony earphones. The incident confirmed all his worst fears.

SARAH'S TALE

Sarah listened to the shrill ring of her kitchen phone, nagging her to pick up the receiver. The jangling, heart-pumping sound filled her small apartment and fired off her nerve endings. But at 43 years old she just stood by the demanding instrument, indecisive and wringing her hands. She hoped it would soon stop.

All-encompassing panic had gripped her by the throat the moment the phone had started to ring. Instantaneously dread and uncertainty enshrouded her. In spite of its occasional usefulness, Sarah viewed the phone as her most unwelcome intruder ... next to cockroaches.

But maybe the call is important, she counseled herself. A look at the caller identification screen was uninformative. It read "Unavailable." I can't answer it, she told herself. I don't know who it is or what they want, she replied, her chest constricting. If it's really important, they can leave a message on the answering machine.

It seemed an eternity to Sarah before the answering machine on the night table next to her bed picked up the call on its fifth ring. She turned up the machine's volume so she could hear the beep. Her heart seemed to stop as she waited, petrified of what was to follow. But on hearing a resounding click and soothing hum of the dial tone, she breathed a big sigh of relief. No message. Thank goodness.

Sarah's caller ID had become more essential to her existence than her microwave. When she knew who was calling, she could decide whether or not to pick up. In that few seconds she could begin to prepare herself psychologically for the exchange. Particularly since the phone provided no nonverbal clues to guide her, she needed to be able to exercise some control. Preparation and control were her protective devices.

When she wasn't ready, her tongue would seem to fill her mouth and she jabbered. Words tumbled out helter-skelter. Once she picked up the receiver, there was no refuge. Her incompetence would humiliate her.

Whenever she saw *Anonymous* on the ID readout, she felt palpitations. This meant that someone didn't want her to know their identity. In fact, they had taken measures to block her access to that information. So they had the advantage. She felt one-down: She was a wolf on its back, baring its throat. Anonymous callers who left no message abandoned her to her agony.

But it wasn't just answering the phone that was a problem for Sarah. Placing calls too was a masochistic exercise. She could call her mother and Tanya, her best friend, without discomfort but couldn't call anyone else without a script in hand and a half-hour rehearsal. Even with practice behind her, she felt compelled to read from her prepared text, leaving her sounding as if she were puzzling over a foreign language.

Each time she prayed no one would ask her a question she hadn't anticipated. When they did, it left her flustered, sputtering whatever popped into her head. Sometimes, when things were totally out of control, she had to hang up to keep from destroying all her credibility.

While overall she was glad to have the answering machine to further screen her calls, she hated that others had them too. If she could manage to call people, they could darn well be there to receive her calls. Being pressured to say what she wanted in their prescribed 30 seconds or be cut off in mid-sentence ratcheted up Sarah's anxiety yet another notch. This meant she'd have to say as quickly as possible all the "right" words in the right order.

The "right" words never came easily to Sarah, if they came at all. She could barely walk and chew gum at the same time in social situations. And when the words did appear, they never presented themselves either concisely or quickly.

Moreover, knowing that these clumsy attempts at speech would be recorded for posterity, for all to hear and evaluate, only tightened her throat muscles more. She sighed again as she went back to the protection of her computer. I wish everyone communicated by e-mail only.

HARRY'S TALE

Harry had dealt successfully with people for most of his 56 years. As a pharmacist for 30 of those years, he spent his time checking medication histories and educating customers about drug interactions. He enjoyed this chance for social interchanges. In his off-hours he coached the girls' soccer team and acted as secretary for his local chamber of commerce. Despite his deceptive appearance of being short, heavy, and balding, Harry was on everyone's invitation A-list because of his sense of humor and down-home story-telling ability.

Surprisingly, Harry wasn't always this comfortable and composed in social situations. One situation, in particular, in which he was observed, literally turned him inside out with skull-screaming anticipation of public scrutiny and judgment. As strange as it seemed, this was his acting with the town's little theater group.

No matter how many times he had performed a role, his repertoire ranging from King Lear to the King of Siam, he always nearly missed his entrance. Night after night, just before his appearance, he found himself doubled over, with his head dangling over the dressing room toilet, retching. It didn't matter that he was so prepared he could practically recite his lines backwards. And he didn't care that Sir Lawrence Olivier had suffered the same fate.

When it came time to approach the stage, to stand in the wings to await his cue, he went into deep-freeze suspension. His fear clapped the eraser and wiped his blackboard clean. All that was left him was the vision of hundreds of pairs of eye lasering holes into him, searching for a chink in his armor.

As he gasped for breath, his heart started to rattle the bars of its prison. His head swam and his fingers tingled. Before each performance he was sure this was the "big one," the grand finale, the *Guinness Book of Records* heart attack to beat all others. If he didn't immediately grab his good luck Walgreen's prescription bag and start breathing into it for five minutes, he knew he wouldn't make it onto the stage.

Yet, somehow, he never missed a cue. Furthermore, once he was actually out on the boards, involved in doing what he loved and was so thoroughly prepared to do, he relaxed. Then he could focus on projecting his character to the audience, giving a good performance, and having fun.

MARIA'S TALE

Thirty-seven-year-old travel agent and mother of three, Maria arrived at her church early on Sunday morning. She was going to meet two friends from her church parents' group so they could sit together for the service. Rosa and Jane wanted to sit up front. Consequently they asked Maria to stake out their places for them since they thought they might be delayed. But this was a big problem for Maria, who always slipped in unnoticed into the last row near the door, just before the service began. She did not want to be part of the easily observed advance guard, but complied.

In front of the congregation she felt as if she were leading them in the service. Even with her friends soon to be physically supplying support, she writhed at the idea of being the focus of attention. But no matter how uncomfortable she was about being observed as she communed with God, she found it impossible to say "no" to her friends.

As the time for the service drew near, and the pews behind her were rapidly filling up, Maria twisted around in the front seat. She craned her neck to scan the faces, trying to locate her rescuers. Everyone seemed to notice her frantic behavior. She was sure she could hear them clucking to themselves about her un-church-like antics. Suddenly the music swelled and service began, still with no sign of Rosa and Jane. Maria wasn't ten feet from the altar and the gaze of her minister.

Without warning, her heart exploded in thundering beats like a racehorse out of the gate. She could feel the hooves pummeling her chest. The pulsations cannonaded in her ears as sweat bathed her palsied hands, nearly sending the hymnal crashing to the floor.

She felt inky coldness taking over; she was unable to stand for the first hymn. Curiously, people on either side of her looked down at her. Simultaneously mortified and terrified she was going to keel over, she just hung her head. She was on the brink of humiliating herself before the entire congregation, her pastor, and God.

As all the others around her rejoiced in song, one thing became unmistakably clear to Maria. She was either going crazy or about to die. A heavy blanket of suffocating fear had already enveloped her. Wanting to scream or run, she bit her tongue and clutched her seat to immobilize herself, to keep control until the singing subsided.

She rose just as those around her sat down. Her hymnal, which had been teetering on her knee, finally slid to the floor with an echoing crash. Clutching her purse to her breast, she rushed up the main aisle as the assembled watched her with concern.

Once she was in the safekeeping of her car, away from the judging eyes and knowing looks, Maria calmed down enough to drive home. Slowly her anxiety was shrink-wrapping her world, squeezing it smaller and smaller. As a result, she didn't go to travel conventions any longer. She rarely went on excursions to check out tourist facilities in the many exotic locations served by her agency. Unless she was with her small group of friends, she rarely socialized.

And now she had guaranteed she couldn't go back to her church, one of the main pillars of solace in her life. She had acted like a maniac and humiliated herself. If she went back, if she could go back, she knew she'd have to deal with others' negative judgments of herself as well.

WHAT'S S GOING ON HERE?

Everyone worries occasionally about what others may think of them. Will they like or dislike me? Will they accept or reject me? So it's only natural for you (and everyone else) to be concerned about presenting yourself in social situations in the best light possible. This means you don't wear aluminum foil or Saran Wrap to work. You don't whistle during a funeral. You don't ride your Harley nude or stop bathing.

While a fleeting concern about being evaluated is common, the fear experienced by Joanna, Barry, Joe, Sarah, Harry, and Maria is neither fleeting nor common. Their concerns about being in the spotlight and the adequacy of their self-presentation are more profound. To them the mere possibility of being observed, evaluated, or having their relationships devalued is a threat like being held at gunpoint.

Every time they enter a social situation they perceive as threatening, they feel as though they're walking on a tightrope above the Grand Canyon. Every shaky step is a potential slide into oblivion. Their lives are hanging by each unraveling thread of the frayed rope. Their fear of stumbling makes their making a misstep even more probable. The winds of public scrutiny buffet them, making them sway precipitously above another social disaster … as always, without a safety net.

WHAT DOES IT MEAN?

What Joanna, Barry, Joe, Sarah, Harry, and Maria endure is an intense and persistent fear that is out of proportion to the realities of the situation. Their lives are not in imminent danger, but their bodies, feelings, thoughts, and behaviors are responding as if they were, urging them to flee.

Their arousal system seems stuck in overdrive. They're hypervigilant, alert, and worrying about what "might" happen. This is *anxiety:* What a Gallup Poll says 30–40 million Americans suffer, with 15 million suffering severely enough to warrant treatment.

Anxiety in General in a Nutshell. Anxiety is an inaccurate, unrealistic speculation about threats and potential dangers. When you are anxious, you focus primarily on low probability negative outcomes. Furthermore, you believe you have little or no control. As a result, you are at the mercy of random events and unpredictable people. This means that to survive you have to be constantly on guard.

Psychologists usually talk about anxiety in the context of general arousal or physiological fear in response to perceived danger. In some threatening situations your *parasympathetic nervous system,* the one that slows everything down, takes over. You respond with an automatic inhibition similar to freezing behavior in animals. Everything shuts down, leaving you unable to move, speak, or think clearly.

In other threatening situations your *sympathetic nervous system,* the one that speeds everything up, kicks in, preparing you for action. Your physiology shows a state of high arousal. This arousal reaction includes rapid heart, shallow breathing, sweating, and tremors.

The body's automatic reaction to anxiety is to fight or escape. It compels you to take some action, in the form of a reaction, to reduce the threat. You can avoid going into the threatening situation or escape either physically or psychologically.

Anxiety is a complex blend of a range of emotions, thoughts, beliefs, attitudes, expectations, values, behaviors, and bodily reactions that results in that feeling of discomfort about the future.

When you're anxious, your thoughts become a welter of perceptions of unpredictability and uncontrollability over potentially negative future events. Your attention and focus shift maladaptively toward your inner self and away from others and the reality of the situation. The stronger your perception of uncontrollability in a social situation, the more likely you'll try to avoid the situation.

Thus, your feelings, thoughts, actions, and body response combine to immediately prepare you to cope either effectively or ineffectively with the situation you see as threatening.

Anyone who has experienced this anxiety in social situations, whether in its milder or more severe forms, can strongly identify with Joanna, Barry, Joe, Sarah, Harry, and Maria. This is like a theatrical production where the cast, the props, and the locations may be different, but the story line is basically the same. This is *social anxiety.*

So what is social anxiety? Social anxiety represents a universal concern about what others think. Polls on what people fear most have found consistently that speaking in public, formally and informally, is the number-one American fear. This social fear even out-ranks the fear of death. It occurs in all segments of society, regardless of socio-economic status, race, ethnicity, sexual orientation, religion, or color of skin. Social anxiety is an equal opportunity affliction. It doesn't discriminate … and, unfortunately, no one is immune.

While those of you who have "social anxiety/social phobia" (hereinafter called "SA/SP") share a lot of similarities, you have a lot of differences too. You differ in symptoms, anxiety triggers, and history. You are *not* wearing a one-size-fits-all label. This is because you're a unique individual who's arrived at your current personal state of anxiety through a path that differs from that of others.

Like everyone else in general, you often monitor others' reactions to you at an unconscious level. You look for cues in the social environment to signal how you're being perceived. After all, it's only human to want to influence or control the impressions you make on others. You want to present yourself positively and appropriately to make it more likely others will accept you.

Like everyone else, you also monitor the effect of your presentation at a conscious level. By monitoring and controlling your self-presentation, you try to maximize the resulting social benefits as well as minimize the resulting social costs.

But unlike everyone else, you monitor your presentations to the extent that your thoughts are exclusively about the impression you're making. To you nothing else matters. These negative thoughts take over your every thought and overwhelm you with fear.

Because of this, when you do interact with other people, you tend to behave in ways that reduce the amount of social contact you have with them. You withdraw both physically and psychologically. Typically you stand on the outer perimeter of conversations as long as possible, maybe smiling and nodding, and hoping you won't have to try to contribute anything remotely intelligent.

In general, SA/SPers tend not to initiate conversations. But when you're in them, you engage in less eye contact and speak less. You allow longer silences and take longer to respond. The same holds true when you're before large numbers of people or those perceived to be critical. As a result, you're more frequently seen as reticent, shy, or introverted.

When you do speak, you may tend to try to say everything in one breath. This is to get it all in before the other person stops listening … or before you forget the point you want to make … or both. This causes others to look at you strangely, thus confirming your worst fears.

Yet, some of you, because of the kind of work you do, such as teaching, selling, or consulting, are forced to present a more extroverted face. You have to initiate conversations, speak up at meetings, give talks, and interact with authority figures. This gives you the look of confidence. However, this apparent level of social competence, doesn't necessarily mean that you aren't working very hard to appear comfortable, outgoing, and adequate.

Because you may push through your feelings of dread doesn't mean you aren't struggling with social anxiety. It doesn't mean you're not suffering. It doesn't mean you wouldn't prefer little or no interaction, to work alone with your computer, and never step into the spotlight of public evaluation again.

What's at Its Core? The core of social anxiety is a sense of *vulnerability* that results from the thoughts and feelings that accompany threat. As Aaron T. Beck, the developer of cognitive therapy, suggests, vulnerability can be defined as your perception of yourself as subject to dangers (internal and/or external) over which you lack the control that affords you a sense of safety. In other words, the less control you have, the more vulnerable you feel ... and conversely.

When you enter a socially threatening situation, you feel as if you're swimming among sharks. You see serious consequences for a single slip or inadequate performance. You believe your safety requires adherence to a strict set of rules of appropriate behaviors, such as social expectations, norms, or mores.

Your perception of vulnerability is dependent upon a number of factors. First is what you see as the relative power between the person "evaluating" you and yourself.

Their "power" is in their being able to provide or withhold desired resources, like love, acceptance, or money. The greater you perceive their power to be, the greater your impulse will be to do what is considered to be "socially desirable" to get those resources.

Second is the degree of threat, the severity of the consequences, and the probability of its occurring.

Third is your threshold for threat and your skills to deal with threat. When your threshold to threat is high, you're less vulnerable. When your coping skills and resources are good, your perception of threat is low.

Fourth is your willingness to confront powerful figures and the skills you have to do so. The more assertive you are the less vulnerable you are. A "confident" mask, or presentation, may make you feel more confident and convince your evaluator that you actually are what you appear to be. As your self-confidence increases, your vulnerability decreases.

Fifth is a lack of resilience that allows you to buffer the effects of stress and anxiety. Resilience is based on your beliefs of commitment, control, and challenge. These beliefs are the basis of self-confidence.

Commitment is the belief that persistence in your goals will result in something meaningful.

Control is the belief that you can influence what's going on around you and you are ready to act on it

Challenge is the belief that negative life events can be turned around to result in positive outcomes.

When you hold these beliefs, you're likely to engage in resilience coping behaviors. This means confronting anxious circumstances by changing your beliefs and actions so to reduce the stressfulness of the circumstances. You can do this through *reframing*, or re-labeling.

For example, rather than see an office Christmas party as a personal threat, upsetting to your normal routine interactions, you can reframe it as an opportunity to make yourself visible, with an eye toward future promotions or becoming acquainted with others to lessen your loneliness.

Your anxiety-distorted thinking and erroneous beliefs magnify your vulnerability. As an SA/SPer, you minimize your positive personal resources and focus on your weaknesses. You maximize all potential catastrophes and expect public humiliation.

You have difficulty being objective about yourself so you feel helpless and under attack. You believe you lack important coping skills. You doubt your ability to deal with threat. Your resulting lack of self-confidence holds you back from reaching your goals. Moreover, it doesn't protect you from the effects of failure and negative evaluation.

It's Making the Right Impression, Stupid. It's true. Most of social life is dedicated to influencing others and being influenced by others in return. This means you need to manage impressions. Nearly everything in Western culture depends upon being seen as competent, responsible, ethical, and friendly. The impressions we make on each other determine many of the central outcomes of our social lives.

As you know, your failure to make the desired impression you want has important ramifications for you. Specifically, it means you don't exert the influence you want in situations important to you. As a result, you may not snag a particular job or promotion, be considered for club membership, make the team line-up, or make friends, date, or marry the person you want.

This is the crux of the SA/SPer's problem. You know you have to make good impressions on others, but you don't know how you can do that. To make a good impression you have to be in a social situation. But to be in a social situation is to be at risk of being negatively evaluated by the people whom you want to impress. It's a no-win situation.

All you can think about is how you feel, what you think, what you think others will think about you, and how vulnerable you are. When you focus on yourself alone in this intense manner, you can't likewise focus on others and the environment.

But you feel you need to focus on your thoughts, feelings, beliefs, and behaviors to protect yourself. However, that is not to say you are not constantly monitoring the world around you. You are. But it is *only* in terms of how you think it relates negatively to you.

When you focus on the negative, you are seeing the world through a *negative filter*. This means you don't look for hard, objective evidence as to what is really going on. Instead, you look for anything that will support your negative feelings. For you what you *feel* is absolute truth.

Also, social situations create for you a strong sense of having no control. The greater your sense of uncontrollability in a situation, the greater is the likelihood of your avoidance of that situation. Avoidance or escape becomes a rewarding response for you because it immediately removes your anxiety.

This self-focus creates an ongoing internal dialogue about what is going on, what it means, and how it will negatively impact you. Self-focus perpetuates self-focus. It's a vicious circle.

What is so unfortunate about this is that you really want to put your best "face" forward in order to be seen as competent and socially desirable by others. But, because you're so wrapped up in analyzing and interpreting everything, and assuming it is a threat, you don't project the friendly, approachable image you want and need.

Maybe I'm Just Not Motivated Enough. Motivation is an important part of impression management. How motivated you are in trying to manage your impressions depends upon the degree to which you value the outcomes you hope for.

For example, the more important and valuable the outcome, like getting a date or a job, the more concerned you'll be about obtaining it. The more concerned you are about obtaining it, the more motivated you'll be to create the desired impression. But with SA/SP you can feel very motivated to do it and yet not do it. This is because your negative thinking and avoidant behavior sabotage you.

When Does Social Anxiety Occur? SA/SP is generally anticipatory so it occurs *before* anything actually goes wrong. You *expect* it to go wrong. For example, you would tend to worry now about the speech you are to give in a month's time.

However, on other occasions you may react anxiously to situations that have already occurred. You may see people look at you, hear them laugh, and then become anxious, such as in Barry's dating anxiety. You also may recall incidents from the past that made you anxious and re-experience their associated agony.

WHAT MAKES SOCIAL ANXIETY A DISORDER?

It's important to note that your simply being uncomfortable speaking in public, being observed, or evaluated isn't sufficient to fit the definition of social anxiety disorder. The difference between social anxiety and social anxiety disorder is the degree of its severity and its persistence.

Just-plain social anxiety is like being in a swamped rowboat in a five-foot-deep pond. It's uncomfortable and undesirable but bearable. This feeling lasts just until the situation is over and the survivor makes it to shore.

But the anxiety of social anxiety disorder is like being on the Titanic after it hits the iceberg. It's intense, full of extremes of emotion, thoughts, and behaviors. Its effects can be paralyzing for survivors and last for years.

For anxiety in social situations to become *social anxiety disorder*, there needs to be a (1) high degree of nervousness, uncertainty, dread, and self-consciousness about negative evaluation in social situations that is

(2) severe, (3) lasts at least six months, and (4) significantly interferes with your daily activities.

When this anxiety encompasses three or more situations, it's called *generalized social anxiety disorder.* Generalized social anxiety accounts for about 80% of all those with SA/SP.

Social anxiety disorder may also occur independently where you experience anxiety only with respect to a specific social performance or task. Your response to the situation could be dependent upon the actual presence of others or their implied presence, where you associate negative evaluation with the specific performance or the task's characteristics.

This is *discrete,* or non-generalized, *social anxiety disorder.* It's also called *performance anxiety.* Discrete social anxiety may occur as a single social anxiety, such as in test anxiety or Harry's stage anxiety, or as part of the multiple-component generalized social anxiety like Joe's.

What About How You Look?   Social anxiety can also occur when you're chronically anxious about others' judging your physical appearance. For example, when a chunky child is teased mercilessly about its weight, the adult person will tend to carry a large body image even when they are slim as an adult. The actual weight isn't as important as the emotional image you have of yourself. Being overly concerned about how you look physically can result in imagined body flaws.

As compared with some subjective standard or ideal, you often see yourself as too fat or too thin; too short or too tall; knees too bony or pudgy; nose too crooked, hooked, or bulbous; eyes too close together or too far apart; skin, hair, and eyes the wrong color; body too hairy or not hairy enough; secondary sex characteristics too pendulous or puny.

Your obsessing about these perceived "defects" drives you to constantly monitor others' reactions to see if they're noticing and commenting upon your perceived "flaw." Physique anxiety can create social anxiety and embarrassment. When this condition is severe enough, it is a separate disorder called *body dysmorphism.*

The Vicious Circle. When you're drowning in this whirlpool of excessive concern about being perceived unfavorably, you're often left unsatisfied with your interactions. If you're dissatisfied, you expect those with whom you interact to feel the same. It gets you coming and going. As a result, you see yourself to be less socially skilled … a social flop. It creates a downward spiral.

Even if your social skills are intact, your social awkwardness tends to reinforce and perpetuate your social fear. You doubt you can make your desired impression on others. You fear being embarrassed or humiliated in front of others. And because you have an underlying rigidity in your thinking about behavior, you assume things are black or white: there is a "right" way and a "wrong" way to do things. And, of course, you assume that you're automatically locked into doing things the "wrong" way.

While the cardinal signs of social anxiety are increased public self-consciousness and exquisite sensitivity to evaluation in social situations, the overarching theme is a *fear of being found wanting*. Your believing you're being perceived as inadequate raises all kinds of questions in your mind about your likeability, general acceptability, and self-worth. You will doubt the likelihood of having intimacy and loving relationships as well as general social success.

SITUATIONS THAT TRIGGER SOCIAL ANXIETY

According to Craig Holt and associates, there are four categories of situations that precipitate social anxiety. Knowing which social anxiety category applies to you can be useful in targeting dysfunctional behaviors for treatment:

- *Formal speaking and interaction* (giving a talk before an audience, performing on stage, giving a report to a group, speaking up at a meeting, participating in small groups, and acting)

- *Informal speaking and interaction* (giving a party, calling someone you don't know very well, meeting strangers, trying to pick up someone at a bar, dating, having sex)

- *Assertive interaction* (talking to authority figures, expressing disageement, expressing disapproval of someone, returning goods to a store, resisting high-pressure salespeople)

- *Observation of behavior* (eating while others are watching, modeling clothes, simply being observed while working, taking tests, using a public restroom, or writing).

It's important to note that adults and adolescents may differ on the category of their most feared situations. Adults tend to fear formal speaking and interactions most whereas adolescents and young adults tend to fear informal speaking and interactions most because of their dependence on peer approval.

Avoidance may or may not be a feature of your experience with SA/SP. Some people avoid some or all feared social situations. Others may reluctantly confront the situation and stoically endure the associated distress of doing so.

HOW SOCIAL ANXIETY PERPETUATES ITSELF

SA/SP is a *feedback loop* of the four components of physiology, emotion, thoughts, and behavior. Each influences the others, with no one component *the* primary mover in the process. While physiological arousal is necessary for SA/SP to occur, it is not sufficient to create that sense of vague, unrecognized danger in the future.

How Does the Feedback Loop Work? You begin with a possible hypersensitivity or biological predisposition to arousal. Then some stressful life events involving your performance, such as job loss or relationship failure, negatively interrupt what is your generally functional behavior. Now you're left feeling uncertain, self-conscious, apprehensive, helpless, and vulnerable.

The negative emotion you're experiencing becomes associated with increasing feelings of future uncontrollability and unpredictability. When you encounter a social situation that you expect *not* to be able to handle, you feel apprehensive. You tell yourself, for example, there's no way you'll be able to take part in the organizational meeting or eat with fellow employees. How helpless you feel will be tempered by your coping skills, social skills, and social support network. The better your skills and social support, the less helpless you're likely to feel.

Next your action tendencies are geared up; they are ready to go. Your attention shifts to internal evaluation. You become more aroused as you listen to your negative self-talk, telling you that you're going to muff this meeting too and look foolish.

As you become more aroused, you become hyper-alert, looking for things that trigger negative emotional content. As a result, what you recognize and remember are only those things that support your current negative mood and arousal-interpretation.

You're flooded with memories of inadequacy and rejection that are painful and unacceptable. These are recollections you're usually able to keep under wraps. Your negative emotion increases further as you keep building layer upon layer of anger and fear.

Finally, you're overwhelmed by intense worry that so preoccupies you that you can't perform at the meeting. You stutter, stammer, and blank out. At this point you feel so bad you want to escape.

How Do You Get From Arousal to Emotion? For that feeling of arousal in social situations to have emotional meaning for you, it has to be interpreted and labeled. In general, when you feel heightened arousal, you look for specific cues in the situation to determine what label you should attach and how to interpret it.

For example, if you experience arousal in the presence of an attractive individual, you'll probably label the feeling as "sexual excitement." If you feel arousal after learning of the death of a loved one, you'll probably label the sensations as "sorrow." After receiving a severe insult, you'll probably label it "anger."

This psychological process is called *cognitive appraisal*. You look at the various dimensions of the situation to determine the emotional content of the situation.

For example, in a classic experiment conducted by psychologists Stanley Schachter and Jerome Singer in 1962 participants were injected with adrenaline, producing heart palpitations, hand tremor, rapid breathing, and that warm feeling of flushing. All participants were led to believe the injection was an experimental vitamin supplement. One group (Informed) was told to expect these side effects as a result of the injection.

So when the symptoms occurred, the Informed group would have an appropriate reason and label for their feelings. The second group (Uninformed) was given no prior warning about the symptoms. The third group (Misinformed) was told that the injection could produce numbness, itching, and slight headache, obviously inappropriate reasons to explain the symptoms they actually experienced.

Shortly after the injection, before onset of symptoms, an experimental confederate joined each participant. The confederate had been trained to act in either an angry or happy manner. For participants without an adequate explanation for their symptoms (Uninformed and

Misinformed) the actions of the confederate provided an appropriate label. Results showed that participants in the Uninformed and Misinformed groups adopted the label provided by the confederate's behavior, while the Informed group participants did not.

What Are Some External Situational Cues? Lots of other factors contribute to how you think and feel about situations. For example, you unconsciously look at what you perceive to be *pleasant* about the situation. Pleasantness contributes to a good mood.

You look at *agency* to see who has responsibility or control in the situation. If you perceive yourself to be responsible for a big mistake, you're likely to feel guilt or shame. If you perceive that another person is responsible, you're likely to feel anger or contempt instead. But if the circumstances are responsible, like a rainstorm destroying an outdoor wedding, you are likely to feel sadness.

You also look for *uncertainty*. When events are unpredictable and personally uncontrollable, you're likely to feel fear. You look at *attention* and the degree to which you need to stay attuned. If the situation requires little of your attention, you're likely to feel bored. Or if it requires too much, you'll likely feel frustrated.

However, this process of inference-from-behavior can lead to errors in assigning causality, called *misattributions*, because people can laugh because of anxiety, shed tears when feeling joyous, and eat to comfort themselves in times of stress.

This is particularly important because how you attribute causes to your social anxiety, or shyness, affects how you act. Philip Zimbardo, the leading researcher in shyness, found that when shy people had something other than the labels of "shyness" or "anxiety" to account for their feelings of arousal, they did not feel or act shy or anxious.

What Happens When Situational Cues Are Missing? When strong external cues are lacking, you look to your own behaviors to infer how you feel. For example, I'm laughing so I must feel happy. I'm crying so I must feel sad. I'm eating so I must feel hungry.

But Cognitive Appraisal Differs in Social Anxiety. While most individuals when aroused look to situational cues for labeling, SA/SPers don't. Instead, you ignore the full range of external cues. Instead, you focus on yourself and look internally for thought, feeling, and physical cues. But unfortunately, the cues you see are distorted.

This distortion results from your erroneous thinking and negative self-talk. It also is a consequence of your perceived inability to predict and control future events or obtain your desired results in the future. The upshot is that you narrow your focus specifically on negative emotional content.

In summary, in SA/SPer's cognitive appraisal you unconsciously assess those cues that have personal relevance to your well-being: that is, those that will harm you or help you. You look for coping options. You associate the present situation with past experiences. And you look at what you expect to happen as a consequence of your actions.

However, this process doesn't serve SA/SPers well because you tend to recognize and recall selectively *only* those things that match your negative feelings. You go on auto-pilot, ready to see things as "anxiety" whenever you experience physiological arousal in social situations. It's like having an overnight bag always packed for a sudden business trip.

Social Anxiety Creates Its Own Reality. Your internal focus and your faulty information processing serve to reinforce all your negative attitudes, beliefs, thoughts, feelings, and behaviors. As a result, it eliminates the possibility of your finding disconfirming evidence in the situation outside yourself.

For example, when Barry was debating with himself about the risks involved in speaking to the young woman with the sweet smile, he was so wrapped up in his own concerns about being played for a fool that he never saw her nervously glance away when another young man spoke to her. He didn't see her friends trying to convince her to stay awhile longer. When he saw her shake her head "no" in reply, he interpreted it as referring to him. In fact, she was telling her friends that she really wasn't really interested in the man who had already spoken to her, but in someone else … Barry.

As cartoonist and playwright Jules Feiffer asks, "If you're not able to communicate successfully between yourself and yourself, how are you supposed to make it with the strangers outside?"

Is All Anxiety in Social Situations Social Anxiety? While SA/SP results from social sources, obviously not all anxiety experienced in social situations reflects "social anxiety." If you're alone at an ATM after dark and several members of a street gang are approaching you, the nervousness you feel isn't social anxiety. If you're waiting to hear from your boss about the future of the company, your tension isn't social anxiety. If the plate of spaghetti the waiter is carrying past you starts to dip in your direction, your discomfort isn't social anxiety

HOW MANY SA/SPERS ARE THERE?

Of all the anxiety disorders: agoraphobia, specific phobia, panic disorder, acute stress disorder, generalized anxiety disorder, obsessive-compulsive disorder, and SA/SP, SA/SP is the most common anxiety disorder, the least recognized, and the most under-treated anxiety disorder. It wasn't until 1980 that SA/SP was listed in the American Psychiatric Association's *Diagnostic and Statistical Manual of Mental Disorders, the Third Edition (DSM-III)*.

But it wasn't until 1994 with *DSM-IV*, that SA/SP was carefully defined using restrictive criteria to differentiate it from similar conditions, such as agoraphobia.

Since then, the National Institute of Mental Health has found that over 13.3% of American adults have this disorder some time over their lifetime, making it the third most common psychiatric disorder, after depression and alcoholism.

Millions suffer from this life-pervading personal problem in multiple situations. SA/SP interferes with overall satisfaction and enjoyment in life. In its severest form it can lead to functional impairment, such as alcohol and substance abuse, depression, suicidal thoughts, dropping out of school, unemployment, and financial dependence.

SA/SP also causes fatigue, insomnia, headaches, gas, diarrhea, constipation, and various muscle aches, particularly in the head, neck, and shoulders. It causes you to participate in fewer activities, meet fewer people, and experience difficulties with work, school, and interpersonal relationships.

It causes you to become less outgoing, more solitary and socially isolated, often relying on your pets and the Internet for companionship. You work at whatever is available that requires less self-presentation from you. This means you're likely to go from flipping hamburgers to working in a stockroom, from seeing patients to hunkering behind a microscope, from working with adults to playing with children.

As a result, you frequently feel stuck in a no-win situation. You see your dreams of having a college education and well-paying job, owning a home, or having a permanent relationship, one by one slip away out of reach. As a result, SA/SP has national health consequences.

Perhaps the most significant of these is that SA/SPers frequently turn to alcohol and illegal drugs for temporary relief from this tension, dread, and uncertainty. Because of this, the disorder is now seen as a cause of alcoholism and drug abuse and as a candidate for public health prevention strategies.

The number of SA/SPers is increasing. Over 20 million people in the U.S. alone feel intensely self-conscious or anxious in social situation, from work to relationships. The current estimate is that up to 50% of the U.S. population have experienced social anxiety at some point in their lives.

TEST YOURSELF FOR SOCIAL ANXIETY DISORDER

Do you think you have SA/SP? Answer the following questionnaire **yes** or **no** to find out. (This assessment is for information purposes only and is *not* to be used for diagnosis.)

____Do you experience intense and persistent anxiety when you're exposed to social or performance situations you fear?

____Do you feel nervous anticipating future social or performance situations you fear?

____Do you feel nervous about meeting strangers?

____Do you feel nervous being observed or scrutinized by others?

____Do you feel nervous about being evaluated by others?

____Do you feel your nervousness is excessive or unreasonable for the real danger present?

____Do you avoid these feared social or performance situations or endure them while experiencing considerable distress?

____Does anxious anticipation of the feared social or performance situations significantly interfere with your activities, relationships, or normal routines?

____Does avoidance of the feared social or performance situations significantly interfere with your activities, relationships, or normal routines?

____Have you ruled out a medical condition or the effects of drugs or medications to account for your anxiety?

The greater the number of **yeses** the greater the likelihood you have SA/SP as defined by the *DSM-IV* (inventory adapted from *DSM-IV* definition).

ARE WORRY AND ANXIETY DISORDER THE SAME?

Anxiety and *worry* are often used interchangeably, but are they the same? Worry, like anxiety, has been defined as a narrow, intense emotional focus on the future with accompanying symptoms of physiological arousal. But, in general, worry, unlike anxiety, is like a rehearsal for dealing with a specific problem. You focus your mind on the problem in order to search more efficiently for a solution. Anxiety tends to be more free-floating than worry.

According to clinical psychologist Thomas D. Borkovec, everyone worries. Some degree of worry is expected and normal because it is part of the problem-solving process.

When "normal worriers" encounter a problem, they first assess its magnitude. If they find the problem is trivial or beyond their control, they decide to forget about it. But, if it has significance for them *and* they believe they can affect it, they imagine the things that could happen next. Then they brainstorm some solutions, pick one, and act on it in their own best interest.

It is worry that motivates them to address the problem directly and deliberately. Their worry behavior is directed at and results in finding solutions. They exert only the energy necessary to put the things they want in motion.

But "chronic worriers," those who spend more than one and a half hours a day in apprehensive turmoil about a problem, frequently find themselves unable to deal with it or extricate themselves from thinking about it.

They think about their problems and become anxious. Their worry takes on a life of its own, becomes self-perpetuating and part of the problem. Despite their acknowledgment that the things they worry most about never seem to happen, they become immobilized in the process.

WHAT ABOUT STRESS DISORDER?

Stress is everywhere. It pushes you on and holds you back at the same time. With chronic, intense stress often comes a stress disorder. With chronic, intense anxiety often comes anxiety disorder. However, while stress and anxiety may seem synonymous, they are not.

In anxiety the focus of attention is internal, on yourself, such as on what you think and feel. In stress the focus of attention is external, on the situation or event itself, such as a disintegrating relationship. While anxiety has emotional, cognitive, behavioral, and physiological symptoms of fear, stress has *only* the physiological symptoms, such as rapid heart, shallow breathing, and sweating. Only anxiety is associated with increased worry, negativity, and a feeling of helplessness.

EFFECT OF CULTURE ON SOCIAL ANXIETY

It's important to remember that how SA/SP manifests itself is a function of the culture in which it occurs. The culture gives it form and dictates how and when members of the culture perceive themselves to be the object of threatening social evaluation. Each culture has its own set of social expectations its members are expected to follow. This means that to understand social anxiety in any given culture you have to understand the norms for behavior and social skills, and how deviations are verbally and nonverbally expressed.

In several East Asian countries, such as Japan and Korea, the culture defines the individual not as individual but as a member of a group: family, social group, or community. Consequently, the behavior of the individual, whether good or bad, is seen as a direct reflection of the group. Deviations from the norm ("individualism") are not tolerable.

One is responsible to the group for the welfare of the group and is dependent upon their evaluation. SA/SP in this culture, called *taijin kyofu-sho* (fear syndrome) in Japan, focuses on the specific fear of offending or embarrassing others in public because it brings shame to the social group to which one belongs. This offense and embarrassment may also result from blushing, displaying unsightly body parts, or emitting body odors.

In Western cultures, on the contrary, individuals are defined by their individualism and independence. Being unique, self-aggrandizing, and standing out from the crowd are not only accepted but also expected.

One's primary responsibility is for oneself. In these cultures the focus of social fear is embarrassing and bringing shame to oneself.

BEING OVERWHELMED BY SOCIAL STRESSORS

Defining the present cultural climate in which we in Western societies experience SA/SP is important for your overall understanding of the predisposition and prevalence of the condition. Over the last several decades, the number of social stressors has increased dramatically.

With each successive year things have only gotten worse. This has led to system overload for many, perhaps helping trigger clinical symptoms of SA/SP. Under this accumulating burden, you seem unable to process all the inputs from your environment. This may be because there are either too many inputs for you to cope with or they come too fast for you to process them in the proper order.

This is the situation to which you are forced to adapt. Even though this overload distorts daily life on every level (from the physical to the psychological, from the social to societal) most of the time it leaves the majority of you still able to set priorities and make choices.

But social stressors interfere with the roles you play, whether as parent, child, worker, friend, or lover. They interfere with how you follow social norms, such as becoming independent and productive members of society. They significantly and negatively impact SA/SPers by creating and maintaining a negative atmosphere.

Let's take a look at some of the many factors contributing to this overload.

Value Shift. Everything around you seems to be in a state of flux, producing feelings of insecurity and worry. This has been made worse by 9/11, wars, and the focus on terrorism. There are no stable, consistent socially accepted and socially enforced standards or values by which to live. Over the last 40 years the pendulum of ethics has swung from the position of favoring group/community rights and individual duties to individual rights and group/community duties. The transition for the individual has been from dependence and interdependence to independence. The continuing emphasis on "me" and "self" creates a climate of self-focus and helps perpetuate your sense of isolation, alienation, and loss of community.

Mobility. Sense of community has been rapidly disappearing since the 1950s when increased individual mobility made it easier to travel and travel in ever-widening circles. Always on the move, you've grown accustomed to brief encounters and accept them as the norm. You see time as a precious commodity, in short supply.

You feel pressured … so much to do and so little time in which to do it. As a result, you don't want to have to wait to build relationships in order to communicate your message of who you are. It's no longer a small, closed world where you have known everybody with whom you'll interact since your childhood.

Density. Everywhere you look space is at a premium. New houses are being built closer together with postage-stamp lots. Developments are springing up like crabgrass. In all but the most rural areas the roads and highways are filled to capacity from morning 'til night. People are becoming denser and seem to be carrying this density around with them as they move at a fast clip. This crowding and pace create an unremitting level of arousal, keeping people on edge.

Efficiency. In this big, wide, hurry-up world you need to be both effective and efficient. Efficiency suggests creating and relying upon first impressions to do the job, despite their superficiality and seeming artificiality. You sell cars, food, politicians, movies, and wars through impression management.

Social Support. With mobility comes disconnection, the breaking up of the nuclear family, and loosening of the extended family ties. Rarely do three generations live in the same house, in the same neighborhood, or even in the same town.

Social support networks, interdependent groups consisting of friends and family which are important to your mental and physical health, especially in times of stress, are likewise becoming more difficult to establish and maintain.

Business Trends. Increasingly competition, mergers, outsourcing, economic downturns, and business- and industry downsizing often have debilitating social and economic effects. Competition, mergers, and downsizing are also changing workers' perception of loyalty. Jobs have become simultaneously more demanding and less secure. No longer is it a given that if you work well and hard for a company that you'll be rewarded by being guaranteed a place with them until you retire.

Jobs. You can no longer define your self-image by your job. Competence, experience, and knowledge are no longer the linchpins of your getting the rewards of your labor. It's become harder to hold onto the belief that upward mobility is a "birthright."

Despite this environment, you tend to expect more from your job, not less. You expect your jobs to use your talents, be a challenge, be an avenue of self-expression and meaning, and provide you a means of contributing to society. But the reality is that work has become more routine and specialized, offering less satisfaction and remuneration.

Youth. Particularly hard hit is the younger generation that faces an economic situation for which it has been inadequately prepared. Imbued with the unrealistic expectation of continuing economic prosperity, of having things better than their parents did, they grapple, often unsuccessfully, with underdeveloped self-sufficiency, unemployment, and underemployment in all but a few circumscribed areas. As a result, young adults may tend to feel more disillusioned and alienated.

Privacy. Loss of privacy often looms large in your psyches. Spam, computer data collection, storage, and retrieval by large corporations and the government make personal details of your lives easily accessible to marketers, employers, insurance companies, law enforcement, and a whole host of others. Your "confidential" medical records are still anything but confidential.

Employers listen to your telephone calls, read your e-mail, search your lockers, and require testing of your personality, honesty, and urine. Closed-circuit television cameras monitor your actions everywhere you go, whether in stores, businesses, bathrooms, or on the street. Telecommunications companies monitor and mine data for government surveillance. While there's always been and will continue to be some unwanted intrusion into your life, restricting the access of others to what's intimate in your lives is even less under your control today.

Crime. Fear of crime, violence, and terrorism is at a high level. Even as crime rates are dropping, sales of handguns are increasing because you feel alone, anonymous, unprotected, and unable to predict and control an alien environment. You may feel leery of strangers and concerned about certain ethnic groups. The resulting heightened sense of physical and emotional vulnerability makes you think twice about trusting or reaching out a hand to another.

Technology. Technological changes are occurring rapidly too, barely allowing you time to adjust before the next wave hits. Many of these changes produce a sort of "techno-anxiety" because you are not sure how they'll affect your life, if they'll impact your values, families, or economic status. Many of these changes also reinforce your isolation by further reducing face-to-face interaction.

You no longer need a teller to get your money; you can use a card at the ATM. You no longer need a station attendant or a cashier in order to get gas or pay for it; you can use a card at the pump. You no longer need a telephone operator to make a call; you can dial the pre-recorded information you need and use a card at the phone. You can order nearly anything online and never have to encounter a salesperson, at least a non-robotic one. This automation offers efficiency, convenience, but no human contact.

Computers. Similarly computers are providing you the access to an overwhelming array of information. You can spend hours every day surfing the web, doing research, working on your website or blog, collecting and sending e-mail, playing video games, listening to music, watching movies, or launching product promotions. You can also chat anonymously and superficially with disembodied others. You can do this without interacting face-to-face with another human being.

Because you are unable to observe the verbal and nonverbal aspects of most online social interactions, you may feel a lesser sense of a personal connection. Personal connection mediates your behavior toward others.

Online relationships have a magnetic pull because you can meet large numbers of people, quickly and easily, and be less concerned about negative evaluation. You also can be whoever and whatever you want, as can anyone else. This means that without face-to-face contact you may be more likely to be vulnerable to and at-risk for fantasizing and creating unrealistic expectations about others and relationships, thus setting yourself up for disappointment.

Real-time relationships, which are guided by explicit social norms, are messy, awkward, and sometimes stifling. They require attention, emotion, problem solving, decision making, and work.

But in cyberspace the "rules" governing interpersonal relations and interaction are more ambiguous. You can be whomever you want. You don't have to pay careful attention to what the other is saying or meaning. You don't have to contribute your emotion or work through problems. And, if you wish, you can simply and easily walk away from it all with just a click of the mouse, reinforcing your avoidance of social situations.

Financial and Health Security. Due to economic upheavals there are justified fears that Social Security, Medicare, and Medicaid will not be available when people are of the age or financial situation to need them, depending upon whether or not adequate health care reform takes place. As a result, you cannot be sure if you'll receive health and mental health care or quality care when you need it.

Media Image. All the while the media reinforce and perpetuate unrealistic expectations about what "should be" through TV, movies, and advertising. Perfection is the goal: looking anorexic and beautiful, being rich, famous, and powerful. Life becomes a fantasy of endless possibilities where you're taught to desire more, imagine more, and expect more.

By feeding on your sense of inadequacy, embarrassment, alienation, and withdrawal, the media claim to know and be able to provide you with the panacea. To this end they promote consumerism, materialism, and instant gratification as the solution to the void in your life. But in holding out false hope that the right deodorant, newest athletic shoe, whitened teeth, or enhanced breast size will make you feel better about yourself, they only make you feel even more inadequate and anxious.

SUMMARY

What all this suggests is that there are many social forces currently at work that combine to increasing everyone's stress, fears, and insecurities. However, you who suffer from social anxiety will tend to be more strongly impacted by these forces. Your inability to fully cope with this overload contributes to your predisposition to anxiety and helps set the stage for SA/SP. There are four key reasons these stressors are significant especially for SA/SPers.

*First, they focus your attention on yourself.

*Second, they decrease the amount of face-to-face social interaction.

*Third, they decrease your learning social skills and communication skills or practicing the skills you have.

*Fourth, they reinforce your isolation and loneliness.

Henry David Thoreau writes, "The mass of men lead lives of quiet desperation." Is it any wonder that the number of individuals with social anxiety is increasing?

2

DISSECTING SA/SP—WHAT IT IS & ISN'T

"Why worry about the future? The present is more than most
of us can handle."

WHAT ARE ITS SOCIAL CHARACTERISTICS?

When SA/SP actually begins in your life is unclear, but 47% of you
with it have reported either a lifelong disorder or onset prior to the
age of 10. The general time frame is thought to be between 11 and 17
years old. In my case, however, it didn't reveal itself until I was in my
20s!

What is clear is that since SA/SP involves public self-consciousness
and a concern about negative evaluation, SA/SP can't begin until you
have (1) an awareness of others and (2) an awareness of yourself as
an object that can be evaluated. This public self-consciousness occurs
around 8 years old.

While there has been a great deal of research done on different
aspects of public self-consciousness, unfortunately it has been done
under different labels (shyness, social anxiety, self-consciousness),
with different definitions at different times with different populations
(adults versus children).

Diagnosis of SA/SP in children, for example, has slightly different
characteristics than it does in adults. Because the condition is dependent
upon understanding the impact of social interaction, children must be at
a stage where they are able to have age-appropriate social relationships
with familiar others. That means this anxiety must occur with other
children, not just with adults. While adults are expected to recognize
that their social fear is excessive or unreasonable, children are not.

Despite the disorder's early onset, SA/SPers who present for
treatment tend to do so 15–25 years after onset, around age 30.
For those who don't seek treatment, your public self-consciousness,
concerns over social threat, and fears of negative evaluation will tend

to remain relatively stable over your life span, likely following a fairly chronic course.

In most anxiety disorders there's a marked predominance of females; however, in SA/SP the distribution seems to be equal across the sexes presenting at clinics. While females are more likely to report social anxiety, males are more likely to seek treatment for it. This discrepancy may be attributable to the social influences of sex roles.

Sex Roles. Western society generally socializes its males to be aggressive. That is, males are still expected to be more assertive than females, have higher career aspirations and achievement, and initiate both romantic and non-romantic contact. This means that males who exhibit social anxiety or shyness won't meet those expectations. As a result, they may receive negative feedback from parents and peers that their behavior is inappropriate.

While sex-role stereotypes allow females to be withdrawn and non-assertive, they punish males for it. Parents are more likely to admonish their sons than their daughters for shy and inhibited behavior. Because of a social fear of appearing passive and "feminine," boys may restrict their interests and their ability to engage in a wider range of human activities.

Social anxiety/shyness then may be a major social impediment for males' social development. It may lead to less effective interaction and relationship satisfaction. It may provide more interference with life for them than for females, thus motivating them to seek help.

The female's sex-role stereotype, on the other hand, still expects and rewards reticence, withdrawal, and non-assertiveness to some degree. The so-called "upside" of this is that females can hide their disorder behind these perceptions and expectations. The downside, however, is that these same perceptions and expectations make it difficult for females who seek help to be seen as needing help. Depending upon the health care professional's own sex-role stereotypes, the female with SA/SP may be seen as perfectly "normal," or a little shy.

Relationships and Careers. By its very nature SA/SP interferes with *all* interpersonal relationships, but does so particularly with romantic relationships. In general, SA/SPers are less likely to marry.

For both males and females shyness is also negatively correlated with a number of behaviors considered to be important career-wise.

Shy people are less likely to seek out information, network, look for mentors, work in teams, and make the decisions so instrumental to career advancement.

Likewise, many SA/SPers find it difficult to pick and stay with a career path. In school you're guided by the amount of interpersonal interaction required of you. Consequently, you may change majors, not because your interests have changed, but because your fear of public speaking and evaluation is greater than your desire to pursue a particular field.

The same holds true for work. You tend to have poor work records, with reduced work productivity. This is because you're frequently overwhelmed by the self-presentation requirements of your job. When the pressure is too much, you move on.

In general you have three times the rate of unemployment of non-SA/SPers, with 23% of you reporting substantially impaired working performance due to your SA/SP. Thus, as SA/SP increases, your positive career behaviors and career potential decrease.

ARE THERE DIFFERENCES IN FEAR RESPONSES?

Those of you who react to a single fear situation, like test taking, performing, or public speaking, respond differently from those of you who react to many feared situations. Individuals who are fearful about public speaking, for example, show more rapid heartbeat and palpitations at that prospect than do those who are fearful about being around people in general.

According to social anxiety clinical researcher Stefan Hofmann, it appears that discrete SA/SP may produce a strong fear response (similar to that found in a Specific Phobia, like fear of heights) whereas generalized SA/SP frequently produces a more general, variable, and inconsistent anxiety response, depending upon the particulars of the social situation. Discrete SA/SP is more focused and specific whereas generalized SA/SP is more unfocused and general.

Hofmann also suggests that there may be *three* types of SA/SP: In addition to the two clinical types (discrete and generalized) there may be a sub-clinical (a generalized *non-diagnostic* SA/SP). While people in this third group would show elevated symptoms, the symptoms wouldn't meet the *DSM-IV* diagnostic criteria for SA/SP.

The difference would be that while they experience social anxiety as severely as do clinical-level generalized SA/SPers, they don't consider themselves to be socially phobic. They don't avoid fearful situations or let them interfere with their activities. Instead, while they feel the pain, they stoically push on through it. Consequently, they are less likely to seek the help they need.

HOW ARE HIGH SENSITIVITY, INTROVERSION, AND SHYNESS RELATED?

There seems to be a lot of confusion about the degree to which shyness, high sensitivity, introversion, and SA/SP may be related. Loose definitions have made it seem that all these different entities may be clinical variations of one another, all requiring treatment. On their face, they appear to be the result of a simple fear of evaluation in social interactions. But that is not the case.

Shyness. Shyness is considered a normal personality trait, not a mental disorder. It does, however, share with SA/SP a fear of humiliation, embarrassment, and negative evaluation. Other shyness behaviors include inhibited behavior, wariness of unfamiliar people, timidity and cautiousness in situations that contain risk of harm or failure. But the shy individual does not consider the fear to be unreasonable or dysfunctional whereas the SA/SPer does.

One important difference between shyness and SA/SP seems to be how you process information in social situations. While both shy and socially anxious people experience anticipatory anxiety, shy people tend to check out the situation for cues on how to interpret the situation and respond. As a result, if others' behaviors don't support having negative thoughts and feelings, shy people may simply stop those thoughts and feelings.

SA/SPers, on the other hand, look specifically for cues to support their negative thoughts and feelings. Because of this you are *un*likely to end your negative thinking even if you receive information to the contrary. In general, both shy and socially anxious people appear to have knowledge of appropriate social behavior, but as a SA/SPer, you don't believe you have the ability to use it or you're less willing to do so.

Another important difference, pointed out by clinical behaviorist Samuel Turner, is that SA/SPers have more extreme deficits in daily functioning than do shy individuals. The course of your disorder is more severe. Avoidant behaviors are more extreme. And, furthermore, your physiological reactions to social situations are stronger. Whereas a shy child might hang back from participating in class, a SA/SPer might look for the nearest exit, use it, or at least desperately want to.

Still, it's hard to discern where shyness ends and SA/SP begins. There are no clearly defined clinical criteria for "shyness" since it's not a psychiatric disorder. In most cases, the trait is self-defined. Fifty percent of the population report themselves to be shy.

As Philip Zimbardo says, "If you think you're shy, you are shy." Far-reaching in its prevalence, shyness affects some 84 million people. This is several times as many as are affected by SA/SP.

Developmental psychologist Jerome Kagan's work on the "shy personality" suggests that shyness is the result of fear arousal and *behavioral inhibition* in response to novel objects or events. It occurs with excessive sympathetic nervous system arousal and behavioral withdrawal. This syndrome may begin as early as four months and persist until age 7½ years. While shyness may be a general temperamental factor, there's been nothing to suggest that social anxiety may be as well.

Categories of Shyness. There are two sub-categories of shyness. One is *fearfulness*. This first appears after 3 years of age as a response to strangers, new toys, new locations, and the intrusion of others. Your fearfulness is often exhibited in behaviors such as avoidance, retreat, isolation, clinging to a caregiver, and vocalization.

However, importantly, a history of behavioral inhibition does *not* appear to be associated with anxiety symptoms in general or social anxiety symptoms in particular later on. This means that even though behavioral inhibition is part of shyness, it is unknown *if* it relates to anxiety at all.

The other sub-category of shyness is *self-consciousness* which appears later in development, 4–17 years of age. This is a response to a situation in which you are the focus of scrutiny. Both public and private self-consciousness are characterized by the thoughts you have.

Publicly shy people report being uncomfortable when their behaviors are observed. You feel uncomfortable when you're being awkward, failing to respond appropriately, or being too quiet for the situation. *Privately shy* people, on the other hand, are bothered by their own experience of anxiety *per se* and focus on their body's cues, such as increases in heart rate.

Effect of Family on Shyness. Family environment is important in shyness. High family cohesion, high emotional expressiveness, lower conflict, and emphasis on intellectual, recreational, social, and cultural development *decrease* shyness in children aged 1–2 years. For girls, specifically, the mother's positive responsiveness correlates with decreased shyness. On the other hand, if the mother is nervous, unpleasant, uncomfortable, irritable, or shows shyness-related inhibition, the girl is more likely to have increased shyness. There are currently no data on boys.

Children who are temperamentally fearful and inhibited AND have parents who are unsupportive, perceived to be unavailable, and unresponsive tend to feel insecure and become shy. Your level of shyness has been found to increase with decreased maternal acceptance and increased maternal control.

Mothers of shy children are more likely to believe that social skills should be taught by direction or coercion, rather than by personal experience. They tend to feel angry, disappointed, guilty, or embarrassed by their child's unskilled behaviors. Witness how some parents of Little Leaguers act when their child isn't the latest World Series-winning super-champ.

Both parents of shy children tend to be less emotionally warm, more rejecting, overprotective, and more concerned about others' opinions regarding appropriate behavior. Similarly, when you have SA/SP, you will tend to rate your parents as more rejecting, overprotective, and less emotionally warm.

Peers likewise frequently react to shy children's withdrawal and reticence badly, as if it were a form of deviance from appropriate social behavior. Males and females alike tend to respond to them with rejection. They may tease, pick on, ridicule, victimize, or neglect them.

Even teachers tend to perceive shy children negatively. They become frustrated and annoyed at your reluctant behavior. As a result, they tend to rate shy children as less friendly and sociable.

Selective Mutism. One result of experiencing social distress in childhood is selective mutism (formerly called elective mutism). This is where there's a persistent refusal to speak in selected social situations despite your being able to communicate fluently in spoken language. According to the *DSM-IV*, these children may show excessive shyness, social fears such as fear of social embarrassment, social withdrawal, isolation, and negativism. Because of symptom similarity some believe selective mutism is a variant of SA/SP. But until controlled trials demonstrate this, making the distinction will be difficult.

High Sensitivity. High sensitivity, or hyper-arousability, is also seen as a normal personality characteristic. This is where you're easily stimulated, overly aroused, or stressed by stimuli. It's estimated that 20% of the U.S. population share this trait.

To the highly sensitive person (HSP) lights seem brighter, sounds louder, fabrics coarser, smells stronger, and pain greater. Temperature-, humidity-, and barometric changes may be very noticeable. You startle easily. You tend to pick up on nonverbal and verbal nuances that others miss. You may feel the highs, lows, and subtleties of life more deeply. Music, art, and poignancy touch you. This describes my own experience with it.

For this reason you may avoid violent content in movies, television programs, books, and newspaper accounts as well as other highly arousing situations. Where you find there is too much external stimulation, overload occurs. This may make you appear irritable, touchy, and picky. Environmental overload not only increases your physiological arousal but also interferes with your thinking, recognition, and recall, and may set the stage for conflict with others.

Elaine Aron, developer of this concept, believes everyone has a range of stimulation with which they feel comfortable. Too little and you feel bored; too much and you feel on edge. However, the degree to which you're aroused in a particular situation by a particular stimulus differs from individual to individual.

Highly sensitive children and adults often appear frightened, irritable, apprehensive, with digestive problems, or as loners. But you may also appear as aware, imaginative, and creative. As an adult you tend to overwhelm yourself by working too hard, too long, with too much interpersonal interaction, unaware of your sensitivity thresholds.

When highly sensitive persons are in the midst of too much arousal, regardless of the situation or stimulation, they tend to become confused and distressed. You feel less in control. Increased awareness and reflection only serve to magnify the experience. Without boundaries or safety- or comfort zones, a highly-sensitive person (HSP) may become overwhelmed, avoidant, and exhausted.

As a result, HSPs tend to avoid situations that are over-stimulating. You may also respond negatively to and seek to avoid situations where you may be observed, judged, or criticized. Your hyper-arousal tends to make you look to others as if you're fearful or avoiding specific situations out of fear. However, your avoidance may be merely an effort to turn down the volume.

Introversion. Developed in 1923 by Swiss psychiatrist Carl Gustav Jung, introversion is a psychological temperament used to describe your personality. Introversion represents one pole of the Introversion–Extraversion continuum. Introversion today may be thought of as a social-attitude dimension of subjectivity.

Those who tend to live in a highly personal, contemplative, subjective world of experience may be thought of as closer to the introversion end of the continuum. You orient yourself toward your inner, more introspective world. You're more wrapped up in the intrinsic aspect of things, ideas, thoughts, impressions, reflections, emotions, and your imagination. This inner world is the generator from which you draw your power, energy, and motivation.

Because you prefer and value this inner-orientation, you rely less on socializing for stimulation, meeting your needs, and satisfaction. This doesn't mean, however, that you don't enjoy meeting and being with others. On the contrary, you do, but you enjoy them in smaller doses, and in deeper, longer-lived relationships. Crowds and short-term, superficial connections not only don't interest you but also tend to drain your batteries.

It's important to remember that we're talking about places along a continuum. This means degrees of introversion. At either pole you'll find extremes. You must bear in mind also that the environment in which you find yourself at any given moment has a large effect upon your social attitudes and behavior. When those with introversion are with intimates, for example, you're more likely to come across as very social, although, in more general circumstances, you aren't as likely to appear that way.

Some suggest that "reserved" is a more appropriate and descriptive term than "introverted," which is burdened with negative connotations. Reserved, you don't reveal yourself quickly or easily to others. You tend to be quieter, keep to yourself, and be more a listener than talker. This, however, it is important to note, is a positive quality since conversations and social relationships wouldn't exist long without that behavior.

Because of your reserve you tend to bottle-up unexpressed feelings. As a result, outwardly you tend to seem focused, serious, and cautious, guarding the inner space you hold so dear. If given the option of relaxing with your computer or partying with a group, you'd likely choose isolation and your solitude. According to Aron, approximately 70% of HSPs tend to be "reserved."

Where the Similarities End. Shyness, high sensitivity, and introversion seem very similar yet at present there are *no* data that link these factors. They all have a lot in common with SA/SP, *but* not all individuals who have these personality characteristics develop SA/SP. Conversely, *not* all SA/SPers have these characteristics.

This intriguing puzzle has led psychologist Samuel Turner to hypothesize that (1) shyness is a predispositional factor for SA/SP *but* that other factors, such as traumatic experiences in childhood, trigger development of the disorder. (2) Hypersensitivity and an introverted temperament *may* likewise act as independent predisposing factors to SA/SP. (3) If you add the right environmental elements over time to this susceptibility, you *may* be able to produce SA/SP. However, there is currently *no* proof for this intriguing idea.

ASSESSING THE PLACE OF EMBARRASSMENT AND SHAME

Embarrassment is the emotion that is closely associated with SA/SP. It's an uncomfortable aroused state of awkwardness, mortification, and chagrin. It results from knowledge that others could conceivably notice your doing something you'd prefer them not to notice.

These behaviors can include trembling, stumbling, stammering, stuttering, sweating, blushing, misspeaking, and forgetting. Your doing something in public that you perceive as awkward or stupid upsets your expectations of what's appropriate. You fear communicating unwanted impressions of yourself to others. Because of this, your embarrassment motivates you to repair, if possible, or escape, if necessary, the awkward situation.

Let me share with you one of my most embarrassing moments. It occurred when I was 25, living in San Diego, attending bi-weekly singles' dances. Over the course of 7 months I developed a pure-and-chaste-from-afar crush on a popular man whose look and lithe dance movements seduced every woman on the dance floor. I loved the feeling of oneness when dancing with him.

Suddenly one evening he asked me to coffee at his apartment! This was the place I'd resigned myself to never visiting. After etiquette-required preliminaries, we started to make out on his day bed. I was so thrilled that he finally liked me as much as I liked him.

Then the phone rang. Unperturbed, he took it. To my astonishment he began to tell the caller what he was doing. While looking at me in my disheveled state, he grinned slyly and graphically detailed all his moves and my physical and emotional responses to them. I was aghast. He laughed and handed the phone to me. His male friend on the line was laughing too.

I was the vehicle for their nasty little game. My expressions of anger were barely a squeak above my humiliation. As a result, I never went to the dances again.

Grounded in your public self-consciousness, embarrassment is the ability to be concerned about what others are thinking about you. This ability to look at yourself through the eyes of others is thought to begin around the age of 3 years, when you gain the capacity to understand the abstract idea of "self." Once you develop the concept of self, you can begin to suffer the consequences of trying to see yourself as others might.

Of course, your social image may be accurate or inaccurate. But what you operate on is your belief about it, not its reality. Some suggest that embarrassment may be considered a signpost of what it is to be human. This is because it motivates you to try to correct any awkward social situations. Interestingly, when individuals don't show this emotion when others expect them to, they are perceived to be less human, abnormal, insensitive, thoughtless, and uncaring.

Frequently when you experience embarrassment, you blush. As Mark Twain is often quoted as saying, "Man is the only animal that blushes ...or needs to." Blushing is one of the most characteristic features of embarrassment and the principal physical symptom of SA/SP.

Not everyone blushes. When you're embarrassed, you may engage in a number of discomfiture behaviors, such as agitation and increased body movement, averted gaze, sheepish grin, face touching, and blushing. Exhibiting embarrassed behaviors has an important social function. It shows others that you're aware that you've breached some social rule. These behaviors then influence how others respond to you in those predicaments. People tend to be drawn to embarrassed persons.

While embarrassment and social anxiety share an awareness of and concern for what others will think about you, they are different. Social anxiety is composed of fear, dread, and apprehension. It occurs before the event and depends on what you think about the situation. It begins with public self-awareness and ends with distress.

Embarrassment has no anxiety component. It's composed of startled surprise and abashment. It's reactive, occurring only after the event has taken place. It has nothing to do with what you think about the situation. It begins with your public self-awareness that leads to your distress that ends in your feeling dumb.

The terms *embarrassment* and *shame* are often used interchangeably. Both embarrassment and shame result from events that communicate unwanted images of you to others. Both are found in SA/SP. However, they are two distinctly different emotions.

Embarrassment results from minor breaches of convention, manners, or poise. It's associated with the unforeseeable, mistakes, goofs, and accidents. These events aren't serious and have no moral implications. When you're embarrassed, you feel foolish. Others attribute your embarrassment behaviors to the situation and see it as only a limited and temporary *faux pas* on your part, as when you drop food in your lap in a restaurant.

Shame, on the other hand, is a breach of important and fundamental standards of conduct or rules. It's associated with the awful, foreseeable, serious, or unforgivable actions and dereliction of duty. As such, shame has strong moral implications.

When you're ashamed, you feel regretful, guilty, and depressed. You're afraid of exposure because public revelation of these behaviors leads to extremely unfavorable assessments of you, as when you're caught going through a friend's private financial records. Others attribute shame behaviors to a defect in your personality, morals, or character.

Furthermore, people expect it to be ongoing and likely to recur in all types of situations. Unlike embarrassment that can occur in the absence of others, shame occurs only when others actually become aware of your behavior.

DIFFERENTIATING OVERLAPPING DISORDERS

There are a number of disorders that are similar to SA/SP and may even occur with it (*co-morbid*). Some 70–80% of cases of SA/SP are complicated by co-morbid conditions. These disorders include panic disorder, agoraphobia, specific phobias, school refusal, generalized anxiety disorder, depression, avoidant personality disorder, alcoholism, and schizophrenic spectrum disorder. Their presence increases symptom severity, disability, and suicide potential.

It's important for you to be able to differentiate them from SA/SP, both for understanding and appropriate treatment. Unfortunately, there's a lower recognition rate for SA/SP in primary care due to the presence of co-morbid conditions. It is the co-morbid condition that is more likely to be recognized and treated initially.

Panic Disorder. Panic disorder has as its core element *panic attacks*. Panic attacks are sudden episodes of acute apprehension or intense fear that occur without any apparent cause. Panic usually lasts only a few minutes. During the attack, you're likely to experience any of the following symptoms:

- Heart pounding or palpitations
- Shortness of breath
- Faintness or dizziness
- Sweating
- Shaking or trembling
- Sensation of choking
- Feelings of unreality

- Nausea
- Tingling in hands and feet
- Chest pain or discomfort
- Fear of losing control or going crazy or dying
- Hot and cold flashes.

Individuals with panic attacks can have attacks merely thinking about or encountering any feared situation. These attacks are spontaneous and unexpected.

Panic attacks become *panic disorder* when you have at least three such attacks in a month's time and at least one of these attacks has been followed by a month's worth of concern or worry about having another attack.

As a SA/SPer you may have panic attacks as part of your disorder. Your attack results from apprehension about feared social situations or performance. It's important to note that panic disorder is different from *agoraphobia*.

Agoraphobia. Agoraphobia, which affects one in 20 in the general population, appears to stem from panic disorder and may have a balance-impairment component. Individuals fear having a panic attack in public, being embarrassed by it, and not being able to escape or find help. It's common for agoraphobics to avoid various types of situations.

These include public transportation (subways, planes, buses, trains), confined or enclosed areas (highways, bridges, tunnels), crowded public places (stores, restaurants, theaters, churches), and being alone (anywhere one can't reach a "safe person").

What differentiates SA/SP from agoraphobia is the reason for fearing the social situation or performance. In SA/SP it's the social situation itself wherein you may be evaluated that directly elicits your fear of being embarrassed. In agoraphobia the social situation does not elicit fear of having an attack. Instead the fear comes from being in an unfamiliar, strange, or challenging place or just being away from one's security.

Specific Phobias. Specific Phobias are intense, out-of-proportion fears and avoidance of a specific object or situation. This results in marked distress or impairment. Examples include fear of elevators, small places, dogs, snakes, heights, and blushing. Like SA/SP they may involve panic attacks that are related to particular situations. Even though 33% of those with speech phobia attribute their phobia to panic attacks, it's not known whether their panic attacks are the cause *or* the consequence of their phobia.

While these fears may occur in social situations, social situations are not a requirement. This is not a fear of bring observed, negative scrutiny, embarrassment, or humiliation. Whereas SA/SP requires a combination of arousal, maladaptive thoughts, negative feelings, and avoidance-related behaviors, specific phobias require only fear.

The specific phobia is a result of conditioning, where you associate some neutral object or event with negative arousal, which produces automatic fear and avoidance behavior. For example, you can see either a real snake or picture of a snake, feel instantly afraid, and want to run away or avoid it. As a result, specific phobias are oriented in the present and, thus, are not anticipatory.

Therapy for phobias is primarily behavioral which uses exposure over time to break the connection between the feared object and the fear response. The process is done in the imagination and in real life.

SA/SP therapy uses behavioral techniques, but also relies on cognitive reshaping of your thoughts, beliefs, and expectations, improving coping and social skills, enhancing self-confidence and assertiveness. It also uses nutrition, exercise, and psychotropic drugs.

School Refusal. School refusal was previously referred to as *school phobia*. It is a behavioral symptom of anxiety and other disorders. It may be related to a number of factors, such as avoidance of a negative situation, attention getting, separation anxiety, or getting some reward. Or it may be related to avoidance of a feared social situation or negative evaluation, as found in SA/SP.

Diagnosis is difficult because some children with school refusal show overtones of SA/SP and some don't. Moreover, some children with SA/SP don't show any school refusal. Symptoms for school refusal include the following:

- Refusal
- Tantrums
- Complaint of stomachache, headache, or nausea

- Chronic school absence
- Panic attacks
- Crying
- Shyness
- Petulance
- Opposition
- Cringing
- Unhappiness.

Generalized Anxiety Disorder (GAD). Generalized anxiety disorder is a driven, unending process, characterized by a chronic state of anxiety or worry that lasts for at least six months. It has no accompanying panic attacks or phobias. Focusing on two or more life stressors, such as health, job performance, or finances, GAD results in your entertaining a stream of thoughts and images about possible or traumatic events in the future and how you might deal with them.

GAD individuals spend most or all their time considering feared what-if possibilities surrounding the problem. If they generate solutions, they don't act upon them to actually deal with the future. For a GAD diagnosis there needs to at least three of the following six symptoms:

- Feeling keyed up
- Difficulty concentrating
- Difficulty sleeping
- Muscle tension
- Irritability
- Feeling easily fatigued.

GAD can be aggravated by any stressful situation. This includes ones that elicit fears, such as fear of not being in control and fear of rejection. Both of these fears are seen in SA/SP. There are few differences between GAD and SA/SP so it's easy to misdiagnose SA/SP as GAD.

More common with GAD than SA/SP are insomnia, headaches, and fear of dying. More common with SA/SP than GAD are frequent sweating, flushing, and shortness of breath. However, the primary difference appears to be that GAD has none of the significant fear of evaluation, embarrassment, or humiliation that SA/SP has.

Depression. Depression is the leading psychiatric disorder in the U.S., followed by alcoholism and SA/SP. A large proportion of SA/SPers meet the criteria for depression (*dysthymic mood disorder*) as a co-morbid condition, with 40–50% of SA/SPers presenting at primary care with major depression. Development of SA/SP precedes this major depression by over a year in 75% of patients. Depression is characterized by a persistent

- Sadness
- Loss of interest in all or almost all activities and pastimes
- Decrease in energy
- Feelings of worthlessness or guilt
- Self-denigrating ideas
- Difficulty in concentrating or thinking
- Indecisiveness
- Social withdrawal and avoidance
- Helplessness
- Hopelessness
- Suicidal ideation.

Common to depression and SA/SP is a sense of helplessness, focus on self-denigrating ideas, fatigue, and insomnia. In addition, both depression and SA/SP exhibit social withdrawal and avoidance. But the motivation for that behavior is different in each disorder.

In depression those behaviors generally result from lack of interest and energy. In SA/SP they result from fear of being scrutinized or judged by others. Individuals with both disorders tend to attribute causes for negative events that occur to them to internal factors, like lack of social ability. They see these factors as stable, character-related, and present across situations.

There are two elements that best discriminate depression from SA/SP. One is the presence of a sense of hopelessness. Depressed individuals operate in a continuous state of pessimism. For SA/SPers hopelessness and negativity depend upon the specific situation.

The other discriminating element is the degree of activity present. Individuals with depression don't engage the world. They don't act upon their circumstances in order to try to change or improve things. They can't; they have no energy.

SA/SPers, on the other hand, do engage the world, despite their fears and desire to avoid situations. You do act upon your circumstances to try to change or improve things. Your anxiety is nothing but energy.

Avoidant Personality Disorder (APD). Avoidant personality disorder is a deeply ingrained, enduring, inflexible, maladaptive pattern of fearful perceptions, cognitions, and behavior about social interaction. As such, it's a severe form of social fear. It's characterized by an exquisite sensitivity to rejection or humiliation. Its primary characteristics include

- Avoidance of occupational and other interpersonal activities
- Fear of criticism, disapproval, or rejection
- Preoccupation with being criticized or rejected in social situations
- Restraint in intimate relationships, no close friends
- Inhibition in participating in new interpersonal situations or taking risks
- Feeling of social inadequacy and inferiority
- Fear of embarrassment, shame, and ridicule.

Avoidant personality disorder and SA/SP have considerable overlap. In fact, several studies demonstrate rates in the range of 50-89% of APD among individuals with generalized SA/SP. Individuals with either APD or SA/SP have a fear of criticism and tend to be disturbed by the lack of relationships. However, there do seem to be two significant differences.

It appears that those with APD tend to have little desire to confront their phobic event. As a result, they adopt avoidance as their primary coping mechanism and lifestyle. This allows them to withdraw from opportunities to develop close relationships wherein they fear they'll be criticized, humiliated, or rejected.

SA/SPers, on the other hand, frequently desire to be able to confront the avoided situation. You sometimes do so, but at great sacrifice. Individuals with APD often feel justified in avoiding social activities because of their perception of the criticality and unreliability of others. SA/SPers are distressed that their fears and anxieties keep you away from people and potentially rewarding activities. You want to change and feel better.

It may be that APD and SA/SP are not qualitatively but quantitatively different. That is, they may represent different places along a social approach-avoidance continuum. Specifically, APD appears to have a greater degree of severity, negative emotion, impairment, and co-morbidity with other mental health conditions.

It is important to note that while most personality disorders respond only to intensive psychotherapy, APD, like generalized SA/SP, responds to MAOI antidepressants and cognitive-behavioral therapy (CBT). This suggests that there may be more similarity than dissimilarity between APD and SA/SP.

Schizophrenia Spectrum Disorders (SSD). Schizophrenia spectrum disorders represent a loss of a sense of reality and an inability to think and act normal and respond appropriately to social expectations. There may be mood changes, social withdrawal, delusions, or paranoid social fears. However, this fear and avoidance of social situations is thought to be the result of a lack of social interest or perhaps delusional fears of harm. There are no data to suggest they result from fear of embarrassment, humiliation, and/or negative evaluation.

Asperger's Syndrome. Asperger's is a pervasive developmental disorder that is characterized by an inability to understand how to interact socially. It is a mild variant of autism disorder that may have a social fear component. It is not, however, the same as social anxiety disorder wherein the person suffering from SA/SP knows that their dysfunctional anxious thoughts are irrational. Research has shown that the social anxiety of Asperger's Syndrome tends not to reach the clinical level of true SA/SP.

Asperger's features, which typically occurs around the age of 3, may include uncoordinated or clumsy motion-related movements, repetitive routine behaviors, speech or language peculiarities, angry facial expressions, and intense preoccupation with one or two subjects. They tend to be in their own world. However, higher-functioning individuals with Asperger may have well-developed language skills.

Alcoholism. Alcoholism overlaps SA/SP because alcohol abuse and dependence commonly accompany SA/SP. They also frequently increase with the severity of the anxiety disorder. Consumption of alcohol is a form of self-medication. Short-term it's a particularly effective way to reduce your fear of social threat.

Specifically, it generates a sense of personal power that SA/SPers frequently lack. This accounts for its widespread use and abuse. Under its influence you feel less inhibited and more willing to participate in activities you normally fear but desire, such as meeting people, talking, dancing, and performing.

However, when alcohol's relaxation effect disappears, the anxiety reappears, prompting you to reach for another drink to regain that feeling of adequacy and control. Studies indicate that severely fearful and anxious people develop alcohol dependency more quickly than less fearful and less anxious people.

While alcoholism in the general population has a lifetime prevalence of 8–10% in men and 3-5% in women, in the SA/SP population it's 16–36%. Patients often report that their social anxiety symptoms preceded their alcohol abuse or dependence, yet SA/SP symptoms frequently occur as a consequence of alcoholism. This is where cessation of drinking leads to remission of the anxiety.

Individuals suffering from both alcohol dependency and severe anxiety have difficulty differentiating the symptoms of anxiety from those of alcohol withdrawal.

SUMMARY

The essence of SA/SP is concern about what others may think of you. It is the fear that they will judge you, find you inadequate, and reject you. While there are other conditions that may have similarities, there are generally sufficient differences to allow you to distinguish your SA/SP from them. It is important for SA/SPers to thoroughly understand SA/SP.

First, if you are to work toward recovery, you need to have a solid sense of what is going on in SA/SP in general and in your individual condition in particular.

Second, you need to know that the disorder is treatable and there is help out there.

Third, if you are going to employ the services of a professional (clinical psychologist, psychiatrist, licensed social worker, psychiatric nurse, or primary care physician), you need to know what they may not.

At present even with all SA/SP's visibility, too many mental health professionals are not yet up to speed on SA/SP in either knowledge or experience. You may need to help them in order to help yourself.

Henry David Thoreau suggested that "If a man does not keep pace with his companions, perhaps that is because he hears a different drummer."

3

SEARCHING FOR ORIGINS AND TRIGGERS

"Speak roughly to your little boy, and beat him when he
sneezes: He only does it to annoy, Because he knows it
teases" (Lewis Carroll, *Alice's Adventures in Wonderland*, 1865)

HOW DOES SOCIAL ANXIETY ORIGINATE?

Okay, so how do you acquire SA/SP? Genetics? Stress? Family? Evolution? Physiology? Upbringing? Behaviors? Trauma? Cognitions? Conditioning? The answer is Yes ... and No. The one thing that seems crystal clear is that no one factor creates the disorder.

The condition is generally thought to be an interplay of factors which *predispose you*, factors which *trigger the clinical signs*, and factors which *maintain the symptoms long enough to make them a psychiatric disorder*.

What makes understanding SA/SP particularly difficult is that each clinical manifestation appears to be an individual combination of many of the possible contributing factors. Despite symptom commonalities with others, your SA/SP will be as individual and unique as you are.

Let's take a look at some of the more significant predisposing and triggering factors. Maintaining factors will be found in the next chapter. (This general categorization of factors has been adapted from Edmund Bourne.)

WHAT ARE ITS PREDISPOSING FACTORS?

Predisposing factors are those elements that create your vulnerability or susceptibility to SA/SP. They may include biochemistry, genetics (as demonstrated by genetic tests with twins and family studies), evolution, development, childhood upbringing and experiences, and cumulative stress.

Biochemistry. From the biochemical perspective SA/SP can be seen as a physiological imbalance of your neurotransmitters. Research in neurobiology suggests that SA/SP may be related to one or more neurotransmitter-receptor systems that cause either a deficiency or excess of particular neurotransmitters in the brain. Neurotransmitters that have been implicated in SA/SP include serotonin, dopamine, norepinephrine, and gamma-aminobutyric acid. This biochemical imbalance may be acquired or inherited.

Here's a crash course in SA/SP neurobiology. The central nervous system controls and coordinates your entire body. This includes your brain functions, such as memory, thoughts, emotions, pleasure, sleep, and anxiety. The system uses electrical impulses to carry input from all your sense organs to your brain and then to relay directions from the brain back to your body.

These electrical impulses are generated and transmitted by chemicals called *neurotransmitters*. And run along chains of nerve cells that run throughout your body.

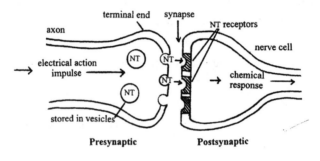

NEUROTRANSMISSION

The presynaptic end of the nerve cell selectively releases neurotransmitters (NT) when it is stimulated by an electrical impulse. The neurotransmitters cross the space between the first cell and the next in line and look for receptors on the adjacent structure to match their chemical composition. The match produces a specific physiological response which signals (1) release more chemical, (2) stop releasing the chemical, or (3) stop inhibiting the release of the chemical so the chemical can continue.

All neurotransmitters derive from amino acids, or *amines*. They're geared either to continuing to send the message forward (excitatory) or to stopping the message right there (inhibitory). Any problem with the storage, release, creation, or break down of the neurotransmitter, or change in the receptor sensitivity, could lead to incorrect transmissions.

As you may guess, these incorrect transmissions result in clinical disorders. Neurotransmission is a very sensitive process. It needs to be incrementally increased or decreased to meet the requirements of any specific situation.

While SA/SP has been *hypothesized* to be the result of a physiological imbalance of neurotransmitters, most studies on the effects of neurotransmitters on mood disorders have been done on depression and panic disorder. It's important to note that what may hold for depression or anxiety disorders in general may not hold for SA/SP in particular.

How do neurotransmitters and the drugs prescribed for SA/SP affect your moods? Let's take a brief look.

Receptors for benzodiazepines (like Valium, Xanax, Klonopin) appear to match those receptors for the inhibitory NT gamma-aminobutyric acid (GABA). The benzodiazepines would enhance GABA's blocking signals to the emotional center of your brain. This would prevent triggering anxiety.

Therefore, if you increase the stopping signal, you produce a calming effect. But if you don't have enough GABA available for the number of receptors, you would trigger anxiety.

Monoamine oxidase (MAO) is a complex enzyme system throughout your body. *Monoamine* refers to the type of amine and *oxidase* (enzyme) breaks down, burns, or deactivates that particular amine. An increase in monoamines leads to a corresponding increase in serotonin, dopamine, and norepinephrine. This, in turn, would lead to a decrease in depression, for example.

This suggests that to decrease depression and some forms of anxiety, you need to stop the oxidase from deactivating the monoamine. You can do this by employing a chemical that inhibits the oxidase, called a *monoamine oxidase inhibitor* (MAOI), like Nardil and Parnate. By inhibiting MAO, the cell prolongs the effective life of these amines in your brain and their calming effect.

Serotonin derives from the amino acid tryptophan. *Selective serotonin reuptake inhibitors* (SSRIs) are drugs like Prozac, Paxil, and Zoloft that have been found to help some SA/SPers. They work by preventing the cell's receptors from reabsorbing the serotonin. This, likewise, continues the calming effect of the serotonin.

Dopamine derives from the amino acid tyrosine. While MAOIs, which have an effect on dopamine, serotonin, and norepinephrine, are useful in SA/SP, the specific role of dopamine, if any exists, in this disorder is currently unclear.

Norepinephrine is made directly from dopamine. SA/SPers tend to have higher levels of norepinephrine in their blood than do those with panic disorder or non-SA/SPers.

Because several classes of drugs (for example, MAOIs, SSRIs, and benzodiazepines) are known to be effective on different aspects of social anxiety, some have suggested that *perhaps*:

1. None of these drugs actually targets a common nerve pathway that creates SA/SP.

2. There is no common pathway.

3. There may be parallel neural pathways.

4. The disorder may actually be a group of seemingly similar but neurobiologically different conditions.

It is important to note drugs are not the only way to positively alter neurotransmitter levels. Research has shown that Cognitive-Behavioral Therapy (CBT) can do it as well.

Genetics. Genetic research has found an association between a personality test result for "neuroticism" (which includes worry, pessimism, and fear of uncertainty) and a serotonin-transporter gene (5-HTT). The "neuroticism scale" is said to predict anxiety and depression.

Results suggested that those who had the presence of a particular form of the 5-HTT gene tended to score higher on the neuroticism test than those who didn't. Therefore, they hypothesized this gene might be implicated in anxiety.

However, relating a gene variation to what one checks off on a personality test is problematic. It is often difficult to assess the meaning of an association, since all it indicates is that two factors seem to vary together in some fashion. Also there are 200 potential neurotransmitter genes that may play some small part in predisposition to anxiety.

Furthermore, what's relevant for anxiety in general, should any gene variant be a factor, may or may not be relevant for SA/SP in particular. All forms of anxiety are not the same.

While there may be a genetic predisposition to SA/SP, the National Institute of Mental Health's 1998 report, *Genetics and Mental Health*, suggests that susceptibility will more likely result from a number of genes working together. To-date no one gene has been found to be *the* cause of any mental disorder though some genes appear to be implicated through linkage and association.

Most conditions will result from a combination of a number of genes and environmental factors. This is particularly true with something as complex as human behavior which is also so closely tied to culture, environmental context, and what you define as "abnormal." Of the many components in the mix some will be discernible, some will not.

Twin Studies. Twin studies have been done to attempt to provide clues to the relative contribution of genes versus environment to SA/SP. These studies compare identical twins (those who share 100% of their genetic information) with fraternal twins (those who share 50% of their genetic information). Generally, these twins have been reared separately.

Twin studies in anxiety, in general, have suggested that members of the identical twin pairs are more likely to suffer from anxiety to a similar degree. However, adoptive studies have shown that shy children have been found to have both biological and adoptive mothers who were more socially anxious and less sociable than those of non-shy children.

This suggests the presence of an environmental influence as well. The similarity of twin environments both before and after separation tends to confound some of these findings. Currently there have been no twin studies on SA/SP reported using the strict *DSM-IV* definition of SA/SP.

Family Studies. Family studies look at and assess your first-degree biological relatives (biological parents, brother and sisters, and children) to see whether SA/SP clusters within families. Some studies suggest a familial transmission of the more severe, generalized form of the disorder. However, to date the studies have been unable to pinpoint genetics, social learning from anxious parents, or a combination of both as the cause of it.

Twins, Families & Genes: What Does it Mean? Twin and family studies suggest the possibility of the existence and presence of a genetic component in SA/SP. But it's important to remember that at one level everything human can be said to have some genetic component.

Genes are what write the software for everything you do and then carry those programs to every cell in your body to make everything work properly. Genes can be altered internally, by DNA replication errors, and externally, by assault by environmental toxins or stress. Not all genetic variations will be passed on from generation to generation. It will depend upon whether the genes in question are in the sex (germ) cells or body (somatic) cells. Only sex cell variations are inherited.

Evolution. Evolutionary theory suggests that early human beings developed the capacity for social anxiety to prepare for and aid their survival. In this vein psychologist Roy Baumeister says that social anxiety is a natural consequence of your concern about your individual and collective social bonds.

Individuals alone in the wild were very vulnerable defending against predators, the elements, and other environmental factors. But individuals in groups could work together against predators, the elements, and environment and, thus, be more likely, both individually and collectively, to survive and reproduce.

Belonging is nearly as necessary as the air you breathe. It shows social approval of you by others, recognizes you, and confers visibility upon you. It legitimizes your existence, implies acceptance, and provides you with a sense of not being in jeopardy of rejection. It establishes social bonds.

Perhaps this is why humans are very social creatures. You're drawn to one another to form all kinds of relationships and bonds, from casual to intimate, in order to accomplish your individual and mutual goals. But to stay a part of a group and derive benefits from the group, early humans had to find ways to prevent their exclusion or rejection from the group.

This could have been done by appeasement, or submissive, behaviors, such as blushing and grinning sheepishly. In monkeys behaviors similar to those observed in humans have been associated with attempts to communicate their lack of threat or their subservience to dominant others. Primate reassurance behaviors, such as greeting, holding, hugging, kissing, grooming, and grinning, likewise appear to be geared to maintaining the connectedness among interdependent members.

An extension of these stabilizing mechanisms may be seen in humans in the systematic use of civility: etiquette, politeness, apologizing, paying compliments, and performing reciprocal behaviors, such as taking turns in conversations. You may then be predisposed to worry when you fail to make the desired impression since self-presentation failures are associated with possible social exclusion.

Dominance, Submission, Status & SA/SP. Those dominance-submission behaviors observed in animals may be an analogue to human status behaviors. The status of those with whom you interact plays a large part in how you respond to one another ... and how you're accepted. High status is synonymous with power, having access to and discretionary use of resources valued by others. These resources today include money, fame, physical attractiveness, knowledge, and competence. For early humans access to food, mates, and protection may have been the primary high-status resources.

When you're in the presence of, or interacting with, someone you consider to be powerful, specifically one who has access to the resources you want, you tend to defer to that person. You tend to take on low-status, "submissive" behaviors.

Today your perception of others' power, who's down and who's up, may play a big role in the pressure you feel to make the desired impression. After all, you want to be accepted. How you see your relative power in an interaction determines your level of self-confidence. If you perceive yourself to be in an inferior position, you're likely to feel less confident, less competent, and more vulnerable. You're less secure about your place in the group's membership. This will affect your behavior and concern about belonging.

If avoidance of social rejection is a human goal, it follows that a fear of social rejection would create social anxiety. This being the case, early people would be motivated not to make undesired impressions on others. They would be motivated to stop any such presentations when they discovered them occurring. And, according to social psychologists Mark Leary and Robin Kowalski, they would want to restore, foster, and maintain supportive relations with others which would increase acceptance and reduce their social anxiety.

This would imply that modern humans were likely to have hardwired tendencies to reinforce and perpetuate social connections, to be aware of others' responses to your self-presentations to them. It would also imply that you would feel anxious when you aren't successful at conveying your desired impressions. Therefore, SA/SP could be thought of as an over-expression of an evolutionary protective, primitive fear.

So What Does Biology Tell You About SA/SP? Biological factors suggest that social anxiety may occur when there's a biochemical or genetic predisposition that affects how your body responds to its environment. But how and to what degree biological, genetic, and evolutionary elements are involved and interact in SA/SP is as yet unknown ... and may be unknowable

This is because it's very much a chicken-and-egg situation. For example, a psychological factor, such as trauma, can affect a biochemical factor, such as neurotransmission of serotonin. A stress factor, such as death in the family, can also affect serotonin levels. Serotonin levels, in turn, can lead to feelings of anxiety. Anxiety can lead to job loss, which, in turn, can lead to greater anxiety, which can further affect serotonin levels.

Each factor can trigger or maintain the others. As a result, it's important to note that addressing or eliminating only one of these factors may not eliminate your problem. Since SA/SP is likely a problem with many components, it likely requires solutions that address its many components.

HOW DEVELOPMENTAL FACTORS AFFECT YOU

How you cope with anxiety may relate to how you pass through developmental stages. Erik Erikson created a psychosocial model of the eight developmental stages through which you will pass.

The stages are biologically-based and constitute a fixed, universal sequence. Each stage represents a conflict of old attitudes and abilities versus new. You must address and resolve the conflict at each stage before moving successfully forward to the next stage. This is because behaviors that served you well at previous stages no longer fit or suffice.

Resolution of each conflict results in your developing a sense of competence. Without this sense of competence, you lack self-confidence, suffer from low self-esteem, and feel anxious and vulnerable.

Throughout your life cycle you acquire a series of competencies primarily through interaction with your physical and social environment. However, in actuality you never totally resolve these conflicts during each developmental phase. As a result, some of the aspects of the competencies to be mastered continue through succeeding stages, like extra baggage. Of all the conflicts to be resolved, establishing both a strong identity and sense of competence are the most critical.

The degree to which you successfully pass through these stages ultimately depends upon your development of this strong sense of identity in adolescence and early adulthood.

Trust vs. Mistrust. Erikson contends that one of the most basic elements of a healthy personality is a sense of trust that you develop toward others and yourself. Trusting is often very difficult for SA/SPers. Your trust develops during the first year of life as you react to your environment.

If your needs are met with warmth, certainty, and regularity, you feel comfort, security, and confidence that significant others will be forthcoming in getting you what you need from the world. If not, you'll have lingering doubts about significant others' willingness to provide necessities for you. Mistrust can result and lead to a sense of loneliness and feeling of isolation.

Autonomy vs. Shame & Doubt. Between 1 and 3 years of age, you begin to act upon the world, to test your capabilities in relation to your parents in order to see yourself as an able individual. Once again, your view of yourself depends largely upon the responses of others to your actions. Your perception of independent action will tend to last throughout your life.

If, however, your attempts to spread your wings and explore are met with disfavor and criticism, as in, "You shouldn't do that," you may be left feeling unsure as to what is appropriate to try. You may be certain that any attempts to be independent will be seen as punishable.

Initiative vs. Guilt. Between the ages of 4 and 5 you expand your testing of your abilities to your trying to influence the outside world (the family). You do this through competition, manipulation, power-seeking, and aggressive behavior. Now that you've discovered that you're a "somebody," you have to determine *who* that somebody is. Now that you know you're autonomous, you want to show yourself to be responsible for actually initiating behavior. However, you learn that as much as you want to act, that some behaviors have negative repercussions. This can produce guilt.

Industry vs. Inferiority. Between ages 5 and 12, you concentrate on mastery of cultural, intellectual, and technical tools in school. It's at this stage that you reinforce your sense of self, your identity, and that you can *do* things. You want to learn things that meet the expectations of your social environment. *This is where SA/SP comes into play.*

Your culture transmits its values and expectations. By meeting these expectations, you hope to build on your "somebody-ness." Critical to your identity development is your awareness of your competencies.

This means that you're especially aware of negative evaluations, where being seen as a "bad" student may create a feeling of inferiority. Teachers and students often label SA/SPers as "bad" or "different." To compensate for this some may feel compelled to be a troublemaker or the class clown.

Identity vs. Identity Confusion. Between ages 13 and 19, you develop a sense of identity with respect to peer- and reference groups and leadership models. You try to discern how you're similar to and different from your parents and what your rights and responsibilities are. It's a confusing and ambiguous time, heavy with mixed messages about freedom and responsibilities. For SA/SPers it's an incredibly difficult time because you're likely to still be lugging around steamer trunks full of guilts, incompetencies, and mistrust You look to your peer- and reference groups as the prime resource of your answers, guidance, and identity options.

But SA/SPers are at a disadvantage in this respect because feeling part of any group is difficult for you. You may not yet see those with whom you feel you can identify. In addition, your more tentative behavior and lowered self-confidence make you less likely to be invited into physical groups.

You can accept a clearly defined self (a parental ideal, for example) or you can expend a great deal of energy experimenting with a variety of roles, even negative identities, to see what really fits you. SA/ SPers may feel locked into developing either a negative identity or shoehorning yourself into your parents' roles. When you don't feel separate from your parents, you tend to not act independently.

Intimacy vs. Isolation. Between ages 20 and 30, you take on the adult role along with its many responsibilities. Close, stable relationships require you to share all aspects of yourself (feelings, ideas, goals) unconditionally without fearing the loss of your identity. They also require you to be receptive to those same things from your partner.

But this moving toward intimate partnerships creates risk for all, particularly for SA/SPers. You're likely to not yet feel secure in your identitiy or your career goals. You don't feel comfortable putting yourself on the line to meet people and get to know them.

If, however, SA/SPers do establish a relationship, your weak sense of self may cause you to demand a great deal of reassurance and praise from your partner. As a result, you may be more willing to go along with what the other wants and decides rather than actively participate to share decisions and reach compromises.

One negative consequence of this is that your partner might quickly tire of your non-assertiveness and dependence. This could leave you exposed and vulnerable. Inability to share and be shared with can put SA/SPers on the sidelines, feeling alone, lonely, isolated, and alienated.

Generativity vs. Stagnation. Between ages 30 and 60, you begin to make your assessment of the fulfillment of your dreams. You look at what's still available and accomplishable. You acknowledge that some things that you'd dreamt of now will never be. You make peace with the reality of these fantasies of youth.

But if you're unable to let go of those old dreams, as most SA/ SPers "can't," and if you're unable to make the transition, you'll be held prisoner by them. Not allowing yourself to close the door condemns you to spinning your wheels, wasting the present in service to the past … a past that you see as empty and full of failure. This leads to a sense of stagnation where you're painfully aware of your weaknesses and defects.

Integrity vs. Despair. Between the age of 60 and death, you look for a meaning to your life and how your life fits globally into some larger whole. You seek to accept that the life you've lived has been worthwhile. You have to find worth and purpose in your life as you have lived it. You have to forgive others and yourself for stupidity, ignorance, imperfections, and mistakes.

But if you can't or won't accept all that has gone on before and feel your life has been wasted, you'll "not go gently unto that good night.... but Rage, rage against the dying of the light" to quote Dylan Thomas. You'll spend your last years, your precious remaining time, bemoaning the lack of time to do all the things you missed because of your SA/SP.

LOOKING AT CHILDHOOD EXPERIENCES AND UPBRINGING

Parents can significantly contribute to your sense of security, self-esteem, and confidence.

Overly Cautious Parents. Parents of children with fears are often anxious, fearful, and overly concerned about potential dangers. They impart this worry to you by how they respond to their environment and their frequent admonitions to you to "be careful," "watch out," "don't talk to strangers," "wear your galoshes or you'll get pneumonia." When this happens, you come to think of the world as dangerous, threatening, untrustworthy, and something to avoid.

Instead of taking risks and exploring the world and the people in it, you tend to become excessively concerned with your vulnerability and personal safety. You may feel less able to rely upon others and feel anxious about their responses. Because you worry about what you can and should do, you don't want to put yourself in harm's way. Therefore, you restrict your activities accordingly.

JOE. Whenever one of 9-year-old Joe's classmates was ill, his mother kept Joe home from school. His father wouldn't let him ride on the school bus because it lacked seat belts. When he started wearing glasses in the 7th grade, which he was sure resulted from his not heeding his father about lying on the floor to watch TV, both his parents cautioned him about dropping, sitting on, breaking, or losing his glasses. Joe began to worry so much about the safety of his glasses and what his friends would say about his efforts to protect them that he finally gave up the neighborhood baseball games that he loved.

Overly Critical Parents. Parents who set very high standards for their children tend to be perfectionistic. For them "good enough" is not acceptable. This leaves you doing whatever you can to please and maintain the approval of your demanding parents. But no matter how hard you strive to look good and "do the right thing in the right way," you never can achieve your goal because they are constantly readjusting the yardstick upward.

For example, when my father made suggestions on how to write a civics essay, I followed his directions religiously, wanting his hard-to-obtain approval. But after several hours of writing and several draft critiques, I received only further criticism for what he considered an unsatisfactory final result.

Nevertheless, you act like a puppy, overly eager, trying to please your master. This leaves you feeling unsure about your own acceptability. It leaves you feeling insecure about your own true emotions and thoughts. It also stifles your capacity for assertiveness, or standing up for your own rights. Because of your being socialized in this environment, you learn to expect this behavior. You learn to respond to it, internalize your parents' values, and incorporate their criticality into your thinking, feeling, and acting.

As a result, you too will likely have very high standards for others as well as yourself. You will likely be perfectionistic and overly critical of everyone. But, as Johnny Carson once suggested, "A perfectionist is one who takes great pains and gives them to other people."

JOANNA. While Joanna's father was very dominant and her mother very submissive, both were very critical of everything she did. Her father concentrated on her schoolwork. He was never quite satisfied with her performance. Rather than praise her for what she did right, he always pushed her to do better.

Her mother instead focused on how Joanna looked: What kind of statement she made to the world about herself and her family. From the barrettes in Joanna's hair to which ankle socks to wear with her patent leather shoes, her mother dictated her wardrobe. The dress-yes/blue jeans-no approach allowed for no expression of Joanna's individuality. Her own acceptability was always in question.

Both overly protective and controlling parents tend to have lower expectations for their anxious children. They expect you to be more upset and less competent to cope in stressful situations. While they tend to attribute your undesirable behavior to your disposition, they attribute your desirable behavior to factors outside you.

For example, if you strike out in softball, you're incompetent or uncoordinated. But if you hit a homer, you're lucky or the pitcher threw an easy one. In other words, they perceive you to have neither ability nor control in the situation. Unfortunately, you tend to take on and fulfill their, and others', lowered expectations of you.

Assertiveness-Suppressing Parents. Parents who still operate under the dictum that "children should be seen and not heard" tend to be overly controlling. They want you to obey and act like miniature adults. As a result, they continually suppress your expression by reprimanding and punishing you for any instance of speaking out, getting angry, or acting impulsively.

This suppression suggests that you don't have the right to state what you feel. To do so puts you in jeopardy. Their behavior leads to your internalizing this restrictive attitude as well as bottling up your feelings. Bottled-up feelings can lead to anxiety, depression, anger, and passivity.

BARRY. When he was a child, Barry often thought he was in the Army. He was told when to get up, what to wear, what to eat, how he could use his time, and with whom he could spend his time ... until he left for college. When he was a teenager, he broke the cardinal rule and he spoke back to his father. "Why," he asked, "can't I go to Friendly's for a Coke after school with my friend?" His father became so enraged at his insubordination that he grounded him for a week, cutting Barry off from his one connection to the outside world.

Parental beliefs affect parental behavior and parental behavior affects what children believe and how they see themselves and the world. What they believe and how they see things affects their thoughts, feelings, and behavior.

Emotional Insecurity. You can develop a sense of insecurity from the experience of neglect, rejection, physical, psychological, or sexual abuse, or abandonment. This abandonment isn't just the intentional physical cutting of ties with you as a child, as in leaving you in a basket on someone's doorstep. It's also the perceived emotional and physical cutting of ties that results from divorce, death, or betrayal.

For example, I learned early that I couldn't rely upon my father to protect me. That was made abundantly clear every time we visited my paternal grandfather who ruled his world literally and figuratively with an iron fist. Part of every audience with him was a ritual greeting that all the grandchildren had to endure. With my father and his two brothers looking away in parental conflict, my grandfather lined the children up then demanded that we each shake his hand. I was first.

Knowing what was about to happen, I started to cry and begged my father not to have to. He half-heartedly commanded me to comply. My grandfather wrapped his meaty paw around my 6-year-old's hand, and began to squeeze ... and squeeze ... and squeeze. As I screamed and writhed, struggling to get away, he riveted his icy gaze at me, smiled, and squeezed just a little more for good measure.

Dependence. Children of alcoholic parents, in alcoholic families, and alcoholics themselves tend to be overly concerned with control. As such, you tend to think about things in terms of black-and-white, all-or-nothing. You may try to avoid your feelings and have difficulty trusting others. At the same time you bend over backwards to please them, even at your own expense.

You passively allow others to assume responsibility for areas of your life. As a result, you may subordinate your needs to those on whom you depend in order to avoid the possibility of having to rely upon yourself. Feeling unable to function independently, you lack self-confidence. As children who respond to insecurity with dependency, you will tend to rely on safe harbors: safe places and safe people.

Overall Parental Effect. Recent research has suggested that when parents are diagnosed with an anxiety disorder, their children are seven times more likely to develop an anxiety disorder as well. Moreover as few as eight family sessions of Cognitive-Behavioral Therapy can reduce children's symptoms and the risk of their developing anxiety.

HOW CUMULATIVE STRESS IMPACTS YOU

Stressors are often conditions of threat or loss that produce varying degrees of physiological arousal. But they can also be anything that places a demand upon you for change, adaptation, or readjustment. According the Holmes and Rahe Social Adjustment Rating Scale, these include death, divorce, marriage, job loss or promotion, financial loss, sexual problems, childbirth, relocation, severe or chronic illness, pregnancy, retirement, physical aging, or menopause.

In addition, you often have to bear the burden of unresolved psychological conflicts (such as identity or love-hate issues with your parents) that you carry with you.

Each of these events, changes, or conflicts has stress associated with it. Sadly, it doesn't take long before these events and their resulting stress begin to accumulate. They create a chronic state of arousal. Its presence is both physically and psychologically felt.

What this means is that when you recover from your arousal for a specific event, your stress level doesn't return to baseline but stops at a higher level. Each time you're stressed, you start higher and higher because your baseline has continued to change. When you can no longer marshal your body's resources or there are too many stressors to which to respond, you will start to succumb to the stress overload.

WHAT TRIGGERING MECHANISMS DO

Triggering mechanisms are short-term events that set the anxiety-producing process in motion. The mechanism may be a single, acute stress condition resulting from a significant personal loss, life change, trauma, or a series of stressors ... or it may be the use of stimulant drugs.

Behavioral Conditioning. SA/SP may be thought of as the consequence of one or more traumatic events that result in your fearing some object or situation. This conditioning occurs when you associate something neutral, such as a dais or podium, with the strong anxiety you experience when giving a speech. While initially only giving the speech elicited anxiety, now the presence of a dais or podium elicits anxiety too.

This conditioning can also occur by avoidance. When you avoid the object or situation that creates your anxiety, you reduce the anxiety. Reducing anxiety is rewarding, thus making your avoidance of it rewarding. Consequently you learn to avoid the situation.

Conditioning may be what's happening in a single acute experience, such as being humiliated by a teacher in front of the class, or chronic experiences, such as moving constantly as a child where there's continual newcomer rejection.

SARAH. When Sarah was 7, her father told her he had wanted a boy instead of a girl. Since she knew that boys weren't supposed to cry, Sarah swallowed her grief and started dressing in a T-shirt and pants like her father. When she walked, she swaggered and spoke to her dog, Ralph, in a deep-pitched voice.

Since she rarely saw her father who traveled a lot, when he was around she tried to participate in whatever he wanted to do. Unfortunately, that included shooting at crows. This created conflict for Sarah who loved animals and wanted to be a veterinarian someday. Would a son object? It didn't really matter because she saw this activity as the only viable connection to her father and she feared severing it.

Vicarious Learning. Observing someone else's fearful behavior in the presence of some previously neutral object or situation also may cause this fear conditioning. Even though research on observational, or vicarious, learning has not been extended to social fears in humans, it's easy to imagine children learning how to respond to situations by watching a parent. I know I learned my mother's fear of heights from her.

With respect to SA/SP, if you see your parent respond to high-status individuals by grinning, nodding, and deferring or respond to crowds by cringing, looking agitated, and withdrawing, you're likely to follow suit.

Research by Ruth Stemberger and others has found a relationship between social anxiety and a childhood traumatic conditioning event. They've also found that this conditioning *plus* shyness tended to predict the likelihood of SA/SP. Since not all who undergo traumatic or vicarious conditioning actually acquire clinically significant levels of fear, you may need to have some prior experience with the conditioning stimulus for the conditioning to have a powerful effect.

Individuals will differ widely in the degree to which your fear is maintained over time. They will also differ widely in whether the fear generalizes to other objects or situations over time. Fear of the public speaking microphone, for example, may or may not expand to include lecterns and stages.

Some of this difference may come from other negative and stressful life events that may prepare you to experience fear. The more prepared you are to experience fear the more rapidly you'll acquire it. Moreover, the larger the number of aversive social experiences you have, the greater the likelihood is that you'll expect these social situations to continue to be negative and feel anxiety when approaching them.

Conversely, the larger the number of rewarding social experiences that you encounter, the greater the likelihood of your not experiencing anxiety in approaching them. That is, if every time you approached the feared microphone you received acclaim, the microphone would lose its negative association and the fear would vanish.

Self-Efficacy. Learning theorist Albert Bandura suggests that whether or not people undertake particular actions, attempt to perform tasks, or strive to meet specific goals depends on whether or not they believe they will be effective, or efficacious, in performing those actions.

Self-efficacy is a control-related belief. It relates to your belief in your ability to manage particular kinds of activities, mobilize your motivation, control your own cognitive and emotional reactions to it, and achieve desired outcomes. Related to goal setting, it's sometimes synonymous with *self-confidence.*

Self-efficacy is a dynamic process that changes over time with new information and task experiences. The more efficacious you see yourself, the more persistent and confident you will be in your effort toward a task. So, if you believe you know what to expect at a group meeting and are prepared to interact with others on particular topics, you are more likely to attempt to do it.

It's important to note that threat is not a fixed property of social situations. Threat exists if you *believe* it does. It's a function of how dangerous you think the situation is and to what degree you see yourself able to deal with it. Your appraisal of the likelihood of a negative event relies on your interpretation of the information you encounter.

Believing you can't cope with perceived potential threats is what makes you anxious and avoidant. SA/SPers experience high levels of anxiety because you envision yourself to be without any control over your situation or future. Bandura has found that this low level of self-efficacy is associated with increased levels of stress, anxiety, and depression.

Self-efficacy is the basis of mastery and, conversely, mastery is the basis of self-efficacy. You learn how to achieve a task or solve a problem then get to experience the thrill of success at your accomplishment. This translates into elevated self-confidence and self-esteem.

People who believe they can exercise control over potential threats don't engage in anxious thinking. They are not disturbed by such threats. They control their arousal by believing in their ability to cope, to forestall or mitigate the negative events. Their resiliency beliefs not only buffer this stress and the aversive psychological effects of failure but also prevent them.

Monkey studies have demonstrated that extensive early experience controlling one's environment prepared the animals to successfully cope with novel and threatening situations. This success experience acted as an immunization against the effects of the stressors. What this indicates is the importance of the perception of controllability *and* an early history of actual control over your environment. It also emphasizes the usefulness of knowing what specifically to expect in social situations and preparing for it. Knowing what to expect and preparing for it can significantly increase your self-efficacy and reduce your anxiety.

Note: While these animal study findings are suggestive, you need to be careful generalizing from lower animals' behavior to that of humans. Since SA/SP is also predicated on self-consciousness, a fear of evaluation, embarrassment, and humiliation resulting from observation, it is difficult to conclude that monkey behavior of confidence or fear is the same thing as SA/SP in humans. Even though the behaviors may appear to be similar, you can't know whether these behaviors are demonstrating a similar biological function or even similar evolutionary origins.

SUMMARY

The search for origins and triggers of SA/SP goes on, with some researchers emphasizing nature and some nurture. But what appears to be the case, in general, is that many different factors work together in different unique combinations to predispose different individuals for SA/SP. However, as you will find out in the next chapter, vulnerability, or predisposition, to SA/SP isn't enough for you to develop this disorder.

4

KEEPING SOCIAL ANXIETY GOING

*"Deep into that darkness peering, long I stood there
wondering, fearing, Doubting, dreaming dreams no mortal ever
dared dream before."* (Edgar Allan Poe, *The Raven*, 1845)

WHAT ARE MAINTAINING MECHANISMS?

As you've seen, once you're primed for anxiety by vulnerability, negative life experience, and cumulative stress, you have to experience a trigger to actually start the process rolling. But simply setting this process in motion isn't enough. Anxiety is a temporary condition unless there are other factors available to keep the process ongoing and in high gear.

What sorts of things do SA/SPers think, believe, and expect others to think and say that keeps the process going? Things such as

Them: "I see you've set aside this special time to humiliate yourself in public."

You: "You're validating my inherent mistrust of strangers."

Them: "Someday, you'll look back on this, laugh nervously, and change the subject."

The primary maintaining mechanisms for SA/SP include your core beliefs, self-presentation, and negative self-talk.

Core Beliefs. You develop beliefs and attitudes in childhood about others, yourself, the way the world is, what it does, and how it *should* operate. These are the foundation of what you think and do. According to psychologist Jeffrey Young, most core beliefs fall into these ten general categories:

- Value (self-worth)
- Security (self-safety)
- Performance (self-competence)
- Control (self-power)
- Love (self-desirability)

- Autonomy (self-independence)
- Justice (life fairness)
- Belonging (being a part)
- Others
- Standards (self-derived norms).

Your beliefs are personally formed thoughts that are often culturally determined and culturally shared. But SA/SP beliefs are systematically different. They are quite specifically negative and maladaptive.

According to cognitive therapist Judith Beck, these negative beliefs represent two basic assumptions about yourself: your "helplessness" and "unlovability." SA/SP beliefs can be broken down by type: *unconditional beliefs* about yourself, *conditional beliefs* about social evaluation, and *excessively high presentation standards*.

Unconditional, unequivocal beliefs about yourself include:

- I'm stupid.
- I'm helpless.
- I'm undesirable.
- I'm a failure.

Conditional beliefs are about the conditions under which you think negative social evaluation will take place. For example, "I'll be seen as stupid, helpless, etc. *if* I speak up in class."

Excessively high presentation standards convey your perfectionistic, all-or-nothing irrationality, as in, "I must be perfect or everything will be ruined."

These are your *core beliefs* ... beliefs so central and fundamental to your SA/SP existence and sense of self that you regard them as absolute truths. They act as a frame of reference for all you encounter. They determine what you see as "fact" and how you interpret its meaning.

When these core beliefs are activated, they become the filters through which you perceive and interpret everything. The truth or falsity of your belief is really inconsequential because your belief focuses selectively on information that supports it. For SA/SPers the selective focus is negative. As long as your belief is "supported" by negative evidence, it'll continue. This means that irrespective of what predisposes you to SA/SP and triggers your disorder, it is your system of negative beliefs that will lead you to view yourself as at-risk and will maintain that anxiety.

Core beliefs result from a variety of sources: parental and cultural values, group stereotypes, and conclusions drawn from specific incidents about what happens and why. You frequently don't know whether your beliefs are correct or not because you don't test them. If you see social situations as being inherently dangerous and feel you have to be perfect to be acceptable to others, you're less likely to feel comfortable in social situations and less willing to take risks regarding them.

Similarly, you may believe that you are "personally responsible for everything that happens to you." This belief implies that "illness," like SA/SP, is a personal failure. If you're responsible, you caused it, and, therefore, can cure it. Even though a belief such as this could be harmful, you tend to take it at face value, accept it as gospel, and operate on it. As a result, mistaken beliefs may become self-fulfilling prophecies because you look for information to support them.

As you work from your inner mind to your outer limits, you can see the expression of these core beliefs in your *attitudes, expectations, rules,* and *assumptions.* If you break the core belief "I'm a loser," for example, into its components, you're likely to see the following:

- Attitude: *"It's perfectly awful that I'm a loser."*

- Expectation: *"I have to do everything I can to prove that I'm not a loser."*

- Assumption: *"If I do everything I can, I might be able to just get by."*

Negative Self-Talk. What you say to yourself is self-talk. It represents your core beliefs. For SA/SPers it is the automatic, pre-conscious or just barely noticeable negative statements you make repeatedly to yourself about:

- Perceived *inadequacies*
- What *should* be
- *What-ifs* ("What if I say something stupid?")
- *If-then* premises ("*If* I approach a woman, *then* I'll be vulnerable to attack").

They cause you to anticipate worst-case scenarios and embroil you in self-criticism. They compel you to work toward perfection and assume a feeling of helplessness. Just thinking about potential consequences of being in a threatening social situation sets your automatic and habitual anxiety in motion.

Consequently, when you're actually in those social situations, you tend to think of yourself negatively. You *overestimate* the degree of *threat* associated with the situation. You also simultaneously *underestimate* your *ability to cope* with it.

But, it's important to note that this occurs *only* in social situations you fear. When you're alone or in non-threatening situations, you tend to think of yourself more positively and feel more adequate. Thus, when Joe's car is the only vehicle on the road, he doesn't feel stupid or inadequate. When Harry can spin his tales any way he wants, he shines at parties. When Sarah is with her mother or Tanya, she's funny and outgoing.

Since social anxiety is anticipatory, dealing with possibilities and what-ifs, much of what you agonize over is imaginary. This fact makes your automatic anxiety programming ineffective and inefficient at accomplishing anything positive for you. You become caught up in a spider's web of negative social thoughts and self-focused attention. This excessive attention to anxiety cues from your body, your emotions, behavior, and thoughts wraps you then immobilizes you in a silken cocoon of apprehension and dread.

Consequently, when SA/SPers enter a feared situation, you approach it with a distorted view and go on negative cognitive autopilot. You choose negative evaluations for ambiguous situations, catastrophic interpretations for mildly negative situations, and underestimate your presentation confidence and ability.

You no longer focus on others or on the social environment. You think and feel you're the feared center of attention. To you thinking you've done something dumb is the same as your having done something dumb. Similarly, feeling out of control is the same as being out of control. External information that doesn't support your negative views doesn't make it through your negative filter. You either discount or dismiss it so it doesn't get checked out against the reality of the situation.

What sorts of self-deprecating things do you say to yourself?

- "I'm not so much a has-been as a definite won't be."
- "When I open my mouth, it's only to change feet."
- "I have delusions of adequacy."
- "I have a knack for making strangers immediately."
- "If you see two people talking and one looks bored, I'm the other one."
- "The wheel is turning but the hamster is dead."

What sorts of negative things do you believe others are thinking about you?

- "She's a prime candidate for natural selection."
- "He's depriving a village somewhere of an idiot."
- "She brings a lot of joy whenever she leaves the room."
- "Some drink from the fountain of knowledge, but he only gargled."
- "He donated his brain to science before he was finished using it."

Then you look to your physiological symptoms to support your threat perception: "My heart is racing and I'm breathing fast, I must be anxious about the situation." You monitor your thoughts: "Everyone's looking at me. What if I make a mistake?"

The greater your social anxiety, the more likely you'll overestimate the degree to which your anxiety is observable and/or observed by others. You monitor your emotions: "I'm frightened by what others might do. I feel angry that they're evaluating me."

Trying to Meet Standards. Part of your evaluation process is checking to see how your perceived self-presentation matches some ideal. But making this match creates an internal conflict, known as cognitive dissonance. It creates a discomfort that motivates you to reduce it.

To reduce it you can (1) change your behavior to bring yourself closer to the ideal. You can (2) change the situation. You can (3) change your attitudes. Or you can (4) direct your attention elsewhere.

Suppose you want to go to a movie featuring the latest heartthrob but are afraid of being scrutinized by other movie patrons. You're confronted with the unpleasant arousal of dissonance. As a result, you are on the horns of a dilemma about what to do.

You may decide to go but disguise yourself and sit in the back by the exit. You may wait for the film to come out on DVD or go to another theater that is virtually empty. Or you may tell yourself you really don't want to see the movie, because the reviews weren't five-star, or you don't want to spend the money, or you really have to clean the bathroom right now.

In SA/SP you frequently reduce this kind of conflict by making your thoughts and behaviors consistent with the fear-based thought. That is, you find an excuse for not going or doing what you'd like to do.

Typically, following any such conflict-filled social event, you'll review what you perceived to have happened in all its gory details. You'll microscopically dissect and analyze it, not once but over and over and over again, through your negative filter. You'll compare it with past failures. This is especially easy to do since you have a better memory for negative information about yourself than you do for positive information.

When you're done, your sense of social defeat will be amplified and your embarrassment deepened. The negative effect of the event will be chiseled in granite. This means you'll have even more to torture yourself with the next time you take a trip down your memory lane of "failure."

This process becomes a vicious circle of negative self-perception and erroneous feedback. As a result, your self-focused attention leads to self-dissatisfaction and bad feelings. This, in turn, works to increase your social anxiety, which, in turn, further inhibits your self-presentation. And it goes on and on, spiraling downward.

Safety Behaviors. When in social situations, SA/SPers also attempt to reduce the risk of negative evaluation through safety behaviors. For example, when Sarah answered the phone, she adopted a simple vocabulary and one-word answers to avoid misspeaking and self-disclosure. When Joanna gave a class presentation, she spoke rapidly without pause so classmates wouldn't think the pauses meant she was unprepared. When Barry feared he would tremble in the presence of an attractive woman, he braced himself against the nearest stationary object. And when Joe wanted to keep from making eye contact, he'd avert his gaze and fiddle with the radio buttons.

These behaviors feel comfortable. They serve a useful purpose and seem to be only minor distractions for preventing feared outcomes. But they are, in fact, forms of avoidance. They actually reinforce your overestimation of negative evaluation by others and its consequences.

They reinforce your negative thinking and feared behaviors. Their use makes some anxiety-reducing techniques, like exposure, less effective. The problem with safety behaviors is that when Joanna races through her speech, she doesn't allow for audience feedback that might disconfirm her fears. She doesn't get to see how her classmates would actually respond if she paused at expected intervals. When this behavior reduces her fear, she feels rewarded for doing it. Therefore, she is likely to continue doing so. It's the same with Barry and Joe.

Others too may perceive safety behaviors as negatives or deficits. For example, those listening to Joanna will likely feel disconcerted that she doesn't pause where they expect she should, according to generally accepted standards of presentations. In this case, her safety behavior may create a negative pattern of interaction and have a negative effect on the way she appears to others. If Joanna sees her audience's frowns, looks of puzzlement, and sighs, it will likely confirm her worst fears about public speaking. This then will further reinforce her SA/SP. In effect, it becomes a self-fulfilling prophecy for her.

Self-Presentation. As Mark Leary and Robin Kowalski argue, social anxiety is essentially a reaction to real or imagined self-presentation difficulties. The impressions you make may cause others to devalue, avoid, or reject relationships with you. The possibility of your relationships being regarded as not as important, close, or valuable as you desire makes you anxious.

While it would be nice to be certain that you'll make the impression on others that you desire, unfortunately there's no way to do that. This is because you're dealing not only with your performance but also with someone else's perception of it. While you may have some control over the former, you have very little over the latter.

In order for you to influence others to see and evaluate you in certain ways, it is necessary for you to determine what factors will produce the reaction you want. This means paying careful attention and devoting time, effort, and thought to creating the desired impression. You need to seek information and look for clues in the social situation to do this. This allows you to know what to expect and prepare for it.

When you know what to expect and are prepared for it, your expectations of conveying the desired impression will increase and your anxiety will decrease. When you're uncertain, your anxiety increases. When the situation is unstructured, ambiguous, or lacking clues altogether, your anxiety increases. When this results in awkward, stilted interactions, your anxiety increases.

JOANNA. When Joanna began as a volunteer at the local homeless shelter, she found her boss, Irene, worked from a wheelchair as a consequence of an automobile accident. From the moment of their introduction, Joanna never knew where to look when talking with Irene. If she looked at her face, she'd be staring at the scar tissue that covered Irene's right cheek. If she looked lower down, she had her eyes on Irene's right arm that was amputated at the elbow. What are the rules? Joanna asked herself. Where are the clues?

Joanna didn't know how to handle the situation. Because of the uncertainty and ambiguity she was wracked with questions and guilt. Should I stoop or squat when I talk to Irene so she won't strain her neck looking up? Do I pick up things for her or wait for her to ask me first? Joanna wanted to escape interactions with Irene and would talk with her only when it was absolutely necessary. She kept her conversations short, touching only the essentials. Whenever possible, she would try to avoid Irene altogether if she thought she could do so without seeming to reject her.

Joanna's anxiety shot sky-high everyday she went to work. She so wanted to make a good impression but hadn't the slightest notion how to do it. There was no question in her mind that she was doing everything wrong and looking like an insensitive jerk as a result.

This is similar to Barry's questions in the singles' bar. How should I act? What's expected of me? Should I simply mimic others' behavior here? Without the necessary preparation both Joanna and Barry will worry about breaching mores and rules of etiquette and, consequently, experience anxiety.

As poet T.S. Eliot says, "Prepare a face to meet the faces you meet." According to the self-presentation model of social anxiety, you experience social anxiety when you are motivated to make a particular impression on others but doubt you'll be able to make that desired impression successfully.

In other words, if you don't care if you make the desired impression, you won't experience social anxiety. If you're sure you'll make the desired impression, you won't experience it either. What this suggests is that any factor that increases your motivation to succeed or decreases the probability of your succeeding will precipitate or heighten your social anxiety.

Status. The identity of the person who'll evaluate you is important to your motivation to manage your impression. As a result, you look for significant characteristics, such as status. You assign the label "high-status" to those whom you see as powerful, competent, gifted, attractive, knowledgeable, or socially skilled. You tend to see those individuals as having more value as well as more value to share with others.

You see evaluations by high-status people as being more valid than those from others. Since individuals with these characteristics can influence your getting valuable social rewards (from jobs to friendships), you see interactions with them as having more at stake. Consequently, you tend to be more anxious in dealing with those with high status.

Gender. Gender also is a motivating factor for you. Cross-gender encounters tend to create anxiety for heterosexuals because of personal and cultural rewards. Being seen as desirable not only raises your self-esteem and self-confidence but also makes it more likely that you'll participate in culturally desired relationships (from dating to marriage). Participation allows you to be perceived as meeting society's expectations of what you *should* do and to be rewarded for it.

Social Comparison. As a SA/SPer, you assess your own value by comparing yourself to others. How you see them dictates how you feel about yourself by comparison. In other words, your perception of your acceptability is not within you. It is outside you and dependent upon another person.

But when you make these comparisons, you always come out on the short end of the stick. You see that they're socializing, dating, holding good jobs, going to school, making presentations, and enjoying life … doing and enjoying all the things you're not.

This social comparison process appears to be an intrinsic need for people in general. Everyone wants to feel they're doing things right and that their opinions, beliefs, and behaviors match others for correctness. Furthermore, if you know what is acceptable in any given set of circumstances, you can predict the likely outcome and take appropriate action.

However, SA/SPers tend to take social comparison to the extreme. Whenever any uncertainty exists, you look for information in what others say and do against which to judge yourself. Disagreement with you shakes your confidence. You want and need social agreement.

Number of People. The number of people present in any social situations is important. As the number of people present increases, so does your motivation to make the desired impression. Greater numbers tend to lead to a perception that your impression will have greater impact because there are that many more people to observe and evaluate it.

But greater numbers also lead to a decrease in your confidence that you can make a desired impression. This, in turn, also increases your social anxiety.

The number of people performing with you in a group also affects your level of social anxiety. The greater the number of performers you have around you, the less will be your anxiety. This may result from a diffusion of responsibility wherein no one member is responsible for an unfavorable impression. Instead, responsibility for the result is shared by the entire group. The reduction in anxiety may also be related to the audiences' attention being divided among many group members.

Confidence. The degree to which you feel you can make the desired impression is a measure of your self-confidence. When you evaluate yourself negatively or engage in negative self-talk, you lower your self-confidence and, simultaneously, raise your social anxiety. Likewise, when you raise your self-confidence, you lower your social anxiety.

The more confident you think you are, the more likely you'll feel you can and will make the desired impression. Conversely, the less physically attractive you think you are, the less likely you'll feel you can. Attractive people are given gold stars in most cultures. In Western culture you see them as smarter, friendlier, and more likely to succeed. Interactions with attractive people are seen as more satisfying than those with unattractive people.

SA/SP avoidance behaviors tend to be seen as unattractive. When you avert your gaze, have infrequent eye contact, and demonstrate a general lack of participation in the interaction, you may be seen as aloof and unfriendly. Others may mirror your behavior. This may make you feel even less attractive.

People who respond with clear, effective, and well-timed reactions are thought to possess good interpersonal skills. Your reticence and withdrawal in social situations suggests you lack social skills or those skills are inadequate.

In conversations you tend to speak less, look less, interrupt less, and nod, smile, and "uh-huh" more. You allow yourself to be only minimally engaged in the situation. When you are engaged, you ask more questions but make fewer statements of fact or provide any self-disclosure.

However, if you do engage in conversations in this fashion, give yourself some Brownie points. These behaviors are also skillful ways to handle difficult social situations. If you have any doubt about how to present yourself, these behaviors allow you to deal with the interaction safely.

It's important to note that there are no data to support the notion that these interaction displays of social anxiety have any connection with poor interpersonal skills. While you may believe you're less socially skilled, that doesn't mean you actually are. Since your perceptions of your abilities tend to be so negatively distorted, it's hard for you to see it objectively. What you do know is that encounters will be more effective and satisfying when you participate more equally in the interaction.

Avoidance. Avoidance can be summed up in the following advice, "On the keyboard of life always keep your finger on the escape key." Once you've started avoiding feared situations, you tend to continue to do so. In extreme cases you may simply avoid social encounters altogether. But, as long as you do, your fear will remain a viable and disabling enemy.

Denying Feelings. In SA/SP you experience an array of strong emotions but are afraid to express them because of how you think others will judge you. Denial is an unconscious refusal to admit into your awareness those aspects of reality that you find consciously unacceptable. When this happens, you refuse to accept some particular event (the sadness from the death of a loved one) or to face what seems to be an intolerable situation (not being able to trust and depend upon one's parent any longer).

Put another way, denial is a distortion of reality to make it conform to your individual wishes. When I was afraid to stand up for myself and confront others, I denied my fear by always finding an altruistic excuse for giving in to others' wishes ... and letting them walk all over me. The excuse was geared to make me look good but always made me feel bad.

When you deny your anger, frustration, sadness, and excitement, you often feel stuck, depressed, and vaguely anxious without knowing why. Furthermore, what you deny frequently shows itself in other unexpected and oblique ways.

Lack of Assertiveness. In order to feel good about yourself, to keep your self-esteem and self-confidence high, you need to assert yourself. Specifically, you need to express your thoughts, beliefs, and feelings to others in a direct, firm, socially acceptable, respectful manner.

Assertiveness is a behavioral style which involves your awareness of your right to stand up for yourself, ask for what you want, and act in your own best interests *without* harming others or infringing upon their rights. It's expressing yourself in an honest, appropriate, reasonable, firm, and respectful manner.

Non-assertiveness, on the other hand, is not standing up for your rights. It's an expression of self-denial and fear. When you're non-assertive, you violate your own rights by not expressing your honest thoughts, feelings, and beliefs directly and appropriately. Instead, you're self-effacing, apologetic, and overly agreeable.

You act as if you are not as deserving as others, and, thus, must sacrifice by subordinating your needs and wants to those of others. Your message is, "I don't count so you can do whatever you want, even take advantage of me." Non-assertive behavior allows others to dismiss, discount, and easily disregard you.

A non-assertive person will seldom initiate actions or deal directly with others to address problems. You exert no influence by acting in a diffident, self-effacing manner. When you don't assert yourself because you're afraid, you feel resentment. Specifically, you feel angry both with those against whom you can't assert yourself and with yourself. You feel trapped and helpless. When you lack assertiveness, you're always going to be at the mercy of others.

Non-assertiveness is:

- Suffering silently because you're afraid to assert yourself in public or private, with strangers, family and friends;
- Kicking yourself afterwards for not having said the things you really wanted to say;
- Being afraid people will disapprove of you if you express how you feel;
- Holding your tongue until you can't stand it any longer and then exploding.

Why do people act non-assertively? You may mistake assertiveness for undesirable aggressiveness and, thus, avoid it. You may equate non-assertiveness with politeness and believe this is how you should act. You may not be able to accept that you have personal rights that allow you to get what you want. You may fear the consequences of acting assertively. Or you may mistake non-assertiveness for behavior that's helpful and supportive to others.

Overall, being non-assertive leads to significant feelings of frustration and submerged anger. The cost of appeasing others and avoiding conflict can be loss of integrity and, sometimes, dignity. (See Chapter 9 for how to become more assertive.)

As novelist James Baldwin writes, "Not everything that is faced can be changed, but nothing can be changed until it is faced."

Perfectionism. Perfectionism is setting standards for yourself and others that are unrealistically high. But perfectionism is not to be confused with motivation to do a good job or a heartfelt wish to achieve something as perfectly as possible. Instead, perfectionism is a rigid adherence to strict standards. It's a compulsive striving to achieve unachievable goals. By being "perfect" you try to *guarantee* for yourself the approval and acceptance of others.

The problem with this wishful thinking is that demanding approval from every significant or insignificant person in your life only sets you up for failure because it is physically impossible to achieve. As a result, you are more likely to come to expect the worst so as not to feel hurt and disappointment when your needs, and other expectations, are not met.

In this process you equate your self-worth with your performance, productivity, and accomplishments. You nag yourself about your failures. You think that if you don't achieve your goal, it will be "terrible," a catastrophe. This makes your perceived "failure" even more devastating.

Unrealistic Expectations & Shoulds. You are such a hard taskmaster that you allow yourself no relief from self-condemnation. As you heap on the self-recrimination, your anger, frustration, resentment, depression, demoralization, and stress swell to gargantuan proportions. On the other hand, if your unrealistic expectations are too low about yourself, you'll experience depression, resignation, low self-esteem, and underachievement. It's a lose-lose situation. Unrealistic expectations lead to poor coping.

You express these unrealistic expectations in terms of *should*, *shouldn't*, *must*, and *ought*, or what Albert Ellis, the parent of cognitive psychology and rational-emotive behavioral therapy (REBT), calls "*must*erbation." Your believing that there are rules that are etched in marble that you are expected to follow makes you try to strictly adhere to them.

For example, one rule might be, "I must be able to talk with strangers without having medication or therapy." Another might be, "You must wash those dishes right after dinner." These guilt-infusing rules to which you subscribe require that you work methodically and meticulously all the time … endlessly.

These *musts* and *shoulds* create a mental trap for you. While you are beating yourself about the head and shoulders in order to coerce yourself into motivation, you are inadvertently undermining your efforts to succeed at achieving your original task. You're so stifled by what you *should* do and how you *should* do it that there's little wiggle room for being spontaneous and original. Your work then becomes slow and unproductive, leaving you overworked and exhausted.

Shoulds are synonymous with perfectionism. *Shoulds* lead you to perceive and believe that your performance and you are never "good enough." As a result, you will tend to believe that you *should* be punished for this discrepancy between your real performance and your ideal fantasy of it.

But *shoulds* aren't the only illusions engendered by unrealistic expectations. You may expect that your will power should be able to overcome all. You may expect that there's only one true course in life and you have to find "it" or you will have nothing. You may also expect to define yourself as acceptable only through your actions. This means that if your actions don't meet your standards, you're not acceptable.

However, expectations themselves aren't the problem. The problem is how tied you are to the wish behind them and to the anticipation of the expectation being fulfilled or unfulfilled.

Expectations may be positive or negative. Positive expectations are based in an assessment of the situation and a wish for a particular course of events. When positive expectations, such as being surprised by flowers, are unmet, they result in disappointment. Negative expectations, such as your birthday will be forgotten, on the other hand, are defensive, mirroring fears that your wishes won't be gratified.

Expectations you have for others that are too high likewise produce negative feelings. You expect them to intuitively know what you want and need and then to act on that knowledge. When they are unable to meet that expectation, you resent their failure to do so. You tend to scorn and condemn them.

After all, if *you're* fair and just to them, you're entitled to fair and just treatment from them in return. Your receiving anything less than what you expect feels inequitable because it unbalances your mental accounting ledger. This leaves you feeling angry and disappointed.

You need to remember the words of humanistic psychologist Fritz Perls who wrote, "I am not in this world to live up to your expectations. And you are not in this world to live up to mine."

Perfectionism Decreases Satisfaction. Perfectionism often leads to an inability to feel satisfaction if you perceive that you have to give *more* than 100% *all* the time. Just as you approach the high-jump bar, someone raises it higher so it's once again out of reach. But you can't let go. You can't stop worrying about your errors, obsessing over your failures. Tied up in an emotional straitjacket, you lose your grip on the possibility of self-acceptance and inner peace.

Often characterized by your fear of failure, perfectionism results in immobilization. You can see aspects of perfectionism in procrastination, all-or-nothing thinking, task paralysis, workaholism, anxiety, depression, and lowered self-esteem. If you can't be perfect or do something perfectly, there's no reason to try. This eliminates taking risks or exploring new territory. But without failure and risk of failure you learn nothing and experience no growth.

Anger and Hostility. Anger can be a natural, spontaneous, and unavoidable physiological response to many stimuli. It often originates from a lack of assertiveness and a sense of helplessness that is inherent in your anxious state. It's created and maintained by your belief that something "shouldn't be."

In general, it's short-lived, although it can become chronic. Those who withdraw from social situations, and who cling or try to please others, tend not to demonstrate their anger directly. You fear exposing yourself and alienating those on whom you depend for a sense of security. As a result, your anger is buried and accumulates over time, putting others at risk of an inadvertent explosion.

But dwelling on anger or giving in to ranting or explosions is neither healthy nor useful. When you don't control the expression of your anger, its power increases and you often hurt others as well as yourself. As Aristotle said, "Anyone can become angry; that is easy. To be angry with the right person, to the right degree, at the right time, for the right purpose, and in the right way, this is not easy."

Hostility, on the other hand, seems to stem from a blend of conflicting feelings: anxiety, anger, and unresolved rage. As your anxiety increases, so may your hostility. When you feel yourself to be in constant danger of a real or imagined threat of external attack of injustice, you may adopt hostility to protect yourself.

Hostility may result from your having felt deprived of love, fair treatment, recognition, or opportunities. It may result from your having been made to feel inferior, inadequate, or worthless. It may result from your having been hindered in some way, by rigid discipline, excessive criticism, or lack of respect.

In general, that which initially ignited this persistent feeling of bitter resentment is long gone; however, the resulting antagonism and anxiety live on in your thoughts and feelings. They gnaw at you, constantly refreshed by cognitive distortions and mistakes. In your focus on yourself you assume that if you feel ill will toward them, they feel the same toward you. This further justifies in your mind your negative thoughts, feelings, and behavior.

How hostility is expressed depends upon your personality and behavior. While you may present yourself as cool, aloof, and disengaged or charming and engaging, hostility may slip from behind your mask as cutting remarks, sniping at others, putting people down, or sarcasm. If you are shy, non-assertive, or highly anxious, you may express your hostility as greater fear rather than as anger.

Your only release seems to be indirect or oblique. You become masters of passive-aggressive behavior. You "innocently" do things to thwart those you feel have hurt you. You're late for appointments. You make mistakes that inconvenience others. You send mixed messages (with your words saying one thing and your behaviors saying the opposite) about your concern or support.

Like termites slowly eating away the structure of a house, hostility cuts you off not only from others but also from yourself. You're so preoccupied with anger and defending that you alienate yourself from your own warm and vulnerable feelings. This leaves you even more isolated. Without concerted efforts to identify and understand this state of emotional poverty, you can find yourself in a state of chronic withdrawal and depression.

Cognitive Errors. Cognitive errors are distortions in the way you process information. They systematically bias how you think and show up in your negative self-talk. The following are some of the more common errors (they are addressed in detail in "Self Talk" in Chapter 7):

- Arbitrary inference
- Over-generalization
- Magnification and minimization
- Personalization
- All-or-nothing thinking

- Mental filter
- Disqualifying the positive
- Jumping to conclusions
- Mind reading
- Fortune telling error
- Emotional reasoning
- Should statements
- Labeling
- Rationalization.

Low Self-Esteem. Low self-esteem is a sense of worthlessness and insecurity. It's a lack of uniqueness and belonging. It's based on how you compare yourself with others and to what degree you meet the dictates of your internal standards.

You ask yourself, "Who am I to know?" "Who am I to judge?" "Who am I to decide?" Your self-esteem is determined not only by your feelings about yourself, particularly as children, but also by things that happen to you.

These feelings promote behaviors that tend to reinforce them. If you feel bad about not being able to solve one problem, you're unlikely to want to try to solve another and risk feeling bad again. These feelings may stem from parental criticism, neglect, abandonment, abuse, or overprotection, as well as your not having positive role models for self-nurturing behavior.

They are also the result of what others tell you about yourself and what your observations of your behavior and its consequences tell you about yourself. These feelings form gradually and are cumulative.

Having internalized the standards and beliefs of those who judge you, you come to describe yourself in terms of how you deviate from the norm because you accept your culture's pay-off system: Performance at or above the norm is rewarded. Performance below the norm is punished. Buying into this system puts you in further danger of experiencing the anxiety associated with others' evaluation of your performance.

You're likely to demean your own talents and feel others don't value you as well. You'll tend to believe you'll be unable to cope with different social situations. Furthermore, you'll likely doubt that you'll make the impressions you desire to make on others.

All of this promotes your feeling frustrated, angry, defensive, and powerless. It leaves you without the capacity to care for your needs and nurture yourself, act, and be responsible. This feeling of inadequacy leads to feelings of insecurity, self-doubt, being unfit for reality, and, of course, increased anxiety.

However, having high self-esteem alone is not a panacea for SA/SP in particular or psychological problems in general. You'll get into this in more detail a little later.

Guilt. Guilt is a vague but potentially corrosive feeling that results from self-punishment for your not having met some unconscious or conscious standard of behavior. Expressed in terms of "should" and "ought," guilt is the product of your internalization of others' expectations of "right" and "wrong."

Guilt is the gold standard for your personal behavior. It allows you to recognize your violations of some societal or other rule. When the life you live doesn't match up with the life you want to live or feel you *should* live, your conscience regales you with recriminations and bad feelings.

Even though there's no relationship between what you do and whether or not you feel guilt, you make your meeting these standards the measure of your self-worth. While feeling guilty may not stop you from doing something "unacceptable" or make you do something that's "acceptable," it will make you feel terrible for not having done what's expected.

BARRY. Barry's elderly grandmother is in a nursing home and he has trouble visiting her. One reason is that she taps into his well of guilt and social confusion every time she makes an indirect request of him. "I wish you'd visit more ... but I know how busy you are. I don't ask because I don't want to be a bother." Her mixed message tells Barry she's disappointed he's not visiting more, implicitly asking him to visit, but excusing his not doing so.

Procrastination. Procrastination is your conscious decision to do nothing or to delay doing it. It can occur when you have something that is useful, necessary, or unpleasant to do. It occurs when you wish or agree to do something, but postpone doing anything. You berate yourself for delaying, then delay some more, and berate yourself some more for it.

Your procrastination persists through anxiety and self-recrimination. It's based on self-defeating compulsiveness. According to Albert Ellis and William Knaus, it can be categorized by the behavior involved, such as maintenance, self-development, or irresponsibility to others.

Maintenance is where you put off essential duties, like paying bills or your income tax until the last possible moment.

Development is where you routinely avoid anything having to do with self-improvement activities, where you're constructively working toward meeting realistic goals you desire.

Irresponsibility to others involves sabotaging others by dawdling.

Procrastination can be the result of many factors, such as self-doubt, inadequate time, action management problems, organizational problems, powerlessness, hostility, self-indulgence, low frustration tolerance, perfectionism, need for love, depression, guilt, shame, and fear of disapproval. Irrespective of the source, the behavior creates a vicious circle.

WHAT OTHER FACTORS HELP MAINTAIN ANXIETY?

Many other factors help maintain your anxiety, such as muscle tension, nutrition, stimulants, and life style.

Muscle Tension. This refers to tightness and rigidity in any of the large muscle groups of your body. This extreme, continued contraction restricts your blood flow and reduces your breathing to shallow breaths. It's one of the many physiological changes that occur when you experience anxiety's arousal.

Your muscles tense, readying themselves to spring into action. Like the release of adrenaline and liver-stored sugar into the blood stream, this tension is designed to help you survive by preparing you for fight or flight.

The muscles that are particularly affected are the thighs, back, shoulders, arms, jaw, and face. When stress is prolonged, this tension can become a chronic response. Your muscle tension may also be indicative of suppressed feelings such as anger, frustration, or resentment and may lead to anxiety.

In order to feel less anxious, you need to decrease physiological arousal. One way to do this is by learning how to control your breathing. A second way is by eliminating muscle tension through progressive relaxation. (See Chapter 6.) This way often goes hand in hand with breathing control.

Nutrition and Stimulants. What you drink and eat can contribute significantly to your experience of anxiety. Use of stimulants, such as caffeine and nicotine, triggers the physiological arousal associated with anxiety because they trigger the release of the neurotransmitter norepinephrine. They interfere with sleep and deplete B-vitamins (B1, B2, B6, B12). B-vitamins, which are also depleted by stress and anxiety, are necessary for a healthy nervous system.

Those of you who use mental health services, or need to, tend to ingest a lot of caffeine: From 5–10 times as much coffee as non-patients, averaging 10–15 cups per day. This significantly increases your anxiety, irritability, and your problem with insomnia. These factors work to make your condition worse than it already is. Caffeine can also interfere with some anti-psychotics, sedatives, and lithium.

Low intake of calcium, vitamin C, and amino acids, the precursors to neurotransmitters, also leaves you vulnerable to stress. Moreover, your use of alcohol, which is a depressant, depletes both Vitamins B and C. In excess it can destroy brain cells.

Refined sugar acts as a stimulant to your body's hormone insulin, which breaks down sugars and starches. Excessive sugar sends your insulin level soaring, often overshooting, and leaving you with rapid heart rate, feeling jumpy and irritable, weakness, and sweating. This is very similar to the body's response to stress and mimicking the symptoms you associate with anxiety.

Yet, paradoxically, you find eating sugar somehow comforting. This appears to be related to a selective effect insulin has on amino acids. Which amino acid is transported to the brain depends upon which has the highest concentration in the blood stream at the time. Insulin in the blood stream causes all amino acids *but* tryptophan, the precursor of serotonin, to be taken up by muscles and other tissues.

Tryptophan, as the amino acid with the highest concentration, is then transported to the brain. There the tryptophan is converted to serotonin, which makes you feel rewarded for eating the sugar. As a result, your diet can have a profound effect on your daily functioning in general and on anxiety in particular.

Allergic Reactions and Physiological Dependence. Allergic reactions can cause psychological as well as physiological symptoms, such as anxiety, panic, depression, mood swings, irritability, insomnia, dizziness, fatigue, confusion, disorientation, and headaches. Frequent allergy culprits are wheat, milk, chocolate, peanuts, soy, and citrus. Interestingly, clinical ecologists have suggested that foods to which you're allergic are the ones you tend to crave. Let me share a related experience with you.

It took me most of my adult life to come to the realization that I'm an addict: out of control, unable to resist a seductive, toxic substance. I used it daily and relied on it to make everything right. No matter how bad I felt after the buzz wore off, I didn't stop. I had to have it.

Was I sniffing glue or gasoline or eating marijuana brownies? Was I hooked on cocaine, heroine, crack, or amphetamines? No, it was nothing so obvious. In a way, my substance was more insidious because it's widely used. It's one of those things labeled by the Food and Drug Administration as "generally recognized as safe." It is often invisible. I'm talking about processed sugar.

Unless you're consciously avoiding sugar, you eat it all day, every day of your life. According to the American Dietetic Association, the average American consumes in excess of 130 pounds of sugar a year. In other words, that's 6 ounces a day or 2.6 pounds a week. Over 70% of all processed foods contain some form of sugar because it's used as a preservative, flavor enhancer, fruit plumper, acid reducer, curing agent, fermentation medium, crust colorant, moisture holder, shelf-life extender, and provider of bulk, texture, and body Whew!

I've always loved sugar in any form, from Fudgicles to birthday cake to spoonfuls of brown sugar right from the box. My early love affair with it never seemed a problem, until my 20s when I developed constant headaches. They were present upon rising and upon going to bed, often erupting during the day into migraines.

As a result, I ate Excedrin (which contains 65 mg. of caffeine per tablet) by the handful, upwards of twelve a day, every day. In addition, my periods were getting worse. I suffered simulated labor pains and water-weight gain up to 10 pounds.

Anxiety insinuated itself into my every thought. I worried about the occurrence of the improbable and impossible. Depression slowly settled a dark, suffocating blanket over me. I had become fearful of social interaction. By the time I was in my 30s, I'd run the gamut of neurological tests, but nothing revealed itself or helped.

Note: No medical professional asked me about my diet or life style.

I was tired all the time, weak, and cried at a moment's notice. To comfort myself I ate some Brach's Bridge Mix, Nabisco 'Nilla Wafers, or Breyer's Fudge Swirl Ice Milk, only now in larger portions, more frequently to round off the sharp corners.

I developed night sweats, a 120-beats-per-minute heart rate, and insomnia. A prescription for the beta-blocker propranolol slowed my racing heart in between binges. But by this time I was eating all the sugar-laden food I could lay my hands on. If I didn't have candy around, I'd go to the store at any time in any weather to get it, bake a coffee cake, or eat raw sugar. Heartburn and gas were a constant problem.

Then one day I chanced to see physician on television, talking about the controversy over sugar's hypothesized effect on mood and behavior. I quickly began my research and soon found a description of my own health picture. With a glimmer of hope, I copied all the names in which processed sugar (simple sugar) appears: sucrose, dextrose, lactose, fructose, crystalline fructose, corn syrup, high-fructose corn syrup, turbinado, raw sugar, brown sugar, molasses, malt syrup, maltol, and maltodextrin.

Immediately I eliminated from my diet all processed foods that contained any on the list. The only "sugar" I consumed was moderate amounts of fresh fruits (complex sugars) and carbohydrate vegetables, but only in combination with protein, to mitigate any minor sugar reaction, and lots of water.

For the first several days without my precious sugar I was screaming inside my skull. Something down deep inside me, like a caged rat, gnawed at my soul, eating me alive from within. I'd find myself physically doubled over, hugging myself, rocking back and forth, in psychic agony. Then, on the fourth day as I awoke and habitually reached for my Excedrin, I realized I didn't have a headache. This was the first time in 20 years.

By the end of the first week I actually began to feel "up." The knot in my stomach had untied itself in non-social situations. My life looked brighter and held promise. I've been off sugar for a number of years now and have experienced no recurrence of my previous condition. There's no question that, at least for me, sugar is "addictive" and increased my general anxiety symptoms, making my SA/SP worse. This might be the case for other SA/SPers as well.

Lifestyle. This is how you live. "Many people unknowingly subject themselves to unnecessary stress by adopting and maintaining patterns of behavior, habits, relationships, activities, and obligations that add to their stress scores day by day," says Karl Albrecht, corporate stress-reduction consultant.

When you have a stressful lifestyle, you tend to experience chronic, unrelieved stress. You struggle with stressful interpersonal relationships and feel trapped in continuing stress situations. Often, you're involved in work you find unpleasant and unrewarding. In addition, you worry about potentially negative events in the future.

Type A behavior pattern is an example of a negative or stressful lifestyle. Those with this pattern are embroiled in a chronic, incessant struggle to do more in less and less time. There's time urgency, a fear that there's not enough time for all that needs to be done.

Type A people are faced with environmental challenges. You'll try to achieve work goals to the exclusion of other activities. You tend to accept high-pressure and stressful situations with few complaints, conforming to punishing social roles whenever they're demanded. All this is done without a whimper.

There are several lifestyle and health behaviors that contribute to how you experience stress.

Personal factors include your beliefs about control, your resilience, and your coping skills.

Environmental factors include those physical aspects over which you have little or no control, such as noise, air pollution, high-density crowding, heat, and public and organizational policies.

Cultural factors include those goals of culture toward which you work or the values you want to preserve.

Lack of Meaning. When you live without a sense of purpose or a direction to follow, your life lacks meaning. Your psychological health depends upon your having a "why" to live. It depends upon your finding meaning in your suffering in order to survive. All humans have a need for meaning.

According to existential psychologist Viktor Frankl in *Man's Search For Meaning,* it doesn't matter to what external conditions you're exposed or that affect your life. You are free to choose your reaction to those conditions. That is, you can choose to ultimately rise above your circumstances no matter how bad they are. Your continuing need to search for meaning supplies you with the purpose for your existence.

Research in Positive Psychology has demonstrated that creating positive emotions, engagement, and meaning in your life is significantly and strongly related to reducing depression and increasing creativity, productivity, health, resilience, and longevity.

Spiritual or Religious Belief. For those who value having a spiritual or religious faith, your personal belief has been shown to aid in transcending psychiatric disorders and health problems in general. Numerous studies have demonstrated that religious faith helps people cope with their illnesses and makes them less likely to be depressed when ill or hospitalized. Patients report that their faith provides them with a sense of control and meaning and purpose to their suffering.

WHEN ANXIETY ISN'T ANXIETY

Before you begin your journey toward recovery from your anxiety, you need to be sure the anxiety you feel has a psychological basis, not a medical basis. There are many medical conditions that mimic the symptoms of anxiety disorders. Therefore, before you apply the strategies in this book or any other book, you need to rule out medical conditions as the cause or complicating factors. This requires you to have a complete physical examination plus blood chemistries.

The following conditions are more fully detailed in Mark S. Gold's *The Good News About Panic, Anxiety, and Phobias* and James Morrison's *When Psychological Problems Mask Medical Disorders.* This listing is a heads-up and guide for further investigation. To reiterate, it is not for medical diagnosis purposes. An asterisk (*) marks the most common of the following anxiety-related medical conditions.

Asthma. Unpredictable periods of breathlessness and wheezing that are caused by stress, environmental conditions, or foreign substances. Symptoms include: Difficulty breathing, tight chest, anxiety.

Brain Tumor. Where tissue growth in the brain displaces normal structures. Symptoms include: Headaches, weakness, confusion, seizures, nausea, vomiting, memory loss, cognitive decline, depression.

Cerebral Arteriosclerosis. Thickening, hardening, or loss of elasticity of arterial walls in head. Symptoms include: Headache, dizziness, memory defects, anxiety.

*Chronic Obstructive Pulmonary Disease. Loss of elasticity and absorptive surface area in lungs. Symptom include: Shortness of breath, dusty skin hue, headaches, insomnia, panic, depression, anxiety.

Congestive Heart Failure. Loss of heart's pumping efficiency due to heart disease or arrhythmias. Symptoms include: Shortness of breath, weakness, edema, bluish skin, cold extremities, panic, anxiety.

*Diabetes Mellitus (Hyperglycemia). Reduced effectiveness or availability of insulin to metabolize food. Symptoms include: High levels of blood glucose, increased hunger, increased thirst, increased urine output, weight loss, panic, depression, anxiety.

Emphysema. Air sacs in the lungs that exchange gases become distorted or destroyed. Symptoms include: Decreased oxygen and increased carbon dioxide in blood, increased burden on heart, increased blood pressure, difficulty breathing, fatigue, anxiety.

Epilepsy. Recurrent paroxysmal disorder of cerebral structure of the brain. Symptoms include: Sudden, brief attacks of altered consciousness, motor activity, depression.

Essential Hypertension. Most common type of high blood pressure. Symptoms include: No symptoms, headaches, ringing in ears, lightheadedness, and fatigue.

Fibromyalgia. Ill-defined cluster of body symptoms. Symptoms include: Muscle pain and tenderness in specific areas, stiffness, chronic fatigue, depression, anxiety.

Hyperparathyroidism. Over-reactivity in the parathyroid gland. Symptoms includes: Increased serum calcium, weakness, tremors, nausea, abdominal pain, personality change, depression, anxiety.

*Hyperthyroidism. Increased production of thyroxin. Symptoms include: Heart palpitations, sweating, weight loss, increased temperature, insomnia, depression, panic, generalized anxiety.

*Hyperventilation syndrome. Intense episodes of rapid, shallow breathing. Symptoms include: Decreased carbon dioxide in blood, dizziness, shortness of breath, trembling, feelings of unreality, tingling in lips, hands, and feet, anxiety.

Hypocalcemia. Decreased blood calcium from lack of vitamin D, hypoparathyroidism, kidney failure. Symptoms include: Irregular heartbeat and muscle spasms.

*Hypoglycemia. Decreased blood sugar level from stress, improper diet, severe alcoholism, pancreatic tumor. Symptoms include: Shakiness, weakness, dizziness, disorientation, anxiety.

Hypokalemia. Decrease in blood potassium caused by malnutrition, dehydration, treatment for diabetes, hypertension, and use of diuretics. Symptoms include: Muscle weakness, reduced respiration, low blood pressure.

*Inner Ear Disturbances. Meniere's syndrome, infection, allergy. pressure from swelling in the inner ear. Symptoms include: Dizziness, lightheadedness, ringing in the ears, unsteadiness, nausea, vomiting, panic, anxiety.

Lyme Disease. Tick-transmitted infectious inflammatory disease. Symptoms include: Arthritis, headache, fever, chills, pain, fatigue, depression, anxiety.

*Mitral Valve Prolapse (MVP). Slight defect in valve separating upper and lower chambers of left side of the heart that keeps the valve from completely closing, thus allowing back-flow of blood. Symptoms include: Non-dangerous arrhythmic heartbeat, panic, anxiety.

Myocardial Infarction (MI). Blood clot interrupting the flow of blood in the heart results in damage. Symptoms include: Sharp, intense pain radiating to neck or left arm, indigestion, irregular heartbeat, discomfort, anxiety.

Niacin Deficiency. Occurs where a maise-type of corn has not been alkali-treated and it forms the major part of the diet. Symptoms include: Weakness, headaches, rough and red skin, diarrhea, depression, anxiety.

Pheochromocytoma. Where an adrenal-cell tumor secretes neuro-hormones called catecholamines. Symptoms include: Increased blood pressure, headache attacks, sweating, palpitations, nausea, panic, anxiety.

Porphyria. Genetic metabolism deficiency. Symptoms include: Abdominal pain, dark urine, constipation, nausea, vomiting, increased heartbeat, sweating, depression, anxiety.

Post-Concussion Syndrome (Head Trauma). Injury to the brain that is non-penetrating and has temporary or permanent symptoms. Symptoms include: Headache, dizziness, fatigue, mood swings, anxiety.

*Premenstrual Syndrome. Fluctuations in levels of estrogen and progesterone occurring 7–10 days before period. Symptoms include: Weight gain, breast pain and tenderness, edema, fatigue, irritability, depression, anxiety.

Seasonal Affective Disorder (SAD). Insufficient exposure to sunlight. Symptoms include: Depression, irritability, insomnia, agitation, anxiety.

Vitamin B1 (Thiamine) Deficiency. Inadequate intake of polished rice or where increased requirement due to hyperthyroidism, pregnancy, lactation, fever, severe diarrhea, alcoholism. Symptoms include: Fatigue, irritation, poor memory, chest and abdominal pain.

Vitamin B12 (Cobalamin) Deficiency With or Without Anemia. Inadequate or vegetarian diet, chronic alcoholism, small intestine disorders, hyperthyroidism, liver or kidney disease. Symptoms include: Shortness of breath, increase heartbeat, weakness, edema, sensory changes in extremities, amnesia, anxiety.

Other substances and situations too have the capability of mimicking anxiety symptoms:

- Alcohol
- Amphetamine withdrawal
- Aspertame (sugar substitute)
- Caffeine
- Carbon dioxide
- Cocaine
- Codeine withdrawal
- Diet pills with stimulants

- Heroin withdrawal
- Indomethacin (non-steroidal anti-inflammatory)
- Insecticides
- Laxatives with mercurous chloride
- Lidocaine (local anesthetic)
- MAOIs
- Marijuana
- Mercury
- Nicotine withdrawal
- Volatile hydrocarbons.

SUMMARY

What this all suggests is that it's not enough to be vulnerable to SA/SP. It's not enough to be exposed to situations or factors that trigger feelings of dread about being evaluated, found inadequate, and rejected.

For you to develop SA/SP your thoughts, beliefs, expectations, feelings, and behaviors must be persistently and chronically maladaptive. This is what keeps you in this fearful and avoidant state. (In Chapter 7 you'll learn how to modify those thoughts, beliefs, expectations, feelings, and behaviors.)

However, before you decide your anxiety has a psychological cause, you need to check out your physical health, medications, and exposure to toxins and other environmental substances. Once you've decided you are likely to have SA/SP, you can begin to consider how you're going to approach your recovery.

"I'm not socially-avoidant. I'm fear-approach-challenged."

5

APPROACHING RECOVERY

"Climb high, Climb far, Your goal the sky, Your aim the star"
(Inscription on Hopkins Memorial Steps at Williams College,
Williamstown, MA)

HOW OTHERS RESPOND TO YOU

As those of you who suffer from it know, SA/SP is the source of great distress. It generates discomfort, pain, and incapacity. It damages beliefs and values, commitment, and social relationships. It results in embarrassment, humiliation, shame, guilt, and loss of dignity. It forces you to live with fear, uncertainty, insecurity, dread, and apprehension.

This is something that the majority of family, friends, and health and mental health professionals seem to have difficulty understanding.

Family and Friends. Those close to you often seem unable to understand not only the depth of the distress created by the disorder but also how they can appropriately and helpfully relate to your suffering. While some are apparently clueless about what you're going through, others seem to have at least an abstract idea.

However, both these groups tend to be guilty of trying to get you to "put on a happy face." They downplay your fears, feelings, and thoughts, as if you were exaggerating or just being negative. They want you to "cheer up," "look on the bright side," and "accentuate the positive." Aside from the fact that this approach is highly unlikely to work, it trivializes how you feel and how deeply you feel. It undermines the legitimacy of your claim of suffering.

Their mind-set suggests that you're giving in to silly and easily controllable fears and that you should "shape up" and "pull yourself up by your bootstraps." If only you'd "just do it," you could transcend the problem. It's okay for you to feel your discomfort, but after a reasonable period of time, you should get on with it.

This attitude makes it doubly difficult for you because you feel threatened by others' evaluation of you. As a consequence, you're saddled with the disorder itself as well as others' judgments about how "appropriately" you're dealing with it.

People also urge you to be positive in order to reinforce the notion that you have control over such things in your life. For if you don't have control, they don't either. This means that things may happen randomly to them as well as to you. If this randomness were true, the world would not be the "just place" they'd like to believe it is.

They want to believe the world is a place where you're responsible for what happens to you and you get what you deserve. Because the thought of its being an "unjust world" is threatening, people tend to blame the victim of the misfortune. Not only for getting themselves into the position in the first place but also for not getting themselves out of it in the second place.

Some people are frustrated with your avoidant behavior: your indecision, hiding, and running away. They shake their heads, roll their eyes, and sigh. They feel you're not holding up your end but have no idea what to do about it. Your symptoms and self-presentation don't add up to "illness" in their eyes. Instead, your behavior seems merely out of the ordinary, odd, maybe even a little deviant, immature, and, perhaps, irresponsible.

Sometimes their response is to tell you, "You shouldn't feel that way." If you're not perceived to be ill, you're not entitled to these feelings. Your reaction to this often is to apologize, become defensive, feel guilty, or shut down any attempt at communication. Again you're being told that if only you'd simply control your emotions, you'd fare better.

Some people have well-meaning intentions to help when they urge you to "let a smile be your umbrella on a rainy day." They believe what they're saying will be inspirational, promote a positive outlook, and help lift you out of the doldrums. While this may be useful in some specific instances with SA/SP, to get your attention or encourage you, it's not a good overall approach. It implies that *if* you had the right motivation, you could just "snap out of it."

Unfortunately, even with all the motivation, skills, and help available, you're not going to do that. It takes more than a rub of Aladdin's lamp to move from chaos to self-acceptance and empowerment, even for the mildest case of SA/SP. Positive change takes time.

Trying to be empathetic with your situation, people will often tell you, "I know exactly how you feel." Unless you know this person to be experiencing SA/SP or shyness or to be working with those who do, you know they haven't an inkling of what you're going through. In trying to communicate their perceived understanding of your situation, they often inadvertently deprive you of the unique experience of your private event.

Note: It's important to recognize that all this doesn't make family and friends stupid or truly insensitive. They simply do not know what to say or do. As a result, they resort to using commonplace "sympathy" expressions to relate to this odd, awkward and often incomprehensible situation. However, that doesn't discount the fact that this lack of understanding only adds to your suffering.

Professionals. Health care professionals likewise may tend to or seem to underestimate your distress. In general, they're concerned with the quantitative, objective, and technical so they tend to miss or ignore the qualitative, subjective, and personal. Frequently, they have little or only superficial SA/SP information at their fingertips and minimal experience dealing with it. As a result, when you present at primary care for help, all they are likely to see is your depression or alcoholism, or shyness.

The quality of the physician-patient interaction has a great influence on your therapeutic outcome. While many medical schools are paying lip service to physician sensitivity to your life circumstances and to their actively seeking psychosocial information from you, substantive and probing communication between physician and patient is often lacking.

In addition, physicians will often have difficulty understanding the multiple, and often disguised, emotional meanings of what you say. Consequently, they may reject your diagnosis of SA/SP and, instead, chalk your symptoms up to temporary anxiety or a result of underlying depression. They may prescribe an antidepressant that may or may not be helpful with SA/SP. This can leave you feeling angry, helpless, and questioning whether there's any help available if the professionals don't seem to know or seem to care.

Physicians need to:

- Ask probing, relevant questions to screen you for SA/SP

- Actively listen to your answers
- Look for the real message you're sending
- Understand more of what you're experiencing
- Recognize the fear and brittleness of your defenses
- Attend to your strengths as well as your sense of helplessness
- Make the interaction a communication and sharing process
- Respond to your need for both information and reassurance, that there's real hope for recovery.

Furthermore, they need to acknowledge that **one size does not fit all**, that pat answers, quick and easy solutions, and gimmicks will have a negative impact on you and their relationship with you.

But when they don't hear you, it will be up to *you* to make them listen, understand, and take your pain seriously. In Chapter 13 you'll discover some techniques to help you do this with a minimum of fear.

AIMING AT RECOVERY VERSUS CURE

Murphy's Law:

> Nothing is as easy as it looks.
>
> Everything takes longer than you think.
>
> If anything can go wrong, it will.

SA/SP is not like a having a cut finger. Sewing up the wound, putting a bandage on it, and giving you some antibiotics will not cure the problem or restore you to your "former (?)" state of health. SA/SP, especially the generalized form of it, is too deep and far too complex a problem for such a simple solution. Many of you have literally built your lives around the limitations of SA/SP.

The finger heals and the tissue goes back to normal. But despite all the psychopharmaceuticals and psychological therapies available to you, you won't go back to "normal" (however you arbitrarily choose to define it). Why? Because "normal" is just a six-letter word.

What is "normal" for you as an individual anyway? It's important to remember that there likely will be, at the very least, some lingering imprint (both positive and negative) of the disorder on your thoughts, feelings, beliefs, expectations, and behaviors.

This is because you've lived *with* your SA/SP and *through* it for a long time. What you are today is, in part, a result of it. Specifically, it's part of how you perceive and act upon the world.

It's what you've learned to do to protect and comfort yourself. It's the strategies you use to cope, adapt, and accommodate to change so you can manage to achieve some degree of success in your life. Anything which impacts the psyche so completely and insinuates itself into so many aspects of your life can't be shed like a snake's skin or wiped out by anxiety-targeted penicillin.

It may be useful to think of SA/SP as facet of who you are. This implies that hating your disorder is really counter-productive because it's tantamount to hating yourself. You cannot totally separate the disorder from who you are. Trying to do so creates conflict. Accepting it as an aspect of yourself that you want to positively change shifts your attitude from negative to positive. This makes the change easier and more likely.

But while you can make things significantly better for yourself, function quite satisfactorily, and enjoy your life more, you shouldn't expect to never experience even a hint of social anxiety ever again. For this reason it's really helpful to think of treatment in terms of "recovery," not "cure."

Recovery is not an event like the Fourth of July. It's a series of steps and tasks. It's a journey that leads you out of chaos, darkness, and despair into the sunlight. Like any other journey, it requires your deciding on your destination, anticipating problems along the way, and making careful preparations to arrive where you want.

It's also important to remember that for almost every change process, setbacks occur. They are natural and to be expected. Furthermore, they are *not* your fault. No one (except you) expects you to do it perfectly on your first try. It's normal to relapse many times before achieving a stable change. Each go-around shows improvement and teaches you what you need to do differently the next time.

And because of what you've already learned, you don't go back to the beginning, but only back half a step. Relapse can occur at any stage and, indeed, appears to be a necessary part of the overall process. For this reason you should **not** let this reality dishearten, depress, or discourage you.

A guiding principle of any type of recovery program is what Reinhold Neibuhr penned in the first stanza of his "Serenity Prayer":

"God, grant me the Serenity to accept the things I cannot change;

Courage to change the things I can; and the

Wisdom to know the difference."

(Or, as one wag put it, "... the wisdom to hide the bodies of the people I had to kill because they pissed me off.")

As psychologist and self-efficacy expert Michael Aleksiuk suggests, acknowledging one's sense of powerlessness is the first step toward your understanding that you're not powerless at all, that you only *feel* that way. His 12-step approach "Powerlessness Anonymous" can be adapted for SA/SP.

~ASSIGNMENT~

Create a Recovery Journal, an 8 ½" x 11" loose-leaf notebook is often best, and make a plan to work on each step.

1. Admit you feel powerless.
2. Believe feeling powerful could enhance your self-esteem.
3. Commit yourself to becoming more personally powerful.
4. Assess yourself, your good points, and what you want to change.
5. Accept that you need to change and share this need and desire with others.
6. Prepare yourself to use personal power to work on your negative thoughts, beliefs, feelings, and behaviors.
7. Give yourself to the empowering process and change; don't fight it.
8. List those you've hurt or alienated with your SA/SP behavior.
9. Makes amends to those people. Forgive yourself and forget it.
10. Monitor your SA/SP behavior and continue to make amends where necessary.
11. Reconnect with your intuition and common sense and use them.
12. Keep your personal empowerment an ongoing process toward

health, happiness, and recovery.

The goal of recovery in SA/SP is personal empowerment. That is, it's finally taking charge of your life. Through this book's recovery process you'll examine your beliefs and determine your strengths and weaknesses and learn how to:

- Let go of negative, irrational, or distorted thoughts
- Deep-six stress, guilt, shame, and fear
- Terminate your dependence on others for security and self-worth
- Increase your self-esteem, self-confidence, social effectiveness, and control
- Be more accepting of your ups and downs as well as your human flaws.

Stephen Schlesinger and Lawrence Horberg demonstrate that there are three stages, or *E*'s, to the recovery process: Exasperation, Effort, and Empowerment.

Exasperation. Exasperation is when you're in emotional pain, feeling isolated, and afraid of change. It's when you're locked in a closet of shame, helplessness, hopelessness, and vulnerability. Your conflict interferes with your needs and pleasures. Most of what you do is safe, socially acceptable but bland. Addressing, much less fulfilling, your deepest needs seems totally impossible. You're not even sure you know what would satisfy you. You may dream about having a romantic partner or satisfying job but do not do anything to make it so.

You find little about yourself to be admired and believe that others feel the same about you. What strengths you have are not evident. In fact, when you do recognize any strengths in yourself, you dismiss them and label yourself as an impostor. You do the same with your feelings. You either discount or deny them.

Effort. Effort is when you're going through the motions in order to survive, but you have no clear goal in mind. You're experimenting and exploring but unsure there's hope of achieving anything worthwhile. You still see others doing things you perceive yourself as yet unable to do, but you recognize your having succeeded at some things. You enjoy your success and even venture to share it with others, believing they'll admire your actions.

You have made plans for improvement and have tentative confidence in them. Still not knowing how to appropriately evaluate your strengths, you depend mostly upon the opinions of others. Your feelings now are less negative but fear, emptiness, and sadness cast a pall. Because you're skeptical about positive actions and events, you tend to blunt your positive feelings when you get good results.

Empowerment. Empowerment is when you begin to live with a sense of vitality, meaning, and purpose. You take risks and responsibility, make commitments, and become involved with others.

You have achieved confidence in yourself. You perceive others as less threatening and believe that whatever threats still lurk can be handled. You accept your faults, foibles, and idiosyncrasies, and cut others the slack they didn't seem to give you before you recovered. You still get confused but accept confusion not only as a human inevitability but also as a precursor to growth and change.

Now able to stand up for your rights, you put aside aggression and passivity and begin to assert yourself. In fact, you feel secure enough to share your personal feelings with others. At your fingertips is a full-range of both positive and negative feelings.

Further, you have evolved a sense of purpose and self that allows you to follow your own values, take responsibility for your behavior, and withstand the pressure of disappointments. As your plans and dreams come together, you particularly enjoy the accomplishment. This is because your dreams represent a true understanding of your needs. Commitment to challenges becomes important to you and you follow through on them.

~ASSIGNMENT~

At which recovery stage, or E, are you? What makes you think so? Record this in your Recovery Journal.

Recovery as a Growth Process. Recovery can be thought of as a growth process. This is where you develop and mature emotionally, cognitively, and behaviorally over time. Graduation to the next step is predicated on mastering the step before. With this in mind you need to look at six basic questions that you should keep as your focus as you work through your recovery.

~ASSIGNMENT~

Before you begin to work on your recovery, answer these six questions.

- What kinds of experiences do I want right now?
- What actions would I admire in myself in this situation?
- What strengths that I have would be valuable in this situation?
- How do I feel currently?
- What am I doing right currently?
- What do I expect of myself and of the situation?

Edmund Bourne adds that you must also do the following:

- Take responsibility
- Be motivated
- Make a commitment to yourself
- Be willing to take risks
- Define and visualize your goals.

Responsibility. You must *take responsibility* for making your SA/SP situation better. This means discarding the bumper sticker that reads, "I assume full responsibility for my actions except the ones that are someone else's fault."

Responsibility is the ability to fulfill your needs and to do it in a way that doesn't deprive others of the ability to fulfill their needs. It's learned, and acquiring it is a complicated, lifelong problem. If it were easy to fulfill your needs, your social anxiety would probably not exist.

Taking responsibility for making your SA/SP better does *not* mean you caused or are responsible for its initiation. You need to tattoo across your forehead," My condition is *not* my fault." Placing blame on yourself is an unproductive, no-win tactic in recovery. All it does is bog you down in guilt and immobilize you.

On the contrary, you need to forgive yourself for real, not imagined, errors … and you need to award yourself the credit you deserve. You've done the best you could under the circumstances. Limited knowledge of the disorder and available resources set the boundaries on what you could achieve. But in spite of this, you're the one who'll determine if you're going to continue to suffer with it or if you're going to make your life more productive and enjoyable without it.

When you're responsible, you do things that give you a feeling of self-worth and being worthwhile to others. But self-condemnation makes it difficult for you to see the connection between your behavior, thoughts, and feelings and the disorder. It also makes it difficult for you to see the connection between your behavior, thoughts, and feelings and your recovery. Not seeing the connection or shirking the responsibility for the change makes it harder for you to face and overcome the problem.

It may be useful to think of responsibility as "response-ability": the ability to respond. Once you have it, you then have the power to change your behavior in the situation, to act constructively to benefit yourself.

Responsibility also means that if you are to get what you want from life, you must master your destiny by making choices and decisions and standing by them. President Harry S Truman's succinct pronouncement applies: "The buck stops here." This means if you make a mistake, you make a mistake. So what? It's a fact of life. You're a fallible human being and fallible human beings make mistakes … lots of them.

Let me share with you that, in fact, I've made some doozies, like the time I was part of an informal awards ceremony at the college where I was doing my post-doctoral clinical studies. When the clinician who sponsored me introduced me to the college president, he extended his hand and asked what award I was to receive.

I stood there, "Twilight Zone" theme music *booby-booby, booby-boobying* in my ears, with my mouth agape. Rendered mentally comatose by my social anxiety, I couldn't even think to feign deafness or an asthma attack. Still the compulsion to respond was over-powering. Some place in the darker recesses of my brain a small voice commanded me to speak, to say something, "Say anything, stupid!"

What unconsciously rolled off my tongue stopped the interaction cold. "Beats the hell out of me!" I said automatically. The president did a double-take and my mortified sponsor whisked me away … to find a sock to stuff in my mouth, an exorcist, or both.

Responsibility means you mustn't make excuses for your mistakes. You mustn't try to shift the blame to something outside yourself ("The Devil made me do it!"). It's far easier and less painful in the long run to accept responsibility for an error, learn something from it, live with it, and move on. Consider that even executives who make only 50% of their decisions correctly can be successful.

Since part of accepting responsibility is learning from your mistakes, you need to *treat mistakes as occasions for learning*. Even though you do learn through insight, most of your learning is through trial and error. The reality you should etch inside your skulls is that "you are not perfect and will never be." Believe it or not, people, in general, really do not expect you to be perfect.

According to philosopher and architect R. Buckminster Fuller, "Mistakes are sins only when not admitted." Accepting responsibility for your actions means allowing yourself to be human and make errors. "If-onlys" apply only if you have the power to go back in time to alter events. But you don't. So you need to change what you can, stop dwelling on what you can't, put the issue aside, and get on with your recovery ... and life.

Motivation. *Motivation*, as defined by the *American Heritage Dictionary*, is "the possibility of contemplating, determining, acting upon, and maintaining a specific strategy for change." This means, the greater your motivation, the greater your likelihood of sticking with your action plan. However, motivation isn't just sitting around waiting for you to apply it any time anywhere. Instead, motivation depends upon the specific situation, your relationships in it, and the environment.

You must be motivated to put aside whatever rewards you're getting from your present painful behavior. For example, avoiding a negative social situation makes you feel better so you're likely to continue to do it. Likewise, being perceived by others as snobbish or a loner may keep you from having to deal with social interactions you don't want to participate in.

These are payoffs, or *secondary gains*, that erect highly resistant barriers to your recovery. Knowing your payoffs is essential. You have to identify those things that temporarily relieve your anxiety but keep it in place in the long run. Then you have to substitute positive behaviors for them that work toward your goal.

You tend to do things when there are enough incentives to do them. This means that when (1) there are no incentives, (2) the incentives aren't strong enough, or (3) there's punishment involved, you'll tend not to do them. Psychological pain will increase your motivation because positive change ultimately will decrease the pain.

However, pain can motivate you only if the pain of being helped is less than the pain of having the problem. If the reverse were true, where fear or risk or the unknown is more painful than your SA/SP, you're likely to resist change.

Issues that are of intrinsic importance to you, like saving an intimate relationship, protecting your children, or not losing your home, will tend to motivate you, unless you're also severely depressed. Similarly, how much psychological and physical effort is demanded to effect the change affects your motivation. If you need transportation, have to travel long distances, locate child-care, or don't have the money and time readily available to go through therapy, you'll feel less motivated. The easier the process is for you, the more likely you are to work at it.

Expectations of the likely results of a particular course of action also act as incentives. If you expect the positive results to outweigh the negative, you'll tend to be more motivated to work toward recovery. If, on the other hand, you expect the negative to take precedence, you'll resist efforts toward positive change.

Negative expectation can also quickly become a self-fulfilling prophecy. If you anticipate and believe you won't do well, you won't do well. Unconsciously you'll set yourself up to fail.

How much you require of yourself makes a difference. If you demand too much, you may become demoralized and quit. But if you demand too little, you may see no progress and quit.

Other factors that interfere with your motivation include your beliefs. You may believe you're undeserving of a life without SA/SP. As if to punish yourself, you hang onto guilt-inducing behaviors, such as failing to make a scheduled meeting and, therefore, disappointing your team. Or you may hurt yourself in order to punish someone else, such as losing job after job so your parents, who were never there for you as a child, have to be there now.

You may also believe that there's too much to do to make any appreciable change. By dwelling on what's entailed overall, you discourage yourself and keep the process at bay. Moreover, you are less likely to change if those in your life make it easier for you to continue with the problem, make it seem normal, ignore it, or protect you from its consequences.

Commitment. You must *make a commitment to yourself to do it and follow through* with the effort once you begin. Commitment is your strong motivation to bind yourself to your decision. In it you create beliefs that sustain future related ideas, activities, or involvement. Commitment means change.

When you make a behavioral commitment, attitude change is likely to follow. For example, as you start setting up recovery goals, you're likely to come to believe you're doing it because you think it's important and useful. You're also likely to start using ingenuity to interpret and implement this change in a way that ensures success.

Commitment means your publicly acknowledging that your recovery requires constant attention. The more public you make it, by sharing it with others, the more committed you'll feel.

Writing down your intention to recover and giving it to those important to you creates a strong social incentive to continue.

Your recovery requires frequent and consistent practice of all the effective techniques, skills, and strategies available to you. It's like you are preparing for the Boston Marathon. You have to work out every day, doing your running, then doing your weight training. First working on this group of muscles, then working on that, but always working on breathing, relaxation, nutrition, coordination, and timing. Commitment is essential because the motivation required to lift yourself back out of SA/SP into the sunlight is difficult to sustain over the long haul without it.

~ASSIGNMENT~

Write out your intention to recover in your Recovery Journal. State what that means behavior-wise and how it will affect you. Put a date and time on it for when you are going to start your recovery. Share this statement of intent with someone close to you.

Taking Risks. You must be *willing to take risks*. To experiment with and to explore your feelings, behavior, and life is to take a big risk.

Not taking risks means doing things the same way. Not taking risks means always knowing what's going to happen. It's rigidly adhering to a life plan you can count on. But the result is a life that offers no surprises, no challenges, no growth, no joy … just sameness. Still this predictability does provide some semblance of security when you're wallowing in insecurity. It's sort of like an insurance policy.

But, as you know, in reality no such plan can truly exist because it requires the outside world to conform to your wishes. It mandates that no one ever require you to give a presentation, participate in a group, stand in a line at the bank or store, go to school, eat in a restaurant, use a public bathroom, or sign a check in front of others.

Like it or not, you have little control over those things that happen outside yourself. You can't always predict and control the behavior of others. You can't always find a job or relationship that's totally satisfying. Trying to make the world conform to your expectations is an exercise in frustration and futility.

External Security is a Myth. As deaf-blind author Helen Keller said, "Security does not exist in nature. … Avoiding danger is no safer in the long run than outright exposure. Life is either a daring adventure or nothing."

The only real security you have is internal security: Your confidence in yourself to adapt, survive, and succeed.

Your reluctance to try something new is the result of your fear. It can be fear of failure, disapproval, humiliation, rejection, abandonment, loss of self-esteem, and loss of love. It also results from your concern with loss of control and predictability of the situation. You respond with avoidance and look for old, familiar ways to accomplish your goals rather than attempt new ones. As a result, instead of approaching others and introducing yourself to make friends, you stand on the sidelines and do nothing.

It's important to remember that even when the amount of risk taking seems small, the benefits derived can be significant. Robert Frost crystallizes this awareness in his poem "The Road Less Taken,"

"Two roads diverged in a wood, and I—

I took the one less traveled by,

And that has made all the difference."

The road to recovery isn't always smooth. There will be frost heaves, potholes, and boulders to recognize and get beyond. One such obstacle is ambivalence.

Ambivalence. *Ambivalence* is a state of mind wherein you have coexisting but conflicting feelings or thoughts about something. "I want to, but I don't want to." You feel it when you seek help for your SA/SP. One part of you says, "I want to be rid of the pain the SA/SP causes," but the other part counters, "But making changes is frightening and how do I know it will work and things will be better afterward?"

You can see it in your everyday interactions where you feel unhappy and lonely. You want to be with people in a closer relationship yet fear rejection because you feel you won't be seen as attractive or worthwhile.

You're not exactly sure what you should do about the situation because your SA/SP offers you some positive rewards. You're in a constant state of conflict, but the degree of conflict varies with the situation and over time. The more attached you are to the behavior the more difficult it is to move away from it.

A good way to think of this conflict is an *approach-avoidance* situation. This is where you are simultaneously both attracted to and repelled by aspects of your SA/SP. If it weren't so serious, if you didn't feel so stressed and stuck, it would be almost funny. Yes … no. Yes … no. All your thoughts, emotions, and behaviors are locked up in this state of ambivalence. Even though this is a normal part of the process, you end up feeling like a yo-yo.

It's important to remember that the competing sides of your conflict each have both perceived costs and benefits. For example, recovery from SA/SP means you have to go through a lot of fear and pain (–) in order to have more friends or work at a job, but you can enjoy life more (+). Not recovering from your disorder means you stay lonely or have difficulty working and maintaining financial independence (–), but you don't have to expose yourself to fear and pain or give up protective devices (+).

This conflict is analogous to the situation of a fictional Southern Congress member who was asked about his attitude toward whiskey. He replied,

"If you mean the demon drink that poisons the mind, pollutes the body, desecrates family life, and inflames sinners, I'm against it. ... But if you mean the elixir of Christmas cheer, the shield against the winter chill, the taxable potion that puts funds in the public coffers to comfort little crippled children, then I'm for it. This is my position and I will not compromise!"

The value of each item in the conflict may shift over time from positive to more or less positive, negative to more or less negative, positive to negative, or negative to positive. As a result, sometimes you'll be willing to try, and other times you just won't care. You seem to seesaw, going back and forth, making yourself crazy by this unexpected, but normal, state of affairs.

~ASSIGNMENT~

Look at the pros and cons of working on recovering from SA/SP. Write down all the thoughts that come into your head. Then put a plus (+) or a minus (−) beside each to designate whether it's a pro or con. Make a column of all the pros and a column of all the cons. Now assign a value of importance to each.

For pluses, it's +1 to +5 with +5 being the most important positive reason. For minuses, it's −5 to −1 with −5 being the most important negative reason.

When you finish, count the assigned numbers for pros and the number for cons. Irrespective of the + or −, which is more? If your positive total is greater than your negative total, you are more likely to be ready to commit to working on your recovery.

FINDING THE KEY TO MOTIVATION

People often think that self-esteem is the key to motivation and recovery from SA/SP. While bolstering self-esteem may be useful and occasionally necessary to creating motivation, self-esteem is *not* the real key.

Why is Self-Efficacy Important? The real key to motivation is *self-efficacy*. It's your expectation of success in the tasks you undertake. It's grounded in self-confidence. Self-confidence is the positive appraisal you make of your personal assets and resources in order to master a task, solve problems, and deal with threats. It's your belief in your ability to carry out plans, meet challenges, reach goals, protect yourself, and succeed.

If you believe you can't accomplish something, you'll have no hope of achieving that goal. When there's no hope, you'll expend no effort. Making no effort means no change. *But* if you believe you have the ability to do it AND that it's possible to do, you'll feel the hope, make the effort, and effect the change.

Changes in self-efficacy cause changes in behavior and self-esteem. Increased self-efficacy leads to an increased coping ability and decreased anxiety. This is particularly important where your activities depend upon your perceived competency level.

Self-efficacy has many benefits. It

- Creates positive emotions
- Increases effort
- Increases resilience
- Improves concentration
- Reinforces setting and pursuit of goals
- Develops strategy
- Increases psychological momentum.

Even if you have low self-esteem, you will do it.

Social and Cultural Factors. Your culture and social group also affect all aspects of your recovery process. They affect how you feel and think about SA/SP. They suggest if you'll to see it as a real dysfunction. That is, as a mental or behavioral problem, or as immaturity or escapism. Those factors determine not only what labels are applied as well as the implications of using them.

For example, certain labels carry a certain stigma in the public mind. Having a "mental illness" is seen more pejoratively than "being shy," "having stage fright" or desiring to avoid a social situation. Everyone can relate to and identify with some instance of shyness as a child and the stage fright or fear of public speaking or making small talk as an adult. Unlike "mental illness," they are seen as behaviors within the "normal" and "acceptable" range.

Social and cultural factors affect how you evaluate the costs and benefits of change, when it should occur and how. They affect your assignment of the responsibility for change. This is whether the individual is seen to have the free will and competence to make decisions and bear their consequences. They also affect your willingness to commit to projects, others, and yourself.

Your family, friends, and community, likewise, have an impact on the decisions you make, how you make them, and the values you adhere to in the process. Since these factors interact and influence you, you can't fully understand your motivation outside the social context.

Conflicts. As you begin to consider making a change, you move along a continuum from being vaguely unaware of your conflicts to being more fully aware of them. But the more aware you become the greater the ambivalence you experience. As you come to understand and work through your ambivalence, you then come closer to determining what you want and making a decision. When you resolve your conflicts, your motivation emerges. This resolution promotes your readiness for change.

So how do you resolve your conflicts? How do you decrease your ambivalence? How do you ignite your motivation? The first thing you need to do is express *acceptance* of yourself.

Acceptance is telling yourself and believing that you are okay. Conversely, non-acceptance is when you tell yourself that if your behavior is bad, you're bad.

Real, stable change must occur from within. It can't be from without. And, it can't be the result of coercion. When you feel genuinely accepted, you'll feel free to change.

To accept yourself you need to do three things:

- Separate yourself from your behavior
- Assess your behavior non-judgmentally
- Accept and respect yourself … irrespective of your behavior.

In other words, you may hate the behavior, but you love the person. When you do this, you act to support your own self-esteem. You reinforce and perpetuate your notion of your worthiness. In essence, you're giving yourself *unconditional positive regard.* That is, you're acknowledging that you have value and worth as a human being no matter what you do.

Unconditional positive regard is analogous to respect and love. It's a valuing of people for who they are. You have a compelling and pervasive need to seek positive regard in order to make yourself feel accepted, approved of, and loved. But, unfortunately, you don't always receive it.

In your infancy, for example, you may have received only *conditional positive regard*. Specifically, the love you received may have been conditional upon your "proper" behavior. So if you repeatedly dropped your bottle out of the crib or cried "too much," you likely would have received disapproval.

As a result, you would tend to see love and positive attention to be predicated upon your doing the "right" thing. After a while, you would internalize this attitude and begin to even disapprove of yourself when you acted in an "unacceptable" way. The message that would continue to ring out loud and clear would be, "I'm okay *only* when I don't make mistakes or do things *wrong*."

The upshot of this is your developing *conditions of worth*. These are the particular situations, and the only times, in which you can and do feel worthy. A child of perfectionism-demanding parents, for example, may experience a condition of worth when she brings home a "B" instead of an "A" on her test. Her worth as a child and human being is being based upon her test grade.

When you perform unacceptable behaviors or perform acceptable behaviors unacceptably, you feel guilty and unworthy. These are feelings you *must* defend against. When you feel defensive, you feel anxious.

This suggests that the primary requisite of a healthy personality is receipt of unconditional positive regard. Even if you didn't secure it in infancy or early childhood, you can *still* achieve it! One way is to start looking carefully and objectively at your behavior, thoughts, beliefs, and feelings and ask yourself if you are providing yourself with unconditional positive regard through what you feel, think, and do.

~ASSIGNMENT~

Put on the white lab coat of a scientist and objectively assess what you say, do, and feel. Ask yourself the following:

- "Is it true, representing reality?"

- "Is it helpful to getting what I want?"

- "What is its overall impact on me?"

- "Would I be acting this way if I didn't have SA/SP?"

- "Do I want to keep these negative thoughts?"

JOANNA'S POSITIVE REGARD ASSESSMENT

Joanna often found herself thinking, "I can't do anything right. I'm a failure." Assessing her thoughts, she answered each question as objectively as possible.

"Is what I'm saying true?" "No, not exactly. I do some things right. For example, I tutored a high school student in math. I get good marks in college when I don't have to make presentations. I help save unwanted animals. I'm a loving daughter. I'm not really a failure because I have succeeded at achieving goals, like going back to college and making a living for myself."

"Is saying this helpful to get what I want?" "No, it just makes me feel bad and not want to try."

"What is its overall impact?" "It makes me less confident and unworthy."

"Would I be acting this way if I didn't have SA/SP?" "Probably not. I'd feel pretty good about myself, about working, making friends, and having fun. I wouldn't be beating up on myself or putting myself down."

After doing this assessment, Joanna had to decide if she wanted to keep and repeat such negative thoughts. Her answer was, "No."

You can show yourself this respect by seeing yourself as a unique human being. You can care about your welfare and demonstrate a willingness to work toward it. You can become free of your present inhibitions and the unreasonable expectations imposed by your parents, society, and yourself. You can support your desire for self-determination and assume the best of your intentions.

You can suspend critical judgment and take the time and effort to listen to what you're really saying to yourself and about yourself. You can become flexible and open to all new experiences, including formerly threatening social situations. And, once you become accepting of yourself, you can address the factors that make up your conflicts.

MAKING THE RECOVERY DECISION

According to 19th Century psychologist William James, "There is no more miserable human being than one in whom nothing is habitual but indecision."

Before you can make a change, you have to have a solid foundation for it. This means you need to become acquainted with your expectations as well as the process and content of that change. Being able to identify what's happening to you at any given stage of recovery enables you to take steps toward positive and lasting improvement. The change process requires you to go through four basic steps:

- Awareness
- Understanding
- Acceptance
- Change.

Awareness of the problem precedes change. Psychologist Fritz Perls describes this as the "aha!" experience. The light bulb flashes on and you say, "Yes, a problem exists and I want to do something about it."

Understanding comes from discovering something about not only the problem's present manifestation but also the problem's origin. This doesn't mean you have to have total insight into your intrapsychic processes or early childhood experiences. It does mean you should have at least a clue: that you had specific traumatic experiences, that your parents were overly critical and suppressed your assertiveness, that you were shy or hypersensitive as a child.

Understanding, then, is an integration of new and old knowledge. It's your seeing how they interact. It's your realizing that the whole of your problem is greater than the sum of its parts.

Acceptance is taking responsibility for the change. It is being both willing and able to respond.

Change is a decision-making process that starts with inspiration and ends with action, implementation, and success.

STARTING THE DECISION MAKING PROCESS

Author and philosopher Henry David Thoreau captured the essence of recovery when he said, "If you build castles in the air, you need not be lost; that is where they should be. Now put foundations under them."

Decision making puts the necessary foundation under your dreams, wishes, hopes, and plans for the future. To overcome SA/SP you need decision making information. But what information is that?

1. What are the viable alternatives from which you can choose?

2. What is the predicted outcome of each of these alternatives?

Before you can make decisions, you need to know what kinds of decisions there are that might be helpful. There are three categories of decisions.

When the problem is simple and the outcome of each alternative is known because information is available, the decision you have to make is generally considered to be *routine*.

For example, your physician asks if you want to increase your medication. You've been on 20 mg/day and find it working well, so you decide not to change dosage.

When the problem is more complex but the outcome of each alternative can be computed because information is available, the decision is straightforward and *analytical*.

For example, if you wanted to estimate the statistical probability of maintaining your B+ in your history class while skipping an oral presentation, you could employ a probability formula and plug in information about your grade so far, what percentage of the grade the presentation represents, the number of tests remaining, and their percentage of the grade.

These types of decision are described as well-informed, certain, structured, and objective. As such, they involve little risk. However, when you address SA/SP recovery, you have to make decisions in the absence of complete information. In this situation it's not clear what the outcomes of each of your possible actions will be. It's likely that each alternative has several possible outcomes, not just one.

When the problem is as complex as SA/SP, your decisions about your recovery will be subjective or *judgmental*. Nothing is certain. There is no pre-determined *right* structure to follow. Moreover, it's not obvious exactly what you individually have to do to achieve your goal.

Choices. For each problem you have a set of choices for actions. These are possible ways you can achieve your goal. The same is true for the goal of recovery. The first choice you need to make is to choose a recovery that is right for you. The second is to determine very specifically how you want to achieve it

It's important to remember that what works for others may not work for you in the same way. This is because each of you is a unique individual with a unique combination of needs, desires, thoughts, beliefs, attitudes, values, expectations, experiences, history, feelings, behaviors, physiological responses, and life circumstances. All of these have to be factored into the recovery mix.

You have only some information about the outcomes of these choices. To assess and evaluate the relative merits of the choices available, you must recognize their limitations.

For example, do you want to try medication, therapy, both, or neither as part of your recovery? Medications don't work on cognitive distortions but they can have a fairly rapid effect on reducing anxiety (when they work). Cognitive-behavioral therapy doesn't provide immediate relief but it can provide enduring relief. Together they're twice as expensive but potentially more effective. Self-help doesn't work for everyone, but it offers you more control over the process.

You must then establish your preferences and your means of dealing with them and their uncertainty. All decisions on your choices will carry varying degrees of risk. The degree of risk depends primarily on your goals and the environment in which the decision is being made. As you go through this rational assessment process, you will determine the value of the contribution of each of the various alternatives to the process.

It's important to remember that since you can't be sure of the consequences of any given action, you can't make a perfectly rational decision. What you want to strive for is "good enough." This, of course, is not easy when many SA/SPers suffer from the demands of perfectionism.

Level of Risk. Decision making requires that you first distinguish between alternatives which have acceptable and unacceptable levels of risk. *Risk taking* is the ability to make decisions in the face of uncertainty of the outcomes.

Reluctance to take risks drastically reduces your decision-making effectiveness. Taking moderate, calculated risks and trying new things is a prerequisite for recovery from SA/SP. For example, you may be eager to tell a new significant other about your SA/SP. What should you do?

Three alternatives are

(a) Telling the person now and possibly losing the embryonic relationship: *unacceptable*

(b) Waiting until the relationship is more secure before telling: *acceptable*

(c) Deciding that your significant other would never accept your problem anyway, therefore, you should act immediately to break off the relationship so as to avoid rejection later on: *unacceptable*.

Next you need to distinguish between real unacceptable risk and the irrational fear of taking any risk at all. Your fear of risk-taking is like all the rest of the fears that you experience in SA/SP. They're inappropriate, self-defeating, and arising from the inaccurate negative statements you make to yourself. In other words, your risk-taking fear is, likewise, the result of your distorted thinking.

When you're experiencing a negative mood like anger or fear, you tend to employ more rigid strategies in dealing with social situations than when you're in a positive mood. The more positive you are, the more flexible and creative you are, and the more aware you are of multiple ways of dealing with the situation.

If, however, the fear of risk is not a big consideration for the given decision, then you can choose the alternative with which you feel comfortable. You need to choose an alternative, such as answer (b) in the problem above, something that intuitively appears either to be "good enough" or maximizes your expected positive outcomes. Comfortable decisions strive to maximize the benefits and minimize the costs.

RISK TAKING ASSESSMENT

Fear of risk-taking inhibits your ability to grow, develop, and achieve in all aspects of your life. Consequently, you need to reverse this thinking and become aware of how your emotions impact your thoughts and the exercise of self-control. A lot of things that seem like threats can be turned into opportunities. However, change means risk. This means *there is no such thing as a risk-less recovery.*

~ASSIGNMENT~

To make decisions you need to ask yourself, "How willing am I to confront the unknown?" Test yourself by replying **yes** or **no** to each of the following questions and record the results in your Recovery Journal.

1. Are you afraid to try a new activity because you can't do it well? You say, "I don't know what to do so I'll watch." Or you dismiss it by saying, "It's not a very intelligent thing to do anyway."

2. Do you stay with the same old job even though you dislike it because you feel apprehensive about exploring the unknown of a new job?

3. Do you find yourself unable to change your plan when an interesting alternative comes up, for fear that the new situation will not conform to the way you do things?

4. Do you hang around with the same group of friends or associates and never branch out to become acquainted with new and different people?

5. Do you hang back because of fear of what might happen if you started talking with a stranger on new topics?

If you answered **yes** to any of the above questions, you need to look specifically at your risk-taking behavior. You need to determine the particular types of situations in which you are unwilling or reluctant to take risks.

In order for you to make the decisions necessary for recovery you must:

- Surrender the notion that it's better to tolerate the familiar than confront the unknown;

- Allow yourself to be spontaneous and not cling to accustomed and standardized behavior;

- Allow yourself to act independently rather than adhere to what you think is expected of you (by others, society, and yourself).

FORMULATING RISK TAKING BEHAVIOR

Taking risks isn't easy but it's essential. It involves knowing what to do and when to do it. Of course, knowing these things is rarely clear-cut. Thus, in order to do it you need to make your risks more calculated and better grounded.

You can do this by perceptively assessing the problem, sizing up the situation, and recognizing the real risks involved and what's at stake. You need to become a scientist again, to look at yourself under a microscope. "There's an erroneous belief. Sweep it away. There's a distorted thought. Push it aside. Oops, there's a cluster of negativity. *Hasta la vista*, baby."

You have to conceptualize the dimensions of the problem. You have to feel the urgency to solve it. You have to assess the impact of the probable consequences of not solving the problem. So to make moderate and calculated risk-taking decisions you must follow a logical process. This process requires that you:

- Ask the right questions
- Make a rational assessment of the answers before acting.

Once you've recognized that a problem exists and have identified it, you need to assess whether or not it's a situation for which you have a ready and appropriate solution … or one that requires a subjective or judgmental approach.

Goal Visualization. You must *establish*, *define*, and *visualize* your goals for recovery. Generally speaking, a *goal* is a statement describing a long-range outcome you desire. *Objectives*, on the other hand, are the short-range steps that work toward your reaching your goal. Goals must be based in an understanding of yourself and a determination of what resources and assets you have.

It's important to make your goals and expectations as *concrete* and *specific* as possible. You need to be able to identify with and relate to them, to hold and examine them as if they were a diamond you're about to cut and polish. You need to be able to experience the final faceted gem with all your senses.

Goals come from your heart as well as your mind. So achieving your goal is the end product of an emotional and cognitive problem-solving and decision-making process.

Concretizing Goals. In setting goals you need to look at both the present and the future and ask yourself:

- What do I want to do or achieve now?
- What do I want to do or achieve in the future?

Next you need to spell out the *whats* and *whens* of those goals in clear, concrete, specific terms:

- What exactly do I want?
- By what date do I want it?

Goal setting and -achieving are part of a solution-focused approach. To be solution-focused goals have to be

- Positive (it's what you want, not what you *don't* want)
- Specific and concrete (you know the boundaries and substance)
- Attainable (it's within your control)
- Observable (you know what it is when you see it)
- Measurable (you can precisely determine that you've achieved it)
- Stated in terms of the present (it's what you want to do here and now)
- Action-oriented (it's stated in terms of what you'll be doing to achieve it).

These are the standards by which you'll judge the effectiveness of your decisions.

It's important to remember that once you're satisfied you know *exactly* what you want to achieve and when you want it, you need to determine what resources are necessary to actually achieve the goal. Do you already have all the resources you need? If not, who has them? How do you gain access to them?

For you to accomplish your goals it's essential that you not confuse wishes and complaints with goals. "I wish I could go to parties" or "I never meet anyone" won't get you any closer to being social. You have to translate wishes and complaints into what it is you want and are willing to go after.

For example, "I wish I could go to parties" translates into "I want to go to parties." But what does that mean specifically and concretely?

"I want to be able to feel comfortable talking with others." What does "feel comfortable" mean? "I want to feel less anxious and concerned about what others think." This then breaks down actually into two goals: (1) "I want to reduce my physiological arousal in social settings" and (2) "I want to think positive thoughts about my self-presentation." This then is your goal.

~ASSIGNMENT~

Answer the following questions and record them in your journal.

1.What are your goals: the most important positive changes you want to make?

2. What do you need to achieve those goals?

3. What are your expectations of how you'll feel, think, and act when you've achieved them?

Spelling Out Objectives. With your recovery goal established, you need to look next at how you're going to get there. The "how" is a set of specific steps that will lead to reaching your goal. These steps are your objectives. They are the immediate, intermediate, and final specific results you need to achieve to get from SA/SP to "recovered."

For example, saying you want to feel less anxious at work is a vague goal. Less anxious than what? On any given day you're less anxious than on some other day. Less anxious doing what? Everything or something specific? Also, by when do you want to have achieved it? Tomorrow, a month from now, or next year?

If you wanted to be able to give speeches and presentations at work, you would put your objectives into well-defined behavioral steps with deadlines such as, "I want to give an informal 1-minute presentation to my closest colleagues at work by the end of next month."

This is a concrete, specific, realistic, and meaningful objective. It's a step toward the goal of speaking at work. You can determine if you've achieved that step before going on to the next one in the series.

It's useful to think of your objectives in terms of the SA/SP problem components you'll be addressing. They are the physiological, cognitive, emotional, and behavioral elements that make up your SA/SP. For example,

(1) *Physiological objective* would be to "daily work on muscle relaxation,

breathing exercises, and cutting out caffeine and sugar so I can alleviate rapid heart of anxiety."

(2) *Cognitive objective* would be to "use positive self-talk whenever I think others are thinking I'm a failure at trying to speak publicly."

(3) *Emotional objective* would be to "recognize my hostility, sarcasm, anger, and frustration when I have to deal with others whom I think may be negatively evaluating my speaking attempts."

(4) *Behavioral objective* would be to "construct a hierarchy of anxiety-provoking situations and gradually expose myself to them so that I can gradually work my way up to speaking comfortably and confidently for 30 minutes before the entire office."

Then you need to compile a creative and complete list of all possible ways to handle each problem. They can be applications of new ideas to the situation to provide the desired response, existing ideas, *or* new combinations of existing ideas.

For example, to handle the problem of relaxation you can do progressive muscle relaxation, yoga, transcendental meditation, biofeedback, self-hypnosis, visualization, and/or autogenic training. The permutations of all the different ways you can address relaxation are sufficient.

When you look at each of your alternatives, you need to ask yourself five important questions:

1. Does this alternative have some lasting value for my situation or me? Is it worth it?

2. Does this alternative help me meet my objectives and goals either directly or indirectly? Will it further my recovery?

3. Is this alternative an efficient and effective approach?

4. Is this alternative necessary and sufficient to achieving my success in general or in this particular situation?

5. How much control can I still exert to achieve what I want if I use this alternative? Or does this take the control out of my hands? If so, how do I feel about it?

It's important to remember that as you move through the five questions, you look for *negative* responses. These signal doubt about the appropriateness of the alternative. What you want are alternatives that generate positive responses for you. As you apply each of these questions, you begin your evaluation of each alternative. Evaluation consists of looking for:

- Effects
- Probability of desired/undesired effects
- Seriousness of these undesired effects if they occurred.

Finally you make your risk-taking decisions by selecting the intuitively-acceptable alternatives which offer you the:

1. Highest probability of working
2. Highest desirability
3. Highest number of positive outcomes
4. Lowest number of negative outcomes.

Making Your Decisions. Decision making is a process made up of logical thinking and intuition that results in making a choice among alternative courses of action for your desired result. At every turn in your recovery you have to make decisions. First there are the decisions to work toward recovery. Then there are decisions about how to do it. There are big decisions and little decisions alike.

Decisions are, by definition, action-oriented. You're either moving toward or away from something. They're the key to your ability to change because they push you along. By implementing each of your chosen alternatives, you can tell if these particular options will help you accomplish your objectives on the path toward achieving your goal. Taking the time, effort, and energy to act on these options will tell you if your desire to achieve recovery is stronger than your desire to avoid risks.

~ASSIGNMENT~

Answer the 5 important questions listed above then apply the 4 evaluation and risk-taking criteria above to your decision options.

As the *Koran* says, "If you don't know where you're going, any road will get you there."

Timeline. You need a timeline. Developing a general timeline for achievement of your objectives gives you something to which to refer and helps keep you on track. You need to specify how long it reasonably will take you to accomplish each of those objectives. To do this properly you need to be detailed. Therefore, you must write in your journal as much as is necessary to describe what you want to achieve.

But paragraphs of description are cumbersome, so you need to go back over and over these paragraphs to distill your objectives to a sentence ... then a sentence fragment ... and finally into a phrase. The more concise and precise they are the easier it'll be for you to remember and achieve them

It's also helpful to list your objectives both in order of *priority* and *chronologically*. Priority shows you what must be done first and chronology tells you when to do it. It guides your everyday efforts.

RECOVERY TIMELINE

Today's Date_____

Goal	Time Needed	Deadline
1. Read book on SA/SP	1 week	May 15
2. Make appointment with therapist	3 weeks	June 5
3. Start relaxation exercises	4 weeks	June 15

PROBLEM SOLVING MODEL YOU ARE TO FOLLOW

Phase I: Problem recognition

1. Identifying, defining, and assessing problem
2. Committing self to solving problem
3. Generating list of alternative solutions to problem
4. Evaluating alternatives
   a. Concrete and specific
   b. Observable and measurable
   c. Achievable
   d. Risk-level
   e. Likelihood of success
   f. Gut-level reaction.

Phase II: Decision making

1. Deciding on solutions
2. Prioritizing elements of solutions
3. Putting elements in workable, meaningful order
4. Creating program to implement solutions.

Phase III: Acting

1. Creating a timeline
2. Implementing solution actions
3. Observing, recording, measuring, and analyzing actions and outcomes
4. Evaluating progress.

~ASSIGNMENT~

Using the outline above go back to what you have answered on previous assignment regarding goals, objectives, and risks. Now create a full-blown recovery plan with a timeline. Be aware that you will tweak it a little bit over time.

How Can You Become a Risk Taker? You become a risk taker by learning and practicing risk-taking behaviors. This learning process begins with your awareness that

- Your fear exists.

- Trying new things can be beneficial.

Over time you can learn to treat stumbling blocks as stepping stones. Peak performers, for example, treat real failure and rejection as only temporary setbacks. You too can choose to replace fear of risk taking with participation in new, exciting activities to bring growth, development, and pleasure to your life through recovery.

CHANGE GUIDELINES

1. *Know yourself and your personal resources: Your time, skill, and courage.* Over-extension of yourself can lead to additional problems, such as stress, burnout, hostility, increased anxiety and depression, negativity about change, and resistance.
2. *Think through the desired change and make certain you're willing to go through*

with it. When you stop in the middle, you generally see your situation negatively. It feels like a failure and you may just feel worse about yourself. "If it isn't worth doing, it isn't worth doing well."

3. *When you decide to change, do it well; that is, pull out all the stops and leave no stone unturned.* "If it's worth doing, it's worth doing well."

4. *Plan and arrange your recovery.* You can't sit back and wait for things to happen. Opportunities don't seek you out and recovery doesn't just happen to you. You create opportunities and you create recovery by participating and effecting change.

5. *Don't try to do too much too fast.* A slower, steadier pace of exercises, practice, new experiences, and rewards will chip away at SA/SP. Think baby steps.

6. *Know and accept the tradeoffs necessary for your change to materialize, such as money, time, effort, and discomfort.*

7. *Visualize what your recovery ideally would be like.* You need to see how specifically your life will likely change for the better. Looking at different aspects of your life, you ask yourself how you'll think, feel, and act. You need to focus on those areas that are important to you (such as, family, relationships, job, school, activities) and picture the details of your new SA/SP-free existence. You do this in a relaxed state that you practice daily to increase your confidence in your successful recovery.

It's important for you to document the *entire* recovery process. You need to list and schedule your goals and objectives through your Recovery Timeline. But this is not enough. You also need to keep track of what specific tasks you're doing to meet those goals. You need to monitor your intermediate progress.

Your Recovery Journal is for assignments, daily progress notes, diagrams, lists, charts, and calendars. Remember that I said that you will be tweaking your plan now and then? Your using an 8 ½" x 11" loose leaf notebook will allow you to add items easily and shift materials around.

Journal notes will detail what you've done, when you did it, and any changes that have occurred. It will also detail "successes" (when things worked out well because of your recovery program) and "stalls" (when things didn't work out because you backslid). The successes and stalls highlight change that's occurring: Where you need to continue what you're doing, or change, and where you need to put in more effort.

The following progress summary page example is to be filled out at the end of each week.

Daily Progress Notes

Today's Date_____

Week's Goals: 1.

                     2.

                     3.

		M	T	W	Th	F	Sat	Sun
Physical:	Do muscle relaxation							
	Do abdominal breathing							
	Cut out caffeine							
Cognitive:	Practice self-talk							
Emotional:	Listen for anger							
Behavioral :	Work on hierarchy							

Positive changes:

Backslides:

Proposal to correct backslides:

NEED FOR BALANCE

Your recovery generally isn't the result of your focusing on a single area of your life. For most your SA/SP shows up in your overall personal satisfaction. Specifically, it impacts your job, your career, your education, interpersonal relationships, participation in community, and how you conduct your life. All these areas contribute to your sense of well-being and level of functioning. As a result, you need to make sure you include all these areas in your recovery plan, in some way, over time.

SUMMARY

Recovery has three criteria.

The first is *objective*: Your SA/SP symptoms and avoidance must have reduced significantly or disappeared.

Second is *adaptive*: You must have achieved a level of functioning that permits you to express your potential.

And third is *subjective*: You must see and feel your having achieved a state of well-being. This personal change requires awareness, time, effort, careful planning, patience, persistence, follow through, and courage. To lose sight of this fact is to doom yourself to disappointment. But, as Abraham Lincoln said, "The best thing about the future is that it comes one day at a time."

6

TARGETING AROUSAL

"What does the baby chick know which we overlook?
The shell around you won't crack of its own accord."
(Anonymous)

WHAT DOES PSYCHOLOGICAL TREATMENT ENTAIL?

Is there a single treatment, psychological or pharmaceutical, that's best for SA/SP? Sorry ... the answer is, No. This is due in part to the fact that SA/SPers aren't a homogeneous group. You aren't anxious for the same reasons. After all, you all have different personalities, backgrounds, predispositions, and experiences that may require different approaches.

Consequently, the next several chapters will cover psychological treatment, from its most fundamental (arousal) to its more complex (thoughts, beliefs, and behaviors). Later chapters will address traditional and alternative drug treatments.

Note: We will cover the components of psychological treatment of SA/SP in a particular order so you can create discernible, positive change quickly. Therefore, it is absolutely *essential* that you learn and practice these treatment skills in the order in which they are presented. Later come more advanced skills that are built upon these earlier, more basic skills.

It's a fact that irrespective of treatment modality you employ, when you're motivated to recover and expect to improve, you're likely to do better than when you aren't. This suggests that most of the credible psychological interventions will provide you with *some* benefit.

It would then follow that when you're motivated and have *many* credible interventions available to you, you're likely to do better. This is, in part, because this allows you to individualize your treatment. Because of this fact, this book provides you with a choice of interventions for each treatment component whenever possible.

Psychological interventions that are the most commonly used for SA/SP fit into four general approaches, according to the SA/SP factor they address:

- Physical (arousal)
- Cognitive-Affective (thoughts and feelings)
- Behavioral
- Social skills (assertiveness, interpersonal relations).

This chapter deals with the physical approach and the basics of reducing arousal.

RELAXING WITH PHYSICAL TECHNIQUES

Relaxation techniques are based on the premise that your physiology forms not only a major component but also the very foundation of your anxiety. According to psychologist William James, "The greatest thing then in all education is to make the nervous system your ally instead of your enemy."

When you anticipate a "fight or flight" situation, you automatically and involuntarily tense your large muscle groups in preparation for action. Simultaneously, your rate of breathing increases to meet the additional demand for oxygen by the brain. Blood moves into larger muscles, making it easier for you to run. These two bodily functions are also under your conscious control and, thus, can be used to modify your physical arousal.

In order to decrease your arousal, to calm and relax yourself, and reduce your anxiety, you have to reduce your physiological signs of it. Specifically, you have to lower your increased

- Heart rate
- Respiration rate
- Blood pressure
- Muscle tension
- Oxygen consumption
- Alpha brain-wave activity.

There are various physical techniques available that are designed to provide you with a method of doing just that. Your goal is to monitor and recognize early signs of your anxiety and find ways to cope with them before they can snowball. This then counteracts the arousal symptoms. The most useful coping techniques are:

- Muscle relaxation
- Autogenic training
- Abdominal (diaphragmatic) breathing
- Visualization
- Meditation
- Biofeedback
- Physical exercise.

Common to many of these techniques is what mind-body expert Herbert Benson calls the "relaxation response." This relaxation response came about because your innate "fight or flight" response generally can't be acted upon in your everyday life.

As a result, you have had to psychologically adjust to the demands of those situations, leaving yourself in a state of tension-filled readiness. What Benson found is that irrespective of the relaxation strategy you use, there are four shared ingredients that make them beneficial and effective. Those common elements are:

1. Situation or environment that is quiet and without interference.
2. Word, phrase, or sound that can be repeated over and over.
3. Passive attitude in order to disregard intrusive, distracting thoughts.
4. Body position that is comfortable.

Relaxation techniques, in general, are at their most effective when you have the opportunity to practice them *before* and *after* the social situations in which you experience the anxiety. Abdominal breathing, however, is most effective *during* social situations.

The process requires that you first learn the technique, let it become a habit, recognize early signs of your physiological arousal, and apply the training before, during, and/or after the anxiety-provoking situations.

It is important for you to try *all* the relaxation techniques to find which ones work best for you. It is essential that you pick at least **one** *plus* Abdominal Breathing for your regular schedule.

Progressive Muscle Relaxation. Relaxation involves learning to alternately tense and relax various muscle groups until you are capable of voluntarily arriving at a state of deep muscular relaxation. This state is diametrically opposed to that of your anxiety. As a result, it can be made to overcome it. Devised by Edmund Jacobson in 1938, the method has been used successfully to slow heart, pulse, respiration, and lower blood pressure rates.

The calming effects of the relaxation strategy are by-products and consequences of your *voluntary* efforts to decrease your muscle tension. Experiments have shown that when muscle relaxation is induced non-voluntarily or passively by injection of a curare-like drug, there is no calming effect on the individual's anxiety. You need to *control* it because, as behaviorist Joseph Wolpe states, there's a definite relationship between the extent of muscle relaxation and the production of positive emotional changes.

Progressive muscle relaxation technique does not require any necessary sequence of steps, but whatever sequence you adopt should be orderly.

EXERCISE

You should begin by finding a comfortable place and position in which to relax. The surface on which you'll perform the exercise should be neither too hard as to be uncomfortable nor too soft as to induce sleep. Clothing should be loose and non-distracting. Undoing belts and other constricting apparel is useful. You should remove your shoes.

Lying on your back is an ideal position if it's comfortable and convenient for you. A small pillow under your neck and one under your knees (this is particularly important if you have a history of low-back strain) may be more comfortable. In the absence of a knee cushion, you can flex your knees slightly and achieve the same effect.

You should avoid falling asleep since the goal of the exercise is to consciously experience relaxation. Keep distraction and disturbances to a minimum. This includes animals, children, television, radio, sunlight, clocks, telephone, cell phones, and pagers.

You're going to tighten certain muscle groups and study the sensations that come from these muscles when they're tense. Then you're going to relax them and notice what changes occur and how they are different.

Note: Individuals with physical problems, infirmities, or limitations should consult their physician before doing these exercises.

It's important to note that as you begin to practice this exercise, intrusive thoughts will occasionally interfere with your focus. Sometimes it will be a lot. Sometimes it will be a little. This is a normal part of the process and is to be expected.

You must look upon the interruptions with dispassion so as not to further distract yourself. You shouldn't take this intrusion personally. Their presence isn't due to your weakness. It's not an inadequacy or failure. At this point, you simply have no control over them. But you will.

What you need to do about these thoughts is calmly, gently push them aside, telling yourself you'll deal with them later. You set a specific time to do just that, then resume the exercise where you left off. If the intrusion recurs, and it will, you should simply repeat the process. Whatever you do, do NOT allow yourself to become angry or frustrated. That will erase all you've accomplished up to that point and you'll have to start over completely after calming yourself down.

Over the coming weeks, you'll find the intrusions gradually fading away as the relaxation deepens. Remember, relaxation comes at its own speed and it can't be forced. Your being patient and passive will allow it to deepen more rapidly.

Start by clenching your right fist while keeping all other muscles of the body relaxed. Study the feelings of tension, where they start, and how they flow. Note the location of the muscles when tensed. Hold the constriction for about 10 seconds. Relax the arm totally, letting the tension drain away, leaving the arm feeling heavy with relaxation. Now do the same procedure with your left fist.

You're going to work from your hands and forearms to your upper arms, shoulders, upper back and chest, lower back and abdomen, pelvis and buttocks, thighs, lower legs, and feet. Then you'll travel to your neck and throat, head and face, eyes and jaw.

Note: Beware of muscle cramps particularly in the legs and feet when tensing muscles.

In each muscle group you should concentrate on locating separate muscles. See how many you can find. Tense and relax each. These muscle actions should even include raising eyebrows, wiggling ears, frowning, wrinkling the nose, retracting the upper lip, puckering the mouth, and clenching the teeth. Muscles that need special attention are the head, neck, shoulders, and jaw since that's where stress resides.

Note: If you're doing this exercise sitting in a chair, relaxing your neck muscles may make your head fall forward. The head's weight pulling on the muscle fibers that are still contracted may result in discomfort or pain.

Continual practice should lead to relaxation of these neck muscles as well, allowing the chin to rest on the breastbone comfortably. If, however, this forward thrust of the head is too uncomfortable, you can practice relaxing with the back of your head resting against a high-back chair.

When you finish this sequence, consciously relax your whole body, starting at your toes and working your way to the top of your head. Tell yourself that your muscles are becoming heavy with relaxation. Visualize each of your muscle groups as white, knotted, and feeling cool.

As you further relax them, visualize the muscles as unknotting, becoming smoother, longer. As the blood can flow more freely through them as you relax, you see them as becoming redder, warmer, and heavier. See the relaxed muscles as large rubber bands, hanging loosely between bone attachments. See your whole body as limp.

~ASSIGNMENT~

Practice this relaxation technique for 30 minutes per day every day for at least a month to develop the skill and habit. You need to expect only limited success as you begin. Remember that good relaxation takes time.

You can tape record the step-by-step description of what you're doing to play back or you can memorize the sequence. (SA/SPers frequently are more comfortable, at least initially, having a tape direct you so you are less likely to disrupt your concentration by worrying about remembering the next step.) Note your progress in your Recovery Journal.

It's important to note that progressive muscle relaxation *alone* is not considered to be a treatment of SA/SP. While it is useful in *helping* reduce anticipatory anxiety, in general, it should be thought of as primarily setting the stage and removing the barriers of stress. This means muscle relaxation is necessary to SA/SP recovery but not sufficient. Once you have the technique down, you can employ and act upon other techniques.

Autogenic Training. Developed by psychiatrist Johannes Schultz in 1910, autogenic training, also called *autosuggestion*, is a systematic program to teach your mind and body to respond to verbal commands to reduce your arousal. It does this by inducing specific physical sensations that are associated with relaxation.

But this is not the same as autohypnosis, or self-hypnosis, because you do not actually hypnotize yourself in this process. In hypnosis you go into a trance-like state that is characterized by a narrowing of your consciousness. While both the hypnotic and autogenic states are "waking" phenomena, hypnosis relies on active concentration while the autogenic process relies on passive concentration.

Autogenic training allows you to take the characteristics of a relaxed body (that has increased blood flow where the blood flows freely) and superimpose them on your tense body (that has decreased blood flow where the flow is constricted). By using phrases to suggest the sensations, you come to feel the warmth that you associate with blood flowing throughout the body. You come to feel the heaviness you note when your muscles are relaxing.

The key to this process is making suggestions and allowing your body to respond. If you try to consciously control your body, to make it feel what you want it to, you'll fail. Trying too hard creates excess tension that only adds to the stress you're trying to relieve. To be successful you have to let go, to give in to the relaxation. This is often difficult for SA/SPers at first because you need to feel in control.

What autogenic training produces is a state of relaxation that is physiologically identical to that induced by meditation and other Eastern techniques. Where autogenic training differs from Eastern techniques is in its focus on physical sensation and not on abstract mental states. What makes this easy to perform is that it involves concrete tasks and experiences and provides immediate feedback. You can feel that it's working.

Because the technique is easy to learn and easy to do you will experience rapid success in your practice. You can employ it any time you start to feel tense or anxious. You can do it in the car at a stoplight, on the bus, at your desk at work, in a restaurant, in line at the grocery store, before a social gathering, or in bed before going to sleep.

Autogenic training has been used in conjunction with biofeedback as an effective means of directing attention and obtaining relaxation when a biofeedback instrument isn't available.

EXERCISE

You can perform autogenic training when you're either sitting or lying down. If you choose to sit, you should sit comfortably but straight in a straight-back chair with your knees bent at slightly more than a 90-degree angle. Your feet should be planted firmly on the floor, slightly ahead of the knees. In this position, as you relax, you'll tend to crumple straight down with your neck bent forward. You should place your arms on top of your legs, with your hands just behind the knees, with fingers spread apart. This position is thought to create the least muscular tension.

If you choose to lie down, lie flat on a bed or the floor, with a pillow supporting your neck and knees. Let your legs spread slightly and place your arms away from your body, palms on floor with fingers apart. If you're chilly, cover yourself with a light blanket. If you find that lying down makes you more likely to fall asleep, assume the sitting position.

Wolfgang Luthe in *Autogenic Training* suggests that this technique be done before meals or in the afternoon, whenever there is less likelihood of your falling asleep as a result. To prevent interruption or distraction, choose a time when you're likely to have quiet. It may be easier to use a tape recording of the exercise while you're learning the progression, although you may choose to continue to use it as a matter of course. This allows you not to have to think about the sequence.

As with progressive muscle relaxation, you want to let extraneous thoughts flow away. You want to become totally involved in the physical sensations and nothing more. Check to see that you're breathing slowly, deeply, and evenly. Make sure you're comfortable before you begin. The basic procedure requires that you *slowly say each phrase three times,* pausing between repetitions.

Start by telling yourself, "I feel relaxed and calm. I'm feeling more and more relaxed." Note how your body feels as you say it.

Focus on your limbs and feel their heaviness. Start with the right side of your body if you're right-handed, or the left if you're left-handed. Then concentrate on your right arm and tell yourself, "My right arm is heavy. It's getting heavier and heavier."

Concentrate on your left arm, telling yourself, "My left arm is heavy. It's getting heavier and heavier."

Tell yourself, "Both my arms are heavy." Note how they feel.

Concentrate on your neck and shoulders, telling yourself, "My neck and shoulders are heavy. They're getting heavier and heavier." Note how they feel.

Concentrate on your right leg and tell yourself, "My right leg is heavy. It's getting heavier and heavier."

Concentrate on your left leg, telling yourself, "My left leg is heavy. It's getting heavier and heavier."

Tell yourself, "Both my legs are heavy. My arms and legs are heavy. I feel calm and relaxed." Note how you feel.

Focus on your limbs and feel their warmth. Concentrate on your right arm and tell yourself, "My right arm is warm. It's getting warmer and warmer."

Concentrate on your left arm, telling yourself, "My left arm is warm. It's getting warmer and warmer."

Tell yourself, "Both my arms are warm." Note how they feel.

Concentrate on your shoulders, telling yourself, "My shoulders are warm. They're getting warmer and warmer."

Note: The neck area is being omitted from warming for those who are susceptible to headache related to dilated blood vessels. If this is not a problem, do the neck similarly.

Concentrate on your right leg and tell yourself, "My right leg is warm. It's getting warmer and warmer."

Concentrate on your left leg, telling yourself, "My left leg is warm. It's getting warmer and warmer."

Tell yourself, "Both my legs are warm."

Tell yourself, "My arms and legs are warm. I feel calm and relaxed." Note how it feels.

Concentrate on your abdomen, telling yourself, "My abdomen is warm and relaxed."

Concentrate on your heartbeat, telling yourself, "My heart rate is regular and calm."

Concentrate on your breathing, telling yourself, "My breathing is regular and calm."

Concentrate on your head, telling yourself, "My head feels relaxed. My forehead is cool."

Note: The head is treated in a similar fashion to the neck with respect to warmth. Excessive blood flow in the head may trigger a migraine headache in some susceptible people.

Concentrate on your entire body again, telling yourself, "I feel relaxed and calm. I am relaxed and calm. My whole body feels quiet, comfortable, and relaxed. I feel quiet. My mind is quiet. My thoughts are quiet. I am relaxed."

Finish the exercise by bringing yourself back to full wakefulness. Tell yourself, "I'm feeling refreshed. I'm feeling alert. I'm awake and ready to resume my day." Say this slowly three times, then take several deep breaths, stretch your arms and legs, slowly open your eyes. When you feel ready, get up and move around.

~ASSIGNMENT~

Practice autogenic training at least once a day. It may take a month before you achieve a state of deep relaxation. Record your progress in your Recovery Journal.

Abdominal (Diaphragmatic) Breathing. As you know, your breathing responds to your arousal. The tenser you become, the more rapid and shallow your breathing becomes. You begin to breathe only in the upper portion of your lungs. It stimulates the sympathetic nervous system that is associated with anticipation of threat. The mind races and you're unable to focus your attention.

Shallow, rapid breathing produces high levels of oxygen in the blood that contribute to your anxiety. This results in exhalation of large amounts of carbon dioxide, leading to hyperventilation and panic-like symptoms. These symptoms include palpitations, shortness of breath, dizziness, a sense of unreality, tingling in the lips and fingers, and increased heart rate. When severe, hyperventilation can lead to unconsciousness.

Breathing is controlled only partly by your involuntary nervous system and partly by your voluntary nervous system. This is why you're able to consciously control your breathing to some degree. By breathing slowly, deeply, and rhythmically, you can relax. Since the involuntary nervous system also controls your emotions, you can influence your emotions by controlling your breathing.

This is one of your most potent anxiety reduction weapons.

EXERCISE

Note: If you have asthma, emphysema, or other lung-related problems, consult your physician before initiating this exercise.

Sit in a reclining position where you can rest your head, back, and shoulders or lie down, whichever is more comfortable. Rest your hands on your upper abdomen. Your hands will act as monitors of correct movement of your diaphragm as you breathe. Close your eyes.

Inhale slowly through your nose to the count of six (if you can't reach six, aim at four). As you draw air into your lungs, you should be pushing it down toward your lower abdomen. This should make your lower abdomen rise. Inhalation should be slow, unhurried, and unforced.

When inhalation is complete, pause for 2–3 seconds then slowly exhale. As you exhale through your nose to the count of six, you should push from your abdomen as if you were shoving out the air. This should make your abdomen fall. Carefully monitor your abdominal movement to determine if you're using your diaphragm properly.

Repeat the pattern 15–20 times. The exercise may take a total of five minutes. With this breathing sequence comes the total-body heaviness and warmth that accompanies relaxation. After completion of the exercise, become aware of your body and its sensations.

~ASSIGNMENT~

Do this at least three times a day indefinitely. Once you master it, do it sitting up. You will use this at the first hint of anxiety. Record your progress in your Recovery Journal.

Biofeedback. Biofeedback training is like autogenic training in that it aims at making you more aware of how your body responds in specific circumstances. It teaches you to monitor your physiological responses, such as heart rate, blood pressure, muscle tension, skin temperature, and electrical activity of the brain. You do this by means of a specialized instrument, a biofeedback machine, which converts your physiological activity (which is internal) into a bioelectric signal (which is external) and amplifies it so you can detect it.

This signal provides you with continuous visual or auditory external feedback regarding your involuntary responses. For example, when you check your pulse, you're monitoring your heart and giving yourself biofeedback. Biofeedback information helps you learn to bring your automatic responses under your voluntary control.

When you alter your internal state or make it correctly match some predetermined external criterion, you immediately receive visual or auditory feedback via the machine. It indicates that the appropriate response has been made. The technique is frequently used in conjunction with tangible and social "rewards" that reinforce your having made the desired physiological changes.

The most commonly used type of biofeedback is *electromyographic* (EMG). Sensors attached to the skin reveal the electrical activity of nearby muscles, such as that related to muscle tension. By listening to a level of sound, the number of beeps, or by watching a readout screen, you can become aware of the degree of your tension and see how this changes when you relax.

Other types of biofeedback include *breathing patterns* which records the rhythm, rate, and volume of each breath; *finger pulse* which indicates heart rate; *electrodermal* (EDR) which measures perspiration level; and *thermal* which notes changes in temperature as a function of blood flow.

Biofeedback can be used for many conditions, including muscle tension, headache, chronic pain, and teeth grinding. If a body process is measurable, it has the potential for being influenced, or controlled, by biofeedback.

~ASSIGNMENT~

If you have any of the biofeedback mechanisms in your possession, work on biofeedback daily for 20 minutes until you can make your positive physiological changes without the use of the equipment. Record your progress in your Recovery Journal.

Meditation. This is an approach of experiencing your "being" or "existing." This is similar to biofeedback but on an internal level. In place of external feedback from your physiology, you look at internal feedback from heightened awareness. This awareness is not the goal, however. The goal of meditation, in all its hundreds of various forms, is focus on reconnection with "Spirit," God, Universe, or Reality — some ultimate symbol that you value highly.

The process combines physical and cognitive methods. Through mastery of your mental functions, you can decrease your oxygen consumption and increase your skin conduction and alpha brain waves, which indicate a state of deep relaxation. At optimum rest, your muscles are relaxed. Your mind is clear, alert, and creative. Anxiety decreases as your inner control increases.

EXERCISE

Find a quiet space without distractions or interruptions. Sit in a comfortable chair or on the floor. Keep your back straight. Select a word or sound to use as a mantra (what you're going to repeat and focus on), such as "Om" or the word "One." Close your eyes and let thoughts drift away. Concentrate on silently saying your mantra. Ignore distractions; you can deal with them later.

Continue for 15–20 minutes then let your mantra fade away. Quietly sit still as your mind resumes its activity. Slowly open your eyes. Make note of physiological changes that have occurred in your breathing and heart rate, muscle tension, or shift in a sense of your body boundaries. Note also how time has passed.

~ASSIGNMENT~

Practice this technique daily for a month. Record your progress in your Recovery Journal.

Self-Hypnosis. Hypnosis is a state of alertness, producing brain-wave patterns that match that of your ordinary waking consciousness. Hypnosis has not been demonstrated to be an altered state. Rather it appears to be a complex combination of social and psychological factors, such as role-playing, imagination, and social influence. It has three prominent features:

- Selective attention
- Suggestibility
- Dissociation.

Selective attention refers to your narrowly focused attention. You allow yourself to suspend critical judgment. You see certain things clearly and vividly while excluding all other external stimuli or context.

Suggestibility is your willingness to adopt the role of subject and be highly responsive to guidance and compliance through suggestions. Approximately 15% of the population is highly hypnotizable and 25% is not hypnotizable at all. Of those who can be hypnotized, only 10–20% achieve a deep trance.

Men and women are equally good subjects. Children and adolescents, however, are the best. Higher intelligence gives only a slight advantage. The most important qualification for being hypnotized is a willingness to commit your attention fully to the task at hand without any concern or distraction.

Dissociation describes an unconscious process by which one group of mental processes (such as knowledge, memory, or voluntary control) is separated from the rest of the thinking processes. As a result, they function as individual, independent units instead of as an integrated whole. When this occurs, you may not be able to recall your identity and other important information. Your customary sense of reality is replaced by a sense of unreality. You may feel mechanical as if in a dream and perceive yourself as not in complete control of your actions.

Today the primary uses of self-hypnosis are to allow you to control your life better. Within cognitive-behavioral therapy hypnosis is used to

- Enhance relaxation
- Generate imagery
- Heighten expectations of success
- Change self-defeating thoughts
- Pair appropriate behavior with some reinforcement in imagination
- Improve desensitization
- Increase ability to cope with problems of daily living
- Maximize feelings of efficacy and self-control.

Before you consider having a hypnotist initiate this process for you, you need to determine if you are concerned about trusting this person, not having control, or giving over some portion of that control to another. If you do not resolve these issues before the hypnosis session, the session may not be effective for you. You need to feel comfortable with being hypnotized.

It's important to remember:

- You can't be hypnotized against your will or forced to do anything you find very objectionable.
- But if the proposed actions are not in serious conflict with your values and usual standards of behavior, you may perform them.
- While in a trance, you can't be forced to make unwanted self-revelations. In fact, you're still capable of lying either deliberately or unconsciously.

Self-hypnosis induction is similar to that of progressive relaxation and autogenic training. But other methods, such as concentrating on a spot on the ceiling, swinging pendulum, flashing light, or pedaling fast on a stationary bicycle, can be used to focus you as you relax yourself. Once your mind and body are feeling calm and fully relaxed, you shift your focus to concentrate on self-suggestions about improving yourself.

Hypnosis pioneer Theodore X. Barber indicates that self-suggestions are more likely to be effective if you follow a few general guidelines:

1. Use brief and simple words and phrases to transmit the self-suggestion ideas.

2. Word the suggestions "positively" not "negatively." (For example, don't say, "I won't be anxious," say "I will be calm.")

3. Self-suggestions should be straightforward, without doubt or qualification of effort involved. (For example, say, "I will speak to one person at the party," not "I will try to speak to one person at the party" or "I would like to speak to one person at the party.")

4. Don't use "try" because that signals that you may not exert all your effort.

5. Repeat self-suggestions in a manner conveying the feeling behind the statements.

6. Use specific self-suggestions that are sufficiently individualized.

7. Create opportunities to try out the suggestions gradually in real-life situations.

8. Use a tape recorder to improve wording, phrasing, and methods of hypnotic presentation.

~ASSIGNMENT~

Practice self-hypnosis for 30 minutes daily for one month. Record your progress in your Recovery Journal.

Physical Exercise. As you've seen, when you're anxious, you tend to hold tension in your muscles. When this tension is chronic, you experience constrictions or spasms in the muscles. These may immobilize you and create pain. Because the neck is a common site for this tension, you speak of tension-inducing situations as "a pain in the neck." While regular, spontaneous movement is necessary to help you reduce this tension, it often isn't sufficient. In addition, you need extended periods of planned physical activity.

Physical exercise has been found to be a powerfully effective method for reducing both anxiety and depression. When you were young, it was a natural outlet for your arousal. Not only did it reduce all that muscle tension that caused you to feel "uptight," but also it gave you an avenue for discharging pent-up frustrations. It increased metabolism of hormones such as adrenaline, increased oxygen consumption and circulation, and may have stimulated production of endorphins to increase your sense of well-being.

Since the late 1980s, it has been found that exercise increases concentrations of the neurotransmitter norepinephrine in areas of the brain involved in the body's stress response. More recently some have suggested that exercise thwarts anxiety and depression by enhancing the body's ability to respond to stress. Exercise appears to provide the body with the opportunity to positively, dynamically, and efficiently deal with stress.

It's still a natural outlet for adults and has the dividend of providing health benefits. Physical exercise decreases your blood pressure, cholesterol, frustration, and insomnia. It promotes weight loss and improves elimination functions, concentration, and memory. It also creates a sense of control and increased self-confidence.

One reason you may not exercise as much as would be helpful is that you may often forget about it or ignore it. You tend to regard it as "work." This means that if you're going to participate in an exercise program, you have to change how you think about exercise. You need to rethink it in terms of the physical, physiological, and social benefits it'll provide.

As with your recovery as a whole, you have to feel motivated and committed to making this a part of your program. You have to have physical exercise goals that become part of your daily progress notes and Recovery Timeline. It's important to remember that getting started with this may be difficult until it evolves into a habit for you. But once it's a habit (generally in a month or more), it becomes part of your routine and you simply do it as a matter of course.

Warning: If you have any condition for which exercise is contraindicated, or for which there are limits on the type, amount, and intensity of exercise, consult your physician before beginning this or any exercise program.

The type of exercise you choose should depend upon your goal. You need to ask yourself what it's for.

- Muscle tension
- Flexibility
- Strength training
- Cardiovascular conditioning
- Weight loss
- Personal development.

How do you want it to be?

- Alone or with others
- Part of a team or as an individual player
- Strenuous or gentle
- Anaerobic or aerobic.

The exercise(s) you choose can range from ballroom dancing to bowling, swimming to isometrics, basketball to weight lifting, ping pong to fast walking, tennis to skiing, calisthenics to folk dancing to stationary cycling, and all the others in between. Having several types of exercise to do is useful because it reduces the likelihood you'll become bored doing one thing over and over.

Having complementary exercises also may provide a needed balance, for example, a competitive sport, like football, with a solitary activity, like running, or an aerobic sport, like swimming, with an anaerobic activity, like isometrics. Exercise that is rewarding unto itself is more likely to be helpful in reducing stress than exercise that isn't.

No matter what exercise program you follow, you'll receive benefit from the addition of stretching exercises. Stress-reduction therapist L. John Mason cautions that you should never force or strain yourself in trying to accomplish your goal of loosening and making your muscles more flexible. Slowness and proper breathing are the watchwords. Proper breathing means inhaling deeply and exhaling fully and completely. Being aware of what you're doing and how your body is responding is half the battle in stress reduction.

Neck rotation. Drop your head as far forward to the chest as possible then slowly move it to the left or right. See how close you can come to touching your ear to your shoulder. When you feel resistance, stop, take a full breath, and start again. Do it several times and monitor how your neck feels. Rotate the head in the opposite direction.

Neck flexor. Drop your head as far forward to the chest as possible then slowly tilt your head backward as far as possible. Do it several times and note how your neck feels.

Shoulder rolls. Let your arms hang loosely and pull down gently on your shoulders. Rotate both shoulders forward very slowly. Lift to feel the tension. Repeat the process, rotating your shoulders backwards.

Shoulder stretch. Lay your forearms on top of your head and grasp your right elbow with your left hand. Slowly pull the elbow behind your head. Don't force it. Hold several seconds, note how it feels, then switch arms and repeat.

Arm shakes. Let your arms hang by your sides. Lightly shake your right hand and wrist. Slowly let the movement involve the forearm and elbow. Begin shaking your arm more vigorously and do the entire arm for one minute. Now swing the entire arm back and forth from the shoulder while still shaking it. Let the arm hang still at your side and feel the sensation. Repeat with your left arm.

Leg shakes. Balance yourself with a chair or table and begin to rotate your right foot and ankle. Start shaking your foot, ankle, and lower leg. Add the knee then extend to the entire leg. Shake your leg more rapidly. Now swing that leg as you shake it. Stop and notice how it feels. Repeat on your left leg.

Sitting toe touches. Sit on the floor with your legs together, extended in front of you. Reach for your toes with both hands and slowly, gently bring your forehead as close to the knees as possible. When you feel the resistance, hold your position for a minute.

Calf-tendon stretch. Stand 2–3 feet from a wall, lean forwards, placing your palms on the wall at eye level. Make sure your body is straight. Move your right foot backwards along the floor until you feel your calf muscle stretching. Hold that for one minute then repeat with your left leg.

Standing leg stretch. Find a table approximately 3 feet high. Place one leg on the table so that it is extended and parallel to the floor. Slowly extend your fingertips toward your foot on the table and try to touch your knee with your forehead. Hold for one minute, making note of the sensation, then repeat with your other leg.

Side stretch. Stand with your feet shoulder-width apart and legs straight. Place your right hand on your right hip and extend your left arm above your head, slowly bending your arm to the right. Hold for one minute, feel the resistance, and repeat on the other side.

Back stretch. Stand straight with your feet planted shoulder-width apart. Bend forward from the waist, relaxing arms, shoulders, and neck until you feel stretching in back of your legs. Hold for a minute, bend your knees to take pressure off your lower back before you stand up, then stand up.

Scalp massage. With your arms up and elbows out, move your fingers in small circles, pressing gently, around the scalp. Cover your entire head including the nape of neck, your face, particularly around your eyes, and in front of and behind your ears.

RELAXING WITH COGNITIVE-EMOTIONAL TECHNIQUES

Once you've relaxed your body with one or more of the physical techniques, you can make your relaxation more global by bringing your mind into it. Since your thoughts and emotions influence not only your anxiety but also your relaxation, you need to address them as well.

Visualization. One effective procedure is visualizing yourself in a scene you find peaceful and comforting. It should be some place you can look to as a retreat to refresh the soul. It can be real or imaginary, commonplace or fantastical. Whatever you choose, it should be very visual and appealing to all your senses.

As you move through the scene, you need to notice every large and minute detail of the environment and describe it vividly: Colors, subtle shadings, light level, temperature, time of day, types of sounds, loudness, movement of objects, their feel, smells, and how you feel about them. As you do this, you should remind yourself how relaxing this is and how tranquil, comfortable, and secure you feel in this setting. This will be a daytime dream you can choose to enter any time you want to relax and calm your racing mind.

As with relaxation techniques, you need to be in a comfortable position in a quiet, distraction-free environment. The object is to make the images as clear and convincing as possible. This takes time and practice. It's important to regard this as an extension of relaxation. Thus, you should use relaxation-like affirmations, such as "I'm feeling calm," "I'm letting go of tension," "My body is relaxed." Visualization is an important adjunct to abdominal breathing. It may be employed along side other relaxation techniques as well or be used as a replacement for them. As you finish your visualization, you need to guide yourself to a mental state of alertness.

As with other relaxation techniques, pre-recording the visualization makes initial sessions easier, though you may wish to simply continue to use the tape. To allow yourself maximum time to visualize you should read the script slowly, with pauses. You can get a sense of how slow that should be by visualizing as you practice reading the script before you record it.

Here's an example of a visualization script:

"I'm on a wind-swept cliff, surrounded by large boulders and wind-twisted pines, looking out over a large expanse of ocean. The deserted beach below is calling to me. It's 11 a.m. on a glorious summer's day. The sky is pale yellow with fleecy wisps of clouds scudding across it. Everything feels golden and good.

"I spot a path that gradually switchbacks its way down the cliff face to the beach below. As I gently descend this wide, easy path, I feel myself becoming more and more relaxed. The farther down I go, the more relaxed I feel.

"I see red granite rocks covered in orange, yellow, and gray-green lichens lining the trail downward. A speckled squirrel with its cheek pouches filled to capacity, leaps onto a rock to my left, regards me a moment, and scampers away.

"I smile and I feel more relaxed. A soft breeze caresses my cheek. I see small pink flowers poking their petal-ed heads between the rocks. Dark green cushions of moss are everywhere, beckoning me to lie down among them and soak up their coolness.

"As I reach the beach, I feel calm and very relaxed. I lean against a rock to take off my shoes and stockings so I can paddle across the sand in my bare feet. Fine granules of white sand flecked with mica sift through my toes and tickle me. My legs are feeling heavier.

"As I reach the water's edge, I spread out my towel in the dry sand and lie down on my back. I wriggle my body to settle in and feel myself melting into the beach, totally relaxed. I listen to the ocean's roar in the background, smell the salt and seaweed, and hear the water's ebb and flow. Waves playfully slap the beach, foam, and withdraw. The rhythmic motion soothes me. I can hear my heart beating slowly, evenly, and rhythmically too. The sound is comforting.

"An airplane engine drones in the distance and overhead seagulls call as they do sweeping sixty-degree turns on wing tips. I feel at one with the universe. I savor the feeling.

"Now slowly I'm going to return to my waking, alert state of mind. As I count backwards from four to one, I'll become more and more awake and alert. Four: I'm becoming awake, feeling alert. Three: I'm feeing more alert and awake, more aware of my surroundings. Two: I can feel my body becoming alert, beginning to move. One: I'm wide awake and alert. I can fully move my body. I feel relaxed, refreshed, and revitalized by the peace and solitude"

There will be times when you want to do a visualization but don't have time for one this lengthy. At times like this you can do a mini-visualization. Some people picture themselves in the shower, others, soaking in tub, for example. Whatever you choose it has to be something you like.

Here's an example of a mini-visualization script:

"I'm soaking myself in a tub in water that is around 103 degrees. I'm leaning back with a pillow supporting my head, feeling very comfortable. A single lighted candle sits on the edge of the tub; its flame is dancing.

"I'm breathing slowly and evenly as the warm water runs over me and draws away my cares. With each rhythmic breath I'm becoming more and more relaxed. My tension is ebbing. All my worries are evaporating in the rising steam.

"My arms are floating gently, bobbing, totally without weight. The water is soothing, caressing, and massaging my body. As tension releases its hold, my muscles are becoming loose and limp. My body feels cradled. I'm being lovingly rocked to and fro. With every breath I become more and more relaxed."

Visualization also works when you want to keep a confident, success image of yourself in your mind. For example:

Picture yourself dressed in an outfit you associate with a success you've had. This should be an outfit that makes you feel good and confident. Remember that success in all its sensory detail. Re-experience the confidence you felt during that success event: how good you felt, how successful you were, and how proud you were of yourself.

Picture yourself in your success outfit standing within a large force field that looks like a Lucite cylinder. This force field surrounds you and goes wherever you go. Totally invisible to others, it's a shield that is impervious to all the internal and external gremlins that try to attack you.

Criticisms bounce off it. Negative evaluations evaporate in a puff of smoke if they touch it. Humiliation melts and evaporates in its presence. When you turn the field on, no one … and nothing … negative can touch you. No social situation can hurt you.

When protected by this shield, you are someone without fear. You command respect. You can do anything you want to and you can do it successfully. You are in control. You have the power.

SUMMARY

Relaxation exercises, especially abdominal breathing, are at the heart of arousal reduction. Therefore, these exercises should be practiced often. Progressive relaxation and similar methods are best when used *before* and *after* an anxiety-provoking situation. However, *during* the situation, the best approach is abdominal breathing. This is especially true when your arousal is severe. (See Chapter 7)

It is important to do *all* the relaxation exercises for at least two weeks. But remember that it takes about a month for the relaxation techniques to work easily. After that time you can decide which ones work best for you.

However, it is absolutely essential that you continue the abdominal breathing and visualization indefinitely. Employ progressive relaxation or other relaxation methods when preparing for or coming down from an anxiety-provoking or stressful situation. But whatever you choose as your own relaxation regimen, you need to: **Practice! Practice! Practice!**

7

MODIFYING THOUGHTS AND BEHAVIORS

"Out of the whole animal kingdom only humans are
endowed with this capacity to make themselves miserable."
(Sharon A. Bower & Gordon Bower)

WHAT IS COGNITIVE THERAPY?

Some of you may pale at the thought of therapy. You may be afraid
that you'll be exchanging thoughts that hurt with a reality that will
hurt even more. But what effective cognitive therapy does is first make
you aware of those gut wrenching, dysfunctional thoughts, beliefs, and
expectations that underlie your feelings of anxiety and your avoidance
behavior. Second it teaches you how to confront and counter them.

Let's take a second look at how SA/SPers think. SA/SPers make
negative, anxiety-provoking assumptions. These assumptions direct
you to think anxiously and negatively about others, the situation, and
yourself. They determine how you'll process information about others,
the situation, and yourself. This means it's your thinking that gives form
and substance to your physical arousal and keeps it going as anxiety.

Through cognitive therapy, you can identify your negative and
distorted thoughts, evaluate, and modify them. Gradually you can alter
your information-processing biases as well. That is, once you change
these maladaptive thought processes, you can begin to interpret
situations with less distortion and anxiety and, thus, function normally.
The goal of cognitive therapy is to create and develop accurate and
rational thinking. The therapy aims to:

- Determine significant life events and experiences that
  contributed to development of your SA/SP
- Formulate the problem of SA/SP in terms of how your
  thoughts, feelings, and behaviors interact to make you unhappy
- Identify and explore erroneous core beliefs about yourself,
  others, and the world

- Recognize and examine maladaptive thoughts, images, and behaviors
- Identify more realistic and adaptive thoughts
- Accumulate evidence supporting your adaptive thoughts
- Modify your cognitive responses (mistaken beliefs, distorted thoughts, such as attention bias) and behaviors (avoidance) that prevent your disconfirming your fears.

To achieve these aims cognitive therapy uses strategies to:

- Focus on your maladaptive automatic thoughts, the feelings associated with them, and their consequences
- Determine the antecedents of these automatic thoughts
- Determine the frequency and generalizability of automatic thoughts
- Determine associations with these automatic thoughts
- Explore problem-solving possibilities
- Question these automatic thoughts
- Dispute these automatic thoughts by providing contradictory evidence
- Make different explanations for outcomes
- Label your errors of thinking
- Distance yourself from the negative or maladaptive thought
- Track your progress.

Cognitive therapy focuses on your thoughts that are associated with the fear of poor performance, negative evaluation, your expectations of threat in social situations, and your selective attention to threat cues and negative information.

Expectation. What you expect to happen is based, in part, upon how you explain the world. It's how you assign causes to what happens to you and how much control you believe you have. It's what your basic assumptions are. These are the result of your explanatory style that determines how permanent and universal bad events seem to be, and how responsible you personally feel for what happens.

Your *explanatory style* is one important information-processing bias. Learned in childhood and adolescence, it is the habitual, automatic way you explain your setbacks: either with pessimism or optimism. You look at their cause-and-effect and if they will tend to continue over time.

It's the foundation of how you view the world and your place in it. SA/SPers tend to use a *pessimistic* explanatory style. As outlined by psychologist Martin E. P. Seligman, this style is characterized by your inclination to regard bad events as the result of permanent, universal, and personal causes.

Permanence refers to the consistency with which you see the same bad event happening over time. As a pessimist, if you perceive that you do poorly in social situations, you'll tend to see this performance as occurring "all" the time in social situations. You'll explain the negative outcome in terms of "never" and "always," as in "I never get it right. I always look like a fool." Your attributions of permanence are the basis of your *all-or-nothing thinking*. For you, these negative results are practically guaranteed.

The only outcome that you're likely to see as *temporary* in social situations is a positive one. That is, you'll tend to see it as a fluke, a fleeting, random occurrence, something to dismiss or discount. For you "good news is life's way of keeping you off-balance." But, when you can see bad events as *temporary*, you help keep your pessimism at bay.

Universality is your seeing the fear event as occurring everywhere. When you think your self-presentation doesn't go well, your pessimism will tend to make you see your failure as likely to occur in *all* such situations, not just this specific one, as in "Every time I try I mess up." Once again, you see any positive outcome for you as occurring specifically, in a particular situation, and not something you can expect to occur in others or in general. But, when you can see bad events as *situationally specific*, you can reduce your pessimism.

Personalization is where you locate responsibility for the negative outcome in yourself. In SA/SP you tend to blame yourself for bad outcomes rather than assign blame to something outside yourself in the situation, as in "I failed the test because I'm incompetent," not because the test was hard. When you can see the cause of bad events as *external* to you, you can likewise lessen pessimism's hold.

Those who have a pessimistic explanatory style are more likely to become depressed. While depression often accompanies SA/SP, not all SA/SPers are depressed. The reason for this is that depressed people generalize their pessimism to all situations. However, SA/SPers tend to use this style *only* in the social situations they fear. This creates hope for you.

Overall, when you use this pessimistic explanatory style, you see desirable outcomes as: (1) less likely, (2) specific to certain situations only, and (3) the result of luck. This means you'll see undesirable outcomes as *more likely*, *happening across social situations*, and the *result of your ability level*. You see your outcomes, both good and bad, as beyond your control.

The less control you feel you have to change the negative social situations, the more you'll feel anxious, helpless, depressed, and convinced the world doesn't operate in your favor.

Core Beliefs. As discussed in Chapter 4, core beliefs are your unconditional, fundamental, and central beliefs about others, the world, and yourself. They're part of your self-concept. These are the standards against which you judge all situations, thoughts, and actions. They reflect your perception of your value as a human being, your security, and performance. They reflect your sense of control over the world around you. They tell you how lovable and independent you are. They also represent your standards, those of others, and your perception of what justice is and how it operates. They are the basis of your automatic thoughts.

Your core beliefs trigger specific expectations, rules, attitudes, and assumptions about both the situation and how you should act in it. When a core belief is distorted or erroneous, it's considered to be maladaptive. Any thoughts derived from it will likewise be maladaptive.

EXERCISE

Assess Your Core Beliefs

Place a **T** if the statement is true or mostly true about your beliefs or an **F** if it's false or mostly false. (Exercise adapted from Jeffrey Young's Schema Questionnaire)

____1. My needs are legitimate.

____2. I'm unworthy of love and respect.

____3. I can take risks.

____4. I feel unsafe and at risk.

____5. I do lots of things well.

____6. My failures are unforgivable.

____7. I feel pretty much in control of my life.

____8. I feel threatened by others.

____9. Others love, appreciate, and care for me.

____10. Nobody would be interested in me as a partner.

____11. I'm self-reliant.

____12. I generally go along with what others do.

____13. Things generally work out in the end.

____14. It's an unjust world.

____15. I strongly feel a part of a family and community.

____16. I generally feel on the outside looking in.

____17. Most people are trustworthy.

____18. People put themselves first.

____19. My standards for myself are reasonable.

____20. Trusting my own judgment usually ends up wrong.

Scoring instructions: Count the number of **F**s in the **odd**-numbered questions, 1–19. Count the number of **T**s in the **even**-numbered questions, 2–20. These are your negative core beliefs that may contribute to your negative, distorted thinking. Add your **F**s and **T**s, divide by 20, then multiply the decimal by 100% for the percentage of your negative beliefs.

From Thought to Emotion. In general, your emotional response is the result of a chain of activities that you go through when you encounter a situation. Specifically, you (1) *look* at the events and situations that occur in the real world. These may be initially positive, neutral, or negative. Then you (2) *perceive* them, gathering information through your eyes, and record it in your brain as images. You (3) *think* about the events and situations. You (4) *interpret* them, placing your own meanings on them, based upon your core beliefs. Finally you (5) *feel* some emotion that you then associate with the images.

World Events $\longrightarrow$ (Interpretation) $\longrightarrow$ Thoughts $\longrightarrow$ Emotions (Evaluation)

RELATIONSHIP BETWEEN EVENTS, THOUGHTS, AND EMOTIONS

Being a highly analytical human animal, you implicitly ask yourself a series of questions when you enter social situations. This determines what you think about what you see and how you will interpret it. (Adapted from Susan Fiske and Shelley Taylor in *Social Cognition*):

- "What's the situation here?"
- "Who are these people?"
- "What's going on and how do I fit in?"
- "What are my goals in this situation?"
- "Are my goals in conflict with those of others?
- "If there's a choice to make, how do I make it?"
- "How do I choose among available strategies to achieve my goals?"
- "What happens if I'm wrong?"
- "How do I recoup my losses?"
- "How will what I choose affect others?"
- "How do I respond to their reactions?"

It is important to remember that the situation itself doesn't directly determine how you feel. Instead, what you feel is based upon what's going on in your mind as you view a situation.

Suppose you see Joe standing outside a McDonalds' men's room in his unbuttoned khaki long-sleeve shirt over a black tee, with black Levis, and hiking boots. He's shifting from one foot to another, continuously looking around. This is a neutral event. There are no interpretations or evaluation initially attached to the behavior. Therefore, initially you have no emotional response. However, the moment you start to think about the behavior, you start to add an interpretation or evaluation. As soon as you do, your response to the situation changes.

If you interpreted Joe's movements as a sense of urgency to use an occupied bathroom, you'd probably evaluate and label his behavior as reasonable under the circumstances. Your emotional response would follow the evaluation and you'd probably empathize with his distress.

If, however, you interpreted Joe's activities as shifty, anxious, and furtive, that he was likely up to no good, you'd probably evaluate and label his behavior as suspicious and something to be concerned about. Your emotional response would be negative, perhaps fearful. Even though his behavior is the same, your thoughts, interpretations, and resulting emotions are different.

Negative Self-Talk. To reiterate, your automatic thoughts (ATs) are the result of your core beliefs. They create your emotional responses to social situations and things associated with them. Things that have salience for you attract your attention. But this attraction requires your interpretation. The feeling that results is, therefore, logically connected to your thought's content. So, if you believe you're inadequate, you'll feel bad about yourself.

Misinterpreting your physiological arousal symptoms and your avoidance behaviors maintains your negative ATs. The negative things you automatically say to yourself generally represent errors in thinking. Specifically, they are often the result of mistaken or dysfunctional

- Appraisal of the immediate situation
- Perception of long-term consequences
- Other associations with the situation.

You can experience them as what you say to yourself or as images you have. They're brief, fleeting, out of awareness, and not based on reflection or deliberation. They may be general perceptions or situation-specific thoughts. When you encounter a social situation, you begin to process the information that's available to tell you how to interpret it.

SA/SPers and non-SA/SPers alike have ATs. Some are positive; some are negative. They just pop into your head. But SA/SPers have a multitude of negative, inappropriate, self-defeating, upsetting, and destructive thoughts that constantly and magically appear in social situations, creating anxiety for you. It's important to remember that even though you don't *choose* these thoughts, you're the one who is responsible for eradicating them.

HOW DO YOU DETECT THESE NEGATIVE ERRORS?

You can evaluate automatic thoughts by their validity. Most of SA/SPers' negative ATs are distorted and contrary to objective evidence. For example, even as Joe was elected to student council, he believed nobody liked him.

Some can be accurate but have conclusions that are distorted, as when Sarah says, "I didn't get the video back to the store on time so I'm a totally careless, thoughtless person."

Some can be accurate but dysfunctional. For example, Joanna says it'll take her a week to finish her article on the American Cancer Society health fair, and thinking about it increases her anxiety and decreases her motivation to do it.

The following is an expansion of the list of most common cognitive errors, or categories of negative automatic thoughts (negative self-talk), in Chapter 4, as identified by Aaron T. Beck and David Burns:

Arbitrary Inference. This is coming to a conclusion when there's insufficient evidence to do so ("The audience will laugh at me if I make a mistake").

Over-Generalization. This is basing your conclusions on isolated events then applying them across diverse situations ("The audience expected me to talk on measles prevention but heard about measles and managed care. They looked bored. Audiences will find me boring").

Magnification and **Minimization.** This is a way of distorting the importance of events. *Magnification* exaggerates your perceived defects ("I forgot the boss's name and now he'll never give me my pay raise as a result"). *Minimization* inappropriately shrinks your "positive," desirable qualities by discounting or dismissing them ("Yeah, I went to the party and didn't mess up, but it was pure luck"). At the same time it minimizes the "negative," undesirable qualities, of the **other** person ("Sure, Charley forgets the boss's name all the time, but he has a lot of important stuff on his mind").

Personalization. This is arbitrarily and inappropriately seeing yourself as the cause of negative external events for which you're not responsible ("The teacher was gruff, I must have done something wrong"). It's seeing the event as a reflection of your inadequacies ("Little Jennie wouldn't do Show-and-Tell today. It must be because of my SA/SP. I'm a lousy parent").

It's also seeing yourself as the specific object of anything negative even when it's obviously aimed at the group instead ("The boss posted a notice to all employees about taking sick-time, but I know she's really talking about me personally because I don't always show for meetings"). It's an element of pessimism.

All-or-Nothing Thinking. This is seeing things as either-or, black or white, with no shades of gray ("If I don't appear perfectly calm as part of the bridal party, then I'm a total failure and will spoil everything" or "At the office party I'm not very social and I can see that my colleagues think I'm either stuck up or I've had to much to drink").

Mental Filter. This is looking for and selectively picking out a single negative detail, ignoring the big picture, and dwelling on it alone until everything seems black ("Even though the editor bought my article, he wanted me to change one sentence. It means he thinks I'm a hack writer" or worrying that the boss didn't like your speech because she whispered in someone's ear while she was applauding).

Disqualifyng the Positive. This is rejecting or dismissing positive experiences by insisting that they don't count. In this way you can maintain your negative belief even though there's contradictory evidence in your everyday experiences ("Even though I haven't been able to stand in store lines for a month, my trip to the supermarket today wasn't a big deal because I needed food").

Jumping to Conclusions. This is making negative interpretations even though there are no facts that support this conclusion. There are two types of jumping to conclusions:

Mind reading. This is arbitrarily concluding that someone is reacting negatively to you and you don't bother to check it out. ("When I posted a message on the social anxiety list and no one responded, it was because they thought what I said was stupid").

Fortune telling error. This is anticipating things will turn out badly. You feel convinced that your conclusion is already an established fact and you can use it to make predictions. ("Since they didn't care enough about me to respond yesterday when I posted, they obviously don't want me here so I'm leaving the list").

Emotional Reasoning. This is assuming that negative emotions necessarily reflect the truth: how things really are ("I feel it so it must be true").

Should Statement. This is using unrealistically high self-imposed standards of *perfection* to motivate yourself to perform tasks. You express these unrealistic expectations in terms of *should, shouldn't, must,* and *ought* ("I should be able to use will power alone to overcome my SA/SP" or "I must never show anger to my parents").

Labeling. This is attaching a negative label to yourself rather than describe your error ("I'm so stupid" rather than "That was a stupid thing to do"). You attach labels to others ("He's such a moron") when they irritate you and describe an event in emotionally loaded, evaluative language ("He arrogantly shoved my report at me and barked, 'Do it again'"). This is an extreme form of over-generalization.

Rationalization. This is ascribing justifiable and plausible motives to your thoughts and feelings while real motives go unrecognized because they are unacceptable ("I left the meeting to make an important phone call" rather than "I left because I felt they were all staring at me"). There are two common forms of rationalization:

Sour grapes. This is allowing yourself to avoid anxiety, guilt, and shame. To reduce your disappointment you convince yourself that the unattained goal wasn't all that desirable in the first place ("Well, I didn't really want the job anyway"). This is a self-deceptive and ego-enhancing device.

Sweet lemon. This is convincing yourself that your failure in attaining a previous goal may be a "blessing in disguise" after all ("If I hadn't had that panic attack in the mall in front of the guy I wanted to impress, I might have dated him and then been rejected by him because of my SA/SP"). This is similar to sour grapes.

Your recovery demands that you recognize, focus on, and confront your automatic fear thoughts. You need to differentiate the thought from its interpretation, learn about the situations you associate with them, explore the beliefs underneath them, and then counter them with a rational response.

Through your assessment you can determine not only your fear but also the underlying thoughts that generate that fear. You can change the underlying thoughts and, thus, change the resulting emotion. According to Richard G. Heimberg's "Four Steps to Cognitive Restructuring," this means that in order to counter your fear of negative evaluation, you need to:

1. Look at the situation in which the fear of the unknown, failure, or rejection occurs

2. Analyze the thoughts attached to the situation

3. Acknowledge the distortion: your interpretations, meanings, labels, and evaluations

4. Respond to these thoughts rationally by reframing, reinterpreting, re-labeling, and re-evaluating.

This requires your distancing yourself from the thoughts so their emotion won't entangle you.

SARAH'S ASSESSMENT

You can do this by responding as if *someone else* were presenting the thoughts to you for your dispassionate, objective analysis.

Situation: Sarah is a psychopharmaceutical sales representative. She's looking for suggestions on how to sell to a new market. While she's making inquiries of her contacts, she gets a hot lead on the advice she wants. But to get this information she has to pick up the phone and call a stranger. Sarah assesses her unwillingness to make the call. (Format is adapted from David Burns' *Feeling Good: The New Mood Therapy.*)

What is the irrational thought? What is the realistic assessment of the situation? Where does the irrational thought come from? The process works from the outer layer of the automatic negative thought onion to its core. In your realistic assessment you are disputing your irrational fear thought.

Fear Thought: I can't call.

Realistic Assessment: I can call. I can just pick up the phone and dial. I have the person's name, what she can do for me, and I have a reference.

Thought Origin: What is there about calling that bothers me?

Fear Thought: She's busy and doesn't want me to bother her.

Realistic Assessment: She may or may not be busy. Since I am not a mind reader, I have no way of knowing what she will be doing at any given moment. I can't know that she's being bothered unless she says so to me. She might actually enjoy talking to me, taking the opportunity to share. It is her choice how she will respond. I have no right to make her choice for her.

Thought Origin: If she were busy, why would that a problem for me?

Fear Thought: I would be rejected.

Realistic Assessment: If she weren't interested in talking to me at that moment or does not have the time to talk, it does not mean that she has rejected me. She has rejected *talking* to me. By chance I would expect a maximum of half of those I call to talk to me. That means half would not.

Thought Origin: If I were rejected, why would that a problem for me?

Fear Thought: I would be shown to be inadequate.

Realistic Assessment: Just because I don't get what I want on this one occasion does not mean I am inadequate as a human being. I am adequate in many things I do. I'm OK whether or not my behavior works in this situation. If I see a pattern of behavior not working for me, I can consider changing it.

Thought Origin: If I were shown to be inadequate in this situation, why would that be a problem for me?

In this disputation process you're looking for:

- **Evidence.** Is what you think or believe factually correct? You need to question the evidence for believing specific appraisals. What is the meaning? Where is the logic faulty? Then you need to collect contradictory evidence.

- **Alternatives.** What are the other possible causes? Rarely does anything that happens to you have only one possible cause. You need to generate a list all the possible, rational, and relevant contributing factors. You should focus particularly on those that are *concrete, specific, changeable*, and *non-personal*. (*Non-personal* is especially important because you need to begin externalizing your focus.)

- **Conclusions.** What is the worst thing that could happen as a result?

- **Implications.** What is the likelihood of the "terrible" consequences you envision actually occurring (even if the belief or thought were correct)?

- **Usefulness.** To what degree is just holding this thought or belief destructive (whether the thought or belief is true or not)?

Being able to step outside yourself is not easy. Neither is figuring out your attitudes, expectations, and beliefs. They're generally hidden from you. Getting to them requires time and effort. However, when you can reach them, even superficially or tangentially, you can get a sense of some of the things that trigger and perpetuate your SA/SP.

EXERCISE

Your Fear-Thought Assessment

- Construct your own Fear-Thought Assessment table.

- Write down a social situation in which you feel fear of evaluation. Begin by writing down the first fear-thought you have when you think about the situation.

- Then, acting as an objective observer, respond realistically and rationally to the thought. Write down your objective response.

- Now go back to your thought and analyze it: What is the basis of the problem for you. What are the assumptions, attitudes, expectations, rules, or beliefs on which the problem is based?

~ASSIGNMENT~

Record this in your Recovery Journal. Every day you need to assess any fear thoughts you've had that day using this process. You want to focus your rational responses to your fear thoughts.

It is imperative that you remember that this negative self-talk is really a *self-criticism*. This means you have to defend yourself and talk back to your internal critic. You do this by dissecting your fear thoughts to get to the heart of the fear that may be many levels (or onion layers) removed from the first fear thought you have. Knowing this underlying, fundamental, fear-generating thought is useful because it'll show up in many situations in many guises.

You can also recreate your reality by altering the verbal instructions you give to yourself when you face feared social situations. You can train yourself to deal with this fear through a simple coaching process. You can give yourself a pep talk, talking to yourself as you would to a best friend.

COPING WITH FEAR PROCESS

Coping with your fear requires that you step outside your emotion and follow a logical, systematic process. The following is the process you will use throughout your recovery:

- Think of a social situation in which you fear being observed, negatively evaluated, or being humiliated publicly
- Visualize yourself in it
- Start talking to yourself as you approach this situation in your mind
- Prepare yourself for the stress that looms ahead
- Confront and handle the stressful situation
- Listen to your negative self-talk.
- Cope with the feelings of being overwhelmed by responding with coping self-statements (listed below)
- Talk yourself through the problem
- Reward yourself for having coped. (See you can be and **are** your own best friend!)

Positive Affirmation. It's important to recognize that your negative bias rejects positive statements about yourself. For this reason it is essential that you anchor any positive affirmation in a *concrete, specific* positive experience from your past. When you provide evidence to support the positive statement, it is harder for your mind to discount or dismiss the statement. You want to remind yourself, "I've done it before. I _____. So I can do it again."

FEAR DEFENSE STATEMENTS

(Adapted from Donald Meichenbaum and Roy Cameron in *Self Control*)

When you start talking positively to yourself, you need to use statements that counter the different aspects of your negative self-talk. The following takes you from fear assessment to success reward.

1. **Assess the reality of the fear situation**: Is the situation really dangerous so I should be afraid? What is it that I really need to do? I can concentrate on what I have to do; that's more constructive than being afraid.

2. **Control negative, self-defeating, fear-provoking thoughts and images**: I can erase my worry. Worry isn't helpful. Worry is passive, negative, and not constructive.

3. **Re-label fear**: Maybe the feeling I'm calling "fear" is really eagerness to get the situation over with.

4. **Psych yourself up to perform well**: I know I can confront this situation. One step at a time. I'm taking care of it. I'm going to think only about what I have to do and stay relevant. I can relax by taking slow, deep breaths.

5. **Cope with intense fear**: I can focus on what I have to do right now. It cannot and will not last forever. I can wait. I don't need to worry about fear. I can do something else. I feel bad only when I think about it. What's the worst that realistically can happen? How likely is it to occur? Could I cope with it? Yes, I could and can cope.

6. **Positively reinforce yourself for having coped**: I did it. It worked. It wasn't so bad after all. I blew it out of proportion. It wasn't worth the agony. Every day in every way I'm getting better. I'm proud of myself for my continuing progress.

~ASSIGNMENT~

Practice these statements daily and apply them every single time you approach risk taking or any fear situation. Create your own list of Fear Defense Statements using concrete, specific examples of success in your Recovery Journal. Use them with your abdominal breathing whenever you feel even slightly anxious.

Note: It's important to remember that concentrating on negative aspects of a situation, whether real or imagined, only serves to promote more negativity and stunt your spirit, growth, and life possibilities. Negative thoughts affect you more deeply than do positive thoughts; therefore, you have to work that much harder to keep positive.

Concentrating on the positive, whether real or imagined, promotes positive feelings and growth. Being rational and positive, you can choose to think your way to a successful recovery.

COPING WITH PANIC ATTACKS

Not every SA/SPer experiences panic attacks. Perhaps less than 50% of you do. So for those who do and those who may, there are some basic things you need to remember when you find yourself in the throes of panic when you anticipate or encounter a social situation.

- Even though your heart is racing and you're sweating and trembling, you're not going to have a heart attack. Your mouth may be dry but you're not going to choke. Your body is simply overreacting to a stressful situation. While the feelings are unpleasant, they're not harmful and will subside quickly if you let them.

- Look at what your body is doing. You're hyperventilating which is making your heart race and making you feel dizzy. You need to use your abdominal breathing exercises. Breathing into a paper bag to balance your CO_2 loss may also help reduce your arousal but not as much as will abdominal breathing.

- Listen to your thoughts. You're creating worst-case scenarios about what's happening and how others will respond. What you're saying doesn't represent reality. These thoughts create a vicious circle because they engender fear, blame, frustration, and anger that then make you more anxious. You need to talk to yourself. You need to address these negative automatic thoughts, counter them, and then dismiss them.

- Trying to escape will make the situation worse. Instead, make yourself as comfortable and secure as possible. Look for ways to distract yourself until your body shortly returns to its normal state.

- Recognize that you not only survived the attack but also made it through by maintaining control. You should be proud of yourself. You've demonstrated that you don't have to let the panic control you; you can control it.

~ASSIGNMENT~

Put these steps for dealing with panic on an index card that you carry with you and pull out when panic threatens. Then record the event, what you did, and the consequences in your Recovery Journal.

WHY YOU NEED TO CONTROL WORRY

SA/SPers fret endlessly over anticipated negative outcomes. This fretting does nothing to deal with the problem but only makes you feel bad. There are steps you can take to reduce the levels of this ineffective behavior. They involve your recognizing first that you're worrying then interrupting the thought before it can build anxiety. By putting aside those things over which you have no control, you reduce the amount of time you spend brooding about what *might* go wrong. With less time for worry, you have more time and energy to actually solve the problem.

JOE. The first thing that strikes you about Joe, who is reasonably attractive, is that he rarely smiles. There seems to be a perpetual dark cloud playing across his face. He speaks with a refrain that colors his every conversation on a social phobia online list, echoing like a broken record: "Nothing ever works out the way I want because of this problem. Life is so unfair."

For Joe life is a series of possible social catastrophes. In fact, he spends his days and nights conjuring up "what ifs" about anticipated situations. Then he plots strategies to either avoid them or steel himself against their occurrence.

He's interested in stunt flying, but thinks, "Even I can make myself go to the air show this weekend, I can't make myself meet that group of pilots Tom said he'd introduce me to. I know meeting them would be my big chance for success. I can't become a stunt pilot if I can't get in with them. But they wouldn't be interested in a dumb kid like me anyway. They wouldn't want me and I'll be stuck forever in my dead-end job. I'll never get into air shows and my life will be ruined."

Most of the time Joe is tense, frustrated, angry, and fearful. A chain of negative and seemingly uncontrollable thoughts and images bombard him. Consequently, he frequently experiences a sinking feeling in his stomach, gastrointestinal distress, tight shoulders, and rapid heart rate. His body speaks of his distorted beliefs with his furrowed brow, hunched shoulders, clenched fists, and furtive glances.

Because he's distracted, introspective, and often sullen, his work and relationships suffer. A high-level worrier, Joe spends most of his time fretting about things that have little or no substance, or likelihood. His untested speculations are inaccurate and unrealistic, yet he feels immobilized by them and the social situations that precipitate them.

As a result, he won't assert himself or take risks. He avoids such situations but agonizes over the effects of his avoidance. The penalty of his isolation is more acceptable to him than suffering the anxiety of encountering these situations, and any rewards that would be brought to him by new experiences.

Sometimes SA/SPers, such as Joe, experience anxiety about future occurrences that are unrelated to social situations – e.g., finances. This is Generalized Anxiety Disorder and may or may not occur with SA/SP. When it does, there may be an overlap between the social and non-social things you worry about.

EXERCISE

Worry Reduction

If you find you worry excessively about low probability events in the future that are unrelated to social situations, you need to do the following exercise. (Adapted from Thomas Borkovec)

- Establish a minimum 30-minute "worry session." This should be an uninterrupted period of time in the same place at the same time each day. Scheduling is important. It gives you a sense of control. You're in charge of those otherwise aimless, involuntary, and bothersome thoughts.

- Monitor your behavior during the day and identify "worry episodes" by their negative content. They can be a negative thoughts or negative feelings.

- Jot down in your Recovery Journal the thoughts you consider to be a problem. These are what you'll use in your worry session. Writing down worrisome thoughts or feelings is very reassuring. It gets the problem out of your thoughts, where you'll ruminate upon it, and onto paper. Once you've committed it to paper, you can forget it.

- The moment you start to worry, stop yourself. Postpone the worrying until the worry session. You can worry about it at the prescribed time *only*.

- Substitute something positive for the worrisome thought you just had.

- Concentrate on the task at hand to distract yourself from worrying.

- Make full use of your worry session. This is the time at which you can worry intensely about all those thoughts you jotted down in your journal. Tape and listen to your worries.

- Look carefully at each thought and try to determine what it is you really fear.

- Assess how likely it is that such an event would occur.

- Discard problems about which you are unable to do anything.

- Pinpoint those that are under your control then decide: what you can do, what you want to do, and what you will do about the situation. Record this in your journal.

Note: This process can also be very useful when you ruminate over future or past events having to do with social situations.

COUNTERING FEAR THOUGHTS SHORT-TERM

There are a number of strategies that counter these fear thoughts in the short term. While all these techniques work well individually, they'll be even more effective when they are used together. It is essential that you have a lot of strategies available to allow you to short-circuit your fear thoughts. These techniques can be used, especially with abdominal breathing, anytime anxiety rears its ugly head.

Thought-Stopping. This is a simple but highly effective technique that stops thoughts and interrupts habitual thought patterns. Strategies include:

- Saying "Stop! I'll think about it later," and scheduling time to think about it

- Carrying 3"X 5" card with the word "STOP" in enormous red letters

- Writing the thoughts down the moment they occur

- Ringing a loud bell
- Wearing a rubber band around the wrist and snapping it hard to stop ruminating
- Detailing all the ways to change the situation in the future.

Distraction. You can interfere with your fear thoughts by ignoring or forgetting them, deliberately thinking about something non-arousing, or doing something else. You can fantasize or visualize about a favorite subject. However, distraction needs to be used with caution. It's for *temporary* reduction of symptoms and not for alleviating the disorder itself. Alcohol use, substance abuse, aggressive acts, or sex, for example, are distraction techniques that should **not** be employed to take your mind off your anxiety. They are inherently destructive.

Distancing. A belief or thought may or may not represent fact. So your believing or thinking something is so doesn't make it so. You need to stand back, suspend your judgment, and look objectively and critically at the belief or thought.

Substitution. Substituting an emotion that competes with your fear allows you temporarily to go beyond your immobilization or avoidance. When you choose an activating emotion like humor, you focus your attention and energy outward, on the environment. Because you can't respond to humor and fear at the same time, humor affords you a refuge from fear's perceived danger.

Humor substitution. Humor is often employed as a coping mechanism in life-and-death situations, such as in war or medical emergencies. It also provides you a way to respond without fear so you can continue what you're doing.

It's useful to remember that laughter not only takes your mind off your fears but also does a number of other positive things. It boosts your immune system, lowers your blood pressure, and increases your disease-fighting T-cells. And, of course, laughter just plain feels good.

BARRY. Barry's handwriting totally disintegrated whenever he had to write in front of others. It was a situation that mortified him, leaving him agonizing for days on end about what others thought of him. So this time, after signing his name to a company blood-drive volunteer list with his colleagues, he made a point of drawing the others' attention to his signature. Chuckling, he said, "Look at that chicken scratch. What does that say? Boy, aren't you glad I'm not your doctor." Everyone laughed and went about their business.

As you get older, you tend to laugh less. Non-SA/SP children laugh about 400 times a day whereas non-SA/SP adults laugh only about 15 times a day. While there are no figures on laughter in those with SA/SP, you can assume it's, unfortunately, significantly less. To address your laugh-challenged state you need to:

- Be more playful
- Surround yourself with playful, funny, or humorous others
- Do one playful thing a day
- Watch children and/or animals playing
- Collect cartoons to post or jokes to share
- Look for humor in SA/SP and in the absurdity of life
- Listen to humor tapes and/or watch comedies to relieve stress.

Take care not to let humor disguise anger or aggression.

Anger substitution. Anger as well may be substituted for fear because it's energizing. But if you use it, you must do so very carefully. Inherent in the use of anger is the question of at whom the anger is really directed. Directing anger at others when you're angry with yourself only creates more problems both for others and you. SA/SPers already have more anger than they can handle so this may not be a good first choice for substitution for you. Note: If you do use anger, you should direct the anger toward the *situation* and **not** toward *individuals*.

MARIA. When Maria thought about not being able to go to church any longer because she felt she'd made a fool of herself with her frantic behavior, she became incensed at the whole situation. I can go to church if I want, she snorted. Nothing that's happened can keep me away. No matter what, I won't allow my past performance to spoil everything.

The next Sunday she went to church, revved up. She slid into her regular place in the back, noting that no one paid any unusual attention to her. She was glad to be back and her anger disappeared.

Identification. When you determine that a thought or belief isn't correct, you need to label it as a *thinking error*.

Reframing. Framing is how you perceive, interpret, label, and categorize your actions, their outcomes, and contingencies. It's your perspective. That is, it's where you place your emphasis. For example, do you see social events as a threat of negative evaluation or a possibility for making friends.

How you frame things is dependent upon social and cultural norms, your habits, personal characteristics, environmental factors, and, your SA/SP. Like a picture frame, thinking frames put boundaries on what and how you think and feel about a subject at a given time. They restrict or enhance your options. Reframing is turning your negative thinking about events around to look for positive outcomes.

JOANNA. When Joanna entered her English class, she immediately saw her physiological arousal in terms of her anxiety about giving a speech. This was because she thought she would be evaluated, humiliated, found wanting, and rejected if she attempted to speak before the class. She had framed her arousal as negative and the associated situation as something to be avoided.

She could, however, reframe her physiological arousal in view of what she knew to be true about the environment. Her classmates have always been supportive of one another's efforts. A number of them look up to her for continuing her education. She knows her material and has a script from which to read. As a result, she could legitimately reframe her arousal as eagerness to finish the requirement for keeping her grade point average high. Through this positive re-labeling, she's allowing herself to respond to the situation in a new, more adaptive way.

Albert Ellis, the progenitor of cognitive treatment and developer of Rational-Emotive Behavior Therapy (REBT, formerly RET), says: "People and things do not upset you. Rather you upset yourself by believing that they can upset you."

EXERCISE

Maladaptive Thoughts Record

There are numbers of ways to dispute your irrational thoughts and beliefs. Answer the following questions (Questions adapted from *A New Guide to Rational Living* by Albert Ellis and Robert Harper)

1. What irrational thought or belief do I have that is maladaptive and I want to eliminate?

   (For example, "Everyone must evaluate me in positive terms.")

2. Is this belief or thought correct, factual, or rational?

   (For example, "No.")

3. What evidence exists that this thought or belief is incorrect, not factual, or irrational?

   (For example, "People will judge me based upon their own agendas, biases, values, and experience. I have no control over that. There's no natural law that says they have to regard me positively. If one person doesn't evaluate me positively, there are many others who will.

   "I'm not diminished as a person if any one person doesn't value me as I'd like them to. If a person values me negatively, it doesn't mean I'm a bad, incompetent, or worthless person. It *may* mean I have a skill deficit that needs work, but *not* necessarily.")

4. What evidence exists that this thought or belief is correct, factual, or rational?

   (For example, "None really. I'd like everyone to think highly of me. But if they don't, it won't be terrible. I can live with it, but I will feel disappointed, frustrated, and maybe somewhat deprived.")

5. What type of maladaptive thinking is this?

   (For example, "*Should* statements.").

6. What is the worst thing that could actually happen to me if people don't respond to me as I think they must?

   (For example, "I could spend all my time trying to make them think well of me. But some people may never think well of me, might even reject me. I might be alone as a result which would be uncomfortable and unpleasant, but I could survive.")

7. What positive things can I do for myself if I don't get what I think I must?

   (For example, "I can focus and work on my recovery so I can be more comfortable and satisfied with myself and life. I can look for others who might regard me positively. I can devote more time to pleasing those who value me, thereby pleasing myself.")

~ASSIGNMENT~

You need to spend 15 minutes a day disputing your irrational thoughts and beliefs. Answer the seven questions above and record both the questions in the following table. When you copy the table, give yourself plenty of room in which to answer each question.

Maladaptive Thoughts Record

Date_____

Question	Response
Q#1	R#1
Q#2	R#2
Q#3	R#3
Q#4	R#4
Q#5	R#5
Q#6	R#6
Q#7	R#7

This process, according to Rational-Emotive Behavioral Therapy, is as easy as **ABCDE**: (1) **A**dversity: What triggers the anxiety process; (2) **B**elief: What you think about the situation; (3) **C**onsequences: What you expect to result; (4) **D**isputation: What you do to challenge the validity of the thoughts; and (5) **E**nergization: What you experience as a result of countering distorted thoughts.

WHAT IS COGNITIVE-BEHAVIORAL THERAPY?

Cognitive-Behavioral Therapy (CBT) is a combination of therapies that works on your fearful thoughts, beliefs, feelings, *and* on your avoidant be-haviors. Generally, in CBT you work extensively on the cognitive aspects of your SA/SP first to restructure your thoughts and provide you with cognitive strategies. This prepares your for using the behavioral therapies.

The behavioral component is based upon learning theory. It focuses on observable behavior: What you can measure and analyze directly. This behavior, however, is not to be considered maladaptive without reference to the (1) situation in which it takes place and (2) your thoughts and attitudes that are objectionable or unpredictable for you. The aim of these behavioral strategies is to inhibit or remove your maladaptive behavior by directly applying conditioning principles and techniques.

Assessment is a continuous part of the behavioral approach. It asks:

- **What behavior is maladaptive?** (This is the behavior to be increased or decreased, such as Harry's eating only soft food with lots of liquids because he's afraid of choking.)

- **What in the environment either maintains this undesirable behavior or reduces the likelihood of your performing a more adaptive behavior?** (When Harry eats soft food and drinks a lot of liquid, he doesn't choke and isn't embarrassed in public.)

- **What environmental factors can you manipulate to alter this behavior?** (Harry can gradually change the food consistency to show that he doesn't need to eat soft food to prevent himself from being humiliated.)

BEHAVIORAL TECHNIQUES

Behavioral techniques investigate your *present* unwanted behavior only. What may have reinforced that behavior in the past is not knowable. Moreover, it may not be the same thing that keeps it going now. This therapy is more interested in "what" behavior needs to be changed than in "why" you're behaving as you do. Being fully functional in the present is more important than having deep insight into your past.

Behavior therapy is aimed at determining where behavioral change needs to occur in the present then helping you acquire a new, positive, substitute behavior. This approach uses positive reinforcement (rewards) that increases the likelihood of your acquiring the new behavior in social situations. Slowly it increases your comfort level in the situation until you can encounter it without anxiety.

Exposure. This is the primary group of behavioral techniques used in CBT with SA/SP. It involves confronting the feared social situation either in a step-by-step, graduated fashion or at its full intensity. With either, you remain in the situation until arousal reduction occurs and the stimulus no longer elicits your anxiety. When habituation occurs, your physiological arousal, such as pulse rate and blood pressure, drops and you feel less distressed.

Exposure is more effective when you use abdominal breathing, but **no** other relaxation techniques, during exposure to reduce arousal.

Graduated exposure. You can encounter your fear in two ways. One is in your imagination (**imaginal exposure)**, where you envision the anxiety situation. The other is in the actual situation (**in vivo exposure**) where you experience it first hand. Both are done in a graduated manner.

Once you feel comfortable at a minor level of anxiety, you move on to the next level or change point. Exposing yourself to the anxiety situation in your mind first prepares you to feel more comfortable duplicating this process in the real situation. While some therapists focus on doing this only in the actual situation, many others combine these two approaches.

JOANNA. Joanna tried imaginal exposure therapy for her fear of public speaking. She began by imagining herself in her English class when her report was due. Standing at the podium, she felt her heart racing, her legs tremble, sweat pouring down her back, and her mouth dry. Lost in the role-play, she struggled to envision herself in a near-panic state, on the verge of collapse. But despite generating all the emotion she did, her image was still standing at the podium, unscathed by the anguish she regularly felt in real-life. Joanna made a game of it and she practiced it daily. The next time she was to give a report, she managed not only to stay in the classroom but also to stand up at the podium.

Full-bore exposure. An alternative to the graduated approach is experiencing anxiety at its full intensity (**flooding**). With no preparation you expose yourself to the full impact of your fear. While this may sound traumatic, some believe this may work more quickly for some people. The behavioral premise is that being smacked in the face by the intense anxiety where escape is impossible will quickly decrease or extinguish the anxiety because you're forced to see that your negative thoughts and fears are unfounded.

Another type of flooding is Viktor Frankl's **paradoxical intention.** This is where you intentionally try to bring on your anxiety symptoms in the most full-blown way possible. If you tremble, sweat, or blush when anxious, you try to simulate these feared symptoms. But the harder you try, the harder it is for you to do. Not being able to experience what you expect to experience in a feared situation changes your beliefs about the likelihood of its really happening.

HARRY. Harry tried paradoxical intention. Before he was scheduled to go on stage, he'd try to make himself anxious enough to vomit. He began the process in his dressing room, even carrying the wastebasket around with him, willing himself to regurgitate into it … to make the grossest mess possible. He continued as he proceeded into the wings. "I'm an actor," he thought, "surely I can do this." But by the time of his stage cue he hadn't succeeded and was chuckling at the intensity of the silliness of what he was doing. When he walked onstage, he felt more comfortable.

Intentional errors. In addition, you can deal with your fear by purposely creating and acting on those situations. You choose some minor anxiety-provoking behavior, like dropping papers in front of others, then imagine your intentionally doing it and successfully handling the consequences. You rehearse this incident in your mind until you feel comfortable doing it in a real situation. Then you do the actual behavior.

Since you created the incident and have practiced the action and your response to it, you're the one in control of it. This allows you to step back to objectively observe how others *really* respond to your behavior. Thus, you can test your unrealistic expectations. Doing so also allows you to experience yourself as more confident and successful.

SARAH. Being in a restaurant paralyzed Sarah, who feared acting like a klutz. The possibility of her dropping her silverware and drawing everyone's attention to her lack of social aptitude made her anxious. So she decided to become the fork-dropping queen. After practicing her clumsy act in her mind, she tried it out for real at a luncheon with colleagues. As her fork clattered to the tile floor, a good-looking waiter who was passing hurriedly replaced it for her. At which point someone joked that Sarah was just trying to make an impression on the waiter. Sarah smiled and winked, as if they shared a secret, and lunch continued confidently without a hitch.

While both imaginal and in vivo exposure are very useful in reducing fear, in vivo is *the* central behavioral component in effective CBT.

SAFETY BEHAVIORS

Safety behaviors are those avoidance behaviors that you use to protect yourself from anxiety. Some safety behaviors help you avoid the feared situation altogether. Whenever Joanna is invited to a party, she finds an excuse to keep from going so she can't be embarrassed.

Other safety behaviors reduce the risk of being negatively evaluated. When Maria goes to church, she takes the last seat in the back. The problem with safety behaviors is that in anxiety-provoking situations they not only reduce your fear but also reinforce that fear. That is, they can actually cause or exaggerate some symptoms of SA/SP.

BARRY. When Barry braces himself against the singles' club bar, he's automatically preventing the things he fears from happening. He doesn't allow himself to see what actually would happen if he didn't brace himself. As a result, he can't unambiguously disconfirm the belief or the expected consequences of his trembling.

This means he doesn't really know what would happen: If he'd shake, if anyone would notice, and if anyone would negatively evaluate him for it. Instead, he's anxiously preparing for humiliation or rejection that may have a low likelihood of occurring. Furthermore, as he braces himself, he's straining his muscles to keep himself immobile. This strain itself makes the muscles even more likely to tremble.

Your believing others will negatively evaluate you and your mentally preparing for it may make it a reality. It's like a self-fulfilling prophecy. Studies have shown that when you anticipate a negative interaction, you tend to be rated by others in the interaction as less warm, friendly, and disclosing. This is opposite of when you anticipate a positive interaction.

Safety behavior studies conducted by Adrian Wells looked at whether the use of safety behaviors had any effect on the effectiveness of behavioral therapy. Two groups of SA/SPers participated in one session of exposure to a feared social situation. One group was instructed to intentionally drop their safety behaviors. The results showed that while exposure-alone reduced anxiety and negative belief ratings, *exposure-plus the dropping of safety behaviors very significantly reduced anxiety*.

What this suggests is that your safety behaviors can interfere with your recovery. That is, these behaviors allow you to be disengaged from the situation and, thus, ignore the cues to which you need to adapt.

To make your cognitive and behavioral treatment strategies more effective, you need to identify your key safety behaviors. Then you need to assess how they're tied to your anxiety-related beliefs. This means discovering how they act to increase symptoms and/or prevent your disconfirming your mistaken beliefs. It means examining and eliminating them.

Safety behaviors include:

- Avoidance of social situations (not going, not accepting engagements or opportunities to interact with others)
- Social withdrawal within situations (not speaking, making eye contact, or listening, being outrageous or aggressive, standing apart)
- Drinking alcohol
- Using recreational drugs.

ANXIETY HIERARCHY

To address your anxiety through exposure in a step-by-step fashion you need to construct a hierarchical list for your anxiety-provoking social situation. This hierarchy lists all the relevant factors, or steps, in your experiencing that anxiety and ranks them by their severity, from the most disturbing to the least disturbing.

BARRY'S HIERARCHY

Barry doesn't like being scrutinized by others in most situations, but particularly at work. He constructed the following hierarchy of what makes him fearful at work, in descending order from the most disturbing to the least.

Most stressful

Scene #	Scene Description
1.	Being watched working by his boss
2.	Being watched working by ten fellow employees
3.	Being watched working by six fellow employees
4.	Being watched by an expert in his work area
5.	Being watched by three fellow employees
6.	Being watched by one fellow employee

Least stressful

To address your anxiety in a graduated fashion you need to look at the least disturbing item on your anxiety hierarchy. You need to imagine yourself in the situation, visualize it in great detail (as you did in your visualization exercise), and monitor your anxiety. The smaller the increments (or steps) of anxiety, the less intensity you have to experience at each step, and the greater your likelihood of success. It's necessary for you to remain at that step until you can experience it without anxiety.

Once you've achieved this step, you progress to the next step on your list and repeat the process. It may be better if you address no more than three steps in any one session. Once you can comfortably enter the situation in your mind, you're ready to approach it in real life.

Note: If you can, you should look for real-life situations that simulate or closely approximate each step of your hierarchy and experience those.

EXERCISE

Construct your own anxiety hierarchy using no more than ten steps. Do one step at a time in your mind before doing it in real life.

Employ only abdominal breathing to help control your physical arousal during the anxiety experience.

After each successful step, praise and reward yourself for achieving it.

Systematic Desensitization. This is Joseph Wolpe's behavioral therapy model which employs both exposure and relaxation exercises. It involves:

- Constructing an anxiety hierarchy
- Training in deep muscle relaxation and breathing
- Opposing anxiety-provoking elements with relaxation.

While SD may not work for SA/SPers in general, it may work for co-morbid panic. Even though many people have heard of it, there have been few research studies that show SD as effective as plain exposure in CBT for SA/SP. I have found this to be true. One reason SD tends not to help SA/SP is the use of its physical relaxation techniques.

This may be because use of relaxation techniques during exposure may actually interfere with the habituation process. Physical relaxation exercises require you to concentrate on specific aspects of your body and think about how it feels. This distracts you from fully experiencing the anxiety. When you can't fully experience your anxiety in exposure, the exposure becomes much less effective. Breathing exercises, on the other hand, don't require thought or body focus. As a result, abdominal breathing lets you experience your anxiety and work successfully through it.

Virtual Reality Therapy. When real-life exposure is not easily accessible, exposure may be done via virtual reality. Specifically, you can encounter your fears through a series of computer-generated anxiety-provoking scenes, experience graded anxiety, adapt to it, and move on to the next step. One big advantage of virtual reality therapy (VRT) is the freedom it gives to both your therapist and you to control the anxiety-provoking situation.

Since 1992 VRT has been employed with success in the treatment of specific phobias, such as fear of flying, agoraphobia, fear of heights, spiders, and closed spaces. A study conducted at the Virtual Technology Laboratory at Clark Atlanta University looked at fear of public speaking and similarly demonstrated a significant reduction of self-reported anxiety. As yet no studies have been done on generalized SA/SP.

HOW EFFECTIVE IS COGNITIVE-BEHAVIORAL THERAPY?

SA/SP improvement is the result of a reduction in both your fear of negative evaluation and your desire to avoid fear-producing situations. Since your fear of negative evaluation is made up of cognitive distortions and is supported by avoidance behavior, any therapy to be effective in dealing with SA/SP *must* address both components.

Richard Mattick and others have demonstrated that exposure plus cognitive restructuring tends to be more effective than either exposure or cognitive restructuring alone for SA/SP. It is likewise more effective than relaxation alone or systematic desensitization. The use of CBT has been shown repeatedly to lead to significant improvement for over 89% of CBT study participants.

Approach behaviors increased while avoidance decreased. SA/SP symptoms interfered less with work, social activities, and family life. Moreover, these improvements were maintained.

INDIVIDUAL VS. GROUP THERAPY

If CBT is the therapy of choice, what is the most effective way to present it? Is individual therapy better than group therapy? Clinical researcher Richard Heimberg has designed Cognitive-Behavioral Group Therapy (CBGT) to assess that question.

His approach maximizes the integration of cognitive and behavioral procedures. Employing two co-therapists (one male and one female), it works with six patients/clients over twelve weekly sessions. Essential to his approach are the following:

- Training skills in the identification, analysis, and the disputation of maladaptive thoughts through structured exercises
- Exposure to simulations of anxiety-provoking situations within the group setting to receive feedback, the opportunity to learn from others' simulations, and the availability of an audience
- Cognitive restructuring procedures used before, during, and after the simulated anxiety-situation exposures
- Real-life exposure homework assignments which mirror the in-group exposure simulations
- Self-administered cognitive restructuring tests used before and

after the behavioral homework assignments.

The "group" element can provide a number of significant benefits. As group participants, SA/SPers can identify with one another. You can form bonds and share: Ideas, insights, perspectives, feedback, advice, and support.

This group therapy is more cost-effective than individual therapy. Moreover, this process has also been adapted for adolescents so that it takes into account their cognitive and developmental levels, behavioral-skills level, and social milieu. However, access to CBGT may be more difficult because it tends to be less available than CBT.

But not everyone is comfortable in a group. Some SA/SPers find it difficult enough just to speak with the therapist alone. The presence of other individuals, even those who are SA/SPers like you, may dampen your enthusiasm. You may feel expected to ask or answer questions, make suggestions or comments. You may feel pressured to respond then fear being evaluated in whatever you say or do by the group. However, for those who feel you can benefit from the group, CBGT is a good way to go.

Comparison of individual CBT and CBGT has found that outcomes of group and individual treatment are not significantly different. This means that if both are available, you have a choice.

WHAT REALLY GOES ON IN CGBT?

CBGT for SA/SP typically runs 12–14 weeks with small numbers of SA/SPers meeting once a week, often in the evening. In between meetings group participants are expected to engage in 20 minutes of therapy practice each day in a peaceful, stress-free, and positive environment at home. Meetings themselves operate on a stress-free rule wherein you're not pressured, not put on display, or asked to do things you don't want to do.

However, as you move up in your anxiety hierarchies, you do voluntarily allow yourself to be put on display and do things you don't particularly want to do. You do this because this is the only way you can get better.

According to clinical psychologist Dr. Thomas A. Richards of The Social Anxiety Institute, in Phoenix, AZ, who conducts CBGT for SA/SP, the group spends a great deal of time practicing cognitive strategies. These include becoming aware of and disputing negative self-talk. The group also participates in behavioral therapy, such as doing presentations or simulations.

During these sessions, you watch each other. Afterward, you discuss the presentations. You also watch a videotape of yourself to see how you're doing, what's right, and what needs work. You work on your hierarchies then do practical exposure "experiments" in the real world. It's working first with others than on your own. The approach employed is slow and gentle.

Real-world experiments often begin as group exercises where you do those things that make you anxious. You say "hello" first to strangers, raise your voice in public, or drop things in front of others. Each experiment is detailed ahead of time with a handout to follow. Then when you're ready, you do these actions on your own.

There is cognitive preparation before and re-interpretation with group members afterward. This is one reason this method is especially effective. Throughout the process there is a summarizing of what you've done to date and what you still need to do.

CBGT also can be done in an intensive format of four full weeks (with weekends optional). When you follow this course, you need to be ready, willing, and motivated to immerse yourself deeply in the concentrated material and go at a fast pace. Dr. Richards stresses that a four-week intensive program will not totally alleviate your SA/SP but will get you going along the right path with well-established positive therapeutic habits.

It's important that you continue to use your CBT techniques after termination of regular group sessions and regularly continue your exercises for several months thereafter. *Persistence* is the key. Once SA/SPers have returned home following the four-week program, Dr. Richards provides continuing e-mail contact with you to help keep you on track.

SUMMARY

It's necessary to do every exercise and practice every cognitive and behavioral technique in this chapter. Not just once but **over and over and over again**. These and the arousal-reduction strategies *must* become second nature to you. You should also continue to record what you do and your results in your daily Recovery Journal.

These are *the* building blocks of your recovery. Therefore, **before you move to more advanced strategies, you absolutely must have the basics down cold.** This means you must become adept at:

1. Using abdominal breathing
2. Using relaxation exercises
3. Using visualization
4. Countering your erroneous core beliefs
5. Constantly and consistently disputing your fear thoughts
6. Using success-experience-based positive affirmations
7. Employing anxiety hierarchies in specific situations
8. Exposing yourself to feared situations and coping with them
9. Praising and rewarding each and every success you have.

Important Note: If you want to go ahead and read the rest of the book before you master these basic SA/SP techniques, you can go ahead. *BUT* if you want to effectively and significantly alleviate your SA/SP, **I strongly recommend that you come back to these chapters to master their strategies before going on to work on the more advanced techniques in the following chapters.**

In the words of writer Somerset Maugham, "The common idea that success spoils people by making them vain, egotistic, and self-complacent is erroneous; on the contrary, it makes them, for the most part, humble, tolerant, and kind. Failure makes people cruel and bitter."

8

BECOMING SOCIALLY EFFECTIVE

"Tiny differences in input could quickly become
overwhelming differences in output."
(James Gleick, *Chaos*, 1987)

WHAT IS SOCIAL EFFECTIVENESS?

Once you have truly mastered the basic SA/SP arousal and CBT coping strategies in Chapters 6 and 7, you can begin to look at addressing some of the limitations of your SA/SP-shrink-wrapped life. You can begin to see that social effectiveness is the primary skill area on which you need to work.

Social effectiveness skills are aimed at increasing social awareness and interaction. They include a range of cognitive and behavioral abilities, social perception, and information processing. They focus on how you select relevant and useful information from social situations and employ it toward reaching your goals.

To increase your social effectiveness you need to improve your (1) interpersonal skills, (2) verbal and nonverbal communication, (3) social performance, (4) image, and (5) social participation. Doing so further decreases your SA/SP.

Interpersonal Skills. Interpersonal skills are what create and maintain relationships and help you meet your goals. They include holding conversations, listening, speaking, nonverbal behavior, image, assertiveness, and a sense of what's appropriate for the situation. It's generally thought that most of the skills you will need for adult social interaction and successful relationships are learned during adolescence. This appears to be true even for SA/SPers.

But, if you have the skills, then what's your problem? The problem is you *believe* you lack these important skills. You think this because you tend to respond inappropriately in social situations ... when you respond at all. You may display undesirable mannerisms, such as low eye contact, closed body positions, and anxious hand movements. Or, you may have difficulty pulling your conversational weight, such as not volunteering information. As a result, your communication likely will be less effective.

Interestingly, there are few meaningful behavioral differences between those who are high and low in social anxiety. Yes, you tend to speak less about yourself in conversations, ask more questions, and look less at speakers. But, on the positive side, you also smile and nod more, interrupt less frequently, and seem more attentive. It's apparent that many of these so-called "socially anxious" behaviors actually facilitate conversations even more than behaviors of the "socially confident."

When you're anxious in a social situation, you doubt that you have the social skills to convey the desired message or impression of yourself to others. Once you believe you lack the necessary skills, you conclude you're unlikely to make that positive first impression or receive a positive evaluation in a situation where those skills are needed.

It's true that skills you use infrequently may become rusty. It's true that they may suffer from the impact of your continuous negative thinking. But it's also true that sometimes your low self-esteem causes you to underestimate your ability to deal effectively with social situations. This means that even when you are socially adept and do successfully execute these behaviors, you'll see yourself as socially deficient.

To bear this out you need only to look at yourself in non-threatening social situations. Generally, your self-esteem is high. You feel comfortable and are likely to both feel and appear to be socially skilled. But, the moment you see the social situation to be threatening, your distorted thoughts and feelings immediately take priority. They submerge your recollection of your skills and your successfully exercising them.

Social Effectiveness Skills Training. This is an effective method of both enhancing your social behavior and social effectiveness and reducing your social anxiety. Based on the "Social Effectiveness Therapy" model developed by Samuel Turner, Deborah Beidel, and Michelle Cooley, it uses the techniques of:

- Education about anxiety
- Observational learning of a socially skilled model

- Direct instruction in skills
- Videotaped evaluation of social behavior
- Behavioral rehearsal
- Social reinforcement
- Corrective feedback
- Homework assignments
- Flexibility exercises
- Real-life exposure.

WHERE AND WHEN DOES SOCIAL ANXIETY INCREASE?

Your social anxiety increases in novel, ambiguous, and unstructured situations. It increases when you don't know what to expect, as in your interactions with strangers. It increases when you don't have a script prepared for the encounter.

Social effectiveness skills training helps make you become aware of your social environment. It briefs you on what to expect so as to reduce your uncertainty. It teaches you about the formation and termination of interpersonal relationships, the skills needed to carry on relationships successfully, and how to speak and present yourself in public, both formally and informally.

It instructs you how to formulate appropriate scripts for these situations then provides you an opportunity to practice your social skills. Through exposure, it subjects you to feared situations in which you can employ your skills and knowledge and can test your readiness. And, perhaps most importantly, it increases your confidence that you'll present yourself in an acceptable manner, thus decreasing your social anxiety while increasing your social activity.

By improving your social skills, you

- Improve your self-esteem and self-confidence
- Improve the image you present
- Increase your effectiveness in interactions
- Decrease your social anxiety
- Increase the number of interpersonal relationships you have
- Increase the potential for intimacy.

Currently there is more therapy available for SA/SP that there is for social effectiveness skills for the SA/SPer.

HOW IS COMMUNICATIONS INVOLVED?

Communication is the process by which you establish contact with one another. Through symbols you exchange perceptions, knowledge, ideas, and experiences. You share feelings, beliefs, values, and decisions. The aim of communication is to help you and the other influence each other's behavior to understand and mutually achieve your goals.

Effective communication is a blend of applied observation, verbal and nonverbal   skills, behavioral psychology, and common sense. Without effective communication you can't convey your message and your intentions. You can't develop good rapport and relationships. You can't understand and do your work. And you can't present the image of yourself you want others to see.

For most SA/SPers, communication feels like a non-starter. The moment you become anxious, you either jabber or become tongue-tied. Your brain selectively erases your memory banks and you blank out. You can't retrieve the words you want when you want them. What falls from your lips often sounds *to you* like gibberish.

Let me share with you an example. I was giving a presentation at Simmons College in Boston that was going along pretty well until I came to an anecdote I wanted to use. To make a point, I introduced it by saying, "I'll never forget the words of my mentor, Dr. Clara Mayo."

No sooner had I uttered those fateful words than my anxiety-attacked brain stopped dead in its tracks. The "I'll never forget" statement reminded me of being worried about forgetting what I was going to say. It completely severed the connection between my cerebrum and tongue. An hour-long minute passed as I stared blankly at my notes. Finally, I mumbled, "Well, so much for not forgetting her memorable words," and read her quotation to them with an embarrassed laugh.

How Do You Start Addressing Social Effectiveness? You'll start by looking at your communication. To make your communication effective you need to spell out clearly, in behavioral terms, what you want to achieve. As noted before, your goal and objectives must be realistic, concrete, and specific. They must also be achievable, observable, and measurable. This means you need to be working on the four aspects of communication:

Self-awareness. Self-awareness refers to your understanding who and what you are, how you think, and how this is likely to affect your communication.

Attitude. Attitude refers to developing a more flexible, reality-based and assertive style of communication. It also means a willingness to influence people to behave in desired ways.

Knowledge. Knowledge refers to understanding communication concepts and methods, from definition to analysis to insight. It also means understanding how your and the other's message is influenced by the sender's characteristics, the medium through which it's conveyed, and the receiver's characteristics.

Skill. Skill refers to learning how to express yourself, specifically your thoughts and facts clearly and concisely. It means checking that the message has been received and interpreted correctly. It means learning to diagnose, analyze, and solve practical communication problems.

While communication is the key part of every interaction, no two people communicate exactly the same. Therefore, there are no specific, hard and fast rules to follow. Rather, there are guiding principles that apply to all situations and people:

- Think before communicating. Plan what you'll say and how you'll say it.
- Decide on the purpose of your communication. Know what is to be achieved.
- Take into consideration the situation and circumstances in which the communication is to take place.
- Make the message complete and specific, using a frame of reference.
- Make verbal and nonverbal behaviors congruent and consistent.
- Make the message appropriately fit the receiver.
- Describe feelings clearly.
- Listen carefully to what is said and how it's said.
- Provide feedback to the sender of the message.
- Describe behavior without making evaluations or judgments.

- Don't jump to conclusions.
- Respect the ideas of others.
- Acknowledge your feelings and those of others.
- Control your emotions.

Use a win/win approach where you both get something you want.

PINPOINTING BARRIERS TO COMMUNICATION

There are a large number of behaviors and attitudes that prevent communication from taking place.

Assumptions Made Without Any Basis in Fact. You assume a lot of things about individuals, groups, society, and institutions. For instance, you tend to assume that others understand what you mean and that you understand what they mean. You tend to assume that most people in authority or all people with a college education are good communicators. You may assume that newspapers, magazines, and television provide you with facts and truth: accurate, unbiased, and complete information. One of the most common mistakes you are likely to make is assuming that others perceive the world exactly as you do.

Resistance to Unfamiliar Concepts. Often you prefer to deal with the known and avoid the unknown. This may pertain to new subjects or new ways of thinking about old subjects. Resistance may show up as skepticism about everything new or different.

Use of Jargon. Jargon is like a secret code. Its use separates individuals into in-groups and out-groups. Even though each group and profession has its own jargon that is used among insiders, outsiders must use it carefully.

Lack of Knowledge. When you have inadequate training or lack knowledge about the sender, receiver, subject, or medium, you can't transmit or receive the message fully or accurately. When you don't understand the communication process, you can't transmit or receive messages adequately. As a result, there may be big differences in the interpretation of the sender and receiver's words and their implications.

Stereotyped Thinking. This is generalizing and, thus, treating all members of a group (of ideas, objects, or people) as if they were the same. While this short-cut method may be useful in sorting through all the information that bombards you, stereotyping reduces your ability to recognize differences.

The same is true when you use evaluative labels based on these generalizations. You close yourself off to new information. This breeds oversimplification, selective attention, and leads to distortion of reality. Moreover, it encourages your jumping to conclusions.

Sender—Receiver Barriers. Senders and receivers have behaviors and characteristics that can interrupt the communication process. One such barrier is the sender's lack of a goal or reason for offering the message. Another is lack of communication skills. Incorrect word usage, grammatical errors, and poor timing or delivery may also make it difficult for others to understand what you're trying to say.

Thinking About What You're Going to Say Next. Since you can't concentrate on two things at once (their words and your thoughts), it's better to listen, to focus on their words. Similarly, when you're concerned about your role or how you appear, you're distracted from receiving the sender's message. Anything that directs your attention inwards takes it away from your understanding of what the sender is saying.

Judging and Evaluating Others. When you make judgments about the sender or the message, you automatically distort the meaning of the message. If, for example, you don't like the person, it's difficult for you to hear the message correctly. The same is true for the subject. If you are *pro* or *con,* you'll automatically rally, to some degree, to that mindset. Doing this distorts your understanding.

Not Putting Yourself in the Other Person's Place. When you don't see something from the point of view of the sender, you can't hear the message correctly. Likewise, when you listen selectively, you hear only what you want to hear. In doing so, you deny, reject, or distort the message.

Having Preconceived Notions. When you have already decided what the message will mean, the sender's intended meaning will be lost, obscured, or distorted.

Lack of Responsive Feedback. When you reply with a non-responsive or inappropriate response, it may discourage, frustrate, or insult the sender. For example, you ask another person with SA/SP who's on the antidepressant Parnate, "How likely is it I'll have problems with certain foods?" If your listener merely grunts or responds, "Ask a psychiatrist," you'll most likely be taken aback and the communication will cease.

Lack of Trust. When you don't have confidence that the other person will protect your welfare and provide acceptance and support of what you communicate, you may reduce the amount of information you share. This may lead to distortion of your message. Likewise, if you feel the other is disengaged, unreliable, or seems to have ulterior motives, you'll receive what they send with suspicion. Lack of trust is a primary obstacle to effective communication.

EXERCISE

Write down the Communication Barriers in your Recovery Journal and supply one example of each that you have demonstrated at one time or another. Then for each example write down (1) what you think you can do to avoid each barrier in the future, (2) how you will do it, and then (3) create a plan to do just that.

IMPROVING YOUR ORAL COMMUNICATION

Language carries communication, but it also interferes with it. What can you do to minimize this interference when you're trying to communicate?

- Direct your audience's attention to where you want by emphasizing the point, enumerating it, repeating, and/or restating it.

- Convey forcefulness and clarity through the use of short, simple words and sentences.

- Avoid distracting language, punctuated with fillers, such as "uh," "hey," "like," "I mean," "right," "you know," and "okay."

- Use understandable language, not loaded with ambiguities, technical terminology, jargon, acronyms, and abbreviations.

- Use appropriate language. This means avoiding profanity, irreverent, discriminatory, or suggestive speech or dirty jokes. It means avoiding political, ethnic, religious subjects, and derogatory comments.

SPOTTING THINKING PREFERENCES

You can be limited or liberated by the way you think.

- Do you ever feel you're on a different wavelength from your audience?

- Do people ever look at you blankly when you share information with them?

- Do people show frustration when you describe a problem or its solution?

If you answered **yes**, then you may be a victim of what's called "incompatible hemispheric thinking."

Communication theory has been reborn in the form of a neuro-scientific concept called "whole-brain thinking." Proponents of the left-brain/right-brain approach, such as Ned Herrmann, author of *The Creative Brain,* and numbers of Fortune 500 large corporations, believe that this cerebral training increases skills in communication, problem solving, collaboration, and productivity. They also believe it helps them determine and predict the best use of their abilities and that of their employees.

What is whole-brain thinking? What can it possibly really do for you? The whole-brain concept states that the hemispheres of the brain process information in different ways. The left hemisphere processes verbal, logical, quantitative, and analytical thought, while the right addresses visual, spatial, creative, and holistic thought.

Each of you has a "brain-dominance" causes you to lean toward and prefer one style of thought processing over another. The hypothesis is that if you're predominantly left-brained, for example, you're oriented toward logical reasoning, sequences, facts, and conceptual structures. Left-brains, then, are likely to become engineers, accountants, lawyers, or managers.

If you're right-brained, your statements reflect an orientation toward people, feelings, experiences, patterns, and relations. Right-brains, then, are likely to become artists, salespeople, social workers, or entrepreneurs.

Left-brain and right-brain thinking styles are considered equally valid and valuable.

How you think and prefer to think affects your perception of the best ways to communicate and collaborate. How you communicate can cause people to move toward you or away from you. If, for example, you talk to people who have a preference for right-brain creative thinking about details, numbers, facts, and sequences, they will tend to turn off. They'll experience actual physiological stress and want to shout, "What is the point you're trying to make?"

On the other hand, if you talk to those who have a preference for left-brain analytical thinking about pictures, metaphors, analogies, and the "big picture" first, they'll feel like hopping up and down in frustration, screaming, "But ... how are you going to get there?"

EXERCISE

Thinking Preferences

Answer the following questions by picking A, B, or C to determine your probable thinking style.

1. In a conference, where do you prefer to sit?
   - A. Left
   - B. Right
   - C. No preference

2. How do you prefer to work?
   - A. By myself
   - B. On a team

3. When you're given an assignment, which do you prefer?
   - A. Highly specific instructions
   - B. Rather flexible instructions

4. How do you make your own decisions?
   - A. By careful analysis
   - B. By gut feeling

5. How do you motivate yourself?
   - A. By competing with yourself
   - B. By competing with others

6. Which would you prefer to be married to? Someone who

A. Is a thorough planner

B. Has unusual ideas, daring concepts

7. How do you shop?

A. By reading labels and comparing costs

B. On impulse

8. When you meet someone, what do you remember?

A. Name

B. Face

C. Both

9. Which do you prefer at a meeting?

A. Dynamic speaker

B. Imaginative slide presentation

10. When driving in a city you don't know well, do you

A. Get a map and ask for specific directions

B. Navigate on your own sense of direction

11. Mark the word in each line that better describes you.

A. Logical   B. Creative
A. Analytical   B. Intuitive
A Factual   B. Holistic
A. Rational   B. Emotional
A. Linear   B. Spatial

Scoring: Each **A** = 4 points. **B = 1** point. **C = 0** points. If your score is **47–60**, you tend towards left-brain thinking. **46–40** you are left-brain and right-brain equally, switching back and forth depending upon the situation. If you score **39–15**, you tend towards right-brain thinking.

Individual thinking preferences are important because each person approaches problems differently and describes the problem, the process, and the solution differently. As a result, you will tend to find collaboration and communication difficult if these differences are not acknowledged and addressed.

It's important to note that thinking preferences do not represent skills, intelligence, or level of competence. Rather they are pathways by which you and others are predisposed, socially and genetically, to solve your problems. Knowing and experiencing different styles allows you to appreciate how you and others think, learn, and create.

When thinking styles collide, you tend to experience a vague sense of conflict or tension. You don't understand how the other is looking at the situation. The other person seems, at the very least, obtuse, maybe even stupid. As a result, you will feel frustration and tend to stop trying.

BARRY. Barry's boss, for example, used to provide Barry with lists of things to which to attend. "It used to drive me crazy. I don't use lists. I don't need them." Having patience under these circumstances is often very difficult until you realize that your thinking styles are conflicting. Understanding that lists are very useful for Barry's boss made it easier for Barry not to take personally his being given these lists.

What you must recognize and appreciate is that there are many ways to not only approach and describe information but also process it. Knowing what differences exist, each person must make an effort to get ideas across in a form the *other* person can easily grasp. Until this translation medium is on place, accountants and engineers will tend to throw up their hands and say they can't work with salespeople and artists, and *vice versa.*

The whole-brain approach presents a simple model for explaining and understanding behavior and for looking at others and yourself. It also is a model for generating awareness and valuing the perceived diversity. Differentiating and classifying thinking styles provides you a point of common reference that can facilitate communication and collaboration. The process fosters creativity and openness to trying new things.

RESPONDING TO INTERPERSONAL CUES

Another popular approach for developing your communication skills is neuro-linguistic programming (NLP). Based on the study of linguistics, body language, and communications systems, NLP is a way of increasing your sensitivity to interpersonal cues and learning how to respond to them. It's a way of increasing flexibility and responsiveness to change. The aim of NLP's behavioral training is mastery of new ways of:

- Reading another person's internal processes by identifying language patterns and observing nonverbal behavior

- Influencing another person's responses.

According to reported NLP observational data, you organize your experiences, your behavior, thoughts, and feelings, through three primary perceptual systems: visual, auditory, and kinesthetic. Therefore, there are three basic language patterns that reflect these styles.

Visual. Visual people focus on sight. They prefer to read information rather than hear it. When they recall a scene, they do so vividly, in color. They listen for and speak in visual terms: "I see what you mean" and "I get the picture." To make contact with visually-oriented people, it's best to use words related to sight.

Auditory. Auditory people orient themselves to sound. They prefer to hear information rather than read it. Sounds trigger memories and associations for them. They listen for and speak in hearing terms. For example, "I hear what you're saying" and "Sounds good to me." To establish rapport with auditory individuals, you need to use hearing-related words.

Kinesthetic. Kinesthetic people relate to how things feel, taste, and smell. The physical world in all its dimensions evokes strong sensations for them. They listen to and speak in body terms. For example, "I have a good grasp on the problem," "It's a pain in the neck," and "I feel you ought to go forward." To communicate with kinesthetically-oriented people, you need to use feeling-oriented words.

How else can you know how others receive their experience and process information? NLP hypothesizes that eye movement is an indicator of the individuals' primary perceptual system. Specifically, you glance in the direction opposite the hemisphere that's most perceptually active at that moment. Currently there are no empirical data to support this.

- Eye movement up and to your right suggests visualizing something new (*constructed imagery*)

- Up and to the left suggests recalling a visual memory (*eidetic imagery*)

- Eyes staring into space with pupils dilated suggests visual recall or imagining (*imagery*)

- To the left suggests recalling a sound (*internal auditory*)
- To the right suggests imagining a sound (*internal auditory*)
- Down and to the left suggests talking/listening to yourself (*internal dialogue*)
- In general, however, eye movement down suggests sensing how the body feels (*kinesthetic access*).

Knowing How Listeners Receive Information. Knowing how your listeners receive information allows you to present it in such a way that they are more likely to attend to it and understand what you're saying. Matching your language style to theirs enables you to more easily gain rapport and a sense of trust and competence.

You can establish rapport with the other person by a form of matching, called *mirroring*. You do what the other person does. Mirroring is a behavioral conditioning technique. Specifically, you subtly imitate the nonverbal behavior of others: Their gestures, body rhythm, voice tone and tempo, body postures and orientation, breathing rate, and word choice. You synchronize your behavior with that of the other person so that you're presenting yourself similarly. Similarity creates attraction and liking.

You can take mirroring one step further to influence the other person's behavior. Through *pacing*, a form of behavior shaping, you gradually change the degree of matching to effect a new behavior. For example, in a meeting with your boss, he becomes angry because of repeated staff interruptions. He begins breathing in a more rapid and shallow fashion. To establish rapport you could assume the same breathing pattern, putting you in *synchrony*. Then you could gradually decrease your breathing rate. As you do this, your boss likewise will do this, to the point of eventually relaxing and, once again, being in rapport with you.

EXERCISE

Perceptual Preference System

What perceptual systems do you tend to use? Have a partner ask you the following questions then observe the movement of your eyes as you answer. The correctness of the answer is not as important as how you process the question.

1. What was the name of your best childhood friend?
2. What are the three meanings of the word pronounced "2"?
3. How many are five times four?
4. What did you wear yesterday?
5. Which way does Abraham Lincoln's profile face on the penny?

If your eyes looked to the right, you're left-hemisphere-activated. If your eyes looked to the left, you're right hemisphere-activated. Eyes up, visual. Eyes level, left or right, auditory. Eyes down, kinesthetic.

WHY IS LISTENING IMPORTANT?

Communication is a shared experience. You listen to understand the others' needs. You listen to influence others. You listen to learn. To do this you have to correctly interpret and understand what the other person is saying. Listening is not a character trait but a skill that can be developed. You listen only 25% of the time, while the other 75% you're just hearing.

Listening and hearing aren't the same things. Hearing is the passive physical process of receiving sound. Listening is the active cognitive process of searching for the meaning of what you hear. Where listening occurs, the exchange of words and feelings can help you achieve better interactions, relationships, and greater productivity because it encourages action, not passivity.

EXERCISE

Listening Habits

How would you rate your listening habits? Which of the following apply to you? In the space provided, put a **Y** for **yes** or **N** for **no**. (Adapted from work by Eugene Raudsepp of Princeton Creative Research)

____I never let others finish their thoughts before interrupting them

____I'm eager for them to finish

____I don't let them explain their problem fully

____I look at them in disbelief when they talk

____I finish sentences for them

____I constantly do other things while they're talking

____I keep trying to get them off the track by making comments and asking questions

____I kid around or am flippant when they're being serious

____I look at them critically while they're speaking

____I rephrase their words, distorting their meaning.

Score: Count the number of **Ys**: **1–2** = Good. **3–4** = Needs improvement. **5–6** = Poor. **7–11** = Very poor.

HOW TO LISTEN EFFECTIVELY

Effective listening, also called *active listening,* is an art unto itself. You have to train yourself to listen to receive the messages a speaker is sending to you. This requires that you specifically learn to focus to what the speaker is saying. You listen for the main points the sender is making.

You then begin to analyze what is being said. By the time the sender has completed the message, you have thought through the points made and have reached a tentative conclusion. It's tentative at this point because you still need to check to see if you have received the message accurately.

But words are not all you have to attend to. You must attend to the three parts of the message. Each component communicates important information. Words often do not tell it all:

- Words (data)
- Feeling content (tone)
- Nonverbal behavior (delivery).

Active listening requires that you keep an open mind. This means not trying to second-guess the speaker. Your goal is to understand what is being said, not what you think should be or is likely to be said or meant by this speaker.

To listen actively is to check to see that *your impression equals the sender's expression.* You do this by giving feedback. Giving feedback is reflecting to the sender what you heard being said. Not the words *per se,* but what they're intended to mean. Feedback is tangible evidence that you have correctly decoded the message. The sender then confirms the accuracy of your impression or corrects it.

For listening to be effective you need to

- Listen with interest
- Absorb the content
- Actively grasp the facts and feelings you hear
- Listen for total meaning (content and feeling)
- Note all subtle cues
- Sense underlying meaning
- Intuit what person is really saying (not saying in words).

Active listening is the act of looking for congruence between what the person is saying in words and is communicating nonverbally through posture, gestures, mannerisms, and voice inflection. You need to look for the underlying feeling message.

While listening, you respond with nodding and expressions of attention, such as, "uh huh" and "I see." Nodding and other expressions of attention indicate understanding and approval. They encourage the other person to continue speaking. Frequency of these behaviors depends upon what is being said and how it's being said.

When you listen effectively, you communicate:

- I hear what you're feeling
- I understand how you're seeing things
- I see you as you are right now
- I'm interested and concerned
- I don't judge or evaluate you as a person
- You don't have to be afraid of my censure for your speaking out.

Being a good listener helps you better identify those with common interests, those who can help you, those to whom you can be helpful, and what others really want. Being a good listener creates a good impression and visibility.

~ASSIGNMENT~

Assess your current listening skills:

1. Pick a conversation that went well and analyze it. Look at your behavior and that of your partner. What worked?

2. Now pick a conversation that didn't go well. What didn't work? What could you have done to positively change it?

ACTIVE LISTENING SKILLS

There are six active listening skills that you need to master.

Reflecting. Reflecting is feeding back to the speaker the essence of what is being communicated. However, as I've already mentioned, it's not simply repeating verbatim what has been said. If a spouse said, "I really don't want to go to work today. I have a presentation due and I'm freaked out," reflecting would **not** be repeating, "You really don't want to go to work today. You have a presentation due and you're freaked." Instead, a reflective response would be, "You're feeling really anxious about doing the presentation and would rather avoid the situation."

Clarifying. Clarifying focuses on the key underlying issues and sorting out confusing, conflicting feelings. When a schoolmate says, "I hate this class. I wish I didn't have to be here. Nothing I do satisfies anyone," you might respond, "It sounds as though you have questions about the value and acceptance of your work in this class."

Interpreting. Interpreting offers possible explanations for certain behaviors or symptoms as an hypothesis, not a fact. If accurate and well timed, it can be very useful. For example, "I've noticed that when you say you like living with your parents, you shake your head 'no.' Could this indicate that you'd really like to have other living arrangements?" This observation gives the person a chance to consider the validity of the hunch and confirm, deny, or clarify.

Questioning. Questioning gets you in touch with the other's underlying feelings. To do this you need to ask "what" and 'how' questions. They are open-ended and can be responded to in many ways. By not implying that a "right" answer exists, open-ended questions provide rich and wide-ranging information. As a result, they are more informative than closed questions, such as those requiring a "yes" or "no" answer or those posed by the question "why."

"Why" questions imply that some limited number of "right" answers exist, that there must be an acceptable "because" explanation and you need to find it. For example, if you ask, "How do you feel when someone unexpected comes to the door?" you get more and very different information than if you ask, "Why do you feel uncomfortable when someone unexpected comes to the door?"

Empathizing. Empathizing is sensing the subjective world of the other person and being aware of what the other is experiencing. For example, if a friend says, "This week's schedule is very frustrating," you might respond by saying, "Juggling family responsibilities, job, and doctor's appointments must be anxiety-provoking and tiring."

Confronting. Confronting is challenging some specific behavior. It's done in such a way that the focus is on the behavior and your feelings about it, and *not* on the person who does the behaving. Thus, you share your feelings, but avoid evaluation, judgment, and labeling the person.

For example, "When I asked you about the library hours, you said, 'Shut up' and waved your hand at me as if dismissing me. That made me angry. I felt I wasn't being treated respectfully."

When you confront, you:

- Present data upon which your inferences are based before stating inferences
- Are clear, specific, and concrete
- Tentatively present information that is not fact as an inference
- Use *I-messages* throughout confrontation, being the three C's: **c**areful, **c**aring, and **c**onstructive.

~ASSIGNMENT~

For 10 days **observe** how you respond to others in interactions and how they respond to you in turn.

(1) What Active Listening skills do you use?

(2) What don't you use?

Log your observations. You'll see the Assertiveness Assessment in the next chapter for how to use this information.

WHY IS IMAGE ESSENTIAL?

Poet W. H. Auden writes, "The image of myself which I try to create in my own mind in order that I may love myself is very different from the image which I try to create in the minds of others in order that they may love me."

Let's take a look at the image you want others to see. A good image is like investment in gold bullion: Highly regarded, valuable, and solid, no matter where you are. But a negative image is like a building situated on quicksand: Doomed from the beginning, sinking fast, and irretrievable. You can't afford not to have a good image.

The saying "You don't get a second chance to make a first impression" is pretty much on the mark. The first impression is often the most lasting so you have to give it your best shot the first time around. This doesn't mean, however, that if you shot yourself in the foot in your first meeting that there's no hope. You can probably recover from most *faux pas* but you will have to work harder and longer to do it.

Image gets your foot in the door in any situation so you can make your presentation and promote yourself as someone they would like to know. These impressions are so important that you can succeed or fail by them even BEFORE you open your mouth to speak.

Effectively getting your message across requires your creating a positive and affirmative image. It should engender identification with your attitudes, values, interests, and background. You need to establish the perception of similarity because this leads to greater attraction and liking. The greater their similarity, the greater their liking. And, interestingly, the more your audience likes you, the more similar to you they see themselves to be.

Your image determines how much power, visibility, and credibility others perceive you to have, helps you accomplish your communication and other interpersonal goals, and enhance your relationships. It creates the picture you want others to see and act on.

The more interested you are in your listener, and the more you tailor yourself to that listener, the more interpersonally attractive you'll be to them. The more "attractive" you are, the more socially desirable qualities others will see you as possessing (such as, competence, friendliness, intelligence, and influence). The more "socially desirable" you are, the greater your impact in your initial encounters.

JOE. While Joe tried to present himself as one who was unconcerned, this presentation initially had its drawbacks. It made him feel even more like a fraud. He was always acting whenever he was around anyone, including his family. He exerted great effort trying to look calm in situations that churned his gut. He hated himself for doing it. But the longer he did it, the more comfortably he wore his new image.

This is precisely what Cary Grant did. Leaving school in England at age 14 to become a stilt walker then actor, he decided to become a debonair leading man, someone charming, charismatic, handsome, virile, and cultured. And that's what he did. "I pretended to be somebody I wanted to be and I finally became that person … ."

It's your image that determines how people value you, to what degree they're attracted to you, like you, trust you, and want to interact with you.

Image Assessment. You need to assess your present image and communication skills by answering:

- What image do you want (in concrete, specific terms)?
- What image are you currently projecting?
- What elements make up the image you want?
- What do you need to do to create the image you want?
- How are you getting your message across at present?
- What do you need to do to project the image you want?
- Do any of these methods create both visibility and credibility for you? Which ones?
- Where do you talk informally with individuals, besides your family and office colleagues?
- What do you do when you talk with those people?
- What results do you get?
- What results do you want?

~ASSIGNMENT~

Now go back over your answers and reduce each to its key words. These words are the basis of planning your image change. Record them.

Fantasize or brainstorm all the different ways you could create the (a) visibility and (b) credibility of a positive image.

EXERCISE

Planning Image Change

If your image assessment suggests you need to improve your image, answer the following questions as fully as you can. Be specific and concrete.

- What presentation or image elements do you want to work on?
- How do you plan to work on them?

~ASSIGNMENT~

Now pick five image behaviors you want to work on. Set up a chart like your Recovery Timeline, with "Goal," "Action," "Deadline," and "Results." Under "Goal," list the behaviors that need work. Under "Action," describe how you want to change your behavior. Put down a specific date, "Deadline," by which you want to have this accomplished. When you have met your deadline, note what happened as a result of your actions. Post this chart where you can frequently refer to it and monitor your progress. For example,

Goal   Make eye contact

Action   Write down when I don't. Have friend tell me when I'm not.

Deadline 2 months

GRABBING ATTENTION WITH NONVERBAL BEHAVIORS

A first impression is made up of several elements, most of which are nonverbal:

- Facial expressions
- Eye contact
- Posture
- Gestures
- Movements
- Tone of voice
- Physical appearance
- Clothing.

Remember, whether you're voting for President, buying dish soap, or looking for a mate, you identify with and relate best to those who present themselves (and are perceived) as likable, warm, sincere, competent, and confident. Of course, perception doesn't necessarily mirror reality. In general, what you want to create is the image of one who is

- Up, alert, and enterprising
- Enthusiastic
- Interested
- Involved
- Relaxed (not frantic, frenetic, or frenzied)
- Trustworthy.

You need to create a positive, non-threatening aura. "Looks" and "sounds" communicate over 90% of the meaning of human interaction when people meet for the first time. The words you speak initially, while important, may represent only 7% of the meaning. So you need to look carefully at the specific nonverbal behaviors that contribute to a positive first impression.

Smile. A smile is your most important facial expression, even though it's often difficult for SA/SPers to create. When it's natural and spontaneous, it warms people. It indicates your interest and willingness to interact. It inspires confidence, trust, and understanding.

But, you don't want to continuously grin. The effect of a "permanent" smile is a negative one. It creates the appearance of your striving to placate to be liked, submissiveness, and powerlessness.

Both men and women should smile at strategic points during the conversation. For example, you want to smile before and after your message, while making direct eye contact. This establishes sincerity. It emphasizes your point. You also want to smile as a reward, when you want to reinforce and encourage an interest in what you're saying.

Even if SA/SPers can't produce a full smile, you should try at least to get the corners of your mouth to turn up. Often the act of moving your facial muscles into a smile positively affects your desire to smile.

Eye Contact. Eye contact is a very powerful nonverbal behavior. Using the eyes alone, people and lower animals can express emotions, conveying attraction, fear, and aggression. Eye use can open and close the lines of communication. It can also regulate the flow of communication by providing turn-taking signals and a way to monitor feedback.

Furthermore, eye contact can reinforce your other nonverbal as well as verbal behaviors. However, it's important to note that not making eye contact also conveys information. It signals disinterest in or avoidance of an interaction. You need to be aware of the eye use of the other person as well and what that likely conveys.

High- and low-status people use their eyes differently. People who perceive themselves to have little power (low-status) tend to look at others a lot, watching for signals. These signals tell them what's going on in the situation and how they should safely respond. Even when they're speaking, they tend to look at their listeners more often.

This is precisely what SA/SPers do. You're ever-vigilant, always looking for clues in the encounter that you're being seen as acceptable, attractive, or interesting, while expecting the opposite.

Confident people and those in authority (high-status), on the other hand, appear not to monitor the behavior of those around them the same way. They look more at the other when they're speaking than when they're listening. They also tend to look at others at strategic moments

When they start to speak, they look at the other person briefly, then look away. They look back when they've finished to signal that it's the other person's turn to speak.

It's better to assume the role of someone in control. When you combine eye contact with appropriate smiling behavior, you create a stronger positive impression. Therefore, you should begin your conversations with direct eye contact to open the communication line then smile to show your friendliness and interest. When you start to speak, you need to look away to maintain your speaking role. As you finish, you look back so that you end with direct eye contact to signal you're done. Then you conclude with a smile. This is not easy for SA/SPers at first.

If what you're saying is very lengthy, you'll want to look at your listener occasionally. This is to make personal contact, make sure you're being heard, obtain feedback, and see if the other will let you continue. Because you're taking turns you will want to encourage reciprocity of behavior. But you need to remember not to hold your gaze at the other person too long. Two–to–three seconds is good. If you wait longer, your listener might misinterpret it as a go-ahead to begin talking.

When you assume the role of listener, your eye contact changes to show your interest in what the other is saying. After all, everyone likes to be listened to. Since you gaze more at people you like, you should look at the speaker intently, but short of staring at them. Staring is generally interpreted as aggressiveness and produces considerable discomfort on the part of the recipient. This is a fact of which SA/SPers are well aware. To prevent staring, you need to look away fleetingly once in awhile.

But what if you can't make direct eye contact? Indirect eye contact will do. You can look at one eye or the bridge of the person's nose. If that's still too uncomfortable, you can catch an eyebrow, tip of the ear or the mouth. Sweeping your eyes over those of the other person, whether you actually look or not, is important to give the impression of eye contact which non-SA/SPers expect.

Posture and Body Position. Your posture reveals how you think of your listener and yourself. If you slouch, with your head down, talking to your feet, you look as if you don't hold yourself in very high regard. Whereas if you stand tall, shoulders back, with military bearing, you look confident and competent. You're like someone with whom others would want to interact because of your attitude of self-assurance and pride.

Your body orientation also suggests your availability for interaction. If your position is closed with arms and/or legs crossed or close to the body, leaning back, turning or looking away, you're not available or interested. If, however, your position is open, with arms and legs apart comfortably, leaning forward, facing the other person, or making eye contact, you're available and interested. These positions hold equally for your conversation partner.

Voice. Your voice quality conveys a lot of things to others, like enthusiasm, sincerity, informality, and interest in your subject. Your belief in what you're saying will be reflected in your voice. If you believe, are interested and enthusiastic, your listener will follow your lead. If you're not, your listener will pick up on it immediately. Their eyes will glaze over and they'll tune you out.

Whenever possible you should stand when speaking. Doing this allows you to project your voice better. You can gesture more easily and emphatically when you want to make a point. This particularly applies to telephone conversations, which many SA/SPers hate.

On the phone you should stand, smile, and gesture too, speaking at a moderate rate. Too slow is better than too fast. If you get a frog in your throat, it's probably a sign of poor breathing that is most likely related to tension. If this happens, you should excuse yourself for a moment to take a sip of a warm drink, take a deep breath, or picture yourself in the most relaxing situation possible. If necessary, you can tell the other person you'll call back in an hour, giving you time to reduce your mounting anxiety.

Having a phone script may be beneficial, but having a list of points to cover may be more useful. This is because it's less rigid and allows you to wander without guilt or fear of losing your place. Limiting the time available to talk limits your anxiety and helps others get to the point. When the time is up, you can then summarize what has been said to confirm understanding. Getting feedback reduces the number of calls needed to correct impressions and information.

Clothing. Your clothing and accessories indicate your status. They also indicate how you care about yourself. Your attire is the first thing others notice about you after the basics of race, gender, and age. You want to dress appropriately for the occasion, the people present, the surroundings, and your goal. Some SA/SPers dress to attract attention while others of you dress to blend in with the background.

Irrespective of clothing intention, you need to look comfortable. If you're uncomfortable, others will be uncomfortable too. On a job interview, you wouldn't dress for the decision maker the way you would for a beer bash with friends. The occasions, people, surroundings, and goals are different.

Movements. Your walk should look unrushed and purposeful, with no exaggerated motions ... not like the White Rabbit in *Alice in Wonderland.* To keep motions to a minimum, you should keep elbows close to the body and gesture from the elbows down primarily. If you keep your body relaxed and relaxed-looking, you'll tend to feel more relaxed. Aroused behaviors can precipitate general physical arousal.

Even facial expressions should be used conservatively so that it's not expressions that carry the communication. A pleasant face is a good goal. All movement should appear confident, deliberate, poised, and relaxed, with gestures subtle, minimal, and used sparingly.

ANYTHING MORE ON NONVERBAL BEHAVIORS?

Of course, language is important. It's especially so when you've gotten past the first impression. Powerful language attracts others, as do powerful voices and body language. Verbal behavior conveys ideas: Your experience, knowledge, and expertise.

Language is powerful when it's direct, assertive, simple, brief and to the point, and conversational. It's powerful when it's free of fillers, like "um," "ah," "ya know," and "I mean," "okay." When it's free of qualifiers and hedges, such as "I may be wrong, but" or "I'm right, aren't I?" It's powerful when it's free of profanity and prejudice, and doesn't interrupt the other.

EXERCISE

Image Behaviors

Stand in front of a mirror or have yourself videotaped as you respond to interactions with others. If you're doing this by yourself, make a list of questions and comments others are likely to make in an interaction. You can also do this for job interviewing. Assess and make note of your nonverbal behavior:

- Do you make eye contact?

- How do you stand?

- How much do you gesture?

- How often do you use facial expressions? Are they only for appropriate emphasis or all the time?

- Are your expressions appropriate?

- Do you frown or wince?

- How assured do you look?

- How relaxed do you look?

- How enthusiastic do you look?

- Is there anything you do repeatedly that has no real purpose or may be distracting?

CREATING A 30-SECOND GRABBER

When making a first impression, you have up to 30 seconds to grab and hold your listener's attention, to create positive expectations, and set the tone for the potential interaction. That's up to 30 seconds to convince and others that they want to talk to you. Up to 30 seconds to make your point effectively.

Why 30 seconds? That's the TV sound-bite attention span. People often have a sense of time-urgency, busy schedules, and other things to think about. They're impatient to get to the heart of the matter, to see if it's in their vested interest to listen. In general, they're not willing to wait 10 minutes for you to get around to your point. Conventional wisdom for SA/SPers and non-SA/SPers alike is that "if you can't say it in 30 seconds, you can't say it at all."

In that brief span of time you should give your name, tell something significant and relevant about yourself, and state what you're interested in or want to achieve in the interaction. The exact subject matter and objective will vary with the circumstances. Then once you've gotten the listener's attention, you still have only 3–4 minutes in which to effectively tell your story or convey your message. That's the who, what, where, when, why, and how of your message.

Preparation. Before the conversation starts, you need to prepare. This means you need to address each of the following elements that make up an effective message.

Objective. You need to know what specifically you want to achieve as a result of this conversation. For example, do you want information, a referral, a job, a friend, a date, or to influence this person in some way? You also need to determine the right questions to ask, based on your goal.

Audience. You need to know who your listener will be, what their interests are, or what's important to them.

Right Approach. If you have a specific goal to achieve in your conversation, you need to determine:

- What single, simple, direct sentence best leads to the goal?
- What will build a case around this statement?
- How can you find common ground that is *related to the interests, needs,* and *experience* of your listener?

You have to know *what* you want, *who* can give it to you, and *how* to get it.

Hook. Whether you're promoting yourself, a product, service, or course of action, you need to capture your listener's attention. The hook is a statement or object used specifically to garner that attention. Finding a hook means looking for something unusual or intriguing about your subject: Something exciting, dramatic, humorous, or personal. For example with business people, "I turn self-conscious self-promoters into confident marketing successes in only 12 weeks... guaranteed!"

Questions are also effective. Whatever the hook is, it must relate to your *objective*, your *listener*, and *lead to the point* you want to get across.

Supporting Material. Every point you make needs support. It can be documentation, amplification, or clarification. The more personal or visual it is the better. Facts, figures, examples, testimony, anecdotes, imagery, and visual aids give the points substance and life. It's important to relate to both the rational and emotional. Also you need to make it relevant to your listener.

Asking. Knowing what you want from the interaction, you need to ask for it. Do you want an action or a reaction? You must always decide on your strategy in advance.

What all of this tells you is that if you're going to grab their attention, make a positive impression, and get your message across, you have to know:

- What image you want to project
- What your communication goals are
- Who your target audience is
- How you're going to accomplish the goal, then promote the message in 4 minutes maximum.

EXERCISE

Creating a Grabber

1. *Create a 30-second grabber for meeting others at a singles' bar.* For example, "Hi, I'm Barry Ratliff. I heard this place has good pizza, good music, and good company. I'm new in town, from L.A. Since I want to make some friends, I thought I'd give it a try. You seem to be enjoying yourself, what do you think?"

2. *Create a 30-second grabber for meeting others at a business conference.* For example, "I'm Sarah Folsom, sales manager with Nirvana Drugs. I'm here to introduce "Grinnalot," our new anti-anxiety medication which was just approved by the FDA and has shown 87% improvement in SA/SPers in nation-wide clinical trials."

3. *Create an all-purpose 30-second grabber. Rehearse this daily. Have it on the tip of your tongue. Use it every opportunity you get.* For example, "My name's Joanna and I'm an aspiring writer. So far I've had four articles on the life of an older college student published in regional papers. When I'm not working on my writing, I'm finishing my B.A. in English at the local college."

APPLYING PUBLIC SPEAKING IMAGE TIPS

When you're giving a speech or presentation, there are a few additional tips that can make it easier to deal with your SA/SP:

- Make sure your speech has a beginning, middle, and end
- Write it the way you'll speak it. Written and spoken languages have different cadences and tones

- Have no more than 2–3 key points to make

- Put key words, phrases, or concepts for speech on note cards. Using a fully prepared text may be appropriate for some situations but tends to compel you to read it, become anxious about losing your place, and lose your place

- Practice in front of a mirror to become comfortable with phrasing, pace, and gestures

- Practice enunciating more clearly and projecting your voice

- Use a lectern or podium. It provides a barrier between your audience and you, gives you a resting place for your notes, a place to put your hands, and something to grip if necessary

- Use a microphone and test it well before beginning your speech

- Begin with confidence

- Scan your audience occasionally as if you're including all of them as your listener. If you can see them, look at their foreheads rather than their eyes. If you find a particularly receptive audience member, look at them occasionally for feedback

- Talk "to" the audience not "at" them

- Wear comfortable, loose clothing in non-sweat-staining colors, such as black or white

- Wear shoes that don't cause you to teeter

- Have the podium light *on* for your notes and turned in such a way that there's no glare

- Adjust the lighting on you so that it makes it difficult for you to see your audience

- Breathe slowly

- Speak at a slow–to–moderate rate. Don't rush, but keep a steady pace

- Speak as if talking to friends, use anecdotes as examples

- Smile

- Gesture for emphasis, clarification, or expression, but control unneeded movements

- Pause for emphasis

- Involve the audience by asking a question that requires a show of hands, if you can see them, or a vocal "yes "or "no" if you can't

- Have a glass of water available
- Wear the glasses that enable you to see your notes
- Consider green-tinted powder to counteract the redness of blushing
- Keep muscles loose. Don't clench fists or lock knees. Muscles under tension tire and tremble. Keep knees slightly bent
- Concentrate on the ideas you want to convey, **not** on the precise words
- Take any prescribed benzodiazepine or beta-blocker, for specific events, 30–45 minutes before the speech
- Correct and accept mistakes, go on with confidence, then forget them. They're bound to occur even to the best speakers
- Reframe your "nervousness" as "energy," preparing you to knock 'em dead.

SUMMARY

In the words of Albert Einstein, "Everything should be made as simple as possible, but not simpler." Becoming more interpersonally effective encompasses a wide range of communication, presentation, and interaction skills. You need to work on these methodically, one at a time. You need to become comfortable with them before you move on to more advanced skills and their applications.

9

SHARPENING PERSONAL EFFECTIVENESS

"If I am not for myself, who will be for me? If I am not for
others, who am I for? And if not now, when?"
(Hillel, the Elder)

WHAT IS ASSERTIVENESS?

Assertiveness is another name for having standards and limits on what is acceptable and tolerable in your relationships
with other people. It's your determination to be firm and enforce those standards and limits. SA/SPers are likely to be less determined and firm than those who don't have social anxiety.

This is because you're more concerned about getting approval and
not being evaluated negatively. This makes setting your boundaries,
standing up for yourself, and asserting your rights in an appropriate
manner very difficult. When you're unable to be firm, your behavior
tends to create confusion and friction, making interactions with others
even more anxiety-provoking, frustrating, and unsatisfactory.

For example, an assertive person would say, "This is what I think
about that approach" whereas a non-assertive SA/SPer would either
say nothing or hedge about giving an opinion, "Well, it could be okay.
John says he likes it."

Assertiveness is expressing how you see the situation, how you
feel about it, and what you'd like to see happen. It's expressed in *I-
messages*. For example, "When you didn't show up for your date or call
to explain, I felt angry and disappointed. I want you to call when you're
going to be late or not show."

As you can see, it doesn't use critical or accusing *you-messages*. For
example, "You didn't show up for your date. You didn't even call.
You're a thoughtless creep."

Assertiveness is significantly different from aggressiveness and
non-assertiveness (passivity). Assertiveness is the middle ground be-

tween them. Aggression makes you feel better about yourself at the expense of the other person. It's a dominating, controlling, and attacking behavioral style. While it indirectly lets you stand up for your rights, it does it by violating the rights of others, denying and devaluing them. Its aim is humiliation and winning.

While assertiveness exerts a positive influence, aggressiveness exerts a negative one. Aggressiveness presents itself through blame, negative evaluation, and labeling of others' behavior and attitudes. It says, "This is what I think and what you think is stupid or doesn't count."

Let me share an example with you. In order to produce and host a program on cable television in Massachusetts, I had to be trained in all aspects of production and be available to crew on other shows, which I did. The evening of my first produced show, my own "Inside Track," I arrived about 15 minutes before my guests, checked with the director about the script I'd created and I'd supplied earlier, checked graphics, slides, videos, props, then greeted my guests and got them settled. The interview went okay and everything seemed fine, except for my throat-clutching SA/SP, of course.

For my second show I arrived 15 minutes early as I had for the first and was immediately attacked by the director/program manager for the station. Shouting at me in front of the entire crew, she challenged me, "Who do you think you are arriving so late for this shoot! Everyone else has been here 45 minutes already and you waltz in just before you start!" I was shocked, mortified, and abysmally confused.

"No one told me I was expected to crew my own show as well as do everything else," I sputtered impotently, "or I would have been here." She continued belittling me for my "arrogance," stating that I "should" have known (though I didn't know how I "should" have known). When she finished, I greeted my guests and stumbled through the show.

Why do some people act aggressively? You may feel threatened and powerless. Perhaps you fear losing your control over others. You may be expressing frustration from prior non-assertive behavior. You may be overreacting because a present association brings back memories of past negative emotional experiences.

You may believe that the only way to get what you want is to attack. You may feel deficient in appropriate skills and find aggression easier to act on. You may find that aggression evokes an immediate "positive" response from others that is satisfying. Others of you may find your culture reinforces aggressiveness as a sign of status and power.

The overall consequences of aggressiveness, however, are negative. The behavior leads to tension, hurt feelings, misunderstandings, hostility, lost relationships, alienation, and retaliation. Only in the short term does this behavior seem rewarding to the aggressor by creating a feeling of power.

Being assertive rather than aggressive will help you gain control of yourself. Being assertive rather than non-assertive will help you increase your self-respect. When you're confident and in control, you are more likely to be able to positively influence the way others act toward you.

EXERCISE

How Assertive Are You?

How you feel about the way you handle the following situations indicates how assertive you are. Answer the following questions as honestly as possible. (Adapted from the book *Stand Up, Speak Out, Talk Back!* By Robert Alberti and Michael Emmons)

Do you:

- Generally express your thoughts and feelings?
- Protest verbally when someone takes your place in line?
- Often approach people and situations without fear of embarrassment?
- Insist your spouse or roommate take their fair share of the household chores?
- Speak up in discussions when you want to make a point?
- Express your anger in a timely fashion and never fly off the handle?
- Say so when someone is very unfair to you?
- Say "no" with ease when a salesperson makes an effort to help you but doesn't have the right merchandise?
- Speak up for your own viewpoint when you and a person whom you respect differ?

- Refuse unreasonable requests made by friends?
- Feel it's unnecessary to justify or make excuses for your not wanting to comply with a friend's wants?
- Address issues that bother you rather than just put up with the situation because it's easier?
- Ask friends for small favors or help?
- Avoid shouting or using bullying tactics to get others to do what you want?
- Insist that service people who are responsible for doing so make repairs, adjustments, or replacements?
- Speak up when you have been waiting and a latecomer is served first?
- Comfortably accept praise for accomplishment, feeling it's deserved?
- Ask the person who continuously kicks your chair in the theater to stop?
- Feel comfortable when someone is watching your work?
- Have confidence in your own judgment?
- Ask the waitperson in a restaurant to correct an improperly prepared or -served meal?
- Take the first step to introduce yourself to a stranger in a gathering?
- Openly express anger without using *you-messages*?
- Find it easier to tell family and friends how you feel than to tell strangers?
- Find it easy to maintain eye contact when talking with others?

The more **no**'s you answered, the more likely it is that you are acting in a non-assertive or aggressive manner and not feeling good about your actions.

~ASSIGNMENT~

To create assertiveness scripts you need to list situations in which you have experienced discomfort because (1) you didn't do or say what you really wanted to or (2) you felt compelled to justify your behavior.

For example, what might you have done if someone in your elevator began to smoke, bothering you greatly?

For each uncomfortable experience you detail the situation for which you need to script an assertive response. That is, what you might have said in a firm but civil manner. Use the following format:

- What was the public discomfort?

- What you said or did?

- What you want to say or do next time?

Record the situation, your original response to the situation, and your new scripted response in your Recovery Journal. Then repeatedly visualize the situation using your assertive response. You want to be pleasant but firm. See how it feels.

HOW TO ASSESS ASSERTIVENESS

Being assertive requires first that you know what you want to be assertive about. You have to pick your issues then determine what behavior of others is acceptable or unacceptable. What specific factors do you need to consider in this determination? It's important that you understand the changes you need to make and be sure you feel comfortable with both the process and the goal.

Once you know what you want and feel determined to achieve it, you need to start thinking in terms of how to convey your message. This means thinking and expressing yourself in *I-messages* rather than *you-messages*. *You-messages* are accusatory, critical, and attack the individual personally rather than their unacceptable behavior.

I-messages indicate that you're speaking for yourself, describing how *you* feel about unacceptable behavior, behaviors that exceed *your* standards, limits, or boundaries. You're taking responsibility for *your* behavior, but not for the other person's. You're not imputing blame, motives, or criticizing.

BARRY. Barry doesn't know what to do about a colleague who continually takes books from his office bookcase without asking. He's angry about his office being invaded, is afraid he won't get his books back, and wants the behavior to stop. If he confronted his colleague, saying, "You took my books again. You're always doing it. You have no consideration for my privacy or me. Don't do it again," what might happen?

His colleague would probably feel angry. He'd have no interest in complying with Barry's desire for a behavior change because he'd be too busy preparing to retaliate to the Barry's attack. Barry's speaking in *you-messages* would most certainly be seen to him as threatening and accusatory. It would put the other person on the defensive.

Instead, if Barry said firmly but gently, "I noticed my marketing books are gone again. When you take my books without asking, I can't find what I need for my work. As a result, I feel really annoyed. From here on out I want you to ask me if you can borrow my books," his colleague could then respond. He could tell Barry how he sees the situation, what his motivation may have been, and what he's willing to do as a result of Barry's request. When it's expressed in terms of Barry, *his* feelings and *his* wants, Barry's colleague is less likely to feel criticized and is more likely to consider Barry's request.

Specifically, What Should You Say?

- State what you see (describe the other's behavior objectively). "When you did…"
- State how the other's behavior concretely affects you. " As a result, when I…"
- State how you feel about it. "I feel angry…"
- State what you want to happen or make a suggestion: "I want" or "Perhaps"

~ASSIGNMENT~

Look back at the incidents you addressed in your assertive scripts. Did you respond in *I-messages*? If not, rework your responses in the *I-message* four-stage format. Rehearse the answers at least once a day so they become a natural reaction for you.

SIMPLIFYING ASSERTIVENESS SKILLS

Manuel J. Smith, author of *When I Say No I Feel Guilty*, has designed some simple techniques to help you become more assertive. They're called:

- Broken record
- Fogging
- Negative assertion.

These are skills that prepare and help you stick to your firmness. They are the basic scripted responses you need so you don't have to solve the problem from scratch each time you encounter the situation. Knowing what to expect and how to respond is everything.

Broken Record. This is the calm repetition of what you want. The technique teaches persistence in your achieving your goals. Reinforcing your determination, it also allows you to ignore the other person's irrelevant logic, manipulation, or baiting.

For example, you're looking for a particular reference book at the library, but the librarian says to you, "You don't really want that one. You won't find it useful." Instead of your normal, non-assertive SA/ SPer "okay," you'd respond calmly and pleasantly, "I want that book." You'd repeat this phrase like a broken record for every argument the librarian might pose until you got what you wanted.

Fogging. This is calmly accepting the probability that there *may* be some grain of truth to what another says about you. At the same time, it allows you to be the ultimate judge of what you do. This technique combines an empathetic phrase with the broken record.

For example, you could say to the librarian, "I'm sure you feel that way, but…" then add the broken record phrase here. Other empathetic phrases are "I understand how you might think that, but …" and "You may be right, but … ." This technique acknowledges the other person, shows empathy with them, and reflects what is being said.

Negative Assertion. This is the calm acceptance of your own errors or failings by your agreeing with the criticism, at least in *spirit*. This allows you to look at your negatives without becoming unduly anxious and defensive. At the same time, your agreeing with this accurate assessment will reduce your critic's hostility and anger.

For example, if Sarah underestimated the amount of time needed to finish a project and her boss is angry because of high-level demands for the final report, her boss might say, "You really messed up royally, and now my butt's in a sling." Using negative assertion, she might respond, "You're right. I really under-estimated the time to finish the project."

While she acknowledges the element of truth, she does so in *her own frame of reference*. She redefines the situation from her own perspective and doesn't buy into her boss's exaggeration. In this way her boss feels he is being heard and that she is acknowledging her error. Sarah, on the other hand, sees there's some truth to his allegation and owns up to its unemotional facts only.

~ASSIGNMENT~

These techniques need to be practiced everyday, at least three times per day so they become a habit. Having scripts ready to deal with an unexpected situation, make you feel more prepared. You don't have to scare up something to say in a moment of panic.

Practice by starting small, using them in insignificant situations. Then as you become more comfortable, apply them to more important situations. Every success increases your confidence that you have power and are in control. Be sure to reward yourself for each success. And record your successes in your Recovery Journal.

DECLARING YOUR PERSONAL RIGHTS

Assertiveness researchers Robert Alberti, Michael Emmons, Arthur Lange, Patricia Jakubowski, and Manuel Smith together have popularized the concept that there are basic personal rights that an individual can choose to defend.

These are rights that we deserve and, underneath it all, really want to have. When you accept that you have a right and are willing to act on it, you are the one to choose when you will act on it and when you won't. Assertiveness gives you the power of choice.

I have the right to

- Ask for what I want
- Be illogical
- Be the judge of my own behavior, thoughts, and emotions
- Be listened to and taken seriously
- Be treated with respect
- Change my mind
- Choose not to assert myself
- Decide if I'm the one responsible for finding solutions to other people's problems
- Have and express my own feelings and opinions

- Make mistakes
- Offer no reasons, excuses, or justification for my behavior
- Say "no" without feeling guilty
- Say "I don't care"
- Say "I don't know"
- Say "I don't understand"
- Set my own priorities.

~ASSIGNMENT~

Which of these assertiveness rights do you currently accept and act on? Which rights that you don't currently act on do you want to act on? What's holding you back from doing so?

DEALING WITH PROCRASTINATION

According to Christopher Robin in A.A. Milne's *Winnie the Pooh*, "Organizing is what you do before you do something, so that when you do it, it's not all mixed up."

In order to determine and pursue your recovery goals you must become adept at structuring your time. You must be both efficient and effective. Management guru Peter Drucker says, "Being efficient is doing the job right. Being effective is doing the right job" … doing those things that *really* need to be done.

~ASSIGNMENT~

List and rank all the tasks you currently have to do. Next go back and determine the following:

- What needs to be done first?
- Second?
- What can wait?
- What can be done just as well by someone else?
- What do you often do that wastes your time without contributing to your effectiveness?
- What can be eliminated?

Each morning you need to make out a daily *To-Do* list with approximately eight items on it. List the items that should be done in order of their priority.

How to Manage Your Time. After you have answered the task priority questions, you will find that there are some items you can't do quickly and easily or delegate or eliminate. For those items you must make a plan. Specifically, you must assess how much time each item requires in order to accomplish it. Then you need to chop each item into bite-sized pieces so you can do a little piece of them each day.

In general, it's better to do a little of each task item each day rather than concentrate your efforts entirely on Item A on Day 1, Item B on Day 2, and so on. Doing a little on each gets all the items closer to completion. Doing the hardest or most important first allows you to avoid spending the day anticipating, dreading, and putting off the task, as SA/SPers are wont to do. Then if there's a task you like doing, you can do it after the hard task as a reward.

Rewards are important so you should build them into the list. As you finish a task, you can give yourself a treat. The larger or harder the task, the larger the reward. Therefore, you need to create a graded reward list. This reinforces your accomplishments and keeps your motivation up.

Short-term and repetitive tasks, like planning dinner and paying bills, should take place once a week so you're not continually thinking and obsessing about them. Long-range goals, however, require long-range planning. Knowing where you're going and how you're going to get there makes accomplishing those goals both easier and less overwhelming.

To be most productive you must record the deadlines of tasks to be done on a calendar. You should put this in your journal, along with ideas on different ways to achieve them and the progress you're making. Reminders are helpful, especially sticking "Post-It" notes everywhere.

Your journal should contain not only a listing of your activities but also the time involved. Working consistently and systematically day by day until tasks are completed will allow you to both achieve the success you want and feel in control.

Time management also helps rid yourself of time wasters. You have only to think about the times you gave yourself extra time to do your usual activities. Somehow you managed to fill up all the time with them. You wonder, "Where did the time go?" Unfortunately, if you allow yourself a day to do a task, it'll take a day. If you allow yourself half a day, it'll take half a day. It's Parkinson's Law: "Work expands so as to fill the time available for its completion."

This time management method also keeps your procrastination and stress level manageable. The necessity for time management applies equally to your personal and work life.

EXERCISE

Procrastination

To ward off the problems of procrastination you need to:

- Assemble a list of your tasks and prioritize them. Apply the procrastination questions is the last assignment

- Those tasks you do not delegate or eliminate you need to break down into smaller bite-sized pieces. By seeing the task, its pieces, and even diagrams of it, you'll clarify your thinking

- Set up a schedule for working on the pieces of the tasks

- Eliminate distractions in your work area. Have materials organized and the area uncluttered. Keep temptations to waste time to a minimum. Don't have books, magazines, newspapers, television, radio, iPod, cell, or CD player around. Do whatever is necessary to increase your concentration. Use earphones or earplugs to cut down extraneous noise if you need to.

Note: Some people believe they can concentrate better when they're listening to music. However, in reality, your attention will alternate between the sound and the task to be done. Therefore, it may take you twice as long to complete the task because you are, in essence, trying to do two things at once.

- Assemble the tools you need ahead of time. Whatever they are, have them ready first thing in the morning

- Eliminate looking for things. It's easy to waste an entire day looking for misplaced items. Label files and sections of notebooks by topics. Keep and use a 3" X 5" card system to act as a reminder of item replacement. Also keep a Rolodex or computer list of telephone numbers, filed alphabetically, available

- Discourage interruptions. Let people know you're working and don't want to be disturbed. Have others screen your calls for you. Find an inaccessible place in which to work. When people want you to chat or do things with or for them, be firm. You have to assertively say, "No." You also have to cut down on idle phone conversations, text messaging, cyber-surfing, watching YouTube, or reading e-mail (set your e-mail lists to Digest and general e-mail receipt to once a day).

The more you follow the above-listed time-management suggestions, the more disciplined you'll become. The more disciplined you become, the more you'll accomplish. The more you accomplish, the more confidence you'll gain and the more successful you'll be and feel.

HOW IS SELF-ESTEEM IMPORTANT?

How you perceive the world and how you are perceived is, in large part, the result of your self-esteem. Self-esteem differs significantly from your self-concept that involves your beliefs and thoughts about yourself. Self-esteem is your attitude about those thoughts and beliefs. It's your evaluation of feelings about your self-worth and yourself.

It's thought to be global in scope, representing your self-evaluation across a wide range of different situations. It's based on not only how you compare yourself to others but also whether or not you believe you meet your own level of aspirations. Derived from perceptions about personal characteristics like IQ and integrity, it tends to be stable over time.

Self-esteem initially comes from:

- What parental figures accepted and respected
- What limits they defined and enforced.

With high self-esteem you have the conviction that you're worthy of what you want and that your methods are right and appropriate. You're likely to feel good about yourself, IF

1. Your successes match your aspirations and goals
2. They equal those of individuals you use as yardsticks

3. Others speak well of you.

Your self-esteem depends on how you evaluate success and failure. You become the label of your actions. If you label failure as "bad" and success as "good," you'll see not achieving your goal as "bad" and yourself as a failure. This type of thinking has a strong impact on your behavior. It limits what you're willing to try and to what degree you'll be open to growth.

Your self-esteem also comes from how you were given praise as children. Psychologists Carol Dweck and Claudia Mueller have found that children praised for their effort (what they do) tend to maintain their self-confidence more than children praised only for a trait, like their intelligence (what they are). This may be because they don't see success as being under their active control.

Thus, your self-esteem may be related to your perceived *self-efficacy* (self-confidence). As mentioned earlier, if you believe you can *cope with a threat*, *control your reactions to it*, and *accomplish your tasks*, you're more likely to feel more successful and confident. This sense of worth may relate only to the situation at hand or generalize to others.

Self-esteem is your acknowledgment that no matter what you do, whether or not you're successful, you personally still have intrinsic value as a human being. In other words, it's self-love: unconditional positive acceptance. Only when you feel this way about yourself can you share with others all your good qualities.

What Is "Low Self-Esteem"? Low self-esteem means that you tend to magnify your trivial mistakes and imperfections. You make these things symbols of your feelings of inadequacy or worthlessness. You see your self-image as depending upon the approval of others. You have feelings of self-doubt, insecurity, anxiety, and a sense of being unfit. As Groucho Marx wrote, "Please accept my resignation. I don't care to belong to any club that would have me as a member."

While high self-esteem makes you feel effective, productive, capable, successful, and lovable, low self-esteem makes you feel ineffective, worthless, incompetent, and unlovable. Low self-esteem leads to lack of confidence. You feel doomed to failure and, thus, make little effort toward realizing your goals. Low self-esteem leads you down the road to poor performance and a distorted view of both yourself and others.

You don't give yourself credit for the good you accomplish. You see others as doing things better than you do. You see yourself at the mercy of "fate," not responsible for your behavior and its consequences. Low self-esteem makes you anxious and unwilling to risk developing close relationships. Consequently, you are likely to be lonely and unhappy.

Your feelings of inferiority are from low self-esteem. They are never based upon reality, but instead are grounded in your negative, self-critical, distorted, and illogical thoughts that make up your self-concept. To reverse this you need to look at those maladaptive thoughts, identify the distortion behind them, and dispute them.

JOANNA'S SELF-ESTEEM EXERCISE

Joanna has battled feelings of inferiority since childhood. Having her value dependent upon her living up to her parents' high standards of the right grades and the right appearance had convinced her that she was a second-rate human being … totally inadequate. Nothing she did was ever quite right and she savagely criticized herself for it.

She wondered why she had ever tried as an adult to go back to school and make friends. Sad, discouraged, and frustrated, she was a mental bird of prey, swooping down on herself, picking her esteem's bones clean of flesh.

To deal with these feelings Joanna talked back to her inner critic. She labeled her inner critic as a Vulture and took on the role of her own Coach. Her Coach analyzed and disputed what the Vulture said. She did this every time her inner critic criticized her, when the Vulture expressed negative, distorted thoughts.

She continued this interchange until her Coach prevailed. She then labeled each cognitive distortion and recorded her Coaching techniques in her journal.

Joanna's Vulture: "I can't accomplish anything because I just don't have what it takes." (Over-generalization)

Joanna's Coach: "That's ridiculous. I do lots of things right, such as …)"

Joanna's Vulture: "My parents, teachers, and classmates will see me as a loser." (Over-generalization; Mind reading; All-or-nothing thinking)

Joanna's Coach: "My parents will think I'm a loser no matter what I do. My teachers may be disappointed if I don't do what they expect, but that's not the end of the world. And my classmates won't really care."

Joanna's Vulture: "I'm stupid." (Labeling)

Joanna's Coach: "I am not stupid. I may do 'stupid' things once in a while but this doesn't make me stupid. Everyone does stupid stuff. It's only human."

~ASSIGNMENT~

Do this exercise daily and record what your Vulture says to you and how your Coach counters and disputes it. Record your results in your Recovery Journal. Then, using the list of Cognitive Errors below (from Chapter 7), go back and label each distortion the Vulture utters:

- Arbitrary Inference
- Over-Generalization
- Magnification and Minimization
- Personalization
- All-Or-Nothing Thinking
- Mental Filter
- Disqualifying the Positive
- Jumping to Conclusions (Mind Reading; Fortune Telling Error)
- Emotional Reasoning
- Should Statements
- Labeling
- Rationalization (Sour Grapes; Sweet Lemon)

EXERCISE

Self-Esteem Evaluation

How do you feel about yourself? Do any of the following statements describe you? If they are true of you, put **T** in the blank next to the item. If the statement is false about you, put **F** in the blank.

___I often feel inadequate

___Usually I don't let things bother me

___I like to present my ideas to the group

___It's not easy to be me

___I frequently wish I were someone else

___Often, when I have something to say I don't say it

___My family understands me

___I give in very easily

___There are lots of things I'd change about myself

___I make up my mind without much trouble

___My family expects too much of me

___It takes me a long time to get used to new things

___I often feel upset about the work I do

___My family is pretty considerate of my feelings

___I'm not as well liked as most others

___Generally, I can't be depended upon

___Often I feel like running away from home

___My life is all mixed up

___Others often follow my ideas.

Scoring: Count the numbers of **T**s and **F**s. **10–13 F**s = high self-esteem. **10–13 T**s = low self-esteem.

HOW TO RAISE YOUR SELF-ESTEEM

There are six primary ways by which you can raise your self-esteem.

Make Positive Statements About Yourself. Compose a list of I-statements which reflect how you'd like to describe yourself, such as "I'm confident talking to people I know" or "I do my work well." Ground all these statements in experiences where you felt successful and good about yourself. Read this list aloud to yourself often. Add new ones.

Stop Making Negative Statements About Yourself. When you hear yourself saying something negative about yourself, say, "Stop!" Reverse the statement from "I am a failure" to "I can be a success in (name a specific area)." Say the new statement aloud.

Punish Negative Statements. To reinforce your rejection of negative statements, have a list of boring tasks to perform as punishment when you talk about yourself negatively.

Practice Imaging. Design a mental picture of yourself in an actual, positive situation. Run this mental "film" in times of stress and whenever you relax.

Reassess Your Role Models. Are your role models realistic and appropriate? Do you really want to be *People* Magazine's "Sexiest Person of the Year," or the wealthiest computer entrepreneur or most popular TV host? Or, do you want to be attractive, assertive, confident, or competent like these people? Unrealistic or inappropriate role models are not likely to help you succeed or feel good about yourself.

Check Your Expectations. Is your behavior based on your own sense of competence and worth or on your perception of other people's expectations of you? Remember that *only* your own expectations, when grounded in self-love and self-acceptance, can be met.

~ASSIGNMENT~

Create an index card, one for each of the five ways listed above to raise your self-esteem. Carry these cards with you and read them three times a day.

Also make a checklist for yourself of the five ways. On the left vertical edge list the five ways. On the top horizontal edge, list the days of the week, starting with Sunday. Each evening as you read your index cards for the third time, mark your checklist with what you accomplished from that list during the day.

SELF-EFFICACY EVALUATION

Your beliefs concerning your ability to accomplish tasks and achieve goals (your efficacy) affect how you think about difficult situations with which you have to cope. For example,

- Do you feel you can manage to solve your problems if you try hard enough?

- If you're opposed, do you find ways to get what you want?

- When confronted with a difficult problem, can you usually find several solutions?

- Do you feel resourceful enough to handle unforeseen situations?

To keep building on your Recovery you need to assess your beliefs in your abilities to meet challenges and overcome them. How confident are you that you can manage or cope? Choose **A** or **B** in each of the following situations:

1. Your sister has asked you to be part of her wedding party, to be part of the ceremony and on the reception line. Do you

    A. Look forward to making it a positive and memorable day

    B. Start to worry about how you'll appear and what you'll do wrong and have second thoughts

2. Your manager has out-of-town clients coming that she can't pick up at the airport because of a last-minute department meeting so she asks you to collect them, generally acquaint them with your company, and make them comfortable. Do you

    B. See it as a way to make yourself visible in the organization

    C. Know you don't have what it takes to pull it off and will humiliate yourself in the process and look for ways to get out of it

3. The windshield wipers on your new car don't work. Do you

    C. Go back to the local dealership, explain the problem, and ask them to fix it under the warranty

    D. Become angry but hope the malfunction will correct itself so you don't have to deal with the service people

4. You've done a lengthy written report on an historical figure. Your instructor asks you to give a 5-minute presentation to the class on the most significant thing you learned from your research. Do you

    D. Easily prepare the talk

    E. See yourself standing in a pool of sweat, trembling, feeling like a little kid in a dunce cap

If you chose **A** 3 out of 4 times, you have strong sense of self-efficacy. You envision success scenarios, expect favorable outcomes, and adopt a problem-solving approach to the difficulties you encounter.

If you chose **B** 3 out of 4 times, you are riddled with doubt and tend to concentrate on your personal deficiencies. You see failure scenarios and expect unfavorable outcomes. You let this calamitous thinking undermine effective use of your capabilities.

RAISING SELF-EFFICACY

To raise self-efficacy you need to learn how to access and interpret information and improve your coping skills. *Performance accomplishment* is the single most powerful way to raise your self-efficacy.

"Guided Mastery Therapy," developed by S. Lloyd Williams, is a form of therapeutic performance accomplishment. It has been shown to significantly increase self-efficacy. Through Guided Mastery you can:

- See the skills broken down into components and modeled appropriately
- Learn the rules and strategies for applying these skills in different situations
- Put yourself in a simulated situation you need to manage
- Break the situation into achievable tasks
- Test your capability to consecutively handle each task
- Receive suggestions, encouragement, and reinforcement as you work
- Eliminate safety-, defensive-, and self-restrictive behaviors
- Receive help applying the newly learned skills in a real situation
- Increase independence, feel confident, and fade out use of the assistant.

While this is very similar to CBT and Social Effectiveness Therapy, it differs in that the tasks are not social anxiety related. They can be any kind of task. The object is to create success on each task component that builds general and specific confidence. Furthermore, there is active modeling of the techniques by an assistant and observational learning by the student. This model can be used concurrently with CBT and Social Effectiveness Therapy to develop self-confidence and self-efficacy even faster.

EXERCISE

Creating a Self-Efficacy Plan

- Pick a task that needs to be done or a problem to be solved (e.g., go to Social Security to receive disability payments)
- Set objectives and goals for it (e.g., goal is to get payments)
- Determine the steps involved (e.g., phoning for information; setting up the appointment; collecting information for application; going for the interview; following through on the process; and appealing the initial negative decision)
- Make up a list of rewards for accomplishing each task segment and punishments for not accomplishing the task segment
- Write a behavioral contract with yourself that you'll reward yourself for accomplishing each step of the task or punish yourself when you don't (e.g., "I will apply for SSDI. For each step I'll reward my success or punish my failure")
- Act on the plan
- Monitor your progress and record it in your journal
- Administer your rewards and punishments
- Demonstrate how you could apply this process to two other problems and do it.

~ASSIGNMENT~

Implement the Self-Efficacy Plan for another task. Pick one specific task that is either very simple or can be broken into several small and easily accomplished tasks. Create your plan for it, act on it, and follow it through to completion. Record your results in your journal.

REDUCING DISAPPOINTMENT

Disappointment is a large component of SA/SP. It can interfere with your developing social effectiveness. It is built on unrealistic expectations. To reduce disappointment you need to reduce these unrealistic expectations by becoming aware of each of your expectations and systematically dealing with it. Clinical psychologist David Brandt suggests that you:

- **Acknowledge your disappointment** ("I'm not dating")

- **Feel and express your emotions** ("I feel sad and frustrated about not dating")

- **Become aware of and recognize your unrealistic expectations** ("I should be dating")

- **Attain attitude flexibility**: Separate the wish from the anticipation of its coming true (the wish is "dating"; anticipation is "doing it now")

- **Eliminate**: Expunge rigid, unconditional expectations using "never," "every," and "always" ("I'll never date")

- **Gain perspective**: Focus on the implications of the expectation ("If I don't do it now, I'll be devastated" versus "If I don't do it now, it'll be uncomfortable but okay")

- **Reduce attachment**: Reduce ego identification with the expectation ("I'm okay as a person even if I'm not dating right now")

- **Redefine expectations**: Do a realistic assessment of your capabilities, possibilities, probabilities, and past disappointments to diminish the wish component ("I'll be dating in the future when I'm ready")

- **Prepare for change**: Be willing to give up what you want when you can't have it ("I'd like to date but won't hold it as a realistic goal now")

- **Motivate yourself to change**: ("I want to date and will work toward doing it")

- **Decide to change**: ("I'm going to meet people")

- **Act toward change**: ("I'm working to find people of similar interests")

- **Hope**: Expect some disappointments but maintain a positive belief about the future

- **Accept**: Reach acceptance of the disappointment and move on.

EXERCISE

Disappointment

Have a pencil and journal handy. Get comfortable then start your Progressive Relaxation. When you feel more relaxed,

- Think of a significant disappointment in your life
- Visualize the situation in all its sensory detail and experience the disappointment
- Open your eyes and write down the expectation you had that was behind the disappointment
- Break the expectation down into the "wish"(what you really wanted to happen) and the "anticipation" (what you thought might happen) of it
- Write down the ways in which your expectation wasn't met
- Assess the reality of your expectation
- Write down some of the reasons your expectation wasn't met
- Reduce your emotional attachment to the expectation and express the reality
- Assess what would likely happen next time if you continued to keep these same expectations
- Redefine this expectation for yourself in realistic terms or eliminate it

Record your responses in your journal and repeat the exercise once a week.

RECOGNIZING YOUR ANGER

Even though your anger is a very natural response to things you see as annoying, frustrating, unjust, or threatening, it can still significantly interfere with your social effectiveness. While it mobilizes your body's resources and defenses, it also distorts your thoughts and actions. Expressing tension, it often leads to aggression. As it produces feelings of control, it also causes you to defend yourself when it's unnecessary. Hurting others is a frequent result.

Venting anger must not be done in an uncontrolled fashion, such as shouting, hitting, or breaking something. Instead, it must be done within the context of anger resolution. Only in this way will it be effective and useful ... and not reinforcing of negative, nonproductive behavior

EXERCISE

Anger Assessment

In order to see if you need to address your anger as part of your recovery, you have to assess it first. Complete the following inventory, putting a **T** for *generally true* or **F** for *generally false* in the space provided.

____My relationships with others are sometimes stormy or unstable

____I seem to have an unusual amount of unnecessary guilt

____I don't like to admit to myself that I'm angry

____I sometimes use humor to avoid facing my feelings

____I tend to be hypercritical about others and myself

____I sometimes use sarcasm as a form of humor

____I feel I'd like to get back at those who've wronged me

____When I feel angry, I find myself doing things I know are wrong

____I usually don't tell others when I'm hurt

____I have lots of physical aches and pains, like tight chest, headache, stiff neck and/or shoulders, or stomachache

____Criticism bothers me a great deal

____I sometimes do things to appear superior to others

____I often feel inferior to others

____I'd like to tell people exactly what I think

____I feel unloved and unappreciated

____I feel disillusioned with love

____Sometimes I have difficulty controlling my weight, either losing or gaining

____At times I feel life owes me more than it has given me

____I feel that many of my problems can be blamed on others

____Many of the nice things I do are out of a sense of obligation

____Many mornings I awaken not feeling refreshed

____When something irritates me, I find it hard to calm down

____When others are being unreasonable, I usually take a strong dislike to them

____I've experienced spouse- or child abuse

____I'm bothered when things are not done in a predictable way

____I consider myself possessive in my personal relationships

____People who know me would say that I'm stubborn

____Sometimes I could be described as moody

____I argue or disagree a lot, mostly with family members

____I've experienced poor interpersonal relationships

____I can't let go of the past

____I'm constantly unhappy

____What I do is often self-defeating

____I have difficulty resolving conflicts

____I have difficulty avoiding fights

____I'm frequently angry with myself

____I'm constantly disappointed

____I feel depressed, helpless, and frustrated

____I resent some people for who they are, what they have, or what they do

____I can't seem to solve my problems.

Scoring: Count the number of **T**s. This will indicate how important it is for you to confront your anger. If you scored **less than 10**, you control your anger well (or, may be unable to admit your anger).

If you scored **11–20**, you are within normal range, but need to be aware of your anger. Learning how to address it would be useful for you.

If you scored **21–30**, you probably have had a lot of problems with which to deal. Life may not be as satisfying as you would like. You would benefit from addressing your anger.

If you scored **31–40**, your anger controls your life, prevents you from being fully functional and achieving a satisfying existence. Your recovery from SA/SP requires you learn how to deal successfully with your anger.

CONTROLLING ANGER

Controlling anger requires that you first measure it. You need to know how frequently you get angry, how you demonstrate your anger behaviors, and how long each behavioral incident lasts. You can do this measurement by:

- Keeping track on a pad you carry around for that purpose
- Transferring coins or paper clips from one pocket to another
- Using a golf counter to click-count the incidents as they occur.

Graphing. Graphing these data will clarify what's happening. At the end of the first week you should connect the dots from each day's count to form a line. If you've have been conscientious in your spotting and recording anger data, you'd expect to see the line start to slope down toward the end of the week. This shows a progressive reduction in your automatic anger behavior as a result of your awareness of it. This is an accomplishment that you likewise need to acknowledge and reward.

Visualizing. Visualizing your progress as you continue to work on the count is important. You need to see yourself as feeling more positive and in more control over these thoughts and emotions.

Validating. Validating your data is also useful. You'll know whether or not you've picked up most of it. Having a close, trusted friend do spot-checks at some designated period of time each day can provide you with invaluable information. At the end of each day the two of you would compare counts and data.

Anger therapist Hendrie Weisinger categorizes anger as *just* or *unjust*, *adaptive* or *needless*, depending upon the situation. When someone steals from you, that is *just* anger. But when someone picks up an item you were thinking about purchasing, that's *unjust* anger. When a stranger speaks harshly to you and you feel threatened, that's *adaptive* anger. But when you repeatedly replay perceived mistakes in your mind, making you angry, that's *needless* anger.

It's *unjust* and *needless* anger that create a problem for you when they:

- Occur often
- Last too long
- Are intense
- Lead to aggression

- Disturb relationships and work.

When anger escalates and gets too hot to handle, you have great difficulty thinking and acting effectively. You become a prisoner of your own self-perpetuating negative arousal. At times like these you need to isolate yourself from the anger and the arousing situation. You need to step back and do an objective appraisal. Appraisal is more positive and effective than anger suppression.

Weisinger suggests saying, "I'm beginning to feel angry and I want to take a time-out." The form of this declaration is important. First, it's expressed in *I-message* that place no blame. Second, the word *want* suggests choice and control whereas the word *need* would suggest compulsion instead.

Time-Out. In a Time Out you (1) make the declaration, (2) leave the situation, and (3) cool down. Cooling down can be via exercise or other constructively physical activity, relaxation, visualization, self-talk, listening to music, driving, etc. You need to safely discharge the tension so you can think about the situation. If at any point you again begin to feel anger, you need to repeat the declaration, "I'm beginning to feel angry and I want to take a time-out."

When you return to the situation, you have several options available to you. If there's another involved, you can discuss your feelings at that time. If, however, it's not convenient or the other wishes to postpone it, you two can contract to discuss it at a specific time and place later. Whenever you discuss your feelings, you need to communicate them in I-terms (as described in Assertive Exercises).

Automatic Thoughts. Sometimes negative or distorted self-statements generate anger. Typical among them are *over-generalization, mind reading, magnification,* and *shoulds.* (See Cognitive Errors in Chapter 7.) Acknowledging, labeling, and disputing these cognitive errors reduces their incidence.

The same is true for those other factors which provoke your anger. It's important to pinpoint the specific causes. Generally, provocation can be categorized as the result of:

- Frustration
- Irritation or annoyance
- Abuse

- Injustice or unfairness.

Once you've determined what has provoked your unjust-needless anger, you can use cognitive restructuring or reframing. You can have your Coach dispute your Vulture's emotional and irrational accusations and criticisms. Your employing abdominal breathing simultaneously likewise works.

SAYING "GOOD-BYE" TO ANGER

In situations where you expect anger may develop, you may want to consider cutting short your exposure to the situation. While this is an "avoidant strategy," it isn't avoidance in the sense that SA/SPers use it. This doesn't mean not attending the situation or escaping as soon as possible.

This means that if it realistically appears that extending the exposure will create anger arousal, you need to find a way to remove yourself *before* it happens. By shortening the exposure to provocation, you decrease the chance of your being contaminated by the anger.

EMBACING ANGER GUIDELINES

(Adapted from *If You're So Smart, Why Aren't You Happy?* by Mitchell Messer and Linda Dillon)

- Don't minimize anger by using euphemisms (such as, upset, bothered, ticked off)
- Don't invalidate others' anger by saying, "Don't be so sensitive." "You're always angry"
- Recognize and validate others' anger. Let them know you understand how they might feel and that it's okay to feel that way
- Understand your own feelings before trying to explain and analyze how others feel
- Don't take others' anger personally. It's unpleasant but not a reflection of your worth
- In explosive situations it's best not to argue but to empathize
- Catch yourself as you start getting angry and choose to express yourself appropriately
- Vent your anger in a letter but **don't** mail it until you've cooled off. Then read it again, considering whether it's wise or appropriate to

send it

- Catch yourself when you're afraid of expressing your anger out of concern of offending another
- Question who's the proper target of your anger: Another person, a situation, or yourself
- Prevent your anger from accumulating, building, becoming more toxic, and exploding
- Ask what difference it really makes. If it doesn't make a difference in the real world, let it go.

FORGIVING PARENTS AND MOVING ON

You must let go of your anger about perceived parental mistakes or it'll eat you alive. Whether they abused you or just seemed too critical, overly protective, or insensitive, they acted as they did because who they were dictated their behavior. They too were/are the sum of all their experiences, expectations, needs, wants, beliefs, dreams, attitudes, failures, and successes.

Most of the time they were unaware of their effect on you, as you were of yours on them. But your anger wasn't and isn't the result of their actions alone. You had to interpret their actions and your anger and give the anger meaning in your life. You also had to choose to keep it going after the initiating behaviors have long since passed away.

Let me share with you an example. Because we moved every year or so, I was rarely in one place long enough to become part of any well-established groups. In addition, I was slightly more mature from continual traveling and, therefore, "different." Consequently, I made only one or two friends on each move.

In high school having only one or two friends distressed me greatly, adding further to my loneliness. Still trying to curry favor with my father, I sought his advice. Why, I asked, didn't I have any friends? Rather than suggest that I'd had few opportunities because of his work (something over which he, no doubt, felt guilty), he launched into a catalogue of what he considered to be "my faults."

When he finished to the sounds of my inconsolable sobbing, he threw in a few suggestions by which I might rescue myself by trying to get people to like me. At that moment, and for many years thereafter, I wondered why I should even bother trying if I were such an unpleasant mess. I blamed him for my feeling worthless and harbored great anger at his non-support of me when I needed compassion and support most.

Blame and recriminations won't change the "past" (nothing can), but they will impact your present and future. They're continuing to weigh you down, like concrete blocks tied to your feet. You need to say the blaming is over. You need to forgive them, their humanness, and their all-too-human inadequacies. Then you need to assertively create what you want for yourself *now*.

I finally forgave my father, but only after he died suddenly at age 52. Objectively, I could see he had let his father ruin his life by caving in to all his unreasonable demands. I could see him become more depressed, sabotaging himself at every turn. I just happened to be in the wrong place at the wrong time, expecting him to be something other than what he was.

SUMMARY

The more aware you are of what your emotions, thoughts, and behaviors are and how they impact others and sabotage you, the more personally effective you can become. First you need to raise your self-esteem by experiencing present and past successes. Then when you feel better about yourself and are more confident, you will be better able to control your anger and become more assertive. This, in turn, will further increase your confidence, self-respect, and feeling of control over your life and destiny.

"Do not be too timid and squeamish about your actions. All life is an experiment. The more experiments you make the better." (Ralph Waldo Emerson)

10

NAVIGATING THE MEDICATION MAZE

*"You see things and say, 'Why?' But I dream things
that never were, and I say 'Why not?'"*
(George Bernard Shaw, *Back to Methuselah*)

EYE OF NEWT AND TOE OF FROG?

Sometimes SA/SPers feel that *treatment* for SA/SP is really a matter of witchcraft, wishful thinking, or buying a lottery ticket. Unfortunately, that may not be far from the truth.

First, primary care physicians are the first line of defense for mental health. Surveys have shown that general practitioners prescribe about 80% of all SSRIs (selective serotonin reuptake inhibitors). But those practitioners tend to either under-treat or not recognize SA/SP.

Second, when they do recognize and treat it, their first treatment choice is almost always psychotropic drugs, especially the most heavily advertised ones. American Psychiatric Association's R. Bruce Lydiard, M.D., has stated that even if there is merely a "whiff" of depression in patients with anxiety disorders, antidepressants are probably indicated. As the APA has noted, psychiatrists are doing less psychotherapy and are relying more and more upon medications.

Third, as for-profit managed care prevails the mental health area, it's reducing the number of mental health visits you can have. So even if the physician thinks psychotherapy should be an option, it may not be available or be very limited and/or costly.

As a result, health professionals tend to give out antidepressants freely and, perhaps, somewhat indiscriminately. But frequently there is difficulty matching these drugs to your individual needs and responses. As a result, there is a likelihood that you may shuttle from one drug to another to combinations of them. You may obtain less than optimum relief while you and your doctor are figuring this out.

Unfortunately when these medications do succeed in taking the edge off your anxiety, they sometimes take the edge off your motivation to deal with the underlying problem. This means you may have dealt temporarily with the symptoms but still have not addressed the core SA/SP maladaptive thoughts and avoidance behaviors.

SARAH. When Sarah went to her regular doctor for her fear of answering the phone and meeting people, the physician gave her a prescription for Inderal, a beta-blocker, which slowed her heart. But it did nothing for her fear and avoidance. Then he gave her an SSRI that made her feel jumpy and de-sexed. Several medications later, she was still looking for relief, wondering if he had any idea what SA/SP really was and if she should start prescribing natural supplements, like St. John's Wort, for herself.

From the perspective of many concerned mental health professionals, it would be better for you if psychopharmacological treatment were used *primarily* when the intensity and severity of the disorder were such that you couldn't perform most of your everyday activities and doing even the most basic life tasks would be a struggle.

This is because it's at this time that you find it more difficult to concentrate on psychotherapy due to your level of anxiety. This may be particularly important where disorder onset is early, the disorder is chronic, impairment is extensive, and there exists co-morbidity with other disorders. It's at this point that medication *may* be more appropriate for getting you on an even keel so you can work to reduce your

- Anticipatory anxiety and fear of social situations
- Physiological symptoms (trembling, palpitations, e.g.)
- Avoidance in social situations
- Co-morbid conditions (depression, alcoholism, e.g.)
- Overall social-anxiety-induced impairment.

In other words, allowing you to be back in control, these drugs may help you short-term to get through your days so you can focus on your necessary long-term coping strategies. While drug therapy may work more rapidly and have more immediately potent effects than CBT, the gains made through CBT tend to be more durable because they address the underlying causes and provide you with life strategies.

Note: Like many other anxiety disorders, SA/SP has been found to be responsive to a number of psychotropic medications. But not everyone responds to any or all of these medications in the same way. What is effective for you may not be for others ... and vice versa.

Some of you may experience few side effects, while others may struggle with severe, and occasionally life-threatening, side effects. Some may find one drug works well while others may find that nothing works at all, or a combination of drugs is best. It's important to remember that drugs are a *treatment* for SA/SP, **not** a *cure*. The goal of this treatment is meaningful improvement toward recovery.

Positive response to treatment will be short-term and long-term. Short-term you should experience some symptomatic relief, improved performance and social relations. Long-term, beginning between three and six months, you should experience greater functionality in all areas of your life, especially interpersonal.

No response to an adequate range of dosages of one medication may mean that a change in the class of medication would be helpful, such as from benzodiazepines to SSRIs or MAOIs.

Partially adequate response may suggest change to another drug in the same class may be useful. For example, going from the benzodiazepine lorazepam (Ativan) to the benzodiazepine clonazepam (Klonopin).

Or adding another class of drug to what you are currently taking may be worthwhile to try before making a complete change, like combining an SSRI with a benzodiazepine. Many SA/SPers use a combination of drugs alone, with CBT, or use CBT alone.

How you react to these drugs depends upon a number of criteria. One criterion is correct diagnosis. Because clinicians may misdiagnose your SA/SP as panic attacks, agoraphobia, avoidant personality disorder, generalized anxiety disorder, anxiety accompanying depression, or shyness, you may not be prescribed the medication that's most appropriate for your situation. You need an accurate diagnosis from a professional who is knowledgeable in and experienced with SA/SP.

Then there are individual biochemistries. Each of you responds somewhat differently to drugs. Whether you have discrete or generalized SA/SP also makes a difference. What works for discrete SA/SP (mild performance anxiety) tends not to work for generalized SA/SP (fear of evaluation in social situations, humiliation, and rejection).

Furthermore, when you have other disorders that coexist with the SA/SP (and some 69% of you do), the medication may be working well on SA/SP but seem inadequate because it's not addressing the other conditions. Or, it may be addressing one or more of the other conditions but bypassing your SA/SP altogether.

Fortunately, research data are accumulating as to which drugs are the most effective for it and under what circumstances. However, the data are also demonstrating that medications are not the only answer or necessarily the best answer to treating SA/SP.

CATEGORIES OF MEDICATIONS

Important: The following is for information purposes only and should not be used for prescription purposes.

MAOIs. MAOIs are a type of antidepressant called a monoamine oxidase inhibitors. As you may recall, monoamines are neurotransmitters that carry signals from the central nervous system to the brain. Oxidase is the enzyme that breaks down the neurotransmitter after it has done its job so it can be reabsorbed. The presence of these amines has a calming effect on you.

The hypothesis is that when there's not enough or there's too much present, you may respond by feeling anxious or depressed. One way to keep these amines around longer is to prevent the breakdown and reabsorption. That's what an MAO inhibitor does.

One type of MAOI is irreversible and non-selective. It nonspecifically inhibits both Type A and Type B MAO to block the degradation of norepinephrine, serotonin, and dopamine. Binding irreversibly with the enzyme makes the inhibition more consistent. Phenelzine (Nardil), tranylcypromine (Parnate), and isocarboxazid (Marplan) are the three irreversible MAOIs that are used for SA/SP.

Phenelzine can reduce both social and performance anxiety and improve social and work functioning. Improvement tends to occur as early as the first four weeks of treatment. Studies have found it to be more effective than alprazolam (Xanax), a benzodiazepine, but the same as moclobemide, a reversible MAOI, at eight weeks of treatment.

MAOIs may benefit as many as two-thirds of all individuals who take them. Furthermore, SA/SP tends to respond to phenelzine regardless of the severity of the disorder.

During the first eight weeks of treatment, you may experience side effects. Some of the more common ones, in order of prevalence, are:

- Daytime sleepiness
- Low blood pressure
- Dry mouth
- Constipation
- Reduced libido
- Impaired ejaculation
- Vertigo
- Headache.

Even social anxiety that is secondary to medical problems, such as hyperhydrosis (severe sweating), stuttering, muscle twitching, Bell's palsy, Parkinson's, and Charcot-Marie-Tooth disease, may respond to phenelzine.

Tranylcypromine (Parnate) has similar effectiveness to phenelzine but its side effects, such as sleep disturbances, may be more difficult to tolerate short-term. But long-term, it may be less sedating and not create significant weight gain. In general, phenelzine may be safer, with a lower risk of high blood pressure reactions to tyramine-rich foods, supplements, or medicine. Tranylcypromine also appears to be helpful in situations where phenelzine is poorly tolerated or is unavailable.

Use of Nardil, Parnate, and Marplan may be contraindicated with

- Congestive heart failure
- History of liver disease
- Abnormal liver function
- Pheochromocytoma (tumor of the adrenal gland).

Interactions. These drugs can also create reactions of extremely high blood pressure, stroke, and death when the drugs are combined with numbers of other things: Certain over-the-counter and prescription drugs, such as bupropion and Demerol; foods containing the amino acid tyramine; and alcohol. These reactions can occur both while taking these MAOIs and for two weeks after discontinuing their use. As a result, phenelzine is rarely considered a first-line treatment for SA/SP.

When MAOIs are recommended, it's more likely to be to individuals under the age of 50. Because of their effect on blood pressure, there are specific foods and medications to avoid while taking MAOIs by mouth. (List adapted from *Journal of Clinical Psychiatry* and the *Physicians' Desk Reference.*)

Foods to avoid:

- All cheeses, except for cottage and cream cheese
- Tofu (fermented soybean curd) and soybean paste
- Chianti, vermouth, and beer (including alcohol-free wine, reduced-alcohol beer, tap beer, and wine products). Distilled liquors, such as Scotch, gin, vodka, and rye do not produce hypertensive reaction but increase intoxication
- Whiskey
- Yeast or meat extracts used in soups and stews (brewers yeast, Bovril, Marmite, e.g.)
- Broad beans, fava beans, Chinese pea pods
- Ginseng
- Aged, smoked, or cured meat or fish (including corned beef and dry sausages)
- Sauerkraut
- Pickled fish (herring, lox)
- Protein dietary supplements
- Any other food which has previously produced reactions or unpleasant symptoms
- Any spoiled or improperly refrigerated, -handled, or -stored protein-rich food.

Foods in moderation - to be eaten with caution:

- Avocados
- Bananas and peels
- Caffeinated beverages (coffee, tea, cocoa, colas) and drugs
- Cheeses (cottage, cream, processed, mozzarella)
- Chicken liver (fresh)

- Chocolate
- Herring (fresh)
- Liver (fresh)
- Meat (fresh)
- MSG (monosodium glutamate) meat tenderizer
- Nuts
- Raspberries
- Soy sauce
- Spinach
- Wines (other)
- Yoghurt.

Medications to avoid:

- Cold, hay fever, sinus, and nasal decongestants (pills, drops, or spray), including those with dextromethorphan
- Weight-reduction preparations
- "Pep" pills
- Asthma inhalants
- Other antidepressants, especially SSRIs
- Demerol
- Epinephrine in local anesthesia
- L-tryptophan-containing preparations.

Symptoms of an extreme increase in blood pressure include stiff neck, severe headache, profuse sweating, confusion, palpitations, and nausea.

You should carry this list with you all the time while taking irreversible MAOIs, even for several weeks after discontinuation of the drug. It's safest not to take any other medication without consulting with your physician. You need to report promptly the occurrence of headache or other unusual symptoms to your physician.

Therapy with MAOIs is generally started with a low dose and then adjusted upward or downward over a 2–4-week period according to your response and tolerance to it. To minimize insomnia your dosage may be administered in the morning. Phenelzine therapy usually begins with a dose of 15 mg. and then may be increased to a maximum of 90 mg. when necessary.

The treatment goal is to achieve at least 80% inhibition of the MAO activity. Discontinuation, even after 6–9 months of treatment, may result in substantial loss of gains: at least 50%. Longer drug treatment and the use of CBT may lessen the rate of relapse. When the medication is discontinued, it should be gradually tapered to avoid severe withdrawal symptoms, such as agitation, nightmares, psychosis, and convulsions. Switching to another antidepressant requires a washout period of 14 days.

Reversible MAOIs. Reversible MAOIs actually have little chemical similarity to irreversible MAOIs. Instead, reversibles are selective for the Type A MAO and have effects that can be rapidly reversed. They inhibit the breakdown of serotonin and norepinephrine.

Only one of these is being marketed. It's moclobemide (Aurorix, Manerix). Because it only weakly responds to oral tyramine, dietary restrictions with its use are, for the most part, unnecessary. This gives them a considerable safety advantage. Moreover, the side effects are few, infrequent, and tolerable:

- Insomnia
- Sleepiness
- Dry mouth
- Headache
- Constipation
- Low blood pressure
- Loss of libido.

In studies all these side effects either weakened or disappeared by week 16 of treatment. When treatment is discontinued within four months of starting the drug, there may be relatively high relapse rate. Dosage for moclobemide is on average 200 mg. twice a day. While some studies show moclobemide to be as effective as phenelzine for SA/SP, others show it no better than placebo ("sugar pill"). Reversible MAOIs have shown promise in some studies. At present moclobemide is available for use in most countries but not in the U.S.

The FDA (Food and Drug Administration) has approved an MAOI patch (selegiline) for depression. Wearing the transdermal patch may be like getting the antidepressant intravenously. Testing has shown that those wearing the patch exhibit dramatic improvement in the first week as compared with the 3–6-week response time with oral use. Moreover, food-related side effects don't seem to occur because the drug bypasses the intestine and possible tyramine interaction. Dosage starts at 6 mg. in a 24-hour period This innovation could herald a renewed popularity of MAOIs and increase your willingness and ease in taking them.

Beta-Blockers. Beta-blockers are non-selective beta adrenergic blockers They reduce both the amount of nervous system (electrical) stimulation and adrenaline to the heart and blood vessels caused by anxiety-induced arousal. By interrupting the anxiety-arousal feedback mechanism, they diminish your tendency to have rapid heartbeat and trembling. When your heart is not racing, when you're not sweating or trembling during the actual performance, you tend to feel calmer and more confident.

Used widely for treatment of high blood pressure, angina, and migraine headaches, beta-blockers are often used in treating SA/SP as well at much lower doses. Their primary use is for discrete SA/SP (performance or test anxiety), though occasionally they are employed for generalized SA/SP in combination with other drugs. By themselves, however, beta-blockers are considered to have limited effectiveness in the treatment of generalized SA/SP.

The primary beta-blockers include propranolol (Inderal), atenolol (Tenormin), nadolol (Corgard), alprenolol, oxprenolol, and pindolol (Visken). However, the most widely prescribed are propranolol and atenolol.

Studies have shown that while beta-blockers may be effective at reducing sweating and palpitations, these drugs have been ineffective at reducing anticipatory anxiety, phobic avoidance, blushing, and cognitive symptoms. Intermittent use for specific and circumscribed performance anxiety, especially for tremor, has been found to be beneficial for some individuals, but mostly non-SA/SPers. Long-term use may possibly benefit others.

Propranolol is often prescribed in a dosage of 10–20 mg. to be taken 45–60 minutes before a performance or test. The effects last approximately four hours. Most healthy individuals tolerate propranolol well although those with a resting heart rate below 60 beats/minute are generally discouraged from taking it. After a test dose, the initial dose usually starts at 10 mg., or lower, and builds to 20 mg., if necessary.

Use of beta-blockers may be contraindicated with

- Asthma and other bronchospastic diseases
- Diabetes
- Hypoglycemia
- Impaired liver function
- Hyperthyroidism
- Wolff-Parkinson-White Syndrome.

Note: There may be beta-blocker drug interactions with Reserpine, calcium-channel blockers, and haloperidol, for example.

Benzodiazepines. Benzodiazepines act as a central nervous system depressant. The exact mechanism of their action is unknown, although it appears that benzodiazepines increase the activity of the neurotransmitter gamma-aminobutyric acid (GABA), that inhibits the activity of the brain's limbic system. Of those studied, the shorter-acting alprazolam (Xanax) and lorazepam (Ativan), and the longer-acting chlordiazepoxide HCl (Librium) and clonazepam (Klonopin), only the clonazepam was found to be useful in SA/SP.

While benzodiazepines, in general, tend to have little, if any, effect on anticipatory anxiety or avoidant behavior, clonazepam is very effective for them. They're considered medically safe because they don't harm organ systems and can't be used for suicide. However, some can produce physiological dependence and withdrawal symptoms.

There are two specific drug characteristics that predict likelihood of physiological dependence and severe withdrawal problems. One is the speed with which the drug enters the blood stream. The other is the speed with which it washes out of the blood stream. Alprazolam (Xanax), for example, may cause more withdrawal problems because it is "fast-in" and "fast-out." Clonazepam (Klonopin), however, is slower to act and to wash out, thus creating fewer withdrawal symptoms for you.

Withdrawal symptoms often occur late, according to SA/SP researcher Suzanne Sutherland, M.D. As a result, they don't always seem to be directly connected with medication discontinuation.

Shorter-acting benzodiazepines, like alprazolam, also have problems with rebound anxiety as the dose wears off. With this comes anxious anticipation of the availability of the next dose, severe withdrawal symptoms, possible reactivity with alcohol use, and high relapse rate after the drug is discontinued. The longer-acting clonazepam, when it is dosed appropriately and taken regularly, has none of these problems.

Clonazepam has shown the best effectiveness in all controlled trials for SA/SP. However, there is a high incidence of what are mostly short-term negative side effects:

- Sleepiness
- Loss of libido
- Memory problems
- Irritability
- Lack of coordination
- Weakness
- Light-headedness
- Insomnia
- Weight gain
- Blurred vision.

Clonazepam usually begins at 0.25 mg. three times a day to keep drowsiness under control, for a daily total in adults not to exceed 1.5 mg. Typical dosage may be increased to 2–4 mg. per day total. Unlike alprazolam, clonazepam can depress mood in approximately 3% of patients. However, the withdrawal symptoms experienced during tapering and withdrawal are less uncomfortable. There are limited data on the use of benzodiazepines.

Benzodiazepines need to be evaluated over a longer period of maintenance therapy than MAOIs. For either drug several weeks are needed to withdraw. This is especially true if the dosage has been substantial. The last 1 mg. has frequently been found to be particularly difficult from which to disengage.

Benzodiazepines are contraindicated where there's evidence of liver disease. Alcohol, MAOIs, tricyclic antidepressants, and other drugs may synergistically increase their action, making your dosage too high.

SSRIs. SSRIs are selective serotonin reuptake inhibitors (SSRIs) that act as antidepressants by blocking the reabsorption of serotonin. This makes it available longer. The primary SSRIs are fluoxetine (Prozac), paroxetine (Paxil, Seroxat), sertraline (Zoloft), venlafaxine (Effexor), fluvoxamine (Luvox), citalopram (Celexa, Cipramil), escitalopram (Lexapro), and nefazodine (Serzone). Although they are not as effective as phenelzine, these are considered an acceptable alternative to MAOIs because of their favorable safety and side-effects profile.

In one study of fluoxetine, 58–71% of SA/SPers showed marked or moderate improvements. Fluvoxamine has been shown to reduce SA/SP symptoms up to 50% with benefits reported as early as three weeks. Use of paroxetine for generalized SA/SP has been found to be effective for 55% of those taking the drug at 20 mg./day.

These short-term results have been considered substantial, producing clinically meaningful reductions in symptoms and disability. Because of its extensive SA/SP treatment database and FDA approval for SA/SP, paroxetine is considered a first-line treatment for it. However, there has been concern about possible negative effects for adolescents and children The FDA has also approved sertraline and venlafaxine for SA/SP.

Citalopram, likewise, has been approved by the FDA for use as an antidepressant. It has been prescribed in Europe since 1989 and has been used by 8 million people worldwide. Studies have shown its usefulness in panic disorder as well. While it shares some of the side effects of other SSRIs, citalopram has several advantages over them. Escitalopram, a variation of citalopram, has even fewer side effects and is longer lasting.

While SSRIs, in general, may interact with other drugs, such as MAOIs, tricyclics, lithium, barbiturates, and theophylline, citalopram interacts only with MAOIs. With a chemical structure unrelated to other SSRIs, it selectively results in fewer sexual side effects, such as decreased libido and ejaculation.

There are two benefits of SSRIs in general. One is that they are considered "clean" drugs, working primarily on serotonin and not on several other neurotransmitters that may be unrelated to SA/SP. The other is that SSRIs tend not to leave you feeling drugged, although some who take them may feel sedated or lethargic.

The usual dose for fluoxetine and citalopram, for example, is 20 mg. per day, requiring a 2–3-month trial period. The dose for sertraline and fluvoxamine is generally 70–150 mg./day. SSRIs take 2–4 weeks to take effect, with the mean peak response time around seven weeks. If the drug is working, duration on it is generally six months or longer.

Common initial side effects include:

- Insomnia (trouble falling asleep or frequent awakening during the night, though daytime sedation and insomnia may continue)
- Nausea
- Diarrhea
- Stomachache
- Headache
- Weight gain
- Reduced libido and delayed orgasm
- Anxiety.

Use of SSRIs may be contraindicated with

- MAOIs
- Elevated liver function tests
- Severe insomnia not resulting from depression.

SSRIs should not be combined with any other drugs that increase brainstem serotonin activity or with grapefruit, which does the same thing. Significantly increased serotonin levels can produce *Serotonin Syndrome*, which is a potentially life-threatening complication of drug therapy. It's often not easily recognized because it has varied and non-specific symptoms. They include rapid heart, hyperactivity, high blood pressure, high fever, and severe seizures.

If there's to be medication change from an MAOI to an SSRI, the general recommendation is that at least 14 days should elapse between the discontinuation of the MAOI and the initiation of the treatment with the SSRI. If the switch is from the SSRI to MAOI, the recommended washout period is five weeks for fluoxetine, and two weeks for the others.

Abrupt discontinuation of some SSRIs may result in withdrawal symptom. These include tremor, dizziness, nightmares, muscle aches, crying spells, disorientation, poor coordination, and nausea. It is *essential* that discontinuation be in a tapered fashion, reducing the dosage slowly over time. Tapering requires at least 7–10 days but often requires several weeks.

Interactions. As noted earlier, interactions may occur between SSRIs and other drugs wherein the intensity of the other drug is increased by the SSRI. Listed are just a few of these drugs. (Adapted from a 1996 *Harvard Women's Health Watch*)

- **Prozac/Zoloft**: Anafranil, Clozaril, codeine, Elavil, Haldol, Inderal, lidocaine, Norpramin. Pamelor, Percodan, Risperdal, Talwin, Tofranil

- **Paxil**: Anafranil, codeine, Elavil, Haldol, Norpramin, Pamelor, Percodan, Risperdal, Talwin, theophylline, Tofranil. Warfarin

- **Luvox**: caffeine, Clozaril, codeine, Elavil, Haldol, Inderal, Norpramin, Pamelor, Risperdal, Talwin, Tofranil.

Dual-Action Agents. FDA-approved Mirtazapine (Remeron) is the first agent of this new class of antidepressants. Mirtazapine stimulates the release of both norepinephrine and serotonin while blocking two specific serotonin receptors. The serotonin specificity minimizes common SSRI side effects, such as decreased sexual drive, nervousness, and insomnia, as it speeds up improvement. In studies comparing mirtazapine with fluoxetine, citalopram, and paroxetine, mirtazapine was significantly more effective in the treatment of depression (but not specifically SA/SP), showing greater improvement at the first week.

Dosage ranges from 15–60 mg./day. At lower doses it tends to be very sedating. But it is less so at higher doses, unlike other sedating antidepressants. To date there have been no studies on the use of mirtazapine for SA/SP.

Buspirone. Buspirone (BuSpar) is an atypical anxiety-reducing drug, azaspirone, which appears to act on nerve cell serotonin and dopamine receptors. While it may act something like a benzodiazepine, it's chemically and pharmacologically unrelated to benzodiazepines, barbiturates, other sedatives, and anxiety-reducing drugs.

It has no muscle relaxant or anticonvulsive effects and is less sedating. There's no risk of inducing physical dependency. Its anxiety-reducing effects take 2–3 weeks to be noticeable. A transdermal buspirone patch is being tested and may be useful for hyperactivity as well.

Common side effects include:

- Dizziness
- Nausea
- Headaches
- Nervousness
- Light-headedness
- Excitement.

It's used predominately with generalized anxiety disorder (GAD) and discrete SA/SP. However, it is possible that those with generalized SA/SP may respond. The general response rate is 53%. When the drug is combined with CBT, the improvement rate climbs to 67%.

The initial buspirone dosage is 5 mg. three times per day or less. This can be increased in 0.5 mg. increments to a total daily dose over three days. If this is tolerated, it may be increased to four pills and increased every three days until 30 mg. is reached. After four weeks, if this dosage isn't working, it may be increased in 0.5 mg. increments to a total daily dosage of 60 mg. Maximum improvement is around four weeks. Studies have found that these beneficial results may not be dramatic or consistent. Buspirone should not be taken with MAOIs.

Bupropion. Bupropion (Wellbutrin) is an aminoketone that acts as a norepinephrine and dopamine reuptake inhibitor. It also has a weak effect on serotonin.

Side effects include:

- Tremors
- Agitation
- Headaches
- Dizziness
- Visual disturbances
- Palpitations
- Insomnia
- Dry mouth

- Constipation
- Nausea.

Side effects are less common with use of the "sustained-release" (SR) version of this drug, There is also an "immediate-release" (IR) version of bupropion. However, at higher than recommended doses, the IR version may be contraindicated with

- History of seizures
- History of anorexia nervosa or bulimia (because of higher incidence of seizures).

Dosage may range from 75 mg. twice a day to 300 mg. per day, divided into three equal doses. With the SR formula dosage is 150–400 mg. total, given once or twice a day, with no more than 200 mg. given at any one time.

Bupropion should not be used with MAOIs. Recommended washout period for switching from MAOI to bupropion is ten days. To date this medication has not proven to have much effectiveness for SA/SP.

Other Antidepressant Possibilities. There are new medications for depression appearing all the time, along with new uses for other non-anxiety medications. For example, SSRI duloxetine (Cymbalta) is similar to velafaxine (Effexor) in that it affects not only serotonin but also norepinephrine. MAOI selegiline (Eldepryl), also used in the MAOI patch, is also being used to treat Parkinson Disease by boosting dopamine.

Newer anti-convulsive medications, such as gabapentin (Neurontin), pregabalin (Lyrica), levetiracetam (Keppra), and lamotrigine (Lamictal) are showing promise for generalized SA/SP. Old anti-convulsive agents, such as valproic acid (Valproate), are likewise being investigated. Anti-convulsives have the possible side effects of dizziness, nausea, sleepiness, tremor, increased appetite, and blurred or double vision.

Tricyclic Antidepressants (TCAs). These medications include imipramine (Tofranil) and clomipramine (Anafranil). They act as serotonin and norepinephrine reuptake inhibitors. But, as a general rule, they are not effective with SA/SP. This is particularly true about reducing social and interpersonal hyper-sensitiviy. Clomipramine, however, has shown some improvement in some individuals.

Common side effects include:

- Urinary retention
- Dry mouth
- Constipation
- Blurred vision
- Sedation
- Weight gain
- Sexual dysfunction.

Average dosage is 75 mg. or more per day. Combining TCAs and MAOIs may put you in jeopardy of Serotonin Syndrome. As a result, close monitoring is recommended when combining them.

On the Horizon. Research has shown that an antibiotic used for tuberculosis, d-cycloserine, may help people to cope with anxiety. What is does, according to psychologist David Barlow at Boston University, is help the phobic person learn much faster so anxiety reduction is quicker.

Research on oxytocin, a hormone that is closely associated with labor, lactation, and sexual activity, may help reduce fear and increase trust in humans. Some have called it the "bonding hormone." It acts like a neurotransmitter that makes people more willing to engage in social interaction, bonding, and healthy interpersonal relationships.

PRESCRIBING FOR CHILDREN AND ADOLESCENTS

While children and adolescents receive pharmacological treatment for SA/SP, controlled studies on psychopharmaceutical treatment of children are relatively few in number. In spite of this, use of antidepressants in children has been steadily increasing. As early as in 1994, for example, 200,000 prescriptions for Prozac and 300,000 for Zoloft were filled for children ages 5–10 years old.

The first large-scale study of children and antidepressants looked at Prozac. Of the 100 child participants 58% did well on the medication versus 33% who did well on placebo. Because of the considerable lack of information on safety and effectiveness of psychotropics in children, and suggestions that some SSRIs may increase the risk of suicide, the FDA is urging drug companies to do studies on their use in children.

It's important to remember that once a drug is approved by the FDA, physicians can use it for anybody and for any purpose, irrespective of the condition for which it was tested and intended. It's at the discretion of the physician. At present, the suggestion for use of psychotropic drugs with children is to (1) start with a low dosage (perhaps the smallest amount per pound of body weight), (2) go slowly (use only when necessary and increase it in small increments), and (3) closely monitor it (watch for side effects, drug interactions, and effectiveness).

REVIEWING MEDICATIONS

There are three primary points to remember with respect to medications for social anxiety.

1. MAOIs, clonazepam, and SSRIs are considered best for severe SA/SP if there is accompanying depression.

2. For performance- or test anxiety disorder that involves rapid heart rate, short-term use of beta-blockers may be appropriate.

3. For severe anticipatory anxiety and frequent panic attacks the drugs of choice are benzodiazepines.

Overall, there's little research on the long-term psychopharmacological treatment of SA/SP. Maintenance therapy up to a year may sustain improvement and decrease the rate of relapse, as is true for many other psychiatric disorders. But *if* you've tried non-medical strategies first, without success, and *if* you're in severe psychic pain and unable to function, you may want to at least consider the use of medications as an adjunct to other strategies until you're up and running again.

GETTING HOLD OF PSYCHOTROPIC DRUGS

Psychiatrist and psychopharmacologist Jack Gorman reminds you, in *Essential Guide to Psychotropic Drugs*, that there are important guidelines to follow for gaining access to drugs for any psychiatric disorder.

- Get drugs only from medical doctors (M.D., D.O.) and/or psychologists (Ph.D., Psy.D.) who are authorized to prescribe.
- Talk personally with the professional prescribing the drugs. Don't let someone else get them for you.
- Consider long-term drug therapy only from a physician or

psychologist who is well versed in psychotropic drugs.

- Accept treatment designed for your specific needs and situation only.

- Get an explanation of and justification for a particular drug for you from the physician or drug-licensed psychologist.

- Learn side effects and any potential interactions.

- Get a second opinion from another physician or drug-licensed psychologist if it's desired.

- Make sure there are follow-up visits to monitor the drug's effects and dosage.

- Have a support person with you at your appointment.

LOCATING DRUG ASSISTANCE PROGRAMS

Many find it difficult to afford necessary prescription drugs. In order to have them, you may have to do without other necessities. Or, you may do without the drugs entirely, or stop taking the medication altogether, when funds for them run out. However, if you don't have medical insurance or if your medical insurance doesn't cover your anti-depressant or anti-anxiety medications, you may be able to obtain help from drug manufacturers.

Major pharmaceutical firms offer patient drug assistance programs, with free or low-cost medications. These are not government-sponsored programs. Criteria for qualification will vary from program to program, but the information needed to make an evaluation of your eligibility likely includes:

- Combined household income

- Assets

- Monthly expenses

- Number of people in household

- Health insurance and co-pay information

- Monthly amounts of SSI (Supplemental Security Income)

- Monthly amounts of SSDI (Social Security Disability Insurance)

- Medicaid eligibility

- Prescription drug coverage, if any.

If you think you may be eligible for one of these programs, you can make the initial contact with the manufacturer online or offline. When eligibility is determined, the manufacturer sends the drug directly to the physician's office for appropriate distribution. It's important to remember that not all drugs used for SA/SP may be available through these programs. But many are and new drugs are continually being developed for SA/SP and new programs made available.

Drugs that have been available include BuSpar, Celexa, Effexor, Klonopin, Lexapro, Paxil, Prozac, Wellbutrin, and Zoloft.

The National Alliance for the Mentally Ill (NAMI) (www.nami.org) and Prescription Assistance (www.rxassist.org) are resources. Also you can find information in the *Directory of Prescription Drug Patient Assistance Programs*, published by the Pharmaceutical Research and Manufacturers of America. It's available free of charge by calling 1-800-762-4636.

RECEIVING SOCIAL SECURITY DISABILITY INSURANCE

Those of you who are disabled by SA/SP may be entitled to receive benefits as if your disability were the result of a physical condition. *Disability* is defined in terms of your ability to work. According to the Social Security Administration (SSA), criteria for claiming disability include:

- Inability to work for a year or more
- Inability to do any kind of work
- Severity of condition interfering with work-related activities
- Earnings average under $860 per month for the year 2006, e.g.
- Disability determined by physicians and disability examiners at state agency-based examinations and clinical evidence
- Disabling condition must be on Social Security list or have the same effect as a condition that is on the list.

Applying for benefits requires your applying in person at your local Social Security Administration office. However, if your SA/SP prevents your doing that, a parent or guardian may apply for you. You'll be interviewed at length and in-depth and have to fill out a number of forms. This may be an anxiety-provoking experience for you so having a friend or relative along as a support person can help.

Your eligibility will be determined by three primary factors: Medical status, functional status, and financial status. Medical criteria include anxiety disorders. The whole process takes between three and six months following application and you need to check periodically on the status of your application. As NAMI has pointed out, even if you're rejected, you should persist in seeking funds through the appeals process because 66% of those receiving benefits were initially rejected.

WHAT ABOUT SUPPLEMENTAL SECURITY INCOME?

More than half of the states now provide supplemental income that is state administered to those who are aged, blind, disabled, unable to work, and poor. It provides cash for the basic needs of food, clothing, and shelter. You can find out about SSI at www.ssa.gov/ssi/. It will provide you with information about eligibility, how to apply, work incentives, rights, and benefits. You can get additional information from the Social Security Hotline at 1-800-772-1213 during regular business hours.

SUMMARY

Taking medication is a very individual decision. What you decide will be based upon your values, attitudes, financial status, the availability of mental health professionals, and numbers of other factors. Finding the right medication for your body chemistry can be time consuming, difficult, expensive, and frustrating. But when you find the right one or right combination of drugs, it can make your working on your SA/SP less burdensome.

Gaining access to low-cost psychotropic medications is somewhat easier today because of the increasing number of patient drug assistance programs. However, you need to be prepared for what might be a prolonged process: First, becoming part of such a program and second, following the drug regimen to alleviate your SA/SP. Knowing what to expect and being prepared for it can help you cope with it better.

Bumper sticker: "Therapy and drugs are expensive. Popping bubble wrap is cheap. You choose."

11

MOVING FROM LONELINESS TO DATING

"All the lonely people, Where do they all come from"
(John Lennon & Paul McCartney, *Eleanor Rigby*, 1968)

HOW PREVALENT IS LONELINESS?

Thirty years ago sociologist Robert Weiss found that 50–60 million Americans felt extremely lonely at some time during any given month. One in six Americans didn't have a friend in whom they could confide personal problems. Things have changed little since then. Social anxiety is common among all those who are *chronically* lonely, and conversely.

HOW LONELY ARE YOU?

Answer the following questions with **T** for *true* or **F** for *false*. (Adapted from David Burns' *Intimate Connections*)

____Nothing I do to improve relationships ever seems to work

____I don't feel very attractive, desirable, or lovable

____It's difficult to tell anyone I feel lonely

____I feel I won't have many relationships because there's something "wrong" with me

____When I'm alone, I'm often bored, restless, or anxious

____I don't know how to meet others

____I don't know what to do when I meet others

____I don't try to get to know others for fear of being rejected

____I'll never have someone to be close to

____Everyone should have someone; it's abnormal to be alone

____The people I'm interested in never seem interested in me in return

____I don't seem to have much in common with others to talk about

____I don't see how anyone could love me

____I feel like a failure, a loser, or inferior because I have no one

____It's difficult for me to become intimate

____I feel helpless and vulnerable when I'm alone

____I often feel empty and unfulfilled.

____I'm unhappy doing so many things alone

____I sometimes think an unhappy relationship would be better than none at all

____I'm not really connected to any peer groups.

Scoring: Count the number of **T**s. **0–3** = Minimal or no loneliness. **4–6** = Mildly lonely. **7–9** = Moderately lonely. **10 or more** = Very lonely.

IS ALL LONELINESS THE SAME?

Loneliness is an unpleasant experience of involuntary isolation. It's that gnawing dissatisfaction you feel with the existing state of your social relations, either quantitatively or qualitatively. Some basic human social need isn't being met. For some it may be the result of an interpersonal inhibition. But, in general, loneliness appears to be the result of your individual characteristics in your changing social situation.

Loneliness is associated with many things, such as a tendency to avoid social contact, sadness, anger, shyness, self-consciousness, anxiety, depression, self-deprecation, boredom, and marginality. It's important to note, however, that loneliness is not synonymous with "being alone." Solitude, or simply being by yourself, is not necessarily a negative experience. In fact, it actually may be very productive and energizing, letting you accomplish tasks with no distraction, relax away from stress, put everything into perspective, and recharge your battery.

Remember that social contact for the sake of social contact offers you no assurance of protection from loneliness. Whether or not you're lonely depends on what kind of social contact you have. It depends on your expectations, what you want from it, and what it means to you within your life experience.

Weiss describes two forms of loneliness: Social and Emotional.

Social loneliness is a feeling of boredom and marginality because of the absence of meaningful friendships, social network, or a sense of belonging to a community or peer group. It's associated with a lack of trying to make friends as well as a lack of opportunity. It may be either temporary or situational, such as the result of specific events, like divorce or death.

Emotional loneliness, on the other hand, is that anxiety, restlessness, and emptiness that results from the absence of a single, intense, intimate relationship. You frequently associate this with your perceptions of personal unattractiveness, your fear of rejection, shyness, and lack of social knowledge and/or social skills. This loneliness may include longing for the past, frustration with the present, and fear about the future. When this situation is severe, lasting over two years and having no traumatic event preceding it, it's considered to be *chronic* loneliness.

Chronic loneliness is when you have difficulty making social contacts and achieving intimacy even when the conditions are favorable. You may feel estranged, excluded, isolated, unloved, misunderstood, or rejected by others. You may feel deficient in social skills. You may believe yourself to be undesirable because of what you see as unchangeable personality characteristics. Or, you may pass up desired activities because you have no appropriate social partner with whom to participate in them. But irrespective of the reason, you feel distressed, dissatisfied, and deprived.

To feel satisfied with your interpersonal relationships, you need to have two types of these relationships: (1) Someone to whom you feel attached who'll provide you with emotional intimacy and (2) Social ties which will provide you with a sense of group belonging. Having only one doesn't compensate for not having the other. When you lack either or both of them, you're convinced that there's little or nothing you can do to create these social contacts to improve your condition. As a result, you'll tend to feel pessimistic, perpetually unlucky, and in despair.

Social bonds are essential to psychological well-being. When you have difficulty establishing and successfully maintaining them, you often find yourself vulnerable to stress, emotional disorders, and impaired physical health. Chronic loneliness has been linked to depression, alcohol abuse, and aggressiveness. It's also been linked to low school grades and to increased illness, mortality rate, and suicide. The presence of a social network to which you can turn for support is a strong determinant of your overall health.

Of course, loneliness isn't just the number of social contacts you have. It's also what you think is "normal" for your age, peer group, and culture. But SA/SPers' expectations are filtered through your biased assumptions and negative evaluation process. Consequently, there may be a discrepancy between what you actually have and what you *perceive* you have.

If you perceive the quality of your contacts to be poor, you're likely to feel lonely. If you perceive that the amount of time spent with the other person to be insufficient, you're likely to feel lonely. If you perceive that your two lives don't intertwine or that the arrangement isn't desirable, you're likely to feel lonely. It's "all in the eye of the beholder."

The majority of those who avoid social contact are chronically lonely simply because you find yourself unable to perform up to your own expectations. When you find your behavior unfulfilling in a particular situation, you avoid the situation. Even when you have a chance to make a social contact, you frequently don't take advantage of it because you don't see that the chance really exists.

Your perceived "deficient" social skills further increase your anxiety, leading to your avoiding social contacts. This, in turn, increases your perceived and real social skills deficiencies. Like so many other SA/SP situations, it creates a vicious circle.

Because you aren't fully participating in social interactions, you don't get the opportunity to learn and practice your social skills: Speaking, listening, conversational sharing, compromising, and cooperating. Your perceived inability to perform these skills comfortably can have some deleterious effects on your social life.

Role of Development and Childhood Experiences. One direct impact on your loneliness is what opportunities you had for social interaction during your childhood..

Psychoanalyst Harry Stack Sullivan hypothesized that having a pal is *essential* to your achieving interpersonal competence. This is someone with whom you cooperate, plot and plan, figure out life, share secrets, explore, play, and solve problems. A pal is someone who protects you from pain and whom you protect in return. A pal is someone who teaches you what it means to be a friend. Early friendships prepare the groundwork for having social competence and long-term relationships and marriage later on.

Children need to derive both a sense of emotional intimacy and group solidarity from their early social relationships. Group solidarity comes principally from external relationships while emotional intimacy comes initially from the family unit. In many ways the family is the root of loneliness.

That is, it functions as the primary source of your interpersonal involvement. It provides the context for your acquisition of social skills and attitudes. And, it's the base of security from which you reach out to expand your interpersonal efforts to establish peer relationships.

It's in adolescence when you have to deal with establishing relationships when you become particularly concerned about being unattached. It's also at this time that you're your most sensitive to social rejection because it is a time when the potential for rejection is very real.

Parents who are supportive and accepting will tend to foster higher levels of self-esteem in their children. This includes supporting children's friendship choices. Specifically, those who socialize their children into positive interpersonal attitudes and skills through modeling and direct teaching will help create higher levels of self-confidence in their children.

When parents are cold, rejecting, and unsupportive, when they hinder their children's relationship choices, or when they are socially withdrawn or anxious, their children will likely have lower self-esteem. Low self-esteem is central to both the onset and persistence of loneliness.

When you have feelings of low self-worth, self-consciousness in social situations, and self-blame for social failures, you will tend to look for and employ strategies that will protect you. You may use compliance, rebellion, or withdrawal as your strategy of choice.

- **Compliance** is your conforming to the wishes of others in order to avoid criticism or rejection.

- **Rebellion** is your acting against those whom you perceive to be the source of potential negative feedback. You do this internally by your contrary attitudes and beliefs and/or externally by your appearance and behavior. Your objective is to invalidate the power that you feel the rejecting others have over you.

- **Withdrawal** is removing yourself from social contacts altogether in order to eliminate the criticism or rejection.

Unfortunately, these strategies tend to be dysfunctional. By their very nature they don't enhance self-esteem. Instead, they further isolate you or create relationships that are frequently superficial or problematic.

Role of Culture. As discussed earlier, social and cultural trends, such as mobility and the demise of the extended family, often disrupt your family roots and social ties. They make continuity of your social bonds difficult at best. What further makes the situation exceedingly difficult is the perception that this is a "couples' culture." That is, you're labeled and evaluated by where you fit along a continuum that leads to marriage: Looking for potential mates, dating, getting serious, going steady, making a commitment, being engaged, perhaps living together, then marriage.

Being alone or being single is looked upon as being deviant. In this cultural context your being single represents your "failure" in the marriage market competition. Being seen as a "failure" primes you for loneliness. This notion is reinforced by the fact that married individuals tend to report less loneliness than their single or divorced cohorts. The imperative to meet these relationship expectations shows itself in the social pressure of parents and friends and the rewards associated with being a twosome. This is reinforced by advertising that shows that any fun activity requires a romantic partner.

WHAT IT'S LIKE TO BE CHRONICALLY LONELY

One reason SA/SPers experience chronic loneliness is that they often believe new acquaintances dislike them. But, this perception that others feel negative toward you is not unreasonable from your point of view. After all, you often admit that you don't like yourself very much either. By counter-punching you reject others first. This way you prevent them from having the opportunity to reject you first.

Others respond to your negativity by moving away. Your self-focus tends to make you a poor conversational partner. Your reluctance to disclose about yourself makes it worse. Also SA/SPers and lonely people tend to be socially unresponsive.

Age. One study showed that 13.5% of college students were severely lonely. The highest rate of loneliness occurs between 18 and 25 years of age. This is when your need for positive coping style is greatest. Surveys by psychologist Daniel Perlman suggest that while loneliness peaks in young adulthood, it drops in middle age. This may be due, in part, to when you move from home to school or from a married state to singleness.

Gender. Because women are more likely to label themselves as "lonely," it may appear that loneliness is more common among women than men. But the opposite may be true. Men tend to be less socialized in one-to-one communication than women and, thus, tend to be less effective at it. As a result, those men who are lonely may believe their situation exists because they don't "get along with others," rather than they aren't able to make contact.

Also, because loneliness is frequently associated with social failure and weakness in the minds of many, men tend to deny or not admit their loneliness readily for fear of being stigmatized by it. Instead they report vague feelings of dissatisfaction or physical problems, like headaches and stomachaches. Men, in general, tend to have close emotional relationships only with their female partners, which leaves them more vulnerable.

Chronic Loneliness Factors. Chronic loneliness is the result of many factors, not all of which are personal characteristics or skills. So while your level of self-esteem, social attitudes, knowledge and skills, and loneliness coping techniques are primary factors, you must not ignore the specific circumstances in which you find yourself.

There may be objective obstacles that can make your meeting others difficult. They include time, money, and distance. Because of your work and home situations, you may have little time or money to participate in social activities. You may be at a long distance from others, making travel difficult. In order for social contact possibilities to exist for you, you have to be where the "action" is.

Furthermore, there may be a social mismatch between your social environment and your values, interests, and backgrounds. For example, a member of PETA (People for the Ethical Treatment of Animals) might have difficulties finding someone with similar values in a rural community of hunters. When you're different from those around you, you have fewer opportunities to initiate the relationships you want. The primary reasons for your being lonely are:

- Being unattached (no sexual partner or spouse, or breakup with lover or spouse)
- Alienation (having no close friends, not being needed, feeling different or misunderstood)
- Being alone
- Forced isolation (being house-bound, ill, or without transportation)
- Dislocation (being in a new job or school, moving or traveling often, being far from home).

Unfortunately, the opportunities to encounter and interact with those who are similar to you may be haphazard or random. Often you have to carefully investigate the available circumstances, like searching for clubs where you can meet singles, parents, gardeners, singers, or video buffs.

Note: While many factors may have interacted over the years to predispose you to feeling lonely, this does not mean you can't overcome your loneliness. You can. It's the same with your SA/SP where many factors over time have predisposed you to SA/SP, but you can still overcome it.

EXERCISE

Loneliness Assessment

Ask yourself the following questions and record your answers in your Recovery Journal (Adapted from Ann Van Buskirk and Marshall Duke in the *Journal of Genetic Psychology*):

- What does loneliness mean to you?
- When have you felt lonely?
- How did it feel? (Describe)
- What did you do when you felt lonely?
- To what degree did doing this ease your loneliness?

- What thoughts do you have when you're lonely?
- What have you done to improve your circumstances?

TREATING LONELINESS

Clearly, mindlessly staring at the tube, drinking or eating to excess, and hiding out in your room are ineffective ways of your coping with loneliness. You need to be active, positive, and goal-oriented. You have to believe you can do something that will make a change for the better.

To increase your desired social contacts and reduce your loneliness, you need to do the following:

- Focus on realistic expectations for yourself, others, and the relationship
- Develop awareness of defensiveness, self-deprecation, and self-blame. Use the Disputation method for distorted thoughts
- Modify your dysfunctional core beliefs.
- Determine whether you're depressed because of your loneliness or just depressed
- Differentiate between "being alone" and "being lonely"
- Objectively analyze the number, quality, and types of relationships you already have. Decide what's missing and why
- Assess the situational context of your attempts at social contacts and your opportunities for initiating these social contacts
- Attribute your loneliness to its specific components
- Learn appropriate and effective social skills, such as
  - ➤ Assertiveness (asking for what you want, dealing with criticism)
  - ➤ Active listening
  - ➤ Small talk
  - ➤ Initiating conversations
  - ➤ Positive nonverbal behavior
  - ➤ Enhancing physical attractiveness
  - ➤ Handling periods of silence
  - ➤ Approaching physical intimacy
- Learn more effective strategies for solving interpersonal

problems

- Learn to focus on others empathetically
- Look for new opportunities for social contact.
- Cope with aloneness (being alone) by developing solitary skills
- Increase number of rewarding solitary activities
- Become less dependent on others for activities
- Turn loneliness into solitude
- Become comfortable with being alone in order to become comfortable with others.

MAKING FRIENDS, APPROACHING DATING

Before you look at how to meet people, make friends, and approach dating, you need to look at

1. What factors contribute to your being attracted to others and
2. What factors increase the probability of your initiating a relationship.

Being Attracted. A fundamental prerequisite for developing any kind of interpersonal relationships is physical closeness. The smaller the physical distance between two people, the greater the attraction, liking, and friendship. The same applies to repeated exposure. The more frequently you see someone, the more positive your recognition of that person is and the less uncertainty you'll feel. Therefore, those with whom you interact frequently and those you see at work or where you live are more likely to become your friends. Physical closeness creates familiarity that you prefer. The greater your familiarity, the greater your liking.

Seeking Similarity. As noted earlier, similarity tends to create positive feelings as well. You like people whom you *believe* are similar as well as those who actually are similar. You tend to like those who agree with you and dislike those who don't. Similarities to which you resonate include family, background, age, religion, politics, values, interests, education, jobs, and attitudes. You particularly like those who hold similar attitudes. But it's not the total number of similar attitudes that matters, but the proportion of similar to dissimilar attitudes that creates greater liking.

Interestingly, physical similarity is likewise a factor. You tend to seek out those who appear similar to you, but "better." In other words, you look for an ideal version of yourself. When you find both the attitudinal and physical similarity, your attraction to the other person will increase even more. It's important to note that when you're attracted, even before you've had a chance to check out actual similarities, you'll assume similarities exist. What you may respond most positively to are those who have positive qualities that you admire but believe you lack.

Desiring Physical Attractiveness. Physical attractiveness plays a major role in determining interpersonal attraction. Attraction is an attitude toward another person; it's an evaluation of the positiveness or negativeness of what you're feeling at the time. Once again it's the proportion of positive to negative feelings that counts.

In general, you believe that "what is beautiful is good." That is, you tend to see those who are physically attractive as possessing many positive characteristics. You're likely to see those individuals as more of everything: more socially skilled, strong, positive, outgoing, kind, poised, exciting, sociable, nurturant, with better characters, and having increased sexual activity, warmth, and responsiveness.

Moreover, you see their futures as brighter, that they'll have greater prestige, social and professional success, fulfilling lives, and happier marriages. Because of this you feel being with them is rewarding. In fact, associating with them actually does confer upon you some of their status and social power.

Developing Appearance Preferences. Through your family and cultural history you've acquired a set of preferences for physical appearance, which include facial features, weight, height, hair, eye, and skin color, hair length, facial hair, anatomy shape and dimensions, clothing type, and body adornments. There's an assumption that those who look a particular way will correspond to your positive or negative expectations.

"Beauty" varies with the time and culture. Within each culture at any given period of time there's fairly good agreement about what is beautiful. Western cultures may have a standard of "perfection" such as anorexic-looking females and muscular males during one decade but not another.

Importance of Expectations. Because you like those whom you expect will like you, your expectations of others are important in the formation of interpersonal relationships. When you expect to be attracted to someone, you act in ways to elicit attractive behavior from the other person. You're friendlier and show more socially desirable personality characteristics when with the person.

As a result of your being friendly, positive, and upbeat, the other person is likely to respond to you in kind. This then becomes a self-fulfilling prophecy. Unfortunately, it's the same when you expect you won't be attracted. Your expectations reveal themselves in your attitude and behavior and you send out and receive negativity.

Looking Longingly. Eye contact (gaze) is one of the first nonverbal behaviors to signal involvement. In general, when you look frequently and longer (1–5 seconds) at those with whom you're interacting, that person will tend to evaluate you positively. Gazing behavior does differ by gender.

Women tend to spend more time gazing into the face of the man than the other way around. Men rate these high-gazing women as most attractive because their gaze shows their focused attention on them. Women, on the other hand, rate low-gazing men as most attractive. Women's low-gaze preference may be related to men's long gazes being perceived as sexual, domineering, and/or threatening.

JOANNA'S CONTACT. Joanna felt stuck at the crowded, noisy Christmas office party. She had wanted to leave as soon as she had arrived. Anxious, tired, and bored, she just didn't want to hear another inane discussion about the weather, stock prices, racket ball scores, or daycare costs. She had made her appearance, had a drink, hung around the outer fringes of a few conversations, nodding and smiling on cue. But now she was looking for ways to escape gracefully. As her eyes scanned for her boss and the exit, another pair of eyes caught hers, and held them for a heartbeat longer than a glance.

Joanna looked away, shifted her position, and forgot for a moment what she was doing. She surreptitiously looked back and his eyes clasped hers again. He smiled. Slowly, almost imperceptibly, Joanna returned his smile. Then before she knew what had happened, he had threaded his way through the crowd and was standing beside her. Without either one having said a word, their mutual attraction was confirmed. With a touch on her arm, he said quietly, "Let's go somewhere and talk."

Interaction Distance. Distance between people standing together or in conversation is the result of mutual agreement about use of personal space. *Personal space* is the invisible boundary you maintain between others and yourself wherever you go. It represents spatial zones through which most other people should not pass.

Your personal space expands and contracts depending upon the situation. It serves two primary purposes. One is to act as a buffer against real or perceived threats. These threats may be physical or emotional. Emotional threats may result from too much intimacy, not enough privacy, or too much stimulation. Having a buffer zone enables you to control the intensity of interpersonal relationships, protect yourself, and facilitate communication.

Preference for interpersonal distances in different situations appears to be developed early in life. It remains relatively stable over time. It's important to remember that both individual and situational differences affect your personal space.

There are four ranges of personal space in interaction with others:

- *Intimate (0–1 ½ feet):* This is in intimate contact, physical sports, and aggression. Smell and touch are more important than verbalization for communication.

- *Personal (1½–4 feet):* This is with close friends and acquaintances. Vision and verbalization more important for communication, though touch is still possible.

- *Social (4+–12 feet):* This is for impersonal, businesslike contact. Vision and verbalization most important.

- *Public (12+ feet):* This is for formal contact between individuals and the public, such as speakers. Exaggerated nonverbal behaviors supplement verbalization.

You selectively attend best and most easily recall information at a distance of 5 feet although attraction affects the size of your personal space. The greater the attraction the smaller the personal space between individuals. Women interact more closely with women as the relationship becomes stronger than men do with men. Women, likewise, tend to stand closer to men in initial interaction than men do with women.

Invasion of Personal Space. When you become inappropriately close to another, you're likely to decrease attraction as well as increase negative inferences. You often respond to such *invasions* by turning away, avoiding eye contact, trying to put an object between the other and yourself. Or you may mumble, stammer, stutter, fidget, become restless and uncomfortable. This means you need to be exquisitely aware of you own and other people's personal space to avoid invasion.

Irrespective of group affiliation, SA/SPers tend to keep larger buffer zones. Even accidental touching may make SA/SPers uncomfortable. Violation of your personal space tends to make everyone, not just SA/SPers, angry and hostile.

Interaction distance varies by culture. North Americans and Northern Europeans interact at similar distances. Latin Americans, Greeks, and Arabs, for example, use smaller interaction distances. They also tend to be less rigid in their use of space. Distance also varies by socio-economic status. "Lower-class" tends to interact at closer distances while "middle-class" tends to interact at greater distances.

When you and others differ in your preferred interpersonal distances, you inadvertently create problems. You sometimes find that the person with whom you're speaking keeps stepping closer or farther away, causing you, in turn, to try to adjust your own preferred personal space to them. The phenomenon is called the "diplomats' waltz" because it was something that often happened between representatives of different cultures.

When you're not aware of personal space issues, you may misinterpret the spatial behavior of others. Someone coming too close may be perceived as threatening or dominating while someone too far away may be seen as aloof or disinterested.

Relationship Sequence. Your degree of motivation to interact with others is a function of your need for affiliation and your level of self-esteem. This means that the greater your need for connecting with others and the higher your level of self-esteem, the greater your motivation for creating a close relationship. But before you interact, you look for visible characteristics that will guide you toward or away from the interaction.

First, you match the other person to your cultural norms of attractiveness. Then you initiate a conversation that will probably involve a series of attitude and interest comparisons. While you're looking for similarities, occasionally dissimilar characteristics are seen as attractive because they reward you in some way. Perhaps the person is outspoken and you wish you were. Your emotional state at the time also influences your judgment, wherein positive begets positive.

Once you then reach the stage of "just good friends," you're able to disclose to the other your fears, embarrassments, and fantasies to some degree. As a general rule, you're most attracted to those who match you on not only **what** you disclose but also **how much** you disclose about yourself.

What keeps the budding relationship going is perceived reciprocal and equitable social exchange. In wanting the best relationship you can get, you're looking for one that's the most rewarding and the least costly. It would present you with the best value available as compared with others. Your rewards may be the intrinsic characteristics of the other person that you value (such as beauty, intelligence, or sense of humor. They may be directly rewarding behavior (such as attention or empathy). They may provide access to external resources (such as prestige, money, and other people).

You determine costs relative to your rewards. They represent how much you're willing to pay for the relationship. Satisfaction with the relationship is based on a comparison of your perceived rewards to your perceived costs. If the rewards outweigh the costs, you're satisfied. Instrumental rewards (such as physical attractiveness and sexuality) appear to be more important to men in relationships while expressive rewards (emotional support and affection) appear to be more important to women. Happy couples tend to emphasize rewards.

Equity and Equality. In any relationship you need to feel that what you put into it is balanced by what you get out of it. You pay attention to your inputs and outcomes as well as those of your partner. Both are important in determining how satisfied you are with the relationship. One that is *equitable* is one in which both parties *perceive* they get about the same amount of benefit from the relationship relative to what they put in to maintain the relationship. Equity is subjective and qualitative. That is, it's not the total number of inputs and outcomes that's important. It's the proportion of your individual outcomes to your inputs.

This doesn't mean, however, that *equality* is unimportant. On the contrary, as partners you tend to want to benefit equally from external and tangible rewards to the relationship. You may also want both partners to equally bear relationship burdens, such as expenses, transportation, chores, children, and aging parents. Equality is objective and quantitative.

For example, if you buy a car or sell the house, you want to benefit equally. And when you don't, you're likely to feel dissatisfaction with the outcome. Thus, the most successful relationships will emphasize both equity and equality.

WHERE TO MEET PEOPLE

When your goal is to meet others, you need to look in all the usual places:

Aquariums, art galleries or exhibits, amusement parks, bars, banks, beaches, bicycle paths, blind dates, bookstores, bulletin boards (online), buses, charity events, chat rooms (online), church, classes, clothing stores, club meetings, coffeehouses, coffee shops, community meetings, computer dating, concerts, conferences, conventions, dances, dancing lessons, dentist's offices, discount houses, doctor's offices, e-mail lists, elevators, fairs, flea markets, galleries, garage sales, gardens, gyms, hiking, hotels, job, Laundromats, lectures, malls, movies, museums, news groups (online), online dating, outdoor markets, mosques, parks, parties, pen-pal lists, personal ads, pet stores, planes, plays, political rallies, post office, pubs, resorts, restaurants, running, seminars, social clubs, social networks (online), sports events, supermarkets, support groups, synagogues, tennis courts, theater, trains, work-related events, zoos.

Unless you're very isolated, most of you have a large territory available to you to scour for potential partners. That being the case, why aren't more of you successful with your territory? For one thing, as couples therapist Stephen Johnson points out, most of you don't really cover the available territory. You tend to dismiss out of hand many of the ways to meet others as not being legitimate, or, at least, "superficial" "or "beneath your dignity." As a result, you meet only a small percentage of the numbers of people you could if you were more open to these different possibilities.

Added to that is your fear. You experience a fear of the unknown and fear of being embarrassed. Women have the additional fear of being hassled while men are concerned about being rejected. Your distorted and irrational thinking takes over. It points out all the possible false starts, disappointments, and inconveniences you'll encounter. Wishful thinking likewise intrudes, suggesting that maybe you'll be lucky enough to just stumble over a truly wonderful person and not have to endure what seems like a sweep-and-search operation.

Before long inertia sets in. You do next to nothing. And you're sitting on a bench in the park, feeding pigeons, just as lonely as before.

In truth, finding a partner requires effort, patience, and persistence. It means finding out where people of interest gather and then getting yourself there. It's important to remember that it's all a probability game. The larger the number of people you encounter the greater the probability of your finding people who can be friends or romantic partners. The more people you encounter the more frequently you can try out and practice your social skills. The more you can deal with "rejection" the more desensitized you'll become to it, and the better you can determine what you're really looking for.

Let me share my experience in the dating market. I tried online dating but most of the men I met were either desperate for a mother for their children or just plain desperate. One who didn't seem to come across that way was a dentist. After several telephone conversations, I decided to meet him. Oozing with courtesy and enthusiasm, he wanted to show to me his newly renovated home and office. While his office was aseptic-looking, his home above it was a lavish Moroccan movie set.

Unfortunately, it didn't take long before the pro forma pleasantries were replaced by wrestle mania. And when he saw I wasn't going to be "cooperative," things turned ugly. Rape was a heartbeat away as I tried to calmly reason with him.

After 45 minutes of my verbal anesthesia, he began to talk about the trip he and I would take the next day to the Rocky Mountains on his motorcycle named "Sexy Sarah." There we'd find a cabin and live in it. Then he unplugged the phones, locked all the doors, and curled up in a fetal position on his bed, hugging the phones to his chest.

In the morning he took me to breakfast. He talked animatedly about what a great time he'd had the night before. He made suggestions for our next date and then escorted me back to my car. I couldn't get home and into the shower fast enough.

When my next online-date called, I nearly blew him off until he mentioned he worked with an old friend of mine who had encouraged him to call me. And we hit it off. The 3Ps to finding people of interest are Patience, Practice, and Persistence.

Singles' Bar. The singles' bar is one of the places that you may tend to discount because of its superficiality. While you may believe that only the terminally-desperate and losers frequent these establishments, they do provide you with several benefits in your search. For one thing, they are teeming with warm bodies and people-to-meet. The environment is casual, relatively protected, and allows rapid learning of what works and what doesn't.

Because of its pervasive careless and indifferent attitude, everyone is approaching everyone else, with each encounter having less significance than it might have under different circumstances. Since there tends to be little personal investment in these often half-hearted meeting attempts, you can learn to assertively say "no."

Your sense of personal worth isn't riding on each encounter. Threat of criticism or other negative reaction to your "no" is reduced. You get to talk with many you don't want to know as well as some you do.

Going to a singles' bar is like doing a CBT assignment. It teaches you a lot and gets you incrementally closer to your goal. It may even be enjoyable as when a self-professed pool sharp tore up the table's green felt cover trying overly hard to impress me before I took my turn and calmly ran all the balls on the table.

As you become more involved in activities and interests in general, you give yourself more creative outlets for when you're not actively engaged with another person. As you move from loneliness, you move toward a more enjoyable and enriching solitude, and then beyond, to satisfying relationships of all kinds.

Image. Being seen as positive, independent, self-sufficient, with many interests is attractive to others. But when you appear to be in desperate need of companionship, love, or fulfillment (depressed, angry, cynical, or sarcastic), you're seen as significantly "less attractive." As a result, your efforts will be less effective. When you're consumed by your own needs, you can offer very little to others, except, perhaps, the promise of a strangling dependency. This generally causes others to run, not walk, away from you.

Humor is important. Humor that works best in most situations is humor that is light, nondiscriminatory, and self-deprecating. For example, when I was crossing a busy city intersection, I saw a long, lean, nicely muscled cop standing on the curb, talking to his pudgy partner. His angular facial planes and quick smile further piqued my interest. He truly was a "stud muffin." Fortunately, I was walking on a long walk-light because I couldn't keep my eyes off him. Then ... whomp! I walked straight into a large metal sign on a pedestal in the middle of the thoroughfare that threw me unceremoniously onto my butt.

As I raised my bruised body from the asphalt, I saw that the object of my affection was staring at me with his mouth open. A woman on the other side of the street rushed to my aid, dusting me off, checking the lump on my temple, making my *faux pas* even more obvious to all now assembled on both sides of the street.

Then the light changed and there we were, abandoned. We darted into traffic, dodging and weaving the unforgiving oncoming vehicles. By now the exasperated stud muffin had insinuated himself in the fray, busily directing traffic around us so he wouldn't have a fatality on his watch. Once safely on the sidewalk, I glanced back at him and sighed. After going through all that, I never even got a smile from his sweet lips.

As pianist-humorist Victor Borge used to say, "A laugh is the shortest distance between two people."

EXERCISE

People Meeting

(Adapted from Stephen Johnson's *First-Person Singular*)

- Make a list of all your interests. Include not only hobbies but also work-related interests.

- Make a second list of all the possible places (using the **where to meet people** list as a base) where people who share these interests might gather.

- Analyze the list and rate each activity by (1) your level of interest and (2) how likely it will lead to friends and/or dating partners. Use a 5-star scale, with 5 the highest, and 1 the lowest.

- Activities which are rated 5-5 are your "definitely will pursue" list while those rated 1-1 are your "only for practice" list. Don't discard any possibilities but concentrate on the more likely ones first. Periodically review your lists.

- Record your list in your journal. Make notes about what works and what doesn't. Keep refining the process. Update your records periodically.

Process Orientation. It's essential that you focus on the *process of meeting people*, not on the outcome. In other words, when you start looking for people to meet, don't think in terms of finding a romantic partner. That is focusing on the outcome which is anxiety provoking. Instead, you want to simply become comfortable finding and meeting people.

To make the process more successful you need to know what characteristics, attitudes, and values you want in others. You need to develop your skills in approaching and speaking with them. You need to be able to verbally and nonverbally ask for further contact.

This is a trial-and-error learning process. There is no other way to do it. But once you become more adept at initiating contact, you'll be better prepared to develop your ability to evaluate each person as a relationship potential. **You need to make and follow a systematic plan** to cover all the possible locations and activities now as well as later.

Small Talk Strategies. The best way to initiate a conversation is to

- Make a comment
- Ask a question (open-ended whenever possible)
- End a comment with a question (to put the ball in the other's court).

The basic topics for the comment or question are:

- Environment (location, situation, activity, event, weather)
- Other person (attire, non-sexual physical attribute, skill, environment-related interests, movies, music)
- Yourself (feelings, interests, activities, skills, attributes, current situation, occupation, movies, music).

If you choose the other person as your topic, irrespective of whether you ask a question or make a personal comment, you have to make sure that it's not *too* personal. There's plenty of time for you to get beyond superficialities once you get the conversation up on its feet and trotting along. Until then, a light touch is desirable.

As soon as you hear the other person's name, you need to repeat it aloud. Others like to hear their names and this also gives them a chance to correct the pronunciation if necessary. Moreover, your saying it helps embed it in your memory.

As you know, it's annoying to have someone erroneously call you by the wrong name, even when you try to correct them. For example, I pronounce my name, Signe, as "sig-nuh" But after I introduce myself, I'm regularly called "sig-nee," "sin-yuh," "sid-nee," sig-net", and "son-yuh."

Also you should never assume that it's acceptable to arbitrarily choose to employ a nickname or shortened form of a name for another person. Names are an important part of your identity and are very personal. For example, frequently people who are trying to be friendly decide to call me "Sig." I don't like the nickname. But when asking them to call me by my full name is awkward in the situation, I don't always do it. Their doing that is not the best way to initiate a relationship with me, or anyone else. It's better to ask what a person wants to be called.

Wherever you go to meet others, you need to have a short list of boilerplate small talk initiators with you. This is something you can tailor to the situation and person. For variety you should have both questions and comments, representing the three topic areas. In this way you won't be struggling to create something even remotely intelligible to say when you anxiously need it.

Here are some basic examples that are varied by topic and format:

Environment

Comments: "They have a good band here." "The speaker has a new book out on the topic." "This building used to be a roller rink." "This bank's tellers seem very new." "The weather forecast didn't say anything about this torrential downpour."

Questions: "How long has this band played here?" "What is the title of the speaker's new book?" "How long has it been since this place was a roller rink?" "What's triggered the turnover in tellers lately?"

"What's the latest about when this deluge will end?"

Other Person

Comments: "You really seem to enjoy the band here." "You remind me of the successful lawyer in the speaker's new book." "You move like a skater. I'll bet you used to skate here when this place was a roller rink." "You handled that dispute with the new teller so well." "That shawl you're wearing is beautiful."

Questions: "What do you think of the band?" "How often do you attend these lectures?" "What do you think of the roller rink motif?" "How did you ever get that teller to change his mind?" "Would you tell me about that Irish lace shawl you're wearing?"

Yourself

Comments: "I come here frequently to hear this band." "I've just purchased the speaker's new book." "I used to skate here when this place was a roller rink." "I never handle disputes with the tellers very well." "I gave my mother a shawl like that for her birthday." "I'm a paramedic with the fire department here in the city."

It doesn't matter that the question or comment isn't brilliant or witty. It doesn't have to be. All it has to do is (1) let the person know you're interested and (2) let you know if the potential partner is open to having an initial conversation with you. If you deliver your question or comment positively and respectfully, you enhance your chances that the person will be receptive. Once the person responds, you need to share some information about yourself in return.

Comments: (I come here frequently to hear this band.) "I think it's the best they've had so far."

(I've just purchased the speaker's new book) "I like his style and can't wait to read this one."

(I used to skate here when this place was a roller rink) "... but that was years ago. Now I run."

(I never handle disputes with the tellers very well.) "It's a skill I've been wanting to develop."

(I gave my mother a shawl like that for her birthday.) "I searched all over for it. It was her prized possession."

(I'm a paramedic with the fire department here in the city.) "I really feel I'm doing something important helping others in emergencies."

Note: SA/SPers often regard small talk as too empty, tedious, boring, or stressful to participate in. If given your choice, you'd prefer to sit drenched in honey in the path of a battalion of marauding fire ants to having to think of anything casual to say and keep the "inanity" going.

But since small talk is the one true relationship generator and a social lubricant, something that greases the wheels to keep interactions moving along, you need to pay particular attention to it. You need to think of it in positive terms. Small talk is your VIP pass to real, connection-making conversations and developing relationships.

Each time you draw out the other person and make self-disclosures in response, you provide more fuel for the conversational flame. You should think of small talk as a casual game of tennis. The goal is to keep the conversational ball in the air and make sure everyone has an equal opportunity to hit the ball. For the best results, you need to strive for a comfortable rhythm.

For SA/SPers a good strategy is to keep playing to the other player's strengths, rather than focusing on exhibiting your own strengths. Making fancy shots or acing out the other brings the conversational game to its conclusion quickly. The objective of your game should be everyone's satisfaction, a good workout, and mutual desire for another game.

Your opening conversational gambit needs to be not only situation-specific and non-threatening but also without assumptions. As pointed out in Chapter 8, you carry around a garbage bag full of assumptions that you also project onto each new interaction. You tend to assume that you understand what they think, feel, and want. Furthermore, you tend to assume they understand your motivations and intentions. as well. But neither of you can read minds.

What you're all striving for in conversations is to find some common ground so you have some basis for continuing the interaction. This requires that you look for areas of interest, knowledge, or experience to which the other person can relate. Politics, religion, sexual practices, and your struggle with SA/SP definitely don't qualify as neutral subjects. As such, they generally should be avoided. While partners in established relationships may differ on their philosophical approach or their views on controversial topics and survive, embryonic relationships aren't likely to. Instead, you're likely to reject the other as being dissimilar or be rejected for the same reason.

Conversations don't require that you hold precisely the same views or agree on everything, but some commonality helps. Two big no-nos are (1) trying to change the other person's mind and (2) telling them what to do. Those behaviors are perceived as intrusive and controlling and are not conducive to further relationship exploration. The most important thing you can do is to hold up your end of the conversation and appear socially adept.

However, no matter how carefully you listen, share information, and hold up your end, not every interaction will be successful. It's essential that you view this in its proper perspective. Sometimes things just don't work out no matter how hard you try, how assertive, polished, positive, or clever you are. You have no control over the circumstances or the other person.

This is **not** a personal failure. It's the way things sometimes work out. In the dating process, in particular, you should expect to experience this more often than not. It's essential that you reframe the situation as a learning experience and opportunity to grow, and then move beyond it.

Making Progress. How do you know you're making progress? The best way is to be aware of the nonverbal behavior of the other person. Upon your physical approach, if the person makes eye contact, smiles, nods, makes room for you to sit or stand, and/or allows you into their personal space, they're probably showing interest or acceptance. Women tend to have a smaller personal space than men. A woman may also cock her head to one side, look, glance away, and look again, whereas a man may simply look with a smile playing upon his lips.

If the person isn't interested, they may make no eye contact, clench teeth/jaw/lips, look away, pull away, turn their body away, cross their body with their arms, cross their legs or ankles, or put an obstacle, person or object, in your path.

I experienced this on a blind date. My first and only meeting with an online-date physician was over a tasty dinner in a nice restaurant. However, throughout the hour's conversation of, by, and for him, he kept his eyes closed, looking only occasionally to spear another hunk of steak and lobster. My attempted contributions tended to be ignored or dismissed. I didn't know whether his anxiety was worse than mine or he thought I'd be so honored by his presence that paying attention to me was unnecessary.

It's important to note that sometimes when others quit listening to you or just seem bored, it has nothing to do with you. Instead, it may indicate their arrogance. Arrogance isn't just preening, glancing at one's reflection, and being boastful or flamboyant. It's also demonstrating to you that they believe you're not as important, fascinating, or worthy as they are, and, thus, they do not need to shower their valuable attention on you.

As the conversation continues, your companion and you will begin to turn toward one another. This shows increased interest and blocks entrance by outsiders. Perhaps you touch briefly and casually. But remember, touch is "touchy" because it breaches personal space, suggests intimacy, and has sexual connotations.

Caution About Touching. If touch takes place initially, it should be done very cautiously. In other-sex encounters men touch women twice as much as women do men. It appears to be related to dominance, which may be seen as threatening or annoying. Therefore, it's often better if it's the woman who makes the first touch, as in a slight brushing of hands or a hand to an arm, to signal a developing rapport. As a general rule, heterosexual men are well advised not to take this touching by women as a sexual come on, unless there is good supporting evidence for it.

In same-sex encounters touching may tend to occur less frequently because it has the potential to draw public attention to the individuals involved and, thus, to their sexual orientation. In addition, because of the negative implications of misperceiving the receptivity of the other person to a same-sex relationship, gays and lesbians may be more reticent initially about touching.

In established relationships lesbians may engage in non-sexual touching as a communication device in a manner similar to that found in non-lesbian same-sex relationships. Gays, on the other hand, may be more likely to have their touch represent both sexual and non-sexual messages, depending upon the circumstances.

At this point, whether in other-sex or same-sex encounters, eye contact and smiling become more frequent. Voices show enthusiasm and a behavioral *synchrony* may develop. Specifically, you're imperceptibly mirroring each other's movements, improving communication, and building rapport.

Same-Sex Dating. While gays and lesbians face many of the same challenges as straights in the dating game, they also have to deal with pressures not encountered by straights. While a heterosexual male, for example, may rightly assume that most females are potential partners, homosexual males and females can't make that same assumption about others of their own sex. To heterosexuals the potential dating partner is easily recognizable by gender. Not so with homosexuals.

Each individual of their sex may be heterosexual and probably not interested, bisexual and possibly interested, or homosexual and potentially interested. This means that gays and lesbians have to meet a great many more people in order to identify the same number of potential partners as straights do. The more people they meet the greater is the risk of exposure of their sexual identity and resulting risk of stigmatization.

If gays and lesbians have a smaller potential partner pool by virtue of their sexual orientation, their situation is made worse when they have SA/SP. This restricts their circle of acquaintances even further. To minimize the threat of being rejected by heterosexuals some may seek out same-sex social settings. However, doing so may become an obstacle to the widening of their social circle and meeting desirable partners.

Reframing Dating. Putting dating in another, less anxiety-ridden context may be helpful. When you see dating, love, or fulfillment as the ultimate goal of the people-meeting process, you're likely to invest too much emotion in each interaction and each potential partner. This leads to desperation that can make initiating contacts sheer torture, a matter of life or death. This reduces your willingness to even try. Furthermore, this desperation can be sensed by prospective partners and considered unattractive.

If you reframe the process in terms of looking for others with whom to share understanding, recreational activities, and companionship, you may remove some of this anxiety burden. Then if those relationships develop further and deepen, so much the better. But the less emphasis you place on them as a "date," the less pressure you place on yourself to perform perfectly to attract that special someone right now.

The objective is to meet people and enlarge your social circle. You want to make this process as enjoyable as possible, not something you worry about and sweat over. Reframing "dating" as meeting and getting to know people allows you to expand your interests, your activities, resources, and network of contacts to enrich your life.

Who Asks? The conventional wisdom used to be that the older the individuals the more traditional they'd be with respect to sex-role behavior. However, today people of all ages will likely run the gamut of who asks and under what circumstances. It's important to note that irrespective, asking for a date is full of conflict for those on the sending *and* on the receiving ends.

Asking means you put yourself on the line for rejection. It's useful to remember that on average trying to meet people to date has a **rejection rate of at least 75 percent**. Being asked means you have to be able to say, *no* as honestly and kindly as possible: "I'm flattered you asked but I don't feel we have much in common." But saying *no* straight out is difficult for nearly everyone, especially for SA/SPers, because it makes you feel trapped and guilty.

Telephoning. Once you're able to use the telephone, you can further your interpersonal relationships. When you place the call, the first thing you should do is identify yourself as quickly and completely as possible. If you leave the person on the other end of the line puzzling over who you are, where you met, and why you're calling, you've already dropped the ball.

For example, if you say, "Hi, Sarah, this is Barry. How are you doing tonight," Sarah will likely feel awkward not remembering who you are and where you met. She wonders how she should feel or relate to you as a consequence. She's likely to feel wary and one-down because you know something she doesn't. You're both probably going to feel embarrassed as a result.

Unfortunately, the easiest and quickest way for the other person to relieve this feeling of defensiveness is to get you off the phone as soon as possible. This means the other person won't care very much why you called. They won't be listening to whatever proposal you want to make. At the very least you've created a negative impression.

If Barry had identified himself better, he'd have put himself in a better position. For example, "Hi, Sarah, this is Barry Ratliff. We met last night at Planet Hollywood when I found your handbag for you near the ladies' room." Before moving on to his reason for calling, Barry needs to wait for recognition from Sarah. "Oh, yes, you're the man in the L.L. Bean soccer shirt." At this point, Barry can broach the subject of his call. His call is really a request that Sarah respond positively to him in some way, such as talking on the phone or agreeing to go out with him.

But it's here that everything may become a tangle of confusion if the person called resorts to *polite code* to avoid saying "no." While it's meant to be a kinder, gentler way of letting the other down, saying, "I can't do it tonight." "No, Saturday's not good either." "Monday through next January, I don't know right now." And "I may have to wash my hair" leads to misinterpretation.

What is it they or you really want to say? Is it "yes" or "no"? If the answer's "yes" but the night specified is the problem for you, you need to say so. "I'd like to go to the movies with you sometime, but Monday night is a problem for me." You can then supply an alternate night for consideration.

If the answer's "no," you need to communicate that clearly but not harshly. It's not easy to put oneself on the line, risking rejection, to ask for a date. The response needs to acknowledge that you see that the person is doing something positive. It needs to provide the caller with a reason you aren't complying with the request, one that is both generally true and protective of the other person's ego.

You might say, "It very nice of you to ask me, but I can't right now" then supply a plausible excuse. The excuse might be recently having broken up with a significant other, dating one person steadily, or not adding new people to the list of those you date at the present. Being kind and gentle doesn't mean, however, you have to explain your feelings or behavior or justify your decisions.

Going Out. You want everything about the interaction to be as settled and comfortable as possible. If you confer with your partner about what you'd both like to do, you can arrive at some acceptable compromise. When you don't yet know one another, it's best to pick activities that allow you some quiet time to talk to actually become acquainted. Until you know the other's interests, women's mud wrestling, monster-truck rally, astrophysics lecture, or even a movie shouldn't be your first choice for a date activity.

There are other guidelines for first dates as well. As a general rule,

- Shorter dates are better than longer because they create less pressure.

- Less expensive is better than expensive because it creates fewer obligations.

- Use of two cars is better than one because it creates less threat.

- Meeting in a neutral place is better than on someone's turf because it creates less threat.

- Meeting in a public place is better because it creates less threat.

- Single dates are better than double dates because they allow more opportunity to get acquainted.

- Deciding right away on who pays and when is better because it reduces conflict.

- Learning what the other does for a living and fun, as well as about friends, lifestyle, standards, and values is better sooner because it provides a basis for information to share.

- Learning about the other's personal relationship history is better sooner because it tells their current status (single, going steady, separated, divorced, or married).

Establishing Closeness. Once you've begun to find out about the other person, you can self-disclose. Disclosure is a form of confiding about yourself, your background, your feelings and thoughts about others as well as yourself. Carefully controlled openness begets openness. Controlling the depth and amount of the information you initially disclose is important for everyone, but especially for SA/SPers.

When you feel you've found a kindred spirit, you tend to want to share everything with them *all at once.* You often get a bad case of verbal diarrhea. This can be overwhelming for the other person and even more overwhelming when that confidence includes information about your SA/SP.

You don't want the person to turn off, say to themselves, "Oh, no, what have I gotten into," and look for the nearest exit. You need to measure out your honesty in level teaspoons, not heaping tablespoons. While you have to gauge each individual situation, in general it's better to postpone the subject of SA/SP until much later.

So you need to disclose slowly, somewhat superficially at first, keeping the topics relatively neutral. As you explore the quality of the relationship, you begin to talk more about your hopes and fears as well as those of your companion. Being sensitive to your companion and yourself will guide you as to what level is appropriate and comfortable for you both. The sooner you begin building verbal intimacy into the relationship, the more comfortable you'll be in seeing whether the relationship meets your needs.

When you talk about past or ongoing relationships, you need to be brief, to the point, and take care how you present them. Specifically, you don't want to make models of virtue of them; that's an image no one could live up to. At the same time, you don't want to say negative things about past partners either.

Sometimes it seems that if you show your new companion how terrible the former companion was, it'll make the new companion feel better by comparison. Unfortunately, the opposite tends to happen. The negativity itself will make the person on the receiving end feel bad.

They'll begin to wonder if you'll talk about them too, either behind their back now or later if things don't work out with the relationship. They may wonder what all this negativity says about you for saying it. How did you treat your last partner? Will they be treated the same way? Instead of criticizing a former partner, you need to be kind. The more charitable you are the more likely you are to reassure your new partner.

As you work to create positive first impressions, you need to be mindful of falling into the *pretender trap*. The pretender trap occurs when you're trying so hard to accentuate all those aspects of yourself that you think will be attractive. You exaggerate or lie about your interests and tastes in certain areas. First impressions are lasting impressions so you need to create an honest, positive impression you can live with.

Presenting yourself as something you're not is likely to come back to haunt you. On the one hand, you're going to be stuck doing things you dislike or don't really want to do very often because you've convinced your companion you do. On the other, you may be rejected when your new partner discovers you haven't been truthful. You're not the person they thought you were. Moreover, if you weren't honest about this, what else is there you haven't been honest about? Uncertainty, doubt, and suspicion can quickly become emotional hazardous waste material.

Etiquette. The rules by which you date are very ambiguous at this point in time. Some people adhere to traditional prescriptions about male and female dating roles. These traditional expectations are that the man gets the doors and coats, orders food, pays for meals and entertainment, and is generally in charge. Some subscribe to looser behavioral roles where each person gets their own coat, whoever is at the door first gets the door for the other, cost of meals and entertainment is divided, and both are in charge. Others approach dating behavior from somewhere in between, choosing this from column A and that from column B.

Since there's no way to know initially, it may be best to do three things:

1. Think of etiquette in terms of courtesy, doing something thoughtful and kind for the other person, and be prepared to act in ways to demonstrate that courtesy.

2. Watch for nonverbal behavior that may suggest the expectations of your partner. For example, if you pull into a parking space and your female companion makes no move to open the door, she may be expecting you to open it. If your male companion asks you what you're going to have as the waiter approaches, he may be preparing to order for you.

3. When in doubt, it's best to inquire: "May I get your door (or coat) for you?" "Is it okay if I order for you?" or bring it up for discussion: "We haven't discussed expenses, but I'd like to pay half."

Mutual consideration is your real goal. You don't need rigid rules to enforce it. Knowing what's generally expected from one encounter to another makes dating a lot easier. You can establish your own guidelines within each relationship.

Who Pays? Part of the guidelines you mutually devise will concern money. You need to remember that money isn't neutral. It's symbolic of power, status, and dominance. As a result, you need to address it early before misunderstandings and conflicts result from unmet expectations and hard feelings.

One rule of thumb is that the one who initiates the occasion is acting as host and, therefore, is responsible for the expense. But *initiation* is all in how the subject is presented. When it isn't crystal clear, it's better to inquire than find you've made an erroneous and awkward assumption. You can't assume that the man is the only one with resources and should, as a result, pay for everything.

Sensibilities today more openly acknowledge that this perceived obligation for only men to pay is burdensome. The woman may feel she's being bought and the man may feel he has to purchase companionship. This can leave both partners uncomfortable when further behaviors don't meet prior expectations. Wherever possible, the sharing of expenses may reduce the discomfort.

Ages ago, before I started thinking about discussing sharing costs, a first-time date became furious with me when his after-dinner assumptions weren't met. In the car he demanded sex, "You owe me. I paid for your dinner." When I told him that in buying my dinner he hadn't "bought" me, he furiously ordered me out of his car. Whoa! Fortunately I managed to calm him down and convince him to take me home instead.

This incident snapped me awake to the fact that our respective expectations and assumptions weren't necessarily the same. Even though I *thought* we were on the same channel, I needed to address things well ahead of time to make sure.

Where activities simply come about or are the result of partner negotiation, equitable or equal sharing is fair. Where one partner has more resources than the other, the two can pay proportionately. Or they can participate only in activities that both can afford. Or, they can alternate.

Since money is for some, mostly men, a greater taboo than sex, it's often easier if the woman addresses it first. She can suggest that they pay their own expenses. But if, as time passes, she doesn't, the man may introduce the topic. For example, "I'd feel more comfortable if we could share expenses for these activities in some way because I have a budget to stick to. There are lots of things we can do together, some expensive, some not. How do you feel about it?" However it's addressed, you need to negotiate something with which you both are comfortable.

Ending the Date. For most people this is probably almost as awkward as asking for a date. The cardinal rule is be honest but be kind. If you enjoyed yourself, you should say so, suggest that you get together again, and ask your companion how they feel about that. If you didn't, you should still say you enjoyed yourself but you don't feel you have enough in common to continue dating. If you like the person more as a friend than as a date, you should say so and suggest getting together for some friendship activity.

Then there's the question of intimacy. Should I try to kiss her? What will she think if I do? What will she think if I don't? What should I do if he tries to kiss me? What if he doesn't try?

While you may want your companion to be attracted enough to want intimacy, you may not want your companion to act on it just yet. It's taken a tremendous amount of courage for you to get this far. You're not sure of the "rules" or if your social skills are up to the situation. Furthermore, trust may be a big issue for you. Afraid of messing it up, and/or being exploited and rejected, you may feel divided between approaching and avoiding any kind of intimacy.

Coded signals in the best of situations are often ambiguous. And even if they weren't, you tend to be a lousy social cryptographer. One way to address this issue is to discuss it **before** the end of the date.

For example, "I've really enjoyed your company this evening and would like to kiss you." A response, other than an affirmative, might be, "I've really enjoyed this evening too, but because of my last relationship I'd like to take this a little slow." Or you could use one of the "no" responses you used for telephone calls. Having this settled already as the date ends means there's less probability of having to deal with the embarrassment of the "unwanted kiss" or a grope situation.

What About "You-Know-What"? If you decide to have sexual intimacy, it's best that you know that that's what you *really* want. You don't want your motivation to be an anxious response to what you think is expected of you. You don't want it to be a counter-phobic reaction to your fear of intimacy, to show yourself you're not really afraid so you go hog wild. You don't want to be confusing your fear with attraction and sexual excitement.

SA/SPers are particularly anxious about doing "it" and being rejected, as well as not doing "it" and being rejected. A real bummer either way. Of course, anxiety in such a situation is quite natural and is likely to be experienced, to some degree, by the other person as well.

Everyone is concerned about appearing clumsy or gauche, doing the right thing and doing it well, having bad breath, love handles, imperfect secondary sexual characteristics, flatulence, and sweaty feet. And SA/ SPers have the additional concern about blushing.

In physically close situations I was no different. My concern was chronic post-nasal drip from allergies. Convinced my breath could stop a velociraptor at fifty paces, I sucked on Clorets until my mouth looked algae-fied. It didn't matter that treating my tongue was unlikely to have any effect on my sinuses … or that perhaps I didn't really have a bad breath problem. I felt compelled to do something to keep from being embarrassed, just in case.

But when there was even a remote possibility of anything romantic, I switched to Chanel No.5 since a green oral cavity doesn't whisper, "Come hither." Consequently, before and during the date I surreptitiously gargled with the eau de toilette. Did it work? Well, I did get kissed. I don't know if it was the Chanel No.5 or I would have been kissed, etc. anyway. But what I do know is it was a very expensive way to prevent romantic rejection and humiliation.

Most people are self-conscious about their bodies and feel uncomfortable about being nude. You tend to associate nudity with exposure, powerlessness, deficiency, and vulnerability. Without clothes you lose your specialness. Without clothes your excessive sweating is obvious. Moreover, you likely just don't want to be scrutinized and evaluated.

One reason SA/SPers are anxious about sex is that you tend to feel that the other person knows exactly what to do, how, and when. You see them as calm, cool, collected, and sexually savvy … all the things you're not. You don't have the knowledge or experience. In fact, many of you may still be virgins in your 30s and beyond.

You're not prepared. Your mind is a welter of questions: Am I doing this right? What if they don't like it? Should I lead or follow? How do I decide what to say "yes" or "no" to? Should I go ahead and do it or ask permission?

Another reason for anxiety is your ambivalence. You want to but you don't. You're concerned about what's expected: Women, for example, are expected to be experienced but not "too" experienced. Men are expected to be smooth and in control.

When you're anxious and inexperienced, you may feel compelled to try to appear more savvy and worldly than you really are. This deception is hard to maintain and creates confusion for your partner when you slip. As a general rule, if you're unsure what to do next, you need to say so, no matter how scary doing it is. Your honestly addressing the situation is far better than sending inaccurate signals to the other person and being untrue to yourself as well. It may be a little awkward to do so, but a little awkwardness at this stage is better than a lot of awkwardness as passions escalate.

What Do You Really Want on a Date? Richard Sides and Pat McChristie writing about singles on the Internet suggest that men and women may want different things from a date. According to Sides, **men** want:

- Conversations in which their female companion can speak to subjects and issues in which they're interested, whether it's sports, health, business, or social issues.

- Conversations that have a beginning, middle, and end. Talking about feelings doesn't achieve closure for them so they're less comfortable talking about feelings.

- Confirmation that they have unique strengths that are needed. Not being secure about their appeal, they can't tell what the woman wants unless she says so.

According to McChristie, **women** want

- Advance notice for dates of two to four days in general. Last-minute date requests more often than not receive "no" responses.

- Conversations that are more about the present than the past or future glories at the beginning of relationship, that don't go on and on about previous relationships, work or career, children, grandchildren, pets, relatives, financial problems, or the man himself.

- Conversations in which she's not asked excessive questions about her past loves but is asked about herself.

- Not being interrupted when she talks.

- Cooperation not competition.

I'd like to add to McChristie's list that because a woman talks about a problem doesn't mean she wants the man to analyze it and provide a solution. She is capable of asking for suggestions. Sometimes talking about a problem is just for the purpose of sharing feelings about a situation or hearing it expressed out loud. What is requested is for the man to listen and empathize, not analyze and problem solve. When in doubt, the man should inquire.

One important principle to remember in the dating process is that you're more likely to be successful if you accept those you meet for what they are and **not** for what you want them to be. You can't let your unrealistic expectations creep into the process. Wishful thinking will result in disappointment and disillusionment. When you try to make them change to fit your ideal, you're doomed to failure. Moreover, their worth is not dependent upon their ability to meet your needs any more than your worth is dependent upon your meeting theirs.

EXERCISE.

Dating

1. Identify three activities you enjoy. Compose a brief speech (several sentences) on each, highlighting

    A. What you like about the activity,

    B. How you became interested, and

    C. How often you participate in it.

2. Initiate two conversations a week for three weeks on the topics (one per week). After you get the hang of it, do this whenever possible.

3. Over the next three weeks invite someone to join you in each activity.

Record your results in your journal and continue the process until you are comfortable doing it.

"COMING OUT"

Paraphrasing Hamlet, "To tell or not to tell. That is the question." SA/SPers all have grappled with the conflict of revealing your condition to friends, relatives, dates, colleagues, teachers, and employers. One part of you desperately wants to share SA/SP, your darkest secret. You want to release some of the pressure, to stop feeling like a liar, and make your sometimes-odd behavior understandable. The problem is that as much as you feel compelled to "come out," you also feel equally compelled to stay silent because you fear how others are likely to respond to this disclosure.

JOANNA. Joanna wanted to tell her parents but feared more of the same criticism she'd always received from them. Having SA/SP would be equivalent to receiving a "D" on a test. She wouldn't meet their standards of acceptance.

Her condition would be seen as her fault, something easily remedied if she'd only try harder. While she might feel better saying the words, the relief would be short-lived. She knew she didn't need to provide her parents with more fodder for their demonstrating their disappointment in her. So she decided not to tell them about it.

Parents and Family. Reactions to disclosure can be diverse. Some parents may respond with guilt, making your condition their problem. In doing so, they make themselves, not you, the focus of the situation. Some parents may respond with denial, making your claim invisible. Some may blame you for it, as Joanna fears her parents will. They may tell you not to exaggerate and to "shape up," thus making your problem even worse. Other parents may be relieved that there's a name for "it" and be supportive.

Siblings may worry that the condition is hereditary and that they're at-risk. Some may not want to be associated with this stigmatization. Some may want to support and help. Your condition may strengthen or weaken family bonds.

BARRY. Barry and his childhood friend Chaz had weathered many storms over the years and were always there for one another even though they lived 500 miles apart. When Chaz came to town on business trips, Barry and he always spent time together. Much to Barry's chagrin, Chaz generally suggested they end their evening at a singles' bar where they could pick up women. Barry could never bring himself to address his extreme discomfiture participating in this activity, leaving him to suffer in silence.

But on Chaz's latest trip Barry blurted out how anxious he felt and why. To Barry's surprise, Chaz, after assuring himself Barry wasn't kidding around, clapped his friend on the back. "Hey, that's okay. I was only suggesting we meet some women 'cause you don't seem to know any and look as if you could use a little diversion. Myself, I'd rather shoot pool or go to a night game with you than go to a singles' bar."

Friends. Depending upon their relationship with you, friends may be glad you shared with them. Some may wish you hadn't, feeling uncomfortable with your "psychiatric disorder." They may start analyzing everything you do and have done in the past in terms of your SA/SP, rather than accepting it as an aspect of you. Some may take this revelation personally, feeling insulted and betrayed that you didn't trust them enough to confide in them before, thus creating a new interpersonal conflict.

HOW TO "COME OUT"

If you choose to come out, what should you say and how should you say it? In general, you need to frame your anxiety in terms others can understand and identify with. Few will be able to relate to "social anxiety disorder" or "social phobia" except as they relate to television ads for antidepressants. The terms are too clinical and psychiatric. They can be discomforting for most people.

What you need is something that is user-friendly like "shyness" or "anxiety when you have to give speeches or meet strangers." You need to talk about *behavior,* not negative labels. It's definitely a KISS: "Keep it simple, stupid" situation. If you start small, you can elaborate later as the situation allows. If you start big, you have no place to retreat if the announcement doesn't play well.

With Dates. As mentioned earlier in this chapter, since dates are generally new people in a new relationship, you have to ask yourself if there's a compelling reason to lay something as heavy as SA/SP on them. If you feel you must say something and the timing feels appropriate, you should make reference to a sort of "shyness" and do it as positively as possible.

This actually may be seen as endearing rather than frightening. Then as you get to know the person, they will see examples of your "shyness" and this may be a basis for a discussion of it. However, you're the one who will decide if you'll disclose, to whom, what you'll disclose, how, and when.

With Teachers. When class work and attendance suffer because of your SA/SP, you have to decide how you're going to communicate your underlying problem to the teacher(s) involved. Some SA/SPers may just drop out of class or school rather than address it with teachers. But that isn't the best or necessarily the most viable option for you.

One possibility is for you to approach the teacher during their office hours to explain your no-doubt confusing behavior. Unfortunately the very thing you want to discuss may thwart your best efforts. Your SA/SP may prevent you from ever getting to the topic. It may make your presentation unintelligible and create further misunderstanding.

Another possibility is to send a letter or e-mail to the teacher(s) explaining the problem. While in-person communication is always desirable, using written methods would eliminate the face-to-face freeze-ups you have invariably experienced.

When counseling is available at the school, your speaking with a counselor may provide another avenue of communication. The counselor may speak on your behalf to the teachers in question. Having a credible third-party intervene may add substance and weight to your plight.

If you're already in therapy, you could get a letter from your therapist, explaining your "shy," anxious, or phobic behavior and inability to participate in class discussions or do presentations. You could then show or send it to each teacher at the beginning of the year. Even if you're not in therapy, you could talk with every teacher about your problem at the beginning of the school year, semester, or quarter to prepare them for your behavior. While communicating the severity and seriousness of your condition is essential, you still need to describe SA/SP in *behavioral* terms they're going to understand and that are relevant to your class participation.

With Employers. As a general rule, disclosing your SA/SP to employers is not useful. You want them to see you in a positive light. Using psychiatric labels, or anything that suggests a "problem," recasts who you are, what you do, your corporate value, and your potential contribution to the smooth running of business in a negative light. Only if your avoidance behaviors and anxiety are measurably interfering with your work should you consider saying anything. Then, what you do say is best couched in terms the behavior that is problematic and its impact.

For example, if you're asked to give a speech, you don't want to vomit your social anxiety life history all over the employer: "Oh, I can't talk before a group; I sweat like a pig. I've never been able to do that or answer the door or go the grocery store or even make friends without a stiff drink. That's why I'm still a virgin at 30. I'd spend my days in my room, crying, if I could."

What you might disclose when asked to give a speech is that you're not comfortable doing any kind of public speaking and are concerned you wouldn't do a "good enough job for the company." If pressed on it, you might further volunteer that you tend to stammer and go blank under those circumstances.

These are commonplace difficulties others can relate to. In other words, you should disclose only what's necessary and sufficient about the **specific** *behavior* as it relates to work and present it in the most *non-clinical* and *identifiable* way possible. Some companies have Employee Assistance Programs that have public speaking anxiety programs.

SUMMARY

Loneliness can be become a lethal habit. Once you see this and its effects more objectively, you can begin to plan how you're going to break free from its clutches: How you're going to start meeting people and develop relationships. Whether your ultimate purpose is to meet people for friendship or dating or both, the process is the same.

You need to go to where the people are, be prepared with small talk, know what to expect, and share yourself. You need to think of meeting others as trial-and-error practice. You can then learn what works for you and enjoy your successes.

Once you have alleviated your SA/SP, you can learn more about making small talk at http://www.speakwithoutfearnow.com/smalltalk-ecourse.htm.

"Far away there in the sunshine are my highest aspirations. I may not reach them, but I can look up and see their beauty, believe in them, and follow where they lead." (Louisa May Alcott)

12

OVERCOMING SWEATING, BLUSHING, BUSY BLADDER & IRRITABLE BOWEL SYNDROME

"Thou are not for the fashion of these times, When none
will sweat but for promotion."
(William Shakespeare, *As You Like It*)

Excessive sweating (hyperhidrosis), severe facial blushing, bashful bladder (avoidant paruresis), and Irritable Bowel Syndrome (IBS) are four conditions that create embarrassment and anxiety in social situations. They can add to the discomfort you already experience in SA/SP.

Although hyperhidrosis and severe blushing may occur with SA/SP, they are not necessarily a part of SA/SP., but Specific Phobias. In fact, those **without** clinically-defined SA/SP appear to be the majority of sufferers of these two problems.

WHAT CAUSES EXCESSIVE SWEATING?

Hyperhidrosis is due to over-activity of the sweat glands primarily of the palms (palmar), soles of the feet (plantar), armpits (axillae), face, and groin. Sweating is an involuntary activity that regulates your body temperature by sending signals to the body surface where two types of sweat glands (apocrine and eccrine) are located to produce sweat. There are 5 million eccrine glands in the body, 2 million of which are in the hands.

The sympathetic nervous system controls these glands by way of two chains of knots of nerves (ganglia). Referred to as the *sympathetic chain*, they run on either side of and parallel to the spinal column, with each ganglion above a rib where the ribs meet the vertebrae.

There are two types of this excessive sweating: Generalized and localized. Generalized sweating may accompany fever, a dysfunctional thyroid gland, cardiac infarction or insufficiency, or neurological disorder. Localized sweating, however, particularly of the palms and soles, may be caused by other factors, most of which are as yet unknown.

This localized sweating may be sudden or continuous. It's always worse at higher temperatures, improving during cooler months, and doesn't seem to be related to strenuous exercise. Sweating generally ceases during sleep. Psychological factors are thought to play a part for many individuals. In addition, for a minority sweating appears to run in your families.

The social impact of excessive sweating can be enormous. When you have palmar hyperhidrosis and your hands are soaking wet most of the time, you may be too embarrassed to shake hands, hold hands, or dance, making you appear disinterested, standoffish, or anti-social. You're unable to play musical instruments, work with electrical devices, type on computer keyboards, tie knots, or handle papers.

You won't participate in sports that require holding or catching objects, such as basketball, football, baseball, bowling, tennis, or pool; or play games, such as cards, video games, or chess. Your hands slip on the steering wheel of the car making the situation dangerous.

If you have facial or axillary hyperhidrosis, you'll find yourself continuously anxious about whether others are noticing the constant drip, drip, drip off your face or clothing stains under your arms. You know the sweating makes you look unprepared, unkempt, tense, and perhaps a little bit suspect.

What you can wear is limited by color and roominess, making you less a fashion statement or dress-for-success model. As a result, you tend to be ill-at-ease most of the time and preoccupied with how you look and ways to stay dry. All the while you are watching your self-esteem drip into puddles before your very eyes.

The first-line therapeutic measures to be tried for sweating are aluminum chloride hexahydrate antiperspirants, sedatives and anticholinergic drugs, iontophoresis (electric current in electrolyte solution), botulinum toxin, acupuncture, and classical conditioning. In general, these methods have met with variable success, as I found out. The second line of defense is surgery on the sympathetic ganglia controlling those sweat glands.

WHAT CAUSES EXCESSIVE BLUSHING?

Likewise, excessive and persistent facial blushing erects social and work obstacles in your path. When your face flushes, you become a beacon toward which all others direct their attention.

As a result, they may see you as socially inept. While this may be true, it isn't always true or necessarily so. You may also blush spontaneously, registering a range of colors from light pink to deep red. For example, my face, neck, and upper chest often turned dark red when I least expected it.

Blushing is the result of dilation of blood vessels in the face and upper body and may result from a hyper-reactivity, early conditioning, or both. It's primarily controlled by the sympathetic nervous system at the thoracic (T2 ganglion) level. This relationship between blushing and the sympathetic nervous system is important for the potential of surgical control.

It's important to note that persistent redness of the face may be due to an underlying medical condition. One such condition is rosacea, a chronic inflammatory disease that usually begins in middle age or later and occurs generally in the central area of the face. Visibly dilated blood vessels, redness, and lesions characterize it. Other causes of facial redness are exposure to sun, wind, and cold, excessive alcohol, reactions to drugs, food, environmental or chemical allergens, and carbon monoxide toxicity.

Is Fear of Blushing or Sweating SA/SP? Generally, fear of blushing and fear of sweating are thought to be the result of one of three things: (1) primary Specific Phobias, (2) conditions occurring secondarily to SA/SP, or (3) the result of an underlying medical condition. They are *not* automatically considered to be synonymous with SA/SP.

Anxiety and avoidance associated with excessive blushing and sweating may be considered rational and quite understandable given the embarrassing nature of the symptoms. If, however, the anxiety becomes severe, the thoughts about excessive blushing and sweating may become irrational.

When considering solutions, SA/SP clinical researcher Dr. Richard Heimberg points out that how you solve the problem depends upon what is causing the problem. With SA/SP, the problem is how you think about yourself and others. Removing ganglia that control blushing and sweating remove the stimulus to the physical blushing and sweating but they don't "solve" the SA/SP problem: Fear of being humiliated and being found inadequate, a failure, and/or rejected.

That is, while elimination of blushing and/or sweating will likely eliminate the fear of blushing and/or sweating, there's no reason to believe that eliminating those specific fears will likewise eliminate SA/SP. If it does, then the problem was really a Specific Phobia, such as fear of blushing or fear of sweating, and **not** SA/SP.

CURING SWEATING AND BLUSHING WITH ETS?

Virtually the only effective way to "cure" moderate to severe primary hyperhidrosis and significantly diminish severe facial blushing in most sufferers appears to be ETS. ETS, however, is contraindicated for hyperhidrosis that results from a medical condition. You need to have a clinical diagnostic assessment to determine if the cause of your excessive sweating or blushing is medical. Also you need to consider non-invasive solutions before considering something invasive, like surgery.

ETS stands for **E**ndoscopic **T**ransthoracic **S**ympathectomy. It's a surgical procedure that blocks the upper thoracic sympathetic nervous system ganglia that control the sweating and blushing.

Procedure. Performed under total-body anesthesia, the "keyhole" surgery is done through a ¼-inch incision made in the armpit area. You're lying on your back with that arm outstretched at approximately a 70-degree angle from your body. The lung on the side of the incision is deflated by a small amount of CO_2 to make visualization easier.

Then a long narrow tube, called an endoscope, is inserted into the chest cavity. This instrument contains a fiber-optic video camera on a catheter and an electric wire to destroy (ablate) the specific nerves. Surgery may also be done through two tiny slits, with the second access to the chest for placement of 8 mm. clamps on the offending nerves in order to compress rather than destroy the nerves.

Navigating around blood vessels and other nerves, the camera locates anatomical landmarks as the surgeon seeks the "trouble-making" ganglia. Progress is viewable on a television monitor. Once the individual nerve(s) is found and separated from the surrounding tissue of the ganglion, it's then cauterized with radio frequency or clamped.

This may occur from just above the T2 (*T* for thoracic) ganglion to just below the T4 ganglion. Some surgeons, however, do not include T3 and T4. By not treating axillary sweating, they avoid compensatory sweating in other parts of the body. What nerves are ablated or clamped depends upon the specific areas of sweating.

For the face and hands, the T2 nerve is made non-functional, although some surgeons may destroy the total T2 ganglion for severe palmar sweating. For severe hyperhidrosis of the axillae, it's the T2 and T3, and perhaps T4. It's important to note that for some surgeons facial sweating alone is not the target of this surgery.

When the nerve(s) has been done, that lung is reinflated, the CO_2 removed, and a pneumothorax tube inserted to allow excess air in the chest cavity to escape. This takes approximately 20 minutes. There are no stitches to be removed.

At this point the surgeon performs the same procedure on the opposite side of your body. Some surgeons, however, prefer to do the two sides on separate occasions. Following surgery, you are monitored in recovery, the pneumothorax catheter removed, and the chest x-rayed. Procedures vary from clinic to clinic. In some facilities you can leave that day, in others you're discharged the next day. Mild soreness may be expected to persist for a minimum of four days but you can resume your normal activities within 48 hours and sports activities within two weeks after surgery.

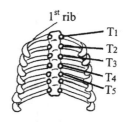

THORACIC GANGLIA

Results. When a skilled, ETS-experienced surgeon performs this procedure, the results are definitive. As you awaken from the anesthesia, your upper extremities and armpits are dry and warm. Statistically, palmar hyperhidrosis is cured in 99% of the cases and facial sweating, 90%. Where there was severe sweating of the soles of the feet too, this is generally addressed. Spontaneous blushing likewise is corrected about 95% of the time.

Isolated plantar hyperhydrosis can be addressed by a lumbar sympathectomy, done as an open abdominal procedure. However, this procedure is not recommended for men. One distressing side effect is retrograde ejaculation into the bladder that may cause impotence. It may also cause low blood pressure with change of position. This can leave you feeling dizzy or faint upon standing from a sitting or lying position. Plantar hyperhydrosis generally doesn't occur by itself.

If the patient with axillary hyperhydrosis isn't responsive to medical therapy, the condition may be treated by removal of axillary sweat glands. Diffuse sweating of the trunk or general sweating is not treated by surgery.

Side Effects. There may be complications and/or side effects of the surgery. One common side effect, occurring in approximately 47% of patients, is called *compensatory hyperhidrosis*. This is where other parts of the body, such as chest and the back of the legs, begin to sweat more. You become more sensitive to thermal stimulation. It appears that compensatory sweating occurs more frequently in those who are operated upon for axillary hyperhydrosis because more ganglia have to be divided to cure the underarm problem. For most people this will be tolerable and may even improve over time.

Another side effect is *gustatory sweating* that occurs when you're either smelling or eating certain foods. This is especially true for foods having a strong, spicy, or sour smell. It may show up as actual sweating or as the sensation of sweating and occurs in up to 2% of patients. These side effects are generally mild to moderate.

There appears to be a direct relationship between the numbers of ganglia treated and the incidence and intensity of compensatory sweating. The more ganglia treated or the more damage inflicted, the greater the likelihood of compensatory sweating. But, at this point in time, there's no clinical way to definitively predict the appearance or intensity of compensatory sweating. When it appears, however, it tends to decrease within the first 6–12 months. There's no reliable treatment for compensatory sweating on the torso.

Complications. Like any invasive procedure, ETS is not without the risk of complications. Its primary surgical complications include:

- **Horner's syndrome**, found in 0.3% of patients, occurs when there has been damage to the T1 nerve (stellate ganglion). This results in constriction of the pupil and drooping of the eyelid (ptosis) on the affected side of the body. These are cosmetic symptoms and do not impair vision. The eyelid can be repaired through reconstructive surgery called blepharoplasty, but the condition may correct itself over time. T1 damage may also cause a slowing of the resting and/or exercise heart rate.

- **Excessive bleeding**
- **Infection**
- **Lung injury**
- **Pneumothorax** occurs where air remains within the chest wall.

Contraindications. ETS should not be used for just any instance of excessive sweating. Specifically, it should not be used when sweating is related to conditions such as:

- Hyperthyroidism (untreated)
- Fever
- Skin diseases
- Severe cardiac, vascular, or pulmonary insufficiency
- Severe pleural diseases, such as tuberculosis, pleuritis, empyema, and emphysema
- Menopause
- Hormone treatments
- Central nervous system disorders
- Psychiatric disorders
- Cancer treatments
- Other medications.

All other causes for hyperhidrosis must be ruled out before ETS can be considered as a treatment. All underlying conditions need to be treated first.

Results Preview. A few surgeons offer you the opportunity to preview the effects of surgery through a procedure called a *stellate block*. This is a reversible process in which the surgeon injects 10 ml. of an anesthesia solution into the left side of the neck so that the solution flows into the muscular area near the stellate ganglion (T1).

While this temporary procedure doesn't affect blushing, it does block sweating on the left side of the upper body. This allows you to experience yourself in the non-sweating state that will result from surgery. The duration of this block is 2–6 hours. During that time period, you're encouraged to put yourself in situations in which you might expect to experience excessive sweating in order to make the comparison. Thus, you can experience what it's like to be free of sweating-associated embarrassment.

Because the block affects the T1 nerve, you experience Horner's syndrome while the block is in effect. Blood pressure and heart rate may drop during this period. It's important to note that the stellate block doesn't predict surgical outcome. It only *suggests* what your surgical outcome will be. There's no way to make an accurate prognosis.

MicroETS. MicroETS is also being performed by a small number of surgeons. What makes it different from ETS in general is that there is a single 1/12th-inch incision on each side, the lungs are not collapsed, nerves and ganglia are not removed, surrounding tissue is not damaged, and there is less chest muscle trauma with less resulting pain. There are no sutures and recovery is rapid.

Cost. The costs of having ETS will vary internationally and by year. It can range from several thousand dollars in other countries to over $10,000 in the U.S., not including airfare and hotel accommodations. Whether the procedure is covered by your health insurance depends upon your policy: (1) If the procedure is classified as experimental or standard procedure and (2) if the referring physician will stipulate that it's necessary, not elective, surgery.

ADDRESSING THE BASHFUL BLADDER

Bashful bladder (BB), also known as shy bladder, shy kidney, shy voiding, pee-shy, phobia of urination, avoidant paruresis, psychogenic urinary retention, sphincteric phobia, and urophobia, is a common problem among SA/SPers (up to 7% of you). This is where you're afraid, embarrassed, or unable to urinate in *public* places. "Public" here means any place where strangers are present, others are in close proximity to you, or you lack visual or auditory privacy.

Though BB is common to both men and women, it appears that men are more concerned about lack of visual privacy whereas women are more concerned about auditory. Speaking for myself, I used to wait in a stall in a restroom until others left then try to convince myself to go as fast as possible, as if I could control the rate. When others were within earshot and I had no choice, I'd wad yards of toilet paper to damp the sound, try to avoid hitting the water directly, or repeatedly flush ... all of which wasted either lots of paper or lots of water.

While BB may even occur in your own home, the most common locations in which it's experienced are public restrooms, restrooms on moving vehicles (planes, trains, boats, and buses), and bathrooms in other people's homes. As with your SA/SP in general, BB occurs when you feel anxious.

Specifically, you experience urinary urgency in other than a "secure" environment. Your autonomic arousal kicks in, your body prepares for fight-or-flight, and your muscles tense. Accompanying this involuntary muscle contraction are the muscles that control urination (bladder and urethral sphincters), thus making voiding impossible. You cannot force yourself to urinate. When BB is severe, it can further interfere with your everyday activities, your relationships, education, career, and job choices.

Treatment. The first thing you should do if you feel you suffer from BB is have s physical checkup. It's essential to make sure that your urinary retention isn't the result of a physical, medical, or medication problem. If, instead, the problem appears to be anxiety-related, you can then see a knowledgeable physician, urologist, or psychologist to deal with it.

It is very helpful to create a BB history. This will give you a clear idea of when the problem first occurred, under what circumstances it occurred, and how, when, and where it has continued to occur. When you do your history, you should also include the thoughts and feelings you have and what you do about it when you anticipate and/or experience having to urinate in public.

Some of the treatments that have been tried include cognitive-behavioral therapy, medications, and mechanical means. The two most useful behavioral methods appear to be systematic (graded) exposure and flooding (no pun intended). Dr. Steven Soifer, author of *Shy Bladder Syndrome*, has found that 8–10 sessions generally work. Paradoxical intention may likewise be effective. Cognitive factors are strong in this condition so CBT can be useful as a treatment.

Also having what is known as a "pee-buddy" may help you practice your desensitization. They can accompany you to the restroom to make the area more secure and to give support. Making noise when you're trying to urinate can make you more comfortable that your urine stream won't be heard. Covering your ears and listening to music likewise can distract you enough so you can relax your muscles.

Relaxation likewise is helpful to remove tension from your bladder and other muscles. Distraction, such as counting, holding your breath, looking at your watch, and listening to tap water run can be valuable. But, these should *never* be used during exposure therapy because they will counteract the positive effects of behavioral exposure.

While some try drugs to assist BB, pharmacological results have been disappointing and don't look promising. Studies have looked at the full-range of medications from antidepressants, anxiety-reducers, sedatives, to urinary-releasers without much success. Drugs that which some BBers have found useful, to some degree, include alcohol, which removes your inhibition, benzodiazepines, and a post-surgery medication for urinary retention, bethanechol. Any of these drugs, however, should be thought of as a *temporary* measure only.

It's important to note that any drug you take for any reason may have urinary-retaining or dehydrating properties. This can be drugs that are prescribed for you for other purposes, over-the-counter drugs, and/or recreational drugs. If you do not know if these drugs can possibly affect your urination, you should consult a pharmacist or physician.

The primary mechanical means available to BBers is urinary self-catheterization. Some urologists suggest this as a way to handle severe BB when you're away from home for extended periods of time or in emergencies. Carrying a "Catheter Pack," consisting of two catheters, water-based lubricant, and topical anesthetic lidocaine, allows you to feel more secure that you can void when you absolutely need to.

However, it's important to remember that self-catheterization poses several potential problems. One is possible infection from an unsterile catheter or its handling, urethral irritation from catheterization, and long-term reliance on mechanical management.

The goal is short-term usage as an adjunct to exposure therapy or cognitive therapy to deal with any underlying SA/SP problem.

This method is not for everyone. This is especially true if you are prone to urinary tract infections or have a urethral or bladder injury or anatomical obstruction.

See Chapter 13 for web sites on hyperhydrosis, facial blushing, and ETS.

IRRITABLE BOWEL SYNDROME

Irritable Bowel Syndrome (IBS) is a very common functional intestinal disorder that is frequently associated with psychosocial distress. It is not, however, a psychiatric disorder. Its predominant symptoms include alternating diarrhea and constipation, gas, bloating, passage of mucus, and abdominal pain. But they can also include nausea, headache, fatigue, depression, anxiety, and difficulty with concentration. From 50 to 100 percent of those with depression or anxiety disorders have IBS.

Two Types of IBS. One is spastic colon and the other is painless diarrhea. *Spastic colon* is often triggered by eating and is a colicky, dull pain with mucus that may be relieved by bowel movement, although there is often the feeling of incomplete evacuation. *Painless diarrhea* is an urgent diarrhea that occurs during or after meals or immediately upon arising.

Psychology of IBS. Thoughts, emotions, and environmental stress affect your gut's function. As in SA/SP, perfectionism often accompanies IBS. This is where you have unrealistic standards for yourself and others and/or others have unrealistic standards and expectations for you. In these circumstances you will suffer significant stress from seeing everything in black or white, as either a success or failure, and being fearful of being imperfect and not living up to all those expectations. This combined with the rational fear of not being able to control your bowels creates even more stress and bowel difficulties. This can significantly interfere with every aspect of your life.

Diagnosis of IBS. As embarrassing as it may be for you to talk to a physician about this problem, you need to do so if you have episodes of either type of IBS because it may be something more serious than IBS. To prepare for your appointment you should keep a running record of those episodes: What occurred (symptoms in detail), when, what was going on in your life before or during the episode, what made it worse and what improved it, how frequent were the episodes, and how long did each episode last.

Diagnosis of IBS will generally include a stool examination, lab tests, and perhaps a sigmoidoscopy. This is where your bowel is fiber-optically scanned for polyps and diverticula (little pouches in the intestinal wall). Abdominal ultrasound may also be used depending upon your symptoms, their severity and location.

Treatments for IBS. There are two approaches to IBS. One is medical and the other is psychological.

Medical. Bloating, belching, and abdominal distension may be related to fermentation in the gut with certain foods but is often related to excessive air intake. This can occur as a result of chewing gum, smoking, and drinking. When you know which foods, such as beans, cause this problem, you can eliminate them. You can stop chewing gum, smoking, and start to drink liquids through a straw.

A diet rich in insoluble fiber (such as green vegetables and raw fruit) and soluble fiber (such as psyllium husks) can transport waste more efficiently. If you're lactose intolerant or wheat gluten intolerant, avoid foods containing milk products and wheat. Anti-cholinergic drugs, tranquilizers, and antacids may help as well.

Psychological. Many approaches have been tried: Reassurance, relaxation, hypnotism, biofeedback, education, and CBT. CBT tends to outperform each of the other individual approaches. Other than CBT, each approach is necessary by itself but not sufficient. What this suggests is that while CBT may be best, the others are a useful adjunct to it to relieve the stress underlying and created by IBS.

TREATING SA/SP WITH SUPPLEMENTS AND NATURAL PRODUCTS

Over the last twenty years there's been a heightened interest in "going back to Nature" to treat health problems. This is due, in part, to the fact that you tend to feel misunderstood, ignored, or excluded from the medical decision-making process. You have turned to these non-medical substances to treat yourself, to demonstrate your control over your health and your independence from the medical system. While the prevalence of natural supplement use as "therapy" is unknown, it has been suggested that one in three individuals has used at least one such natural therapy in the past year.

This may be particularly true for those suffering from psychiatric conditions such as SA/SP. The stigma of mental illness makes it difficult to seek treatment in the first place. Often the medical system is impersonal and off-putting. Health care professionals may not know enough about your condition and the range of treatment for it. This makes so-called natural products and supplements very attractive. And in your desperation you may be willing to try almost anything.

As a result, "natural" products have become abundant. Being heavily marketed as the "real" answer to your health concerns, natural products and supplements have taken on a sort of magical image. They are seen as not being synthesized in a laboratory in beakers of chemicals. Rather, they are seen as taken from plants and other living organisms. This suggests they should be seen as better, safer, and more wholesome than pharmaceutical-created drugs.

Note: The following information is provided for educational purposes only and should not be used for prescription.

St. John's Wort. St. John's Wort (*Hypericum perforatum*) is a perennial herb that has been used for centuries to treat such maladies as depression, insomnia, and nervous conditions. Clinical studies have repeatedly demonstrated that the herb is useful for mild to moderate depression.

Just how hypericum works and how long it stays in your system are not yet known. Some studies suggest that it's an SSRI, like paroxetine (Paxil). But others studies hypothesize that its pharmacological properties are more like that of a low-grade MAOI, perhaps being heavy on both the norepinephrine and serotonin reuptake blockers.

Clinical studies have found that side effects exist though they tend to be mild, such as:

- Gastrointestinal irritation (relieved by intake of food and a large glass of water)
- Dry mouth
- Dizziness
- Skin rashes and itching
- Fatigue
- Restlessness
- Sensitivity to light (usually found at high doses).

Dosage of hypericum extract is usually 300 to 900 mg. for a daily total, divided into 2 or 3 doses. Actual dosage is difficult to calculate since many kinds of hypericum exist. Some are more potent than others. As of 2009, there's been no standardization from manufacturer to manufacturer.

Hypericum should not be mixed with antidepressants or diet drugs. This is because any drug that operates on serotonin (or any other neurotransmitter) in the brain is likely to interact with similar-acting drugs. If you were to mix hypericum with paroxetine, for example, you could over-increase your serotonin, resulting in anxiety, depression, and sleep disorders.

But being short-term ill effects, they would disappear rapidly once the drugs were removed. Combining hypericum with MAOIs likewise creates the possibility of adverse reactions. Substitution of hypericum for a prescribed antidepressant should be done *only* under the supervision of a physician.

Important Note: As a rule of thumb, anyone who's depressed should consult an appropriate health care or mental health care professional. When you're depressed, you're not necessarily the best judge of the severity of your condition. This is especially true if you're severely depressed and/or suicidal. You need a knowledgeable, objective opinion.

Valerian. Valerian (*Valeriana officinalis*) is obtained from the root of the plant commonly called garden heliotrope, all heal, amantilla, and setwall. Having a sedative and hypnotic effect, it's thought to enhance sleep quality, reduce anxiety and nervousness. Few studies have been done on valerian and of those few most of those assessed sleep.

This, however, may be of interest since SA/SPers frequently suffer from insomnia. Currently little is known about the root's pharmacologic properties or how long it stays in the body. There are no reports of adverse effects. Dosage can range from 500 mg. to 12 grams before bedtime.

Kava-Kava. Kava-kava (*Piper mesthysicum*) is the root of a pepper plant found in Polynesia and the surrounding area. It acts as a central nervous system depressant and anxiety-reducer. Several studies have looked at its effect on anxiety syndromes, such as agoraphobia, generalized anxiety disorder, specific phobia, and adjustment disorder with anxiety, and found significant improvement.

Just how it works is not yet known, though there's some evidence that it has a weak effect on benzodiazepine-binding sites even though it doesn't have any significant effect on gamma-aminobutyric acid (GABA). Because of this, Kava may interact negatively with benzodiazepines to produce lethargy and disorientation.

Dosage in one study was 100 mg. three times a day. While no adverse effects have been reported at this dosage level, increased usage may result in a yellow scaly rash referred to as *Kava dermopathy*. Heavy usage may cause metabolic abnormalities, such as increased liver enzymes and cholesterol, and decreased albumin and plasma protein.

Melatonin. Melatonin is a hormone secreted by the pineal gland in the brain which acts on sleep disturbances. The highest level of secretion is at night when you're sleeping. Production decreases with age, a fact that may shed some light on the high incidence of insomnia in older adults.

Its most frequent usage has been for alleviating jet lag and altering circadian rhythms (sleep-wake cycles) for those doing shift work. It has not been used as a "sleeping pill" in the classical sense. Its usefulness for those with chronic insomnia has not yet been determined.

It appears that oral administration of melatonin doesn't precisely duplicate the effect of the hormone as produced in your body. Moreover, while the hormone generally clears the body overnight, when you use it in excess of two weeks, it begins to store in your body's fat tissue.

Short-term studies suggest low-toxicity, but long-term studies have not been done to determine the effect of fat-storage of the hormone. Safety data do not exist. Precise dosage likewise has not been determined, though studies have shown effect between 0.3 mg. and 80 mg. In addition, timing of dosage is important, but the correct timing of it is not known.

What Does "Natural" Really Mean? Most "natural" products or supplements are, in fact, potent drugs. Referring to them as "natural," doesn't mean they're effective or safe. It doesn't mean they can't have medicinal or drug-like properties. Most of these products lack necessary and sufficient information on

- Safety

- Purity
- Dose-response relationship
- Drug interactions.

You need to document and inform your health care professionals about any supplements or natural products you're taking so they can evaluate your health status and concerns more accurately, as well as your use of natural products for the condition.

IS THE ANSWER TO SA/SP IN THE INNER EAR?

According to psychiatrist Harold Levinson in his book *Phobia Free*, 90% of all phobias, anxiety, and panic attacks are the result of a hidden inner-ear dysfunction: Cerebellar-Vestibular Disorder (CVD). His conjecture is based on his research with individuals with dyslexia and learning disorders who manifested CVD and phobias. Levinson then generalized his conclusions about dyslexics to non-dyslexics.

While inner-ear disorders may cause anxiety, this anxiety is generally associated with dizziness, disorientation, unsteadiness, ringing in the ears, and/or blurred vision. Studies of agoraphobia and panic disorder have suggested that vestibular dysfunction and impaired balance may occur in individuals with these disorders. This is particularly in those who report space and motion discomfort, such as fear of small spaces or moving vehicles. To date there are no findings to link SA/SP with CVD.

Levinson's approach to treatment of "CVD-induced" anxiety, phobias, and panic is medication, antioxidants, behavior modification, and psychotherapy. His medication recommendation differs from the general psychopharmacological prescription in that he suggests two levels.

The primary level consists of motion sickness drugs and antihistamines, such as

- Dramamine (dimenhydrinate)
- Benadryl (diphenhydramine HCl)
- Antivert (meclizine HCl)
- Sudafed (pseudoephedrine HCl; brompheniramine maleate)
- Dimitapp (chlorpheniramine)
- Hydergine (ergoloid mesylate)

- Transderm scop (scopolamine).

The secondary level, to be used in conjunction with the primary if the primary alone doesn't resolve the problem, consists of antidepressants and anti-anxiety medications. Because of possible drug interactions, you shouldn't combine primary- and secondary-level drugs on your own. What this line of inquiry suggests is that if you experience both anxiety and balance impairment symptoms, you should definitely contact a physician.

IS THE ANSWER IN THE EYES?

EMDR (Eye-Movement Desensitization and Reprocessing) is a technique introduced in 1989 by Francine Shapiro, to treat post-traumatic stress disorder. According to the EMDR Institute, the technique "accelerates the treatment of a wide range of pathologies and self-esteem issues relative to both upsetting past events and present life conditions."

Its goal is to rapidly desensitize traumatic memories, cognitively restructure memories, and significantly reduce emotional distress, intrusive thoughts, flashbacks, and nightmares. Studies on EMDR have also included persons with phobias and panic disorder. But the technique in these studies appears to be least effective with generalized negative themes, such as fear of social situations.

Over the years EMDR has come to consist of a great many elements besides eye movements, such as: Imagery, cognitive assessment and restructuring, sensory input alignment, targeting information, behavioral exposure, free association, and sensation awareness.

In EMDR therapy the therapist asks you to remember and rate disturbing memories on a subjective distress scale. Focusing on your body sensations, thoughts, and the emotions attendant to your memories, you are to vividly picture the traumatic scene in your mind while the therapist waves two fingers before your eyes (or taps or produces tones). You perform these eye-tracking movements in repeated sets with only short intervals in between. Proponents claim that symptomatic relief may occur in one 30-minute session or may require three such sessions.

Research results on EMDR are mixed. Where studies are carefully controlled, the technique has no effect or resulting improvement is similar to that of existing therapies. Research on EMDR for fear of public speaking supports the hypothesis that its effect is from imaginal exposure. As yet, there are no data for use of EMDR for SA/SP.

INTERACTING WITH PETS

Owning and caring for a pet has long been hailed as therapeutic for those who were old or ill, under stress, dealing with grief, anxiety, or depression. This is because it provides companionship, security, bonding, and affection. Recent research has further suggested that pet ownership positively influences most human beings' emotional state and health.

For example, interacting with an animal can lower blood pressure … while conversing with a human will likely raise it. Interacting with a pet interrupts stressful thoughts. Individuals who have a pet recover more quickly from cardiac surgery than those who don't have a pet. In fact, having a pet has been found to be the strongest predictor of survival in these cases.

However, what makes pets therapeutic for SA/SPers is more subjective than that. A pet can meet so many of your everyday psychological needs that aren't being met by other humans. It can also fulfill those special SA/SP needs.

A pet will love you even if you can't bring yourself to give a speech, if you skip class to avoid people, or if you think of yourself as stupid, ugly, incompetent, or a failure. A pet won't judge you, criticize you, lie to you, or betray your trust. Instead, it'll offer you unconditional love and acceptance. This is sincere affection, unsullied by hidden agendas, manipulation, and desire for control. In exchange for proper care and returned affection, a pet will provide companionship, loyalty, openness, and a friendly welcome home each time it sees you.

When there's no one else to listen to you, a pet will. You can always talk to a pet, confide in it, reveal your feelings, and share your secrets, even the most embarrassing or humiliating of them. And, unlike humans, the pet will act as an attentive and empathetic listener. When you're lonely, it'll be a playful and intelligent companion. Its humorous antics will distract you from your pain. Its nonverbal messages of love and attachment will comfort you when no one else seems to understand.

Because it cares about you, it physically touches you and wants to be touched in return. This offers you the opportunity for the most basic, necessary, and nurturing form of communication. It gladly gives and receives this kind of attention and affection.

Having "someone" to care for and about gives meaning to your life. A regular schedule of pet care provides structure to your time and life and fosters a sense of purpose. This is something you particularly need when your SA/SP makes the world seem bleak and futureless. Reflecting a sympathetic resonance, pets give you the chance to nurture and feel needed.

This was my experience. For eight years one gray and white amber-eyed feline made me feel loved, appreciated, and needed. Found wandering the streets, this lung-scarred, ear-infected furry ball of optimism named "Faust" quickly became my steady companion. When he wasn't draping himself around my neck, he was sitting on his special chair at the dinner table or walking with me down the sidewalk in his harness and leash, greeting passersby.

Unlike most cats, he loved riding in the car, sitting on my lap, looking out the window. But his favorite activity was Hollywood-style training. It was here that he could put Benji and Lassie to shame. On cue he would sit up, stand up, walk across the room on his hind legs, waltz in a circle, roll over, climb a ladder, and talk. It was all for a good scritch between the shoulder blades or piece of chicken, but especially the chicken. Despite the fact he was frequently ill, he never faltered in his attention to our relationship, one that was too short but oh so sweet.

Pet ownership influences you positively in social situations as well. People with animals are thought to be friendlier, happier, more hardworking, and intelligent. This tempers the anxious vibes SA/SPers tend to send out. People walking their dogs, for instance, experience more social contact and longer conversations than those walking alone.

People are attracted to other people's pets. As a result, pets provide a simple and casual method for you to make contact with others and for others to do the same with you. They make available an ever-ready topic of conversation, hobby and interest possibilities. They're also a reason and opportunity to get you out of the house to be where people are, to have fun, to play, and relax.

Because of pet over-population there are many abandoned animals at pounds, shelters, and rescue groups who are in desperate need of loving homes. Be sure to check them out first when seeking an animal companion. If you're not sure about being a permanent pet guardian, you can volunteer to be a foster cat or dog parent.

I've done this for years with the rescue organization C.A.R.M.A. (Companion Animal Rescue and Medical Assistance) in Corrales, New Mexico. In doing this, you help out an over-burdened rescue organization, give the animal a great home until it can be adopted, help socialize the animals to being a pet again, and develop what could be a desirable permanent relationship for yourself. It's the gift that keeps on giving.

OVERCOMING INSOMNIA

About one-third of all American adults experience bothersome insomnia. When you have a sleepless night, this elevates your stress hormones and deteriorates your ability to focus your attention and make decisions. This, in turn, makes you tense and anxious about getting sleep. The more anxious you are the more likely you are to have insomnia. At this rate, it's a wonder SA/SPers get any sleep at all.

However, it's important to remember that insomnia is a symptom of many conditions and not, in fact, a disorder in itself (there are more than 80 known sleep disorders). While it may result from underlying medical or psychological problems, insomnia is often related to taking medication. For example, some antidepressants, anxiety-reducers, anti-inflammatories, such as prednisone, antihypertensives, and alcohol affect sleep quality and quantity. You need to consult with your physician or pharmacist to see if any of the drugs you take contribute to your sleep problem.

Once you determine that your insomnia isn't likely related to a drug or medical condition but is more likely related to anxiety, there are numerous steps you can take to beat your sleeplessness. These steps are based on dealing effectively with *what keeps your insomnia going* rather than on what originally may have started the process.

~ASSIGNMENT~

- Keep a sleep diary. You need to know what your sleep patterns are and how much sleep you really need. For one week record when you go to bed, how often you awaken, for how long, and when you rise in the morning. If you take alcohol or any medication during this time to help you sleep, record that also.

- Keep regular hours. Go to bed and get up the same time each day. Make it earlier rather than later so you don't get overly tired. If you get to bed late one night, don't try to make up for it the next. Keep to your strict schedule.

- Go to bed only when it's time to sleep. Don't read or watch TV in bed. It's best not to associate these attention-focusing activities with where you sleep. Watch TV or read sitting in a chair or do it elsewhere.

- Don't take naps or allow yourself to doze off earlier than your scheduled sleep time. Keep moderately active. If necessary, ask a friend or spouse to help you keep awake.

- Do your relaxation exercises or meditation when you're in bed ready to go to sleep to reduce your anxiety and de-stress your body.

- Think about the day and mentally list three things that went well that day and why they went well. Pick one thing and concentrate on the positive feeling from it. Label it and keep repeating the word to yourself.

- Prepare your mind and body for sleep by doing mild stretching, yoga, taking a hot bath, or listening to soothing music before bedtime.

- Start each day with at least 20 minute of sun. It helps wake you up, energizes you, and tells your internal clock that it's daytime.

- Take carbohydrates before bed. Milk or tryptophan-rich food, like turkey, before bed will not make you drowsy. A light meal of carbohydrates, such as dry cereal or toast and jelly, will however. When insulin is released to metabolize the carbohydrates, it metabolizes other amino acids as well, leaving the tryptophan in your blood stream to make its way to the brain to calm you.

- Don't eat a heavy meal within 4–5 hours of bedtime.

- Restrict your intake of caffeine, nicotine, alcohol, and MSG (monosodium glutamate) late in the day. Caffeine (in coffee, tea, cocoa, chocolate, some soft drinks, over-the-counter medications) takes six hours to leave your system. While alcohol may initially allow you to drift off, it tends to make it harder for you to stay asleep when it leaves your blood stream within several hours.

- Restrict your liquid intake after 6 p.m. If you tend to use the bathroom multiple times a night, drinking less in the evening may help. When thirsty, try sucking an ice cube.

- Eat a light breakfast and lunch.

- Exercise daily (at least 30 minutes) during the day, preferably late afternoon or early evening, but not within two hours of bedtime. Being inactive is considered to be one of the worst things an insomniac can do.

- Make your bedroom very dark. Don't allow moonlight, light from other rooms of the house or outside to penetrate.

- Sleep at a comfortable temperature. Keep the temperature and other environmental factors consistent from night to night.

- Use a white noise generator to block out outside sounds.

- Beware of nonprescription sleep aids. Most of these products consist primarily of antihistamines that are slow to take effect and slow to leave the body. They may leave you feeling drowsy. Aspirin may work for some.

- If you awaken during the night and can't get back to sleep, don't toss and turn. Get up and go to another room to read, watch TV, or do chores until you feel sleepy again, then return to bed.

- Don't let yourself become angry or frustrated by waking up. That will increase your stress hormones, make your heart race and raise your blood pressure, making sleep less likely.

- Use sleeping pills only as a last resort for "transient" insomnia. Transient insomnia results from a temporary situation, such as jet lag or personal loss. These should be used for only a week or two at a time. If you need something more, consult your physician.

SUMMARY

Not all problems associated with SA/SP are obvious. How you'll address symptoms, such as severe sweating and blushing, will depend upon whether they are part of SA/SP or independent Specific Phobias. The same holds true for avoidant paruresis, Irritable Bowel Syndrome, and insomnia. Once it is determined that they are not the result of medical or medication problems, you can address them through cognitive and other means.

Pet therapy is a little-discussed means of assisting SA/SPers to feel needed, wanted, loved, and more confident. Pets also help you reduce your loneliness. Besides being an attentive companion, a pet gives you a means of meeting and interacting with other people in a less threatening situation. If you value animals, you can find solutions to a variety of your anxiety-related problems by sharing your home and life with a pet.

13

ACCESSING PROFESSIONALS AND RESOURCES

"Life shrinks or expands in proportion to one's courage."
(Anais Nin)

HOW CAN YOU TELL IF IT'S TIME TO SEEK HELP?

You need to seek help when nothing seems to be working for you:

- You feel you can't do it alone
- You feel stuck or trapped with no way to turn
- You anticipate and worry all the time
- Everyday life is being affected negatively
- It's not getting better.

LOOKING FOR A CLINICIAN

As pointed out earlier, before you can successfully look for help you need to

- Recognize that a problem exists
- Feel the need for help
- Clarify and concretize the problem so that it's specific, concrete, and solvable
- Decide what you want to be the result
- Learn all you can about your condition and treatment
- Be motivated to act and be responsible *for the outcome of your therapy*
- Find out what's available.

To solve your problem you need to put it in terms of its effect on you. Its seriousness depends upon its production of the **three Ds**:

Disorganization

Dysfunction in everyday habits or living

Disruption (some degree of it).

You also need to choose a problem-solving process that contributes to the development of habits that will help you solve subsequent problems. Problem-solving success in one area often generalizes to other areas and increases your sense of self-efficacy.

Unstructured Self-Help. Self-knowledge is almost always useful. But, unfortunately, self-knowledge alone is no guarantee of effective problem solving and, in fact, may not even be necessary for it. For example, through talk therapy, Maria discovered that she had had a love-hate relationship with her deceased mother, wanting to please her yet never measuring up to her standards for acceptance, and, as a result, hating her for it. While this explained a lot about the dynamics of her relationship with her parent and the guilt Maria felt, it did nothing to help her cope with her feelings of not measuring up in the present day to others around her.

Furthermore, when you follow the self-help path outside a structured approach, you run the risk of going in circles, trying one thing then another, never fully doing what's necessary to achieve progress. For example, you likely have been thrown into social situations that exposed you to your greatest fears. But this so-called "exposure" didn't resolve your SA/SP. Because of this you may believe that exposure is useless. After all, it never worked for you before.

But that kind of "exposure" wasn't presented to you systematically in graduated steps of slowly increasing anxiety. It didn't come with cognitive restructuring to be practiced throughout the exposure. It didn't come with continuous assessment and rewards for each baby step forward.

Often, too, lack of structure in your self-help efforts never gets you outside of your impressions of the problem, either to test the validity of your assumptions or to shape a constructive solution. Structure is essential whether you impose it upon yourself by following a book or series of tapes or a professional imposes it upon you.

Support Groups. Support groups provide minimal structure. For some this is all you need. For others this is a useful adjunct to a structured approach. These are groups of individuals who share the problem and offer the opportunity for:

- Compassion

- Emotional support
- Information
- Advice
- Sharing experience
- Identification
- Resources
- Access to the networks of others.

However, you need to be aware that support groups have the potential for becoming "pity parties" where you share pain, frustration, disappointment, and anger but don't share what works for you and encourage others to try out new positive behaviors.

Professional Help. There are four primary types of professionals from whom you can receive structured help with your SA/SP: Clinical psychologists, clinical social workers, psychiatric clinical nurses, and psychiatrists.

Clinical psychologists generally have a bachelor's degree plus six years of psychological education plus two years of clinical training (one year doctoral-level clinical internship and one year post-doctoral direct supervision, equaling 3,500 hours). On average that's 7.2 years of graduate education and training beyond an undergraduate degree. They may hold a Ph.D. or Psy.D., must be licensed in the state in which they practice. They are psychotherapy-oriented, and, at this writing, most don't have prescription privileges yet. There's a strong movement for clinical psychologists to receive several years of additional training so they can prescribe in limited circumstances. Clinical psychologists may be a member of the American Psychological Association and/or American Psychological Society.

Counseling psychologists who hold an Ed.D. can also provide therapy. To practice independently they must be licensed by the state in which they practice. Other state requirements for practice of psychotherapy may vary. Counseling psychologists may be a member of the American Psychological Association and/or American Psychological Society.

Clinical social workers generally have a master's degree in psychology or social work plus two years of direct supervised training. Not all social workers do clinical work. They may hold an M.S.W. or L.C.S.W., are psychotherapy-oriented, and do not have prescription privileges. They must be licensed or certified by the state in which they practice, except in states which don't offer or require licensing or certification. State requirements may vary.

Master's-level professionals generally have a master's degree from a mental health field (M.A., M.S., M.S.W., M.Ed. or Ed.M.) plus one year of supervised training (1,750 hours). They may be a member of the National Association of Social Workers, American Psychological Association, and/or American Psychological Society.

Psychiatric clinical nurses have an R.N. plus a master's degree in a mental health specialty plus 800 hours of psychiatric practice (direct patient contact). They receive certification for this from the American Nurses Association. This specialty certification may be referred to as C.N.S. (clinical nursing specialist), C.N.S./N.P. (clinical nursing specialist/nurse practitioner), P.N.P. (psychiatric nurse practitioner), or A.N.P.—M.H. (adult nurse practitioner—mental health).

Psychiatric nurses are qualified to do physical exams and order tests and may do limited prescribing. They must be licensed as registered nurses by the state in which they practice. They may be a member of the American Nurses Association and/or American Psychiatric Nurse Association.

Psychiatrists have an M.D. plus four years of medical residency: supervised training in psychiatry. They are generally oriented toward medication but a dwindling few may do psychotherapy as well. Some may further specialize.

They have prescription privileges, can diagnose, and admit patients to the hospital. They must be licensed in the state in which they practice. They may be a member of the American Psychiatric Association and/or the American Medical Association.

What to Look for in a Therapist. Looking for a therapist is a big project. You can't assume Blanche DuBois's approach in *A Streetcar Named Desire* and "depend upon the kindness of strangers." You must know what you're looking for. You want to find professionals who are:

- Familiar with SA/SP diagnosis and treatment

- Experienced in dealing with it and dealing with it successfully

- Philosophically compatible with you in the approach used, whether it's medication, talk therapy, cognitive, behavioral, CBT alone, CBT-plus-medication; whether it's individual or group sessions.

On a more personal level you also want to find professionals who are:

- Comfortable with your checking out different therapists before deciding on one
- Warm, accepting, and non-judgmental
- Respectful and not arrogant
- Comfortable with therapy participants being equal partners in the process
- At ease, friendly, not anxious or depressed
- Open to your explanations, views, and values
- Actively engaged in helping you with your concerns
- Mindful that the message received needs to be checked against what was sent
- Open to your questions and flexible about what may be helpful
- Clear about the therapy process, what it entails, your rights as a client, responsibilities of both parties, boundaries, and confidentiality
- Oriented toward present life pressures, concerns, and daily functioning
- Conscious of the need for regular progress evaluation.

Thus, a good therapist must do three essential things: (1) Know SA/SP and appropriate techniques; (2) Motivate you; and (3) Provide you with emotional support. Anything less and you risk failing to make your SA/SP life changes.

To find these professionals you can ask a trusted friend, your physician, a member of the clergy, the Employees Assistance Program (EAP) at work, or check directly with known treatment centers. You can get a referral from community mental health agencies, the local United Way, or a crisis hotline. Sometimes you can find professionals by their reputation in the community or with their peers (do others refer to them). You may also track down therapists online whose practice is near your location.

But, since SA/SPers may not want to talk to others about this, you'll find them mostly by checking out the phone book Yellow Pages under "psychotherapists," "psychologists," or "psychiatrists" listed under "physicians." If this doesn't pan out, however, you can check with the Anxiety Disorders Association of America (ADAA) online, various "find a therapist" websites, your local professional societies for clinical psychologists, clinical social workers, clinical psychiatric nurses, or psychiatrists, medical schools in the state, hospitals, university psychology departments, and major research and clinical centers.

According to the ADAA, once you have some names, you should speak with several therapists before deciding on one in order to see the range of possibilities available to you. The specific information you need to know is:

- What is their basic approach?
- Is their therapy individual (one-to-one) or group?
- Are additional treatments available? If so, what and how many?
- If necessary, will the therapist come to your house?
- Does the standard treatment have a fixed length? If so, how long is it?
- What if more time is needed?
- Is there a provision for follow-up?
- How is treatment success measured?
- What is the background of the therapist: Training, credentialing (in-field degrees, accrediting agencies, licensure), experience with SA/SP?
- How long has the therapist been treating SA/SP?
- What is the cost of the treatment?
- Is there a sliding scale?
- Is any part of the fee reimbursable by insurance?
- Is it possible to speak with a former SA/SP client, someone who has been through the program?

HOW TO PREPARE FOR THE FIRST VISIT

Before your first visit, it's essential that you be as fully informed and prepared as possible. This means learning all you can about SA/SP and its treatments. Since talking about yourself is often so difficult, you should make up a description of your symptoms to share with the therapist (a copy for them and a copy for you). It's imperative that the two of you have a common understanding of what has initiated this visit and work from common definitions. Clarifications are easier when you're sharing your information.

The description of your SA/SP symptoms should include:

- Thoughts and behaviors you have
- How long you have had them
- When and where you have them
- What precedes your symptoms and what follows them
- How frequently you experience them
- How SA/SP impacts your daily functioning and life satisfaction; that is, what you can do and what you can't.

It's particularly important to emphasize the consequences of your SA/SP. Physicians respond differently to different descriptions. A recent study showed that when physicians heard a description of headache pain as pain, they offered reassurance. But when they received a description of how the pain disrupted the patient's life, they quickly developed a treatment plan to bring the headache under control.

It's very useful for both you and the therapist for you to keep an SA/SP diary. It will reveal patterns: the *what, when, where, how,* and *to what degree* of your SA/SP. These patterns provide the therapist with hints about the cognitive distortions you have and the avoidance behaviors you employ. It suggests the types of social situations where your anxiety is greatest. It reveals your strengths and successes. And it indicates where additional therapeutic exercises may be useful, such as for self-efficacy, social skills, time management, and how to build on current strengths and successes.

When you're not sure the therapist is really well acquainted with SA/SP, you may find it useful to have a photocopy of "frequently asked questions" (FAQ) about the disorder. Hopefully, the therapist will willingly accept this information, but some may resent what they perceive to be "presumptuousness" on your part. They may be insulted or embarrassed.

This doesn't mean that if they seem to know less than you do, you shouldn't share with them to help bring them up to speed. After all, you're really not there to make them feel good, even though you may act as though you are. You're there to make yourself feel better.

It's important to remember that they have a service for sale and you are the person considering buying their assistance. They are not doing you a favor by helping you. Irrespective of how much or how little money changes hands or who supplies it, it is still a sales transaction. And as the potential buyer, you have the choice to accept or reject them.

The part of therapy that most will tend to dislike is being expected to speak. You need to be prepared for all kinds of questioning. If you don't force yourself to provide requested information, you're hindering the therapist's role and, therefore, your progress. Because of your reluctance to speak, you'll find there may be silences in the conversation. While silence may be a therapeutic prompt to urge you to be forthcoming, sometimes it can be too much and can push you to avoid the situation.

Experienced SA/SP therapists will tend to keep the conversation casually moving along. In addition, when the therapist does something with which you're not comfortable, it's best to bring it up for discussion to see if the difficulty can be resolved by mutual agreement. While this may be difficult for you because you don't want the therapist to be angry with you or dislike you, it is essential. When you have questions, it's best to bring them up quickly and directly.

SARAH. Sarah noticed that her therapist looked too young to have had a lot of therapeutic experience. Sarah felt ill at ease about this and needed reassurance. At her next session, she couldn't bring herself to ask for what she wanted to know so she commented on how young the therapist looked.

The therapist looked quizzical, "Why are you commenting on my age?" "I wasn't ... I was just making an observation," Sarah replied with fear, quickly changing the subject. She felt stupid, angry, and embarrassed. What she had really wanted to know was whether her therapist had the credentials and experience necessary for dealing with her SA/

SP. Asking specifically for what she wanted would likely have answered her concerns and not left her anxious about the possibility of having jeopardized her relationship with the therapist.

It's important for you to make your wishes and concerns known and to get the therapist to listen. But you may be concerned that asking questions, correcting, or disagreeing with the therapist's perception may make waves. You don't want to risk making the therapist unhappy with you because you fear rejection and abandonment. But when you act on these fears, you tend to automatically agree to whatever is said or done, irrespective of how it represents the situation or makes you feel. Doing so will frequently leave you frustrated and angry.

When you feel this way, you're likely to act on it indirectly. You may not follow the therapist's suggestions or simply choose not to return. If you're receiving medication from that individual, you may start prescribing for yourself, by increasing, decreasing, or dropping the medication or by adding a new "natural medication" to it. And even if you continue with therapy, you may not inform the therapist of your changes and/or alternative medications. It's important to remember that nearly *everyone* has some trouble confronting medical establishment authority figures.

There are no two ways about it. Initially dealing with a therapist is extremely hard for SA/SPers because it encompasses all the situations that you fear and want to avoid. It requires you to talk with strangers on the phone. It requires you to assert yourself to ask them probing questions about therapy and qualifications. And it requires you to meet the new therapist in person.

And once you're in the therapist's office, you become the center of attention. You're questioned. You have to talk about yourself and divulge personal information under circumstances that sometimes seem like the third-degree. You may be afraid you'll choke up, forget what you want to say, and blank out on questions you're asked. Fearful of being tested and evaluated, you may anticipate feeling criticized and misunderstood.

However, if you know what to expect and prepare for it, you're more likely to survive the "ordeal." It may be useful to ask if you can bring a tape recorder at least for the initial visit when your anxiety is sky-high and you're unlikely to remember, or recall accurately, anything that is said to you. Use of a recorder also allows you to hear how you really sound, what you really said, to confirm or deny your perceptions of your performance and the interaction.

WHAT TO EXPECT ON THE FIRST VISIT

What happens on the first visit can vary dramatically from profession to profession, from setting to setting, so the following includes all the possible scenarios. However, you are unlikely to experience all of them.

Interview is a series of open-ended questions, such as "What's the nature of your difficulty?" "What problem are you having?" "How can I help you?" Or "Tell me what your life is like." Since answering questions is awkward for you because it puts you on the spot, you can have answers prepared, written down, to take with you.

The therapist is really asking what are the salient thoughts, feelings, behaviors, and sensations that occur in social situations that make you anxious and avoidant. You can summarize this information from your SA/SP diary.

History will likely cover not only the disorder's history but also your medical, psychiatric, developmental, family, social, marital, sexual, educational, and occupational histories. The therapist will look for accompanying psychological conditions, like depression and substance abuse. Some of this information may appear inconsistent so the therapist may challenge specific aspects. While this may seem aggressive, it's intended as nonjudgmental clarification.

Physical Examination may be done or recommended to rule out any underlying medical problem.

Anxiety Inventories and/or observation of behavior may be used to determine the manifestation, intensity, and severity of your SA/SP.

Depending upon what's done during the interview, the therapist may then begin to work with you to formulate your goals for therapy and a plan to meet them. This plan will be the basis of all you do in therapy. It will be amended over time as you try different strategies and achieve specific objectives. Ideally, this plan will be the result of a collaboration between you and the therapist, even if treatment consists only of medication.

CHARACTERISTICS OF EFFECTIVE THERAPISTS

You want the therapist to be effective at:

- Attempting to understand your SA/SP behavior
- Identifying your current self-defeating patterns and helping you change them positively
- Knowing what to do about SA/SP
- Helping you look at yourself to ask, "What are my strengths, values, and goals?"
- Reasoning systematically and thinking in systems' terms
- Reaching out
- Caring, respecting you, and inspiring trust
- Being contemporary with world view of events
- Being accessible to you by phone or e-mail.

HOW DOES THERAPY WORK?

The goal of psychotherapy for SA/SP is to help you look objectively at your feelings, thoughts, and behaviors in social situations. In doing so, you learn more effective ways to handle those situations. Together, the therapist and you will identify goals. You want to:

- Significantly alleviate your SA/SP
- Significantly improve your daily functioning
- Effectively work toward your potential.

Then you will agree on the process to achieve them and assess your progress as you move through the process. Psychotherapy requires the therapist's strict attention to your welfare, goals, and confidentiality.

DEALING WITH A THERAPIST AS A BEST FRIEND?

Even though you're seeing a professional, you want that person to be warm, accessible, honest, open, and friendly. You want to feel as comfortable as you can when laying bare your secrets and feelings to this person. You're telling them thoughts and feelings you may not even share with a spouse, family, or close friend.

However, it's important that you not expect your therapist to be your best friend or chum, to reveal intimate aspects of their life to you, or see you outside the therapist-client relationship. They can be approachable, sharing, and somewhat disclosing of themselves to you. They can talk with you in a more natural and casual way. But for your therapist to do their job as a psychotherapist most effectively, they must keep the roles and boundaries of the therapist-client relationship clear.

They're the SA/SP professional, the expert whose professionalism and expertise you're purchasing. If they let you regard them as a bosom buddy too, that changes the dynamics of the relationship. You respond differently (cognitively, emotionally, and behaviorally) to a close friend than you do to an authority figure from whom you're seeking help.

For example, in a business setting if your boss tells you to do something you don't like, you'll probably do it without much of an argument. But if you're intimate with the boss and your superior tells you to do something you don't like, you might well balk, argue, and dig in your heels. That's because the roles of superior and subordinate (like professional and client) are in conflict with the roles of friend and friend.

According to the American Psychological Association code of ethics for practitioners, the client should always be the focus and first consideration of therapy. Therapists should never use their clients to help satisfy their own needs. Multiple relationships, or emotional involvement, can cloud objectivity and interfere with the psychologist effectively performing their functions as a psychologist, and/or possibly harm or exploit you.

It can create misperceptions for you that the friendship will continue when therapy is finished. Your believing that they will always be there for you to depend on can lead to a sense of betrayal and rejection when they aren't when the therapeutic relationship ends.

RESEARCHING INSURANCE COVERAGE

Many insurance- and government-sponsored plans provide some coverage for psychological or behavioral services. Without coverage you have to pay out of pocket. However, some therapists will have a sliding scale of fees or payment plans. An alternative to a private therapist would be help at a community mental health center.

To determine if health insurance covers psychological or behavioral services, the American Psychological Association suggests that you should call your insurance plan representative for the level of coverage you have. Coverage may include outpatient therapy, inpatient treatment, or only "medically necessary" treatment. You need to inquire about:

- What percentage of your treatment will be covered by your plan
- What limits may exist
- What is your co-payment for this service
- What is the total number of visits and is it for a year or a lifetime
- What you should do if coverage is denied or cut off
- What credentials should the therapist have for reimbursement.

If you have coverage, it's important to remember that under most for-profit managed care organizations you need to get "prior authorization" before making an appointment with a psychotherapist. If your primary care professional doesn't authorize it, you'll likely need to contact the plan's customer service people yourself, tell them you want to access your psychological or behavioral (or whatever the plan labels it) benefits, and request a "prior authorization number."

LOCATING PROFESSIONAL AND OTHER ORGANIZATIONS

If necessary, you can contact professional organizations for names. *Note*: Website URLs may change or disappear without notice.

American Academy of Child and Adolescent Psychiatry

3615 Wisconsin Avenue, NW
Washington, DC 20016-2891
(202) 966-7300 (voice) or (202) 966-2891 (fax)
http://www.aacap.org/

American Counseling Association

5999 Stevenson Avenue
Alexandria, VA 22314
(800) 347-6647 (voice) or ((800) 473-2329 (fax)
http://www.counseling.org/

American Psychiatric Association

Public Affairs Office
1000 Wilshire Blvd., Suite1825
Arlington, VA 22209
(7032) 907-7300
apa@psych.org
http://www.psych.org/

American Psychiatric Nurses Association

1555 Wilson Blvd., Suite 602
Arlington, VA 22209
(866) 243-2443 (voice) or (703) 243-3390 (fax)
info@apna.org
http://www.apna.org/

American Psychological Association

750 First Street, NE
Washington, DC 20002
(800374-2721 or (202) 336-5500
http://www.apa.org/helpcenter

Canadian Mental Health Association

180 Dundas Street W, Suite 2301
Toronto, Ontario M5G 1Z8
(416) 484-7750 (voice) or (416) 484-4617 (fax)
info@cmha.ca
http://www.cmha.ca/

Canadian Mental Health Association - BC Division

1111 Melville Street, Suite 1200
Vancouver, BC V6E 3V6
(604) 688-3234 (voice) or (604) 688-3236 (fax)
info@cmha-bc.org
http://www.cmha-bc.org/

Canadian Psychiatric Association

141 Laurier Avenue W, Suite 701
Ottawa, Ontario K1P 5J3
(800) 267-1555 or
(613) 234-9857 (fax)
http://www.cpa-apc.org/

Canadian Psychological Association

141 Laurier Avenue W, Suite 702
Ottawa, Ontario K1P 5J3
(888) 472-0657 toll-free in Canada or (613) 234-2815 (voice) or (613) 234-19857 (fax)
.cpa@cpa-apc.org/

National Association of Social Workers

750 First Street, NE, Suite 700
Washington, DC 20002-4241
(202) 408-8600
http://www.naswdc.org/

OTHER S

American Self-Help Clearinghouse

Northwest Covenant Medical Center
25 Pocono Road
Danville, NJ 07834
(973) 625-3037
http://www.mentalhelp.net/selfhelp/selfhel.php?id=859

Anxiety Disorders Network

1848 Liverpool Road, Suite 199
Pickering, ON, CA LIV 6M3
(905) 831-3877

Association for Advancement of Cognitive & Behavior Therapies

305 Seventh Avenue, 16th Floor
New York, NY 10001
(212) 647-1890 (voice)
(212) 647-1865 (fax)
https://aabt.org/members/Directory/Clinical_Directory.cfm

Anxiety Disorders Association of America

11900 Parklawn Drive, Suite 100
Rockville, MD 29852-2624
(301) 231-9350 (voice) or
(301) 231-7392 (fax)
http://www.adaa.org/GettingHelp/FindATherapist.asp

TO FIND A THERAPIST

Council of the National Register of Health Service Providers in Psychology

1120 G Street, NW, Suite 330
Washington, DC 20005
(202) 783-7663 (voice) or
(202) 347-0555 (fax)
natlregstr@aol.com
http://www.nationalregister.org

Freedom from Fear

308 Seaview Avenue
Staten Island, NY 10305
(718) 351-1717 (voice) or
(718) 667-8893 (fax)
FFFNADSDaol.com
http://www.freedomfromfear.org/

International Paruresis Association

P.O. Box 65111
Baltimore, MD 21209
(800) 247-3864
http://www.paruresis.org/

National Alliance for the Mentally Ill

Colonial Place Three
2107 Wilson Blvd., Suite 300
Arlington, VA 22201
(800) 950-NAMI (6264) or (703) 524-7600 (voice) or (703) 524-9094 (fax); helpline@nami.org
http://www.nami.org/

National Institute of Mental Health

Public Info, MSC 9663
6001 Executive Blvd.
Bethesda, MD 20892
(866) 6157-6464 or (301) 443-4513 (voice) or (301) 443-4279 (fax)
http://www.nimh.nih.gov/

National Mental Health Association

2000 N. Beauregard Street, 6th Floor
Alexandria, VA 22311
(800) 969-NMHA (6642)
(703) 684-7722 (voice) or
(703) 684-5968 (fax)
http://www.nmha.org/

National Panic/Anxiety Disorder News, Inc.

npadnews@ap.net
http://www.npadnews.com/

Phobics Anonymous

P.O. Box 1180

Palm Springs, CA 92263

(619) 322-COPE (2673)

Toastmasters International

23182 Arroyo Vista

Rancho Santa Margarita, CA 92688

(949) 858-8255 (voice) or (949) 858-1207 (fax)

tminfo@toastmasters.org

http://www.toastmasters.org/

Clinical Trials for Anxiety

http://psychcentral.com/cgi-bin/ct-cgi/anxiety

PROVIDING FAMILY HELP AND SUPPORT

When you are working to recover from SA/SP, you need help from friends and family. Their providing this assistance isn't always easy for them. One of the primary reasons is your existing relationship with them. It's built around a history and expectation of certain ways of thinking, believing, feeling, and behaving.

There are two ways in which family members or friends can assist you with your SA/SP. They can help you with exercises and/or they can make psychological room for you so you can change and grow into a more fully functioning person.

Helping, however, means their not taking over, telling you what to do, or trying to make decisions for you. It means their having to step outside their roles in their relationship with you. It means their offering reassurance and encouragement, allowing you to work at your own pace.

What Can Your Family and Friends Do to Help? Frederic Newman, M.D., director of The Anxiety and Phobia Treatment Center at White Plains Hospital (NY), recommends they do the following:

- Become familiar with aspects of SA/SP treatment and encourage the family member or friend with SA/SP to give it a fair trial
- Help where necessary in executing exercises, especially exposure, and tracking progress
- Provide support and minimize acute stresses which aggravate SA/SP

- Avoid ridiculing social fears, anxious feelings and thoughts because they're real to the SA/SPer
- Avoid belittling the SA/SPer's attempts to address SA/SP because progress is made in baby steps, which are often hard for the outsider to see
- Avoid trying to convince the SA/SPer that they can do what they feel they can't. The SA/SPer will do it when they feel ready
- Avoid using guilt as a motivator because the SA/SPer already carries a heavy satchel of it and doesn't need any more
- Avoid scolding, coaxing, cajoling, bargaining, and tricking the SA/SPer into doing more than they planned to do. They're the best judges of how far to go
- Keep promises and don't betray the SA/SPer's trust. Trust is a big issue for SA/SPers and they have few people they're comfortable relying upon
- Avoid trying to protect the SA/SPer from the world by making things "safe." The SA/SPer needs to meet challenges in order to resolve their SA/SP, develop confidence and independence, and build on their strengths and successes.

ACCESSING ONLINE RESOURCES

Having access to the Internet has opened up a world full of opportunities for SA/SPers. Online you can find:

- Information, both general and specific, about your disorder, cognitive-behavioral therapy, medications, and co-morbid conditions
- Support
- Referrals
- Shared experiences
- Friendship (and sometimes romance)
- Links to other sites of interest.

As mentioned in Chapter 1, there are pros and cons to online use. On the negative side there's less of a sense of social presence and less sensory feedback. Online use tends to decrease your real-life social interaction and may lead to loneliness and/or depression. Without face-to-face interaction you tend to receive less of the kind of support and reciprocity that typically contribute to your sense of security and happiness in relationships.

On the positive side, according to psychologist Storm King, it's online where you're able to find peers and interactions no matter what topic is of interest to you. You don't have to search long and hard to find a compatriot. Online provides you with an enhanced opportunity to feel at ease with others. One reason is that you don't have to worry how you look. Furthermore, you can take your time in creating the impression you want others to "see."

Because you're generally in the privacy of your own home, you're at less interpersonal risk than you'd be in a face-to-face encounter. Rude intrusions can be handled easily, unlike someone unexpectedly coming to the front door. Because this medium offers you control of the interaction, you feel a greater sense of autonomy as well. When you can't see one another, your communication is more an exchange of ideas, thoughts, feelings, and impressions. Factors such as gender, race, age, and appearance don't matter because they don't come into play *unless* you choose to have them do so.

You can quickly create a large social circle and network that you would likely find nearly impossible offline. You can create that sense of belonging that you desperately need and want. This is something that can help you keep going.

You can locate these resources via:

- Web sites, including social networking sites
- News groups
- Chat rooms
- E-mail
- Lists.

Note: While SA/SPers gain a great deal from these online relationships, particularly in view of your "real-life" social deprivation, you need to consider the frequency of your online usage and your dependence on it for interaction. Excessive computer use may lead to addiction. For this reason, you need to look objectively at your online use. Do you

- Use online every day?
- Lose track of time when online?
- Spend less time with others or doing other things?
- Deny the time spent online?
- Check your mailbox repeatedly throughout the day?
- Get complaints from others that you're on too long?

Web Sites. For a full complement of useful SA/SP-related sites, including organizations, therapists, and support groups, you can go to my website at www.speakwithoutfearnow.com/links.htm.

News Groups (Usenet). These public discussion groups have pluses and minuses. These will vary from group to group.

Plus side

- Don't need to subscribe
- Drop in any time
- Can ask questions
- Have access to FAQs, specific and general information
- Have access to links, references, and other resources.

Minus side

- Frequently not moderated
- Spawn spammers, crusaders, troublemakers (trolls)
- Posts are archived and open to the public
- Need to be careful with personal information
- News servers may not receive all posts so may be difficult to follow conversations
- Some servers don't carry all groups.

Mailing Lists, Chats, Forums, Social Networks. These are also public discussion groups designed around a particular topic where you send and receive messages by e-mail.

Mailing lists require that you subscribe. You can receive e-mails individually or in digest form. For example,

www.socialanxietyinstitute.org/mailing.html

With chats you can talk in real-time with people from around the world. Some chats have specific topics and provide the ability to have both public and private conversations. Many are available 24 hours a day seven days a week. "Secret" channels also exist. For example, www.gordoni.com/shy/irc-altnet.text (#shyroom in AfterNet)

Forums are like message- or bulletin boards where you post questions, offers, or comments for others to scan. For example,

//healthgroups.yahoo.com/socialanxietydisordersupport/

Social networks, like Facebook, Twitter, LinkedIn, Plaxo (and many more) allow you to connect with others quickly. However, they also encourage you to provide a great deal of personal, private information which others might use so you need to be cautious about revealing too much.

TEN COMMNDMENTS FOR OVERCOMING SA/SP

Your recovery is predicated upon your developing both new ways of looking at the world and new skills with which to deal with it. There are ten areas that you need to continuously address to alleviate your SA/SP. The following are the "Ten Commandments" according to Darrell L.Hill:

1. Thou Shalt Not Let the Evaluation of Others Drag Thee Down.

2. Thou Shalt Not Be Perfect.

3. Thou Shalt Learn to Argue With Faulty Logic.

4. Thou Shalt Know Thyself and Appreciate Thy Gifts.

5. Thou Shalt Learn to Relaxxxxx.

6. Thou Shalt Learn the Art of Conversing.

7. Thou Shalt Rehearse, Rehearse, Rehearse.

8. Thou Shalt Expose Thyself (no trenchcoats need apply).

9. Thou Shalt Be Assertive.

10. Thou Shalt Roam the Social Wilderness (with a smile)

SUMMARY

To derive the maximum benefit from this book you need to read it, embrace it, live with it, and re-read it. You need to fully immerse yourself in the concepts and take action by doing all the exercises and assignments. You need to apply all the cognitive skills, behavioral strategies, and life techniques every single day.

This means you need to master each therapeutic element in a step-by-step, logical fashion, applying each to specific maladaptive thoughts, feelings, and behaviors in specific circumstances. Doing so generalizes those positive and functional results to your overall social response. You need to address and **master the basics before** you begin to work to create your advanced social effectiveness.

You need to keep your Recovery Journal and record everything in it, starting with your anxiety and success instances. You need to track your progress and reward yourself for it. You need to **practice, practice, practice**, using trial and error, to see what works for you.

You need to do this until your positive and appropriate responses become automatic. This means that Abdominal Breathing, Relaxation Techniques, Visualization, Positive Self-Talk, Disputations, and Distraction Techniques become part of you and are *always* available to you for use. Only in this way can you reach toward your recovery and enjoy the satisfying, productive life you deserve.

As Eleanor Roosevelt wrote in *You Learn by Living* (1960), "You gain strength, courage, and confidence by every experience in which you really stop to look fear in the face. You are able to say to yourself, 'I lived through this horror. I can take the next thing that comes along.' … You must do the thing you think you cannot do."

Then, and only then, can you do what Tom Robbins urges in *Even Cowgirls Get the Blues*: **"Be your own master! … Rescue yourself! … And Free the Heart!"**

INDEX

Symbols

A

B

C

D

E

O

P

Q

R

S